The captions for the half-title page and the frontispiece are transposed. The image on the half-title page is of Independence Rock, WY. The image on the frontispiece is of Saint Mary Lake, Glacier National Park, MT.

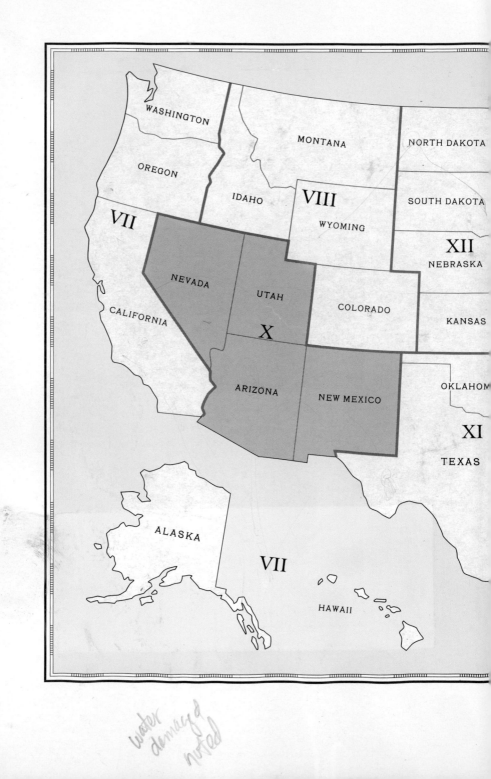

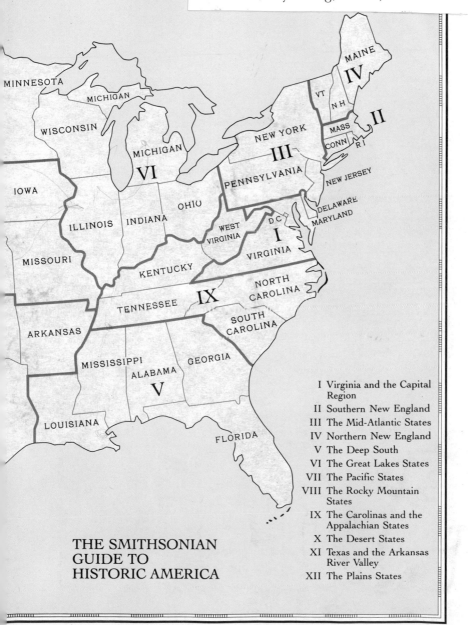

I Virginia and the Capital Region
II Southern New England
III The Mid-Atlantic States
IV Northern New England
V The Deep South
VI The Great Lakes States
VII The Pacific States
VIII The Rocky Mountain States
IX The Carolinas and the Appalachian States
X The Desert States
XI Texas and the Arkansas River Valley
XII The Plains States

THE SMITHSONIAN GUIDE TO HISTORIC AMERICA

THE
SMITHSONIAN
—— GUIDE TO ——
HISTORIC AMERICA

THE ROCKY MOUNTAIN
S   T   A   T   E   S

Text by
JERRY CAMARILLO DUNN, JR.

Editorial Director
ROGER G. KENNEDY
Director of the National Museum
of American History
of the Smithsonian Institution

Stewart, Tabori & Chang
NEW YORK

917.804
SMI
DUN

Text copyright © 1989 Stewart, Tabori & Chang, Inc.

Due to limitations of space, additional photo credits appear on page 463 and constitute an extension of this page.

All information is accurate as of publication. We suggest contacting the sites prior to a visit to confirm hours of operation.

Published in 1989 by Stewart, Tabori & Chang, Inc., 740 Broadway, New York, NY 10003.

FRONT COVER: Jackson Hole, WY
HALF-TITLE PAGE: Saint Mary Lake, Glacier National Park, MT
FRONTISPIECE: Independence Rock, WY
BACK COVER: State Capitol, ID

SERIES EDITOR: HENRY WIENCEK
EDITOR: MARY LUDERS
PHOTO EDITORS: MARY Z. JENKINS, MARION PAONE
ART DIRECTOR: DIANA M. JONES
DESIGNER: PAUL P. ZAKRIS
ASSOCIATE EDITORS: BRIGID A. MAST, PAUL MURPHY
ASSISTANT PHOTO EDITORS: BARBARA J. SEYDA, FERRIS COOK
EDITORIAL ASSISTANT: MONINA MEDY
DESIGN ASSISTANT: KATHI R. PORTER
CARTOGRAPHIC DESIGN AND PRODUCTION: GUENTER VOLLATH
CARTOGRAPHIC COMPILATION: GEORGE COLBERT
DATA ENTRY: SUSAN KIRBY

LIBRARY OF CONGRESS CATALOGING-IN-PUBLICATION DATA

Dunn, Jerry Camarillo.
    The Rocky Mountain States / text by Jerry Camarillo Dunn, Jr. ; editorial director, Roger G. Kennedy. — 1st ed.
      p.   cm. — (The Smithsonian guide to historic America)
    Includes index.
    ISBN 1-55670-103-9 : $24.95. — ISBN 1-55670-107-1 (pbk.) : $17.95
    1. Rocky Mountains Region—Description and travel—Guide-books.
2. Historic sites—Rocky Mountains Region—Guide-books. 3. West (U.S.)—Description and travel—1981-   —Guide-books. 4. Historic sites—West (U.S.)—Guide-books.
I. Kennedy, Roger G. II. Title. III. Series.
F721.D86   1989
917.804'33—dc20   89-4607
                                                      CIP

Distributed by Workman Publishing, 708 Broadway, New York, NY 10003

Printed in Japan

10 9 8 7 6 5 4 3 2 1
First Edition

C O N T E N T S

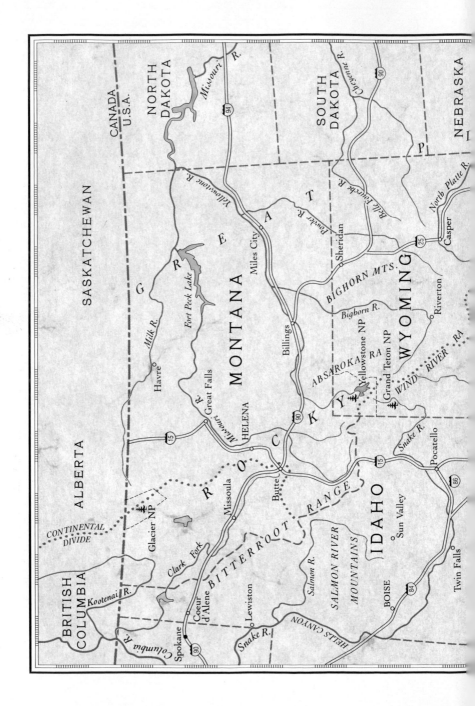

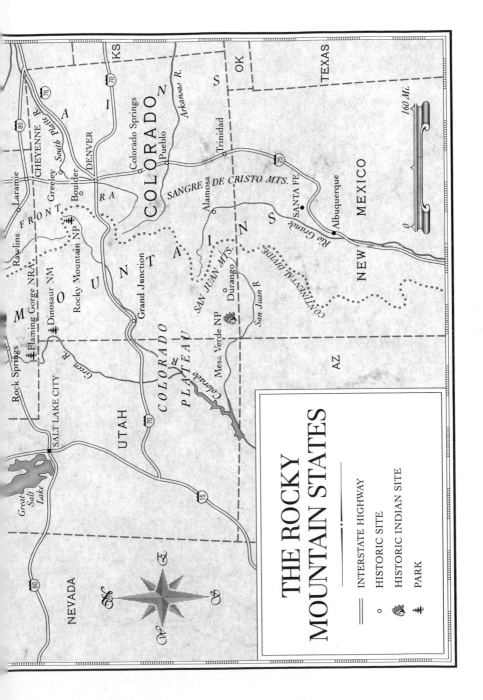

THE ROCKY MOUNTAIN STATES

— INTERSTATE HIGHWAY

o HISTORIC SITE

🌸 HISTORIC INDIAN SITE

⚵ PARK

160 Mi.

INTRODUCTION

ROGER G. KENNEDY

The lone cowboy. He appears from nowhere, provides the plot with a spasm of heroic violence, refuses the tug of domesticity, and rides off into the sunset. "Shane!" the child in us cries after him, but he is gone.

It is just as well. He never was very important in the real West. A single horseman has little chance of inducing very many cows to go anywhere; cowboys worked in groups, often staying in their "outfits" longer than Japanese industrial workers in theirs. But the rest of us want to dream other dreams, for the myth of the lone cowboy is an Eastern creation, arising not from the needs of the cattle business but from the psychological requirements of urban cowboys seeking fantasies of relief from the abrasions of city living.

Chief among those urban needs was a desperate desire to be dumb—dumb in the literal sense: to be able to get by without articulate speech. Brandon De Wilde, the blond boy who called out "Shane!" grew up to become Dustin Hoffman's buddy in *Midnight Cowboy* (Jon Voigt), just as blond and fragile but instead of being solemnly silent in the shadow of the mountains, he talked all the time. Like all city people, he had to. City folk, crowded and beset by the innumerable indignities of urban life, go to the movies to be caught up in the myth of the loneness of the lone cowboy. Forced to explain ourselves at every turn as we shove, prod, and push our way through the day, we yearn for a world in which we might survive without making use of any of the nuances between "yup" and "nope." The Hollywood cowpoke needs but two facial expressions: a squint of disapproval implying an immediate intention to perforate, and a jaunty, asymmetrical grin of beguiling narcissism—no more is needed to communicate with the critters, though occasionally he does vouchsafe a meaningful lurch.

Inarticulate he is, but enormously persuasive. He has convinced us that the high plains and mountain frontier was a place for the lone male—without parents, wife, or progeny. That may have been true for lone American males during the mountain-man generation in the early 1800s, but even then, as we shall see, from an economic point of view that lone American male was far from independent.

It was not only the cinema that distracted us from the true history of the West; before there were myth-making motion pictures there were myth-making historians, apparently moved by the same desire to depict this vast region as if it were largely barren of life except for an occasional lone horseman and farmer. The Harvard historian Frederick Jackson Turner was magnificent in describing the agricultural Midwest—the realm of the family farm—but he faltered in the Southwest and failed as a guide to the high plains because there the frontier was quite different. Turner did distinguish between two agricultural experiences in the East. The first was that of the Southwestern pioneers, exemplified by Andrew Jackson and Sam Houston, who seized the land only after dispossessing a native population that had lived over many generations in densely settled, agricultural villages. These southern pioneers drove their slaves before them into the West, and required a world market for the crops they sweated out of them. This was not the experience of Turner's own Wisconsin parents. The Northern pioneer cleared the forest to make and work his own place and planted for a local market.

Tennessee and Texas, Colorado and Wyoming, were not all Wisconsin. The Midwest had been fertile, well-watered, well-timbered, and divisible into 180- or 360-acre family farms. This, if anywhere, was the natural habitat of a nation of independent yeomen. One might call them, indeed, "lone husbandmen"—each of them constituted an economic unit. But matters were not so simple on the plains and around the Rockies. This was not the agricultural frontier of Turner, nor the West according to John Wayne. There were, and are, few "family farms," in the midwestern sense, just as there were few lone cowboys.

Another Harvard historian, the magisterial Charles A. Beard, proposed a view that was at the opposite extreme from Turner's, suggesting that the real West was so disgusting a place that it justified exploiting. His scruffy sodbusters and savage Indians confirmed the expectations of the Western wilderness that had been held by New England intellectuals since the days of Cotton Mather and Timothy Dwight. The Puritan founders had seen the sunset horizon as red with the fires of Satan. The Harvard faculty, reeling from the presence of Turner in their midst (perhaps that should be "mist"), formed ranks behind Beard and rejected the frontier as a source of anything culturally useful. If the West on its own could contribute nothing important to America's development, one could exploit it without remorse and return quickly to the cultivated side of the hedge. The exploitation goes on, though in our time Turner's sunny view of the agricultural frontier has once again supplanted Beard's crabbed one, and the vitality of cultural life west of Cambridge has recovered from the defoliation of Beard's scorn with sufficient vigor to require no help in these pages.

"The prairie is uncongenial to the Indian . . . only tolerable to him by possession of the horse and rifle." So wrote another influential myth-maker, Lewis Henry Morgan, in 1859. The horse first became available to the Indian in the seventeenth century, the rifle in the nineteenth. If Morgan was right the intolerable high plains would have been unoccupied before those times except for herds of bison and the lone eagle. But archaeology tells us otherwise—for ten thousand years families, tribes, gangs, and more recently corporations have left their remains upon the plains and in clefts of the foothills of the Rockies.

Bighorn Medicine Wheel in Wyoming, seventy-five feet in diameter, presents spokes that form alignments with celestial bodies more accurately than do the spaces between the monoliths at Stonehenge. This was, it seems certain, a ceremonial center for many people, in an area where agriculture was and still is difficult. Not far away at Sheep Mountain in the Absaroka Range, a hunting net was recently discovered that is six feet high, two hundred feet long, and composed of more than a mile of cord. It is thousands of years old. Just over the Canadian border there is the Head Smashed-In kill site where for at least 5,000 years and perhaps as long as 9,000 years large numbers of people kept rock walls and cairns in good repair to funnel lines of bison toward a cliff over which they could be driven by crowds of hunters.

Over thousands of years in this region a substantial population was supported by agriculture and a widely diversified supply of game. Clusters of small circles of stones that once held down the edges of tepees are frequently found throughout even the high, arid fringes of the plains. At the opposite border of the region near Kansas City, there was a mound compound marking the extremity of the densely settled, agricultural woodland culture. In between along the rivers, there were many smaller agricultural settlements where the Mandan and other village tribes lived in earthen houses roofed with sod and built upon massive wooden frames. These were the

Cowboys at a chuckwagon in eastern Montana at the turn of the century. These men worked for the XIT Cattle Company, a famed Texas-based outfit that leased 2 million acres between the Yellowstone and Missouri rivers. One cowboy about to drive an XIT herd from Texas to Montana was given simple directions: "Jean, tonight you locate the North Star and you drive straight toward it for three months, and you will be in the neighborhood of where I want you to turn loose."

prototypes for the "soddies" of European settlers, who for a long time lived less densely upon the ground than did the Native Americans before them.

There is one aspect of the old image of the high plains as a mere bison pasture that has real value in helping us to visualize it as it was and as it is no more. That is the aspect of multitudinousness. Bison beyond counting, in herds so vast as to defy comprehension, moved in masses often a hundred miles across. As a report to the Smithsonian Institution observed in 1880: "Of all the quadrupeds that have lived upon the earth, probably no other species has ever marshalled such innumerable hosts as those of the American bison. It would have been as easy to count or to estimate the number of leaves in a forest as to calculate the number of buffaloes living at any given time during the history of the species prior to 1870." Twelve million animals might move in a herd; one herd followed by Grenville Dodge covered fifty square miles. Bison were not limited to the Great Plains—the Spaniards reported them in Mexico in 1527, as did the English on the Potomac in 1612—but they were to be seen in immense numbers only in the grassy region where the plains approached the Rocky Mountains. The great roundups and drives of the cattle kingdom were the successors to these immense animal assemblies. The West was the unbounded arena for the spectacle of multitudes, not of isolated, singular movement.

The myth of the lone cowboy has distracted us from the real drama enacted on the high plains and the first rearing ranges of the Rockies—a drama of groups, of cowboys whose only real work was concerted, of the crews building railroads to bring the riches of the West to market. And there is the other drama, subtle and invisible, of huge enterprises whose power spanned thousands of miles and controlled the lives of Westerners from the very beginning of European-American settlement. The West's semi-arid terrain lent itself to a kind of dry-country plantation system, a pattern with which the Spaniards were thoroughly familiar from their experiences on their own peninsula. Their ancient predecessors on the Iberian Peninsula, the Romans, had organized the land into *latifundia*, very large plantation units that were owned and ruled from a distance.

In a similar fashion, the West has been exploited by outsiders, from a distance, and organized into very large "spreads." Colorado's own Robert Athearn, a very good historian indeed, made this point thirty years ago. (The Populists had made it fifty years before that.) As Athearn told us, "the most persistent theme" in Western History "is that of exploitation and experimentation carried on by remote control from the more settled parts of America. From the day of the mountain men, down through that of the miner, the cattleman, the land speculator, the timber baron, and the oil wildcatter, the region has been regarded as a place to capitalize upon natural resources with precious little concern about what was left when the stripping was finished."What was left? Raw, sterile tailings on a thousand hills, bleached and yellow and unforgiving, the creaking of doors dangling upon rusted hinges as the high-country wind blows through exhausted grey rows of abandoned houses.

From the tailings and ghost towns, from the saloons of Butte and the shanties at the edge of Denver, there are trails leading eastward to marble fountains, walnut panelling and rich carpets, boiseries and silver wine coolers and opera boxes. At the eastern end of those trails one also can find Western buildings—Western not in architectural style but Western because the West's ore and oil and cattle paid for them. The Guggenheim Museum in New York is as Western in this sense as Fort Laramie, and a dozen "cottages" at Newport are as Western as Main Street in Leadville. In a country retreat just outside of New York City there is an exquisite Japanese garden that is, in its financial origin, not from the Far East but from Montana.

Athearn's "persistent theme" links the mountain man Jim Bridger to Ward McAlister, the New York social arbiter of the Gilded Age—an odd couple to any observer but an economist. The mountain man, gathering his furs in some desolate canyon, served Mr. Astor, sitting in his countinghouse in Manhattan, and was compensated sufficiently to buy himself rum and rough fare in squalid trading posts. McAlister served a somewhat later Mrs. Astor, providing for her needs and being compensated in rich food and champagne, a magnum or two of which were, in effect, provided by Bridger.

The "persistent theme" stretches invisible lines of economic force across the Western landscape, tripping up the horse of the lone cowboy, throwing him to the ground, snarling him in foreign entanglements, and trussing him up so that he can be forever prevented from riding forth again as a symbol of independence. Those lines start, as the cowboy often did, with the cows in Texas. An estimate in 1830 counted only 100,000 head of cattle in Texas, but another in 1860 found an astonishing 3,535,000. Such a rate of increase caught the attention of the shrewd investors of the City of London. The American Civil War, ending in 1865, produced a group of men accustomed to riding long distances, sleeping out, making lethal use of firearms, and unwilling to return to sedentary hardship on the rocky farms of New England or the burned-out cotton fields of the South. Applied to a potential beef crop of such rapid rate of increase, their talents could have substantial money value. The American cowboy was becoming interesting, and so was his native habitat.

The high plains, it was becoming clearer, were not a Great American Desert, but an enormous rectangular pasture, two thousand miles from north to south. Into that pasture cowboys drove 260,000 Texas cattle in 1866. C. W. Dilke told his readers in London three years later that Colorado and Wyoming were destined to be "the feeding ground for mighty flocks." The British landscape was full and Ireland overgrazed, but already there were half a million

OVERLEAF: *Aspen trees in Owl Creek Pass in Colorado's Uncompahgre National Forest. Chimney Rock and Courthouse Mountain are in the background.*

cattle and a million sheep between Denver and the Wyoming boundary. This was true despite the Sioux and Cheyenne, whose livestock interests were confined to bison and horses, and who had not relinquished their claims to most of the pasture.

By 1871 Wyoming cattle were feeding both sides in the Franco-Prussian War; millions were on the plains, driven by tens of thousands of cowboys working in battalions. A hundred thousand ponies went north from Texas in a single year to provide them mounts. A relatively small operation in the Beaverhead Valley of Montana in the early 1870s contained 3,000 sheep and 3,000 cattle, and enough cowboy help to require 500 horses. The valley, bounded by escarpments on either side, enclosed a greensward of 19,200 acres.

By the end of the 1870s, this was a small spread compared to those being financed in the London money market. Huge sums were being aggregated to purchase land, livestock, fencing, and food. Scottish, English, Dutch, and German investors scrutinized cash-flow projections to cover the outgo while the four-legged subjects of all this attention ate themselves closer and closer to the slaughterhouse and toward the income side of the financial statement. At the outset there was considerable skepticism on the part of British cattlemen as to the quality of American cows; but it was a pleasure to observe how they survived on bunch grass, drinking from puddles. A British sportsman observed that "A herd of 5,000 head will feed the year round and grow fat on a stretch of arid-looking table-land, where an English farmer, if he saw it in the autumn, would vow there was not sufficient grazing for his children's donkey."

The Scottish-American Investment Company began borrowing money at low Scottish rates in 1872 to lend to cattlemen. The British-American and Anglo-American companies followed—and then dashed ahead to invest directly in operating ranches. Fifty thousand British-owned cattle grazed along the Tongue and Powder Rivers in Wyoming. Two-and-a-half million acres of Carbon County were British-controlled—about the extent of the Scottish and English holdings (mostly gorse) of the greatest of noble land-owners, the Duke of Sutherland. South of this were the holdings of the Swan Land and Cattle Company and the British-capitalized Prairie Cattle Company, which owned two-and-a-half million acres in Colorado alone and nearly as much elsewhere. In the Dakotas were the Matador Land and Cattle Company and the vast operations of the Marquis de Mores. From horizon to horizon in Wyoming stretched the EK Ranch of Sir Horace Plunkett and the principalities of beef owned by Otto Franc (the Pitchfork) and another German, Charles Hetch.

So much was the power of these foreign investors feared during the late 1870s and 1880s that it was possible for American investors to induce state and territorial legislatures to pass the kind of inhibitory laws against foreigners we tend to associate with Japan in our own time, while huge pools of Boston, New York, and Philadelphia capital were decanted into the cow country. As a result, the chief characteristics of that country were a *lack* of independence in the life of a cowboy, and the military organization of his life. The cattle economy was like the sugar economy of Barbados in the seventeenth century, as enormous remittances flowed back to overseas investors and to the city folk who owned the West.

Cotton had once been king, though its prices were set in Manchester and London; now people said that "grass was king" and they spoke of "the cattle kingdom." It was a kingdom, and remains so in our memories, *not* because it owned more cattle than any other region, but because it was organized like a kingdom, with baronies and dukedoms, vast domains operating on a spectacular scale, using violent means to discipline their realms.

The cattle kingdom, though a potent presence in our national mythology, was in fact not as potent a presence in our national economy, nor even in the cattle economy, as it seemed at the time. Walter Prescott Webb, the historian-laureate of the Great Plains, pointed out long ago, "after all, the West (even including Texas) did not produce many cattle." He cited statistics showing that the plains area, including Texas, produced only about 28 percent of the total cattle in the U.S. in 1880. The plains states themselves, without Texas, rounded up only about 15 percent of the total.

And the era of the cattle kingdom was very brief, lasting only a decade between the internationalization of its economic base and the terrible vengeance wreaked upon its excesses by the weather in 1886 and 1887. Coming out of the world depression of the late 1870s, international investors had expanded the scale of the American cattle business and taken powerful roles in the already oligopolistic organization of the production and marketing of cattle. Their additional power and their traditions of predatory behavior altered the cattlemen's associations of the Great Plains. These associations became organized into cartels as effectively as the railroad

and industrial trusts that came after them. But drought and savage
winters in the middle 1880s could not be organized away. The grass
was seared by unremitting sun; the rains refused to fall; cattle died
of thirst. Then came the blizzards. There are stories of ranchers
driven mad by the sound of their cattle lowing for food. When the
winds stopped, cattlemen emerged to find thousands of carcasses
filling ravines and bunched along fence lines.

The collapse of the bonanza decade was more rapid than its
boom, and the cattle kingdom did not recover. As a depression
diminished the market for beef, many of the great companies, such
as Swan, went to their creditors, who sold the herds into already flag-
ging markets. Some smaller operators managed to hang on, but
many gave up. A pair of apparently colorless statistics tells much: In
1887 one quarter of the cattle sold for slaughter in Chicago were
cows and nearly one in twenty were calves.

There are still large ranches and herds in the West, but nothing
like those of the bonanza years, just as there are no wheat farms
along the Red River of the North to compare to the huge aggrega-
tions of those same years that deployed combines like panzer armies
from horizon to horizon. The 1880s were the decade of agricultural
and pastoral pageants that were never seen again.

Spectacle—it was there overwhelmingly, from the outset.
Nothing mankind could offer could compete with the marvels provided by nature. Perhaps that is why Cecil B. DeMille never attempted a true western—cinematic stunts like Ben Hur's race would have
seemed ludicrously diminutive in Jackson Hole. (The Hudson River
School painters, especially Albert Bierstadt and Thomas Cole, went
west to do their best work—it was not done on the Hudson.) The
great roundups and drives of the cattle kingdom are forever fixed in
our minds—hundreds of thousands of animals moving beneath
clouds of dust rising a mile into the sky, past a backdrop of mountains a mile and a half higher yet. Lost in those clouds of dust is the
truth that these spectacles came about at the behest of distant cor-
porate managers who manipulated the cowboys and the mountain
men and the miners as pawns upon an intercontinental chessboard.

I wonder what John Wayne would say to that.

OPPOSITE: *Bighorn Canyon National Recreation Area, along the Montana–Wyoming border.*

DENVER
AND
ENVIRONS

OPPOSITE: *The seventy-seven-step grand stairway in the Colorado State Capitol, constructed of marble and brass. Murals painted by Alan True, accompanied by Thomas Hornsby Ferril's verse, decorate the rotunda and tell the story of Colorado.*

Colorado's history has been too bountiful for purely local consumption. Over the years it was transmuted into legend and exported to the rest of America and the world: mountain men Jim Bridger and Kit Carson following the fur trade through the Rockies; the Pikes Peak gold rush of 1859, creating boomtowns such as Central City on foundations of glitter and sweat; narrow-gauge railroads puffing over mountain passes two miles high in the sky. Most Americans can conjure up pictures of Indians and cavalrymen in dusty battle, of Doc Holliday betting on the turn of an ace, of cattle barons ruling the plains and cowboys riding the range. Here is a big land with big stories to tell—and in Colorado, most of the legends are true.

The tangible remains of Colorado history include cliff dwellings in the slick-rock country at Mesa Verde; the mine at Cripple Creek; the Georgetown Loop Railroad with tracks circling over themselves on the climb to Silver Plume; Bent's Fort for fur traders on the Santa Fe Trail; and the Denver home of the "Unsinkable" Mrs. Brown, a young store clerk who married a future mining tycoon.

For ages the peaks between plateau and plains barely emerged from glaciers, whose vestiges can still be seen in Rocky Mountain National Park. Colorado has the highest average elevation of any state (6,800 feet), and its ranges contain fifty-three peaks that tower above 14,000 feet. Among these crests four major rivers have their sources: the Colorado, Arkansas, Platte (North and South), and Rio Grande. Only the Colorado drains toward the Pacific; the other rivers flow eastward to the Mississippi and the Gulf of Mexico, as directed by the Continental Divide, which twists down the center of the state and separates it into the eastern and western slopes.

This geography is important in the state's history. Colorado took its name from the Spanish word for "reddish" or "colorful," a reference to the red-rock country. The grasslands once supported herds of American bison, which in turn supported Indians. The early Spanish, French, and American explorers followed the courses of the rivers, as did mountain men in quest of beaver pelts. Prospectors staked their claims along the streams, water being vital for panning and sluicing pay dirt. And water was equally necessary to the cattlemen, sugar beet farmers, and fruit growers who followed.

Wandering hunters came into what is now Colorado about 15,000 years ago. Around A.D. 550 the Basketmaker culture evolved

This 1874 watercolor and gouache view of Denver from the Highlands, painted by Paul Frenzeny and Jules Tavernier, shows some fashionable residents enjoying an excursion in the surrounding countryside.

amid the mesas of southwestern Colorado. Agriculture was introduced, probably by the Anasazi, "ancient ones," who built communal villages high on the canyon walls at Mesa Verde and in the surrounding country. By 1300 they had abandoned their stone cities, probably impelled by drought. Next came the Ute, or "Blue Sky People," who occupied the western slope and moved eastward into the mountains. As a tribal sign they made a sinuous motion of the index finger like a snake writhing, and they fought constantly with the Cheyenne (some of whom painted their bodies red) and the Arapaho, Comanche, and Kiowa who migrated onto the grasslands of the eastern slope.

Then came the Spaniards. Coronado may have crossed the southeastern corner of what is now Colorado on his expedition in 1541, but his failure to find any "cities of gold" in the Southwest discouraged Spanish exploration in Colorado for most of the sixteenth and seventeenth centuries. In 1776 two Franciscan friars, Francisco Atanasio Domínguez and Francisco Silvestre Vélez de Escalante, explored the state's western plateaus and valleys, leaving a legacy in such names as the Río Dolores, or "River of Sorrows"—so called because one of their party drowned there.

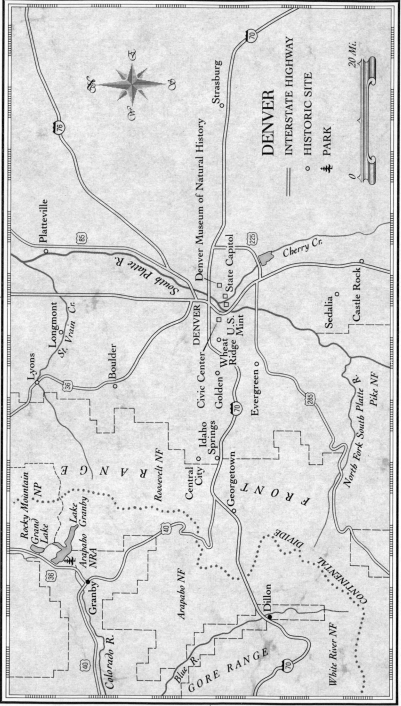

DENVER
— INTERSTATE HIGHWAY
○ HISTORIC SITE
⚏ PARK

0   20 Mi.

70

76

Strasburg

225

Platteville

85

South Platte R.

Denver Museum of Natural History

State Capitol

Cherry Cr.

DENVER

Civic Center

U.S.
Mint

Wheat
Ridge

Golden

Evergreen

70

Sedalia

Castle Rock

285

Longmont

St. Vrain Cr.

Boulder

Lyons

36

North Fork South Platte R.

Pike NF

Idaho
Springs

Central
City

Georgetown

Roosevelt NF

F R O N T

R A N G E

Rocky Mountain
NP

Grand
Lake

Lake
Granby

Arapaho
NRA

36

40

Granby

Arapaho NF

Dillon

White River NF

Colorado R.

40

Blue R.

G O R E   R A N G E

70

C O N T I N E N T A L   D I V I D E

No American explorer penetrated within a thousand miles of the Colorado Rockies until 1806, when a party of sixteen soldiers was dispatched to help find out what President Thomas Jefferson had bought from Napoléon for $15 million. Zebulon M. Pike's expedition made its way up the Arkansas River and managed to reach the site of present-day Pueblo, but failed to climb the peak that now bears Pike's name. Fourteen years later some of Major Stephen H. Long's party did make the ascent, and he made his famous but erroneous endorsement of the view that the plains of Colorado were the "Great American Desert . . . wholly unfit for cultivation."

Unlike most of the world's major cities, Denver was not founded on an important trail, body of water, road, or transcontinental rail line. Instead it was built on gold. In the summer of 1858 William Green Russell, a Georgian with a plaited beard, "struck color" on a tributary of the South Platte River (now in the middle of the city) and started one of history's wildest gold rushes. The nation had been going through an economic depression, and the scent of gold was like perfume. In her history of the period, Sandra Dallas described the first wave of settlers as "a motley hodge-podge of gold-grubbers, gamblers, desperadoes, confidence men, prostitutes, and occasional decent souls who might in fact be called Denver's founding fathers." One of them was William Larimer, a Kansan who claim-jumped onto the land on the eastern side of the Platte. There he organized a town he named Denver City in the hope of gaining political favors from the territorial governor, James Denver, apparently unaware that Denver had already left office. As rumors spread eastward the riches grew with each retelling. One Nebraska man showed off three ounces he "dug with a hatchet in Cherry Creek and washed out with a frying pan." A stampede started toward "Pikes Peak"—a label that outsiders pasted across 200 miles of Colorado's Front Range.

Amateur prospectors poured in, full of hope, but they quickly learned two things—the rumors had been more glittering than the actual ore, and mining was hard work. Libeus Barney wrote a letter home from the settlement of Auraria (now west Denver): "I have had three days' experience in gold digging. The first didn't reach the auriferous color, though I washed about a thousand panfuls. The second day about the same number with a shade of yellow dirt, which inspired courage. Third day, near as I can judge . . . I secured about the sixteenth part of a new cent's worth of the genuine article."

Worthington Whittredge painted Encampment on the Platte, a view of an Indian camp near Denver showing a variety of domestic activities, in 1865. OPPOSITE: *A nineteenth-century engraving of the mining town of Central City, called the "richest square mile on earth" (detail).* OVERLEAF: *The Maroon Bells and Peaks, near Aspen.*

Other fresh arrivals did not see the humor. In rage and disappointment they turned homeward, muttering about the Pikes Peak hoax. Then, in 1859, came news of substantial new finds around Clear Creek, and the rush went wild again. Horace Greeley of the *New York Tribune* went west to visit one of the boom camps at Gregory Gulch. His report was sobering: Prospectors were sleeping under pine boughs, and there was a meat shop "on whose altar are offered up the ill-fed and well-whipped oxen who are just in from a 50-day journey across the plains." But Greeley did confirm the gold strike, and the population of the Gregory Gulch area leaped from 15 to 10,000 in a single month. Later the tent camp grew into prosperous Central City, complete with churches, saloons, three-card-monte dealers, and "soiled doves."

When most of the pay dirt had been staked out, prospectors moved on to discover new diggings and create new towns such as Tarryall, Boulder, Golden, Breckenridge, Fairplay, and Buckskin Joe. The gold camps even had a newspaper by 1859, thanks to William Byers, who published the first issue of the *Rocky Mountain*

News in Denver City less than half an hour before a rival paper appeared. (The other editor agreed to cease publication the same day in exchange for a $30 grubstake from Byers and then vanished toward the gold camps.)

Colorado pioneers organized their own governments in towns and mining districts. The region achieved territorial status in 1861, with William Gilpin as its first governor, but problems soon arose in the Colorado Territory. There was little surface gold left, and hard-rock mining did not pay well. Settlers left to fight in the Civil War. The Indians rose up, ambushing stagecoaches, and at times causing the overland trails to close. The *Rocky Mountain News* opined: "A few months of active extermination against the red devils will bring quiet and nothing else will."

Territorial Governor John Evans had negotiated peace with the Ute in 1863, and the next year he called the Arapaho and Cheyenne to a peace council. After the two tribes set up camp at Sand Creek waiting quietly to sign a treaty with the government, Colonel J. M. Chivington surprised them with a regiment and massacred about 130 men, women, and children, torturing and mutilating with appalling cruelty. By 1869 the army had brought the last of the Plains tribes under control.

During the 1860s silver became the dominant metal mined in Colorado, with bonanzas coming from Georgetown and other camps. A period of prosperity ensued—signs of progress included irrigation farming; mills and factories turning out everything from paper to beer; expanding communications (a branch of the transcontinental telegraph line opened in Denver in 1863); and new roads. The mining industry gained a boost after a Brown University chemistry professor, Nathaniel Hill, built the state's first smelter, at Black Hawk in 1868. When the Union Pacific Railroad announced that it would bypass Colorado and cross the Continental Divide through a lower pass in southern Wyoming, Coloradans put together their own railroad and built a spur to meet the Union Pacific line in Cheyenne. By 1872 the Kansas Pacific had come across the plains to Denver. The Denver & Rio Grande Western Railroad reached south to Pueblo, and soon its narrow-gauge engines climbed over the Rockies like burros.

OPPOSITE: *A grizzled miner swirls water and dirt in his pan, watchful for the yellow glint of gold in this photograph by L. C. McClure.*

The Denver skyline shows that although it is the mile-high city, it is dwarfed by the even

In order to increase business, the railroads encouraged mining, ranching, and tourism. Tracts of railroad land were made available for "colony towns" such as Greeley, an agricultural cooperative organized by Nathan Meeker, an editor on the staff of Horace Greeley's *New York Tribune.* On the plains vast cattle spreads flourished during a brief era of cattle kings, with drives and roundups of Texas longhorns that became part of American legend—even though many of the ranches belonged to investors from Europe.

With its newfound prosperity and population, Colorado Territory clamored for statehood; in 1876 it became the thirty-eighth state, with its capital at Denver. Seventeen years earlier it had been a camping ground for the Arapaho—now it was a city of 35,000. Cherry Creek gold had soon given out, but the town was able to establish itself as a supply center for other mining camps and later became a market hub for nearby farms. Although the great fire of 1863 and the flood of 1864 destroyed most of the early settlement, Denver rebuilt itself more handsomely in brick and stone, earning the nickname "Queen City of the Plains."

higher peaks of the Rockies.

In the 1870s railroads, government business, and money flowing from silver camps ensured Denver's continuing prosperity. Horace Tabor, the Leadville mining king, and his brethren built mansions on Capitol Hill and office buildings downtown. The Tabor Grand Opera House opened, and cable cars shuttled up Larimer and 16th streets. Confidence man J. R. "Soapy" Smith opened a "school to cure gamblers" and sold bars of soap at inflated prices as a sort of lottery—Smith claimed some wrappers contained $100 bills—thereby earning his nickname. Mattie Silks and other madams operated on Market Street, where Mattie's House of Mirrors still stands (although without its glittering fixtures).

When the silver market tumbled in 1893, Denver lost, then slowly regained its economic footing, thanks in part to gold coming from the mines of Cripple Creek. In 1900 the town's first automobile showroom opened on 16th Street, displaying Locomobiles in a salon decorated with Navajo rugs. The city became increasingly respectable; the matrons of Denver society threw parties at the Brown Palace Hotel. But when Dorothy Parker, the witty writer of verses and short stories, visited during the Great Depression, she asked to be spared "stuffed shirts" in favor of "real people." The party given in her honor welcomed prostitutes and pimps, Chinese lottery owners, and gamblers, while Denver society figures were turned away at the door.

Denver has more than twenty historic districts, including Larimer Square and Lower Downtown where the city began. This chapter begins with these two districts, then proceeds to the Civic Center and Capitol Hill areas, and next touches on varied attractions across the city. Then sites outside Denver are described.

D   E   N   V   E   R

L A R I M E R   S Q U A R E

Denver's first thoroughfare was named by the city's founder for himself—Larimer Street. At the corner of 15th Street, William Larimer put up the first building, a log cabin with doors made out of coffin lids, but it was destroyed along with other wooden structures in the 1863 fire, prompting civic leaders to stipulate brick construction for future commercial buildings. The seventeen brick structures in today's **Larimer Square Historic District** (1400 block of Larimer Street) were erected between 1870 and 1890; the district housed Denver's first photographic studio, theater, and bank. After renovations that began in 1965, the buildings have been converted to shops and restaurants. **Lincoln Hall** has a mansard roof and was once a dance hall with the second floor supported by springs. Across the street George Kettle put up the **Kettle Building** in 1873 by erecting only front and back walls and using the side walls of his neighbors. The **Gallup-Stanbury Building,** with its pedestal clock in front, was built in the same year.

DOWNTOWN

In the **Lower Downtown Historic District** adjacent to Larimer Square, the **Denver Union Station** (1701 Wynkoop Street, at terminus of 17th Street) offers one of the city's few examples of Beaux-Arts classicism; it was built as the joint terminal for all railroads with

OPPOSITE: *The Crawford Building in Denver's Larimer Square Historic District. Built in 1875, it was one of the first brick store buildings in Denver.*

service into Denver. Across the street, at 17th and Wynkoop streets, is the 1883 **Denver City Railway Building,** where horse-drawn trolleys were parked on the main floor and horses stabled on the second and third floors. Conveniently close to the train station stands the elegant brick **Oxford Alexis Hotel** (17th Street and Wazee), designed by Frank Edbrooke. The hotel opened in 1891, boasting steam heat and a "vertical railway," or elevator; the guest rooms and lobby have been restored. A reminder of wilder times is the **Elephant Corral** (1444 Wazee Street). The present building dates to 1902, but there were earlier buildings on the site, one of which was the city's "king hell-hole," packing in as many as 800 gold-crazed drinkers each night.

A few blocks uptown, the 330 foot-tall **Daniels and Fisher Tower** (1601 Arapahoe Street) ranked as the nation's third-tallest structure when Frederick Sterner designed it in 1909. It was inspired by the campanile of Saint Mark's Square in Venice, although it functioned more humbly—as part of a dry goods store; it is now offices. The **Trinity United Methodist Church** (Broadway and East Eighteenth Avenue) of 1888 expresses the High Victorian Gothic style in native sandstone. It was designed by Robert S. Roeschlaub, Denver's first significant architect, who practiced between 1873 and 1912.

The **Brown Palace Hotel** (321 17th Street, 303–297–3111) has played host to Denver society, royalty, and presidents. Designed by Frank Edbrooke in the Richardsonian manner, the nine-story hotel was put up in 1892 at a cost of $1.6 million by Henry C. Brown on a triangular parcel of land, which necessitated a triangular building. Its central atrium of Mexican onyx is enclosed by tiers of cast-iron balconies and capped with a roof of stained glass. In the lobby almost every character of note in Denver has made an appearance, from Regent, a National Western Stock Show prize bull, to Evalyn Walsh McLean, wearing the Hope Diamond in her hair.

Museum of Western Art

Legend says that a secret tunnel once connected the Brown Palace to the Navarre, a red-brick Victorian building across Tremont Place that started life as the first coeducational college west of the

OPPOSITE: *The ornate atrium of Denver's Brown Palace Hotel, whose architect, Frank Edbrooke, was so meticulous in his detailing that he used nearly two tons of paper for the plans.*

Mississippi but later became a gambling hall and notorious bordello. This 1880 structure now houses the Museum of Western Art, with three galleries of scenes of buffalo hunts, Indian fights, and landscapes. More than 100 works by such artists as Frederic Remington, Charles Russell, Thomas Moran, and Georgia O'Keeffe are arranged chronologically to tell the story of the West.

> LOCATION: 1727 Tremont Place. HOURS: 10–4:30 Tuesday–Saturday. FEE: Yes. TELEPHONE: 303–296–1880.

At East Seventeenth Avenue and Sherman Street, the **Central Presbyterian Church** ranks as one of Frank Edbrooke's best designs, built in 1892 of stone in the Richardsonian Romanesque style, with a square bell tower and round arched windows. Damon Runyan, the short-story writer, started his career as a journalist while living at **The Denver Athletic Club** (1325 Glenarm Place, 303–534–1211) from 1906 to 1911. Old Fire Station Number One (1326 Tremont Place, 303–892–1436) houses the **Denver Firefighters Museum,** which displays fire-fighting equipment from the 1800s.

CAPITOL HILL

After the turn of the century, the administrative center of Denver took shape on Capitol Hill, a ten-acre parcel given to the city by Henry C. Brown.

State Capitol

Construction of the capitol began in 1888, after Elijah E. Myers of Detroit won the commission with his Classic Revival design, inspired by the U.S. Capitol, incorporating a Greek cross and a central rotunda. Problems with materials and finances plagued the project for a decade, and in 1897 Frank Edbrooke, who had been a runner-up in the design competition, was hired to act as supervising architect. Edbrooke designed the open rotunda, grand stairway, and bronze doors, and suggested the gallery of portraits in stained glass depicting important Colorado figures, including Chief Ouray and Kit Carson. The project exhausted the only known supply of rose onyx

OPPOSITE: *Green lawns separate the Colorado State Capitol from the curved facade of the City and County Building, built in 1932, which was designed by a committee made up of thirty-five local architects.*

in the world, a deposit in Beulah, Colorado. When standing on the thirteenth step of the west exterior stairs, one is exactly one mile above sea level. Capitol tours are available.

LOCATION: East Colfax Avenue at Sherman Street. HOURS: 9–4 Monday–Friday FEE: None. TELEPHONE: 303–866–2604.

In the adjacent parkland, the **Civic Center,** planned by Frederick Law Olmsted, Jr., contains the crescent-shaped, Classic Revival **City and County Building.** At the corner of Broadway and West Colfax Avenue, the **Pioneer Monument** indicates the end of the Smoky Hill Trail, which was followed initially in 1859 by prospectors heading for Cherry Creek.

U.S. Mint

Miners who struck it rich brought their gold dust and nuggets to be cast into bars at the Denver mint. Denver is one of three gold depositories in the United States, along with West Point and Fort Knox. The federal government purchased Clark, Gruber and Company's private mint in 1862, then completed this larger building in 1904, vaguely derived from the fifteenth-century Florentine Palazzo Medici-Riccardi. The government began making coins here two years later. Each day the impregnable-looking granite structure, which completely fills one city block, stamps 30 million metal blanks into coins worth $1.5 million. Tour groups can watch the process.

LOCATION: 320 West Colfax Avenue. HOURS: September through May: 8:30-3:30 Daily; June through August: 8–3:30 Daily. FEE: None. TELEPHONE: 303–844–6202.

Denver Art Museum

The museum displays one of the world's finest collections of North American Indian art—8,500 items, including costumes, pottery, Navajo and Pueblo textiles, Hopi kachinas, silverwork, blankets, and baskets. Spanish colonial art, quilts, and the art of the American West are also well represented, along with European, Asian, and various other American works. There is a museum shop, and free tours are available.

LOCATION: 100 West Fourteenth Avenue Parkway, across from Civic Center Park. HOURS: 10–5 Tuesday–Saturday, 12–5 Sunday. FEE: Yes, except Saturday 10–12. TELEPHONE: 303–575–2793.

The Denver Art Museum, also a part of the Civic Center complex, was constructed in 1971 from the design of the Italian architect Gio Ponti working with the Denver architect James Sudler.

Behind the art museum stands the eclectic **Byers-Evans House** (1310 Bannock Street, 303–623–0709), built by the founder of the *Rocky Mountain News* in 1880 and purchased a decade later by William G. Evans, son of the second territorial governor. Restoration of the house is currently under way, with a public opening planned for early 1990. When opened it will house the Denver History Museum.

Colorado History Museum

Operated by the Colorado Historical Society, the museum traces the state's past through exhibits of Anasazi artifacts from Mesa Verde and the Southwest; dioramas of Indian buffalo hunts, frontier forts, and gold mining; a 150-year time line of Colorado history; and a model of Denver in 1860, when several blocks were set aside as "parking lots" for wagon trains. Other highlights include Tabor family memorabilia (diaries, letters, Baby Doe's wedding dress, business papers of Horace Tabor), prints by the early photographer of the West William Henry Jackson, and mining equipment.

> LOCATION: 1300 Broadway. HOURS: 10–4:30 Monday–Saturday, 12–4:30 Sunday. FEE: Yes. TELEPHONE: 303–866–3682.

Molly Brown House Museum

Margaret (Molly) Tobin was a young girl fresh out of Missouri and working as a clerk in a Leadville store in 1886 when she married James J. Brown, who would later become rich from Leadville's Little Jonny gold mine. In 1894 Molly and J. J. moved with their two children to Denver where, for $30,000, they bought the "House of Lions" designed by William Lang, a Denver architect. They soon joined Denver's prestigious clubs and entertained lavishly in their fashionable home. During their travels in Europe and Asia, it was

Molly Brown's Denver house is built of local lava stone with sandstone trim. The Browns made extensive additions to the house, including a new facade, during the sixteen years they lived there.

leased to prominent individuals, including, in 1902, the governor of Colorado and his wife. The restored house has been furnished in the style typical of the Browns' time, with some objects that belonged to the family. In 1909 the Browns were legally separated. J. J. continued to manage his mining interests while Molly resumed traveling. She became a national heroine in 1912 when she survived the sinking of the *Titanic,* earning her the sobriquet "Unsinkable." Her knowledge of several languages enabled her to help many of the immigrant women and children who also survived the sinking.

LOCATION: 1340 Pennsylvania Street. HOURS: April through September: 10–4 Tuesday–Saturday, 12–4 Sunday (June through August: also open Mondays), October through March: 10–3 Tuesday–Saturday, 12–3 Sunday. FEE: Yes. TELEPHONE: 303-832-1421

An 1889 house down the street at **1200 Pennsylvania Street** (private) is Denver's most noteworthy Richardsonian Romanesque residence.

In 1910, Molly Brown photographed her drawing room to record the lavish decorations in place for a summer reception. She expected 800 guests, but was disappointed by the far smaller number that attended. Brown was unpopular with Denver society until she survived the Titanic *disaster and became a national celebrity.*

The Colorado Governor's mansion, above and opposite, was designed by the Denver architects Marean and Norton for a local industrialist, Walter Cheesman. After his death, it was completed by his wife and daughter, who sold it to Claude K. Boettcher in the 1920s. The Boettcher Foundation gave it to the state, with its furnishings, in 1959.

The **Croke-Patterson-Campbell House** (430 East Eleventh Avenue, private) offers Denver's only example of the French Chateau style; the brick-and-stone pile was erected in 1890 by Thomas Croke, a state senator who was sometimes called America's "Father of Irrigation." The **900 and 1000 blocks of Logan Street** also boast some of Capitol Hill's early homes. Mamie Eisenhower and Douglas Fairbanks were graduated from the **Dora Moore School** at 845 Corona Street.

The **Governor's Mansion** (400 East Eighth Avenue, 303–837–8350), a Colonial Revival house dating to 1908, was given to the state complete with fine furnishings and objets d'art by the family of Claude Boettcher, son of a German immigrant who, according to legend, grubstaked a miner to a $20 cook stove and later sold his share of the discovered claim for $150,000. After becoming an industrialist, he bought the Brown Palace Hotel.

Grant-Humphreys Mansion

Once the setting for dances attended by Denver's magnates, the house was built in 1902 by James B. Grant, Colorado's third governor, and later sold to Albert Humphreys, who had made a fortune wildcatting in oil. Designed in an eclectic Classic Revival style, it boasts grandiose rooms (forty-two in all) and various elements borrowed from European architecture. Tours are given by the Colorado Historical Society.

LOCATION: 770 Pennsylvania Street. HOURS: 10–2 Tuesday–Friday. FEE: Yes. TELEPHONE: 303–894–2505.

AURARIA CAMPUS AREA

In this district on the west side of Cherry Creek, the **Tivoli Brewery** (1342 10th Street) began turning out beer in 1890 in its gracefully composed brick building of Second Empire style; today the building has been renovated for stores and restaurants. Nearby are the 1898 **Saint Elizabeth's Church** (1060 11th Street), the first Catholic church to be consecrated in Colorado, and the **Ninth Street Park Historic District,** which contains one of Denver's oldest intact residential blocks (1873–1905), with a sampling of Victorian architectural trends from Second Empire (1015 and 1027 9th Street) to Italianate (1068 9th Street).

San Rafael Historic District

The district contains many homes built before Colorado achieved statehood, including the **Thomas Hornsby Ferril Residence,** at 2123 Downing Street. A poet from an old Denver family, Ferril one day dared to appear at the dining room of the Brown Palace Hotel without a necktie. The maître d'hôtel insisted he wear a borrowed tie, which provoked a well-publicized controversy in which Ferril described the proffered tie as "a Father's Day clearance sale necktie! A flamboyant necktie of abstract design combining gangrene squid with magenta bar sinister."

Also in the San Rafael District is the **Zion Baptist Church** (933 East 24th Avenue), which was completed in 1892 in rusticated stone. It is the oldest black Baptist church in Colorado.

OPPOSITE: *Corinthian columns like those associated with the antebellum South grace the Grant-Humphreys Mansion, designed by Denver architects Theodore Davis Boal and F. L. Harnois for James B. Grant, a native of Alabama who struck it rich in Colorado.*

Denver's Tivoli Brewery building. The wing to the right of the main section was originally the Turnhalle Opera House where the local turnverein (German athletic club) held its theatrical events.

Four Mile Historic Park

Denver's oldest surviving house, built in 1859, lies on the former Smoky Hill Trail and the Old Cherokee Trail/Denver–Santa Fe Stage Road. Built of logs, bricks, and clapboard, it was a way station for stagecoach passengers. On site are **Four Mile House** (so named to indicate distance from Denver), an apiary, and a working farm.

LOCATION: 715 South Forest Street. HOURS: 11–5 Tuesday–Sunday. FEE: Yes. TELEPHONE: 303–399–1859.

Denver Museum of Natural History

Opened in 1908, this is the largest natural history museum between Chicago and the West Coast. Many exhibits illustrate Colorado's geological history, its dinosaurs (including a 75-foot *Diplodocus* skeleton), and its prehistoric peoples. The museum's unusual collections include flake gold, meteorites, and gemstones (of special interest is a 10,558-carat faceted topaz). There are ninety life-sized dioramas showing animals in their natural habitats.

LOCATION: 2001 Colorado Boulevard, in City Park. HOURS: 9–5 Daily. FEE: Yes. TELEPHONE: 303–322–7009.

Pearce-McAllister Cottage

Harold Pearce, manager of Nathaniel Hill's Argo Smelter, built this home to please his wife, who wanted "a perfect Colonial cottage such as one sees in the older districts of the Eastern States of America." The house was later sold to Henry McAllister, general counsel for the Denver & Rio Grande Western Railroad. The furnishings, tableware, and knickknacks reflect his family's taste and lifestyle from 1900 into the 1920s. The cottage also houses the **Denver Museum of Miniatures, Dolls, and Toys,** whose dollhouses range from a grand Newport mansion to a Santa Fe adobe.

LOCATION. 1880 Gaylord Street. HOURS: 10–4 Wednesday–Saturday, 12–4 Sunday. FEE: Yes. TELEPHONE: 303–322–3704.

Other noteworthy buildings in the Denver area include the **Evans Memorial Chapel** (University of Denver, 303–871–3222), built in 1878 in the Gothic Revival style by territorial governor John Evans and moved to the campus in 1959. The **South Broadway Christian Church,** of 1891 (23 Lincoln Street), is a visually lively Romanesque building of special interest for its craftsmanship and rich carvings. The simple clapboard **Eugene Field House** (Washington Park) was occupied by the poet from 1881 to 1883 while he was managing editor of the *Denver Tribune.* A notorious practical joker, Field once hoaxed a Denver audience by impersonating Oscar Wilde. The house, which was moved here from its original location, represents Denver's first effort at historic preservation, spearheaded by the "Unsinkable" Mrs. Brown.

The **Forney Transportation Museum** (1416 Platte Street, 303–433–3643) houses antique cars, carriages, cycles, a Big Boy locomotive, rail coaches, trolleys, and model trains in the former power plant of the Denver Tramway Company, built in Romanesque Revival style in 1901.

The first famous eatery on the premises of the **Buckhorn Exchange** (1000 Osage Street, 303–534–9505) was the Rio Grande Exchange Restaurant and Saloon, opened in 1893 by Henry Zietz, who worked as a scout for Buffalo Bill and guided Theodore Roosevelt on a hunting trip; the president arrived aboard a private train just outside. Today's restaurant displays more than 500 specimens of taxidermy and serves buffalo and elk steaks at century-old poker tables, amid a collection of old pistols and rifles.

D E N V E R' S   E N V I R O N S

Around the capital lie varied communities whose common element
is a link with the capital—boomtowns tied by early mining history,
farming communities that sold their produce in Denver, railroad
towns linked to big city markets. The sites will be discussed by moving in a counterclockwise sequence, beginning in the north.

FORT VASQUEZ

In 1835 Louis Vasquez and Andrew Sublette built this link in a chain
of fur-trading posts designed to dominate the Indian trade along the
South Platte River. An early traveler reported that Fort Vasquez was
about 100 feet square, with 12-foot-high adobe walls designed to
protect the operations of the Rocky Mountain Fur Company. This
enterprise obtained Indian buffalo robes in exchange for ivory
combs, Hudson's Bay blankets, silk handkerchiefs, and the electrify-
ing liquor known as Taos Lightning. After five years the founders
sold out, and in 1842 the fort was overrun and looted by Indians.
Today's reconstruction was erected by the WPA in the 1930s and is
operated by the Colorado Historical Society; the visitor center has
exhibits on the fur trade and the Plains Indians of the period
1820–1840.

> LOCATION: 13412 Route 85, just south of Platteville. HOURS:
> Memorial Day through Labor Day: 10–5 Monday–Saturday, 1–5
> Sunday; modified hours in September. FEE: Yes. TELEPHONE:
> 303–785–2832.

LONGMONT

This agricultural community was founded in the 1870s on 70,000
acres in the Saint Vrain River valley. Today the town remembers its
history at **The Longmont Museum** (375 Kimbark Street,
303–651–8374), with exhibits that range from Folsom spear points
made by Native American hunters of 10,000 B.C., through the Plains
Indians, explorers, settlers, and town builders, to the belongings of
the astronaut Vance Brand, a native of Longmont. The **Dickens
Opera House** (302 Main Street, 303–772–5167) dates to 1881.

Fort Vasquez, built as a fur-trading post on the South Platte River in 1835, was reconstructed as a WPA project in the 1930s.

LYONS

The **Lyons Depot-Library** (400 Broadway, 303–823–6682), built in 1885, is an example of architecture based on the use of local materials, in this case, sandstone blocks from nearby quarries. The town has served as a stopover for tourists on the way to Estes Park. A school built in 1881 contains the **Lyons Redstone Museum** (340 High Street, 303–823–6692), with displays of Arapaho life, pioneer household items, a large collection of telephone insulators, and a horse-drawn mail cart used from 1907 to 1928. Fifteen buildings in Lyons and the surrounding area, all built between 1881 and 1917, have been designated as a historic district.

BOULDER

In October 1858 a group of gold seekers led by Captain Thomas Aikens camped at the mouth of Boulder Canyon. The Arapaho chief Left Hand visited them there and told of a dream: He had seen the flood waters of Boulder Creek sweep over the Indians,

while the whites were saved. And, as the chief feared, a trickle of pioneers became a permanent flood. They laid out a town in 1859,
called Boulder City for the huge rocks in the nearby Flatirons Range
of the Rocky Mountains. The new inhabitants dug irrigation ditches
and built log cabins along Pearl Street, now a pedestrian mall that is
part of the **Pearl Street Historic Commercial District.** Above Pearl
Street stand a number of grand homes on **Mapleton Hill,** a residential area laid out in 1888. Information about the area is available
from Historic Boulder Inc. (1733 Canyon Boulevard,
303–444–5192).

The **Boulder Historical Society Museum** (1206 Euclid Avenue,
303–449–3464) occupies Harbeck House, the summer home, built
in 1899, of a New York stockbroker. The museum displays dolls,
quilts, glass, and silver, as well as costumes from the mid-1800s to the
present. Artifacts and exhibits representing Boulder's history and
personalities are housed at the **Carnegie Branch Library for Local
History** at 1125 Pine Street (303–441–3110).

In 1860 Boulderites put up Colorado's first building dedicated
to use as a schoolhouse, and in 1877 the **University of Colorado**
opened. The oldest building on campus is **Old Main,** built in 1877
of red brick. On the top floor of this restored building is the **CU
Heritage Center** (303–492–6329), a museum with exhibits illustrating the early days of the university. The **University of Colorado
Museum** (303–492–6892) has exhibits on anthropology, biology,
geology, and zoology.

Within **Chautauqua Park** (11th and Baseline streets) is the
Chautauqua Auditorium, a board-and-batten structure built in 1898
by Texans as a summer study center. In City Park (Canyon
Boulevard at Broadway) rests **Locomotive Number 30,** a relic of the
narrow-gauge (but grandly titled) Denver, Salt Lake & Pacific
Railroad that climbed the "Switzerland Trail" to the high country.

In **Wheat Ridge** an unknown builder constructed the **Wheat Ridge
Soddy** (4610 Robb Street, 303–433–6097) in 1860 by stacking blocks
of native tall-prairie grass sod, a material surprising to find used in a
place where stone and wood were plentiful.

GOLDEN

In 1859 Golden City was organized on the south side of Clear Creek
and named for an early miner, Tom Golden, not for the yellow

metal. A remnant of the town's brief political prominence is the **Territorial Capitol** (12th Street and Washington Avenue), the site of intermittent legislative assemblies from 1862 until 1867, when Denver became the seat of government. Today the building houses a restaurant that claims to incorporate the bar where James Butler "Wild Bill" Hickok downed his last drink.

The **Astor House Hotel** (822 12th Street, 303–278–3557), built in 1867, was the first stone hostelry west of Saint Louis and is probably the oldest hotel remaining in the state. Designed in Frontier Georgian style, the hotel now operates as a museum of frontier decorative art, furniture, and clothing. The interior has been restored in the style of the period 1860–1890. The hotel is adjacent to the **Twelfth Street Historic District,** a neighborhood of homes that territorial-era businessmen built within walking distance of their offices and stores. The nearby **Colorado National Guard Armory** (13th Street and Arapahoe) is the largest cobblestone building in the United States. Its construction in 1913 required 3,300 wagon loads of stream-worn cobble from Clear Creek.

Minerals, gems, fossils, and historical mining artifacts make up the collections at the **Colorado School of Mines Geology Museum** (16th and Maple streets, 303–273–3823). Of special interest here is the Thomas Allen Minelighting Collection of pre-electricity mining lamps. The **Golden D.A.R. Pioneer Museum,** housed in City Hall (911 10th Street, 303–278–7151), displays artifacts from Golden's early days, including an organ brought by wagon train, a metal bathtub, a gold scale, quilts, and oddities such as a chair made of bulls' horns and a picture composed entirely of hair from the heads of one family.

Colorado Railroad Museum

Founded in 1958 to preserve the history of the rapidly vanishing narrow-gauge and steam trains, the museum has assembled railroading artifacts in a replica of an 1880s depot. In the nearby yard stand more than fifty locomotives, railroad cars, and trolleys, including the sole surviving steam engine of the Denver & Rio Grande Western Railroad and a rear lounge/sleeper car of the 1930s from the streamlined Santa Fe Super Chief.

LOCATION: 17155 West 44th Avenue (near Route 70 Exit 265). HOURS: September through May: 9–5 Daily; June through August: 9–6 Daily. FEE: Yes. TELEPHONE: 303–279–4591.

The Buffalo Bill Memorial Museum exhibits items collected by Johnny Baker, a close friend of William F. "Buffalo Bill" Cody and a former member of his Wild West Show troupe.

Buffalo Bill Memorial Museum and Grave

One of the West's most colorful characters, William F. "Buffalo Bill" Cody lived up to his legend. At age 14 he became a Pony Express rider, with great endurance and an unusual memory for terrain. As a hunter supplying meat for workers on the Kansas Pacific Railroad, he gained his nickname after shooting 4,289 buffalo in one season. Dime novels about Buffalo Bill began to appear in 1869, the first of a flood of 40 million words written about him. Generally a friend of the Indians, Cody ambushed and scalped the Indian chief Yellow Hair after the Custer massacre, thereby adding to his fame. Beginning in 1883 Cody toured America and Europe with Buffalo Bill's Wild West Show, an extravaganza featuring 640 cowboys and Indians, as well as horses, stagecoaches, and a buffalo herd. Half the Indians in Cody's reenactment of the Battle of Little Big Horn had actually fought in the battle. Cody himself reenacted his scalping of Yellow Hair.

Buffalo Bill's grave on Lookout Mountain lies beside a museum filled with Wild West posters, Indian artifacts, rifles, early photos, clothing (Buffalo Bill popularized the Stetson hat), and Western art.

LOCATION: 987 Lookout Mountain Road. HOURS: November through April: 9–4 Tuesday–Sunday; May through October: 9–5 Daily. FEE: Yes. TELEPHONE: 303–526–0747.

CENTRAL CITY

When John Gregory hiked up a snowy canyon in early 1859, he found more gold in a week than the prospector who made the strike at Cherry Creek had panned the whole previous summer. That started the real Colorado gold rush, and Central City soon overshadowed Denver. Five thousand people converged within a few months, spawning saloons, gambling halls, and violence. A history of the rush by Sarah J. Pearce reports that during an 1861 election Central City recorded "217 fist fights, 97 revolver fights, 11 Bowie knife fights, and 1 dog fight," although no one was actually killed. The city managed to achieve a reputation as a center of culture, noted especially for its opera house.

Central City was called "the richest square mile on earth," and the hills surrounding it produced more than $125 million in precious metals. Among those who made fortunes there were Henry M. Teller, Colorado's first U.S. senator, and George Pullman, developer of the railroad sleeping car. In adjacent Black Hawk, Professor Nathaniel Hill grew rich after building his smelter in 1868. No sign of the smelter remains, although some historic buildings survive, such as the **Lace House** (161 Main Street, 303–582–5382), a fine example of Carpenter Gothic architecture.

Central City languished after the mines petered out, but rose again after 1932 with the restoration of the oldest opera house in Colorado, the **Central City Opera** (Eureka Street, 303–292–6500). The stone Richardsonian showplace opened in 1878 as the "finest temple of the Muse west of the Missouri." In 1932 Lillian Gish starred as Camille to launch what is now a summer opera festival that continues to lure visitors from July through August every year.

Next door stands the **Teller House** (120 Eureka Street, 303–582–3200), an 1872 Romanesque Revival hotel. Old-time resident Frank Young opined: "From the aesthetic point of view, one may say (with deference to the architect, who, I believe, is still within shooting distance at the time of this writing) that the hotel is not a masterpiece of construction" and "might easily be taken for a New England Factory." Still, it offered the town's finest accommodations—good enough for President Ulysses S. Grant, for whose arrival the townsfolk laid a sidewalk of silver bricks outside the hotel. In 1936 a staff artist for the *Denver Post,* after quite a few drinks in the bar, got down from his stool and painted a portrait of his wife called "The Face On the Barroom Floor," which remains a popular conversation piece.

Other notable buildings in the district include **Saint James Methodist** (123 Eureka Street), dedicated in 1872. The substantial brick **Lee House** (201 West High Street, private) was built in 1878 by Jeremiah Lee, a freed slave who arrived in Colorado after trying his luck in the California gold rush. The **Lost Gold Mine** (229 Eureka Street, 303–642–7533) offers underground tours of two mines that produced from about 1860 to 1913; gold veins can still be seen.

In 1869 Cornish stonemasons constructed the building that now houses the **Gilpin County Historical Society Museum** (228 East High

The Central City Opera House, built in 1878, brought a new level of culture to the gold-rush town known as "the richest square mile on earth." Its stone walls are four feet thick.

Street, 303–582–5283), noted for its collection of cutters and sur-
reys. Other exhibits include a pharmacy, a barbershop, a law office,
and a Victorian home. Another intriguing museum is the **Thomas-
Billings Home** (209 Eureka Street, 303–582–5011/5093), which has
some Greek Revival elements. Boarded up in 1917 with all its furnishings and household goods inside, the house now displays them
virtually unchanged, from kitchen spices to original wallpapers.

IDAHO SPRINGS

In January 1859 George Jackson, an Indian trader, dug his knife
into the frozen ground along Chicago Creek and came up with
gold, making what was technically Colorado's earliest major strike.
Today **Jackson's Monument** (one-quarter mile up Route 103), at the
confluence of Chicago and Clear creeks, marks the spot. Jackson
later organized the Chicago Mining Company to carry out the first
large-scale mining in the state. An early mountain road connected
the camp to Central City via rugged Virginia Canyon. Ulysses S.
Grant and his daughter made a harrowing trip over this **Oh-My-God
Road,** and steel-nerved visitors can drive it today, passing many
abandoned mines. George Jackson also noted the area's beneficial
hot springs, and by 1866 two bathhouses were serving health seekers. The famous turn-of-the-century Radium Hot Springs live on as
Indian Springs Resort (302 Soda Creek Road, 303–623–2050).

A section of town has been designated the **Idaho Springs
Downtown Commercial District.** A brick building constructed in
1912 houses the **Underhill Museum** (1416 Miner Street,
303–567–4100), the rear of which was once a mining engineer's
home, with an office occupying the front. The museum displays
original Victorian furnishings, mining relics, old maps, and photographs of the old-time mining operations. The **John Owen House**
(1334 Virginia Street, private), built of clapboard in the 1870s, once
belonged to a prominent mine owner. Behind city hall is the
Colorado & Southern Engine Number 60, a narrow-gauge locomotive that toiled up the nearby Georgetown Loop.

Argo Town U.S.A. (23rd Avenue at Riverside Drive,
303–567–2421) offers tours of a reproduction of a Western mining
town, including the reopened Double Eagle Gold Mine and the six-
story Argo Gold Mill, which houses the **Clear Creek Historic Mining
and Milling Museum.**

GEORGETOWN

Although Georgetown started life as a gold camp, it grew into a silver center, which the traveling English author Isabella Bird called "the only town I have seen in America to which the epithet picturesque could be applied." Its streets are lined with about 200 Victorian buildings, and it is the only important mining town in Colorado to have escaped destruction by fire. At 507 5th Street is **Alpine Hose Company Number 2,** which sheltered hose carts for one of the four volunteer fire companies.

Churches and substantial homes went up early, since families were part of Georgetown's social fabric from the beginning—a striking departure from the situation in most mining camps. **Grace Episcopal Church** (Taos Street) was built in 1867. When the focus of mining activity shifted to Leadville in the late 1870s, only the speculators departed, leaving a stable community served by the Colorado Central Railroad. With prosperity, elegant homes sprang up, becoming larger as their owners got richer.

Hamill House Museum

Between 1874 and 1885 William A. Hamill, a mining investor, augmented his small Gothic Revival house with a solarium, bay windows, walnut woodwork, central heating, the first gaslights in town, French camel-hair wallpaper, and gold-plated doorknobs. The house is headquarters of the Georgetown Society, which provides visitor information and conducts tours of the house.

LOCATION: 301 Argentine Street. HOURS: June through September: 9–5 Daily; October through June: 12–4 Tuesday–Sunday. FEE: Yes. TELEPHONE: 303–569–2840.

The **Maxwell House** (4th and Taos streets, private) is a fine example of Victorian architecture. It began life as a modest frame house owned by a grocer named Potter. After he grubstaked a lucky prospector in 1890, his house acquired Italianate windows, Greek Revival pediments, a cupola and spire, and a French roof. After the silver crash of 1893, the house was sold to mining engineer Frank Maxwell.

OPPOSITE: *The Hamill House features an ornate fireplace faced with hand-painted Minton and Copeland porcelain tiles manufactured in England in the 1880s.*

Hotel de Paris

Hotelier Louis Dupuy was an oddity in the Wild West: a French philosopher who owned 3,000 books, a legendary chef who served continental delicacies and imported wines by the barrel. Having remodeled a bakery into an elegant inn famous in the West, he often refused to rent rooms to people he disliked. (He also refused to pay taxes, keeping a shotgun on hand to emphasize his philosophy.) A dedicated misogynist, Dupuy nonetheless took in a widow as a housekeeper and willed the hotel to her at his death in 1900. Restored with many original furnishings, the hotel now operates as a museum.

> LOCATION: 409 6th Street. HOURS: June through October: 9–5 Daily; November through May: 12–4 Tuesday–Sunday. FEE: Yes. TELEPHONE: 303–569–2311.

Georgetown's Hotel de Paris, established in 1875 by Louis DuPuy after the citizens of the town took up a collection for his support following a mining injury. OPPOSITE: *Georgetown's First Presbyterian Church, established in 1869 by the Reverend Sheldon Jackson, who organized more than one hundred congregations in Colorado. The native-stone building was completed in 1874.*

A narrow-gauge train on the Georgetown, Breckenridge & Leadville's famous Georgetown Loop, an engineering marvel connecting Georgetown and Silver Plume, built in 1884. Four and a half miles of track had to be laid to cover a two-mile distance.

Georgetown Loop Historic Mining and Railroad Park

The Colorado Central Railroad reached Silver Plume, two miles from Georgetown, by a splendid feat of engineering completed in 1884. The narrow-gauge tracks climbed along steep valley walls, over four bridges, and up the Loop, a section of track on which the climbing train completed a spiral on a trestle 100 feet above Clear Creek. Later the Georgetown Loop became an attraction for thrill-seeking tourists and was abandoned in 1939. It was rebuilt in the 1980s by the Colorado Historical Society as part of the historic park, with steam trains for summer and fall excursionists. Also in the park are the 1871 **Lebanon Mine and Mill,** where visitors don hard hats to go 600 feet underground, and the **Silver Plume Depot,** intact from 1884 but moved from its original location.

LOCATION: Exit 228 or 226 from Route 70. HOURS: Memorial Day through Labor Day: 10–4:30 Daily. Train rides available on weekends in September. FEE: Yes. TELEPHONE: 303–279–6101.

MORRISON

Part of this town, laid out in 1872 at the mouth of Bear Creek Canyon, has been designated as the **Morrison National Historic District,** with buildings of wood, brick, and local stone. The **Morrison Schoolhouse** (226 Spring Street, private) is a two-story limestone structure dating to 1875. The **Red Rocks Amphitheater** (Mount Vernon Avenue, north of the town center) was built in 1938 among towering red sandstone rocks that are 70 million years old and were once the bed of an ancient inland sea. Red Rocks is open daily as a park, except during performances.

EVERGREEN

A resort center occupying a narrow canyon, Evergreen was founded in the 1880s by Canon Charles Winfred Douglas (1867–1940), who wrote and taught plainsong. The **Hiwan Homestead Museum** (4208 South Timbervale Drive, 303–674–6262) now occupies the original Douglas homestead, built in 1886 by the Scottish master carpenter John "Jock" Spence. The seventeen-room log house offers a look at early mountain summer-home living and displays a collection of Indian artifacts, photographs, and period furnishings.

The seven-acre **Evergreen Conference District** (27618 Fireweed Drive, 303–674–3525) is a remarkable assemblage of structures, most of which were built by Jock Spence between 1888 and 1924. Among twenty-one buildings made of native slab lumber and shingle, the meetinghouse (1924), with an octagonal stage and high ceiling supported by massive trusses, is outstanding. The Episcopal music conference founded by Canon Douglas still meets here each summer.

The **Humphrey House** (620 South Soda Creek Road, private) is a chinked-log structure built in 1883 by J. J. Clark, a businessman. Wood for the walls and roof shingles was cut from Clark's own trees and milled on the site. Lucius Edwin Humphrey bought the house from Clark's widow in 1920 and restored it with great care and authenticity. Only two families have owned the house since it was built more than a century ago.

The **International Bell Museum** (30213 Upper Bear Creek Road, 303-674-3422) displays more than 3,000 bells, whose purposes vary from calling cows to summoning worshippers to service, and which range in weight from less than an ounce to a ton. It is the largest bell collection in the United States.

The ten-thousand seat Red Rocks Amphitheater, built in 1938 in a natural formation of red sandstone, has nearly perfect acoustics.

NORTH FORK HISTORIC DISTRICT

Located on both banks of the South Platte River, the district incorporates the little towns of Pine, Dome Rock, Buffalo Creek, South Platte, and others that developed tourist facilities along the tracks of the Denver, South Park & Pacific Railroad in the late nineteenth century. In **Buffalo Creek** the **Blue Jay Inn** (Route 126, private), built in 1880, housed lumbermen and tourists and later was a vacation retreat for girls. A Shingle-style retreat called **La Hacienda** (off Route 285, private) was built in 1902 as a summer home for John L. Jerome, an investor in one of the state's earliest large industrial concerns, the Colorado Fuel and Iron Company. The granite **Green Mercantile Store**, still serving the mountain community, was built in 1898 northwest of Buffalo Creek.

SEDALIA

In this region of broken hills are the **Church of Saint Philip-in-the-Field** and the **Bear Canon Cemetery** (397 South Perry Park Road, 303–688–5444). After a fraudulent circuit rider raised funds for the church and then ran off with the money, the pioneers built this simple clapboard church in 1872, using rough lumber from a Plum Creek sawmill established in 1859, one of the first in the state. The church has been Episcopal since 1889. In the cemetery lie as many as five generations of some early families. The **John Kinner House** (6694 Perry Park Road, private) is a rancher's stone home built in 1896.

CASTLE ROCK

As Major Stephen Long's party passed this way in 1820, a member of the expedition recorded this impression of Castle Rock: "It has columns, and porticoes, and arches, and, when seen from a distance, has an astonishingly regular and artificial appearance." Half a century later, the local lava stone nearby was quarried for use as a building material; it can be seen, for example, in the **Denver & Rio Grande Railway Depot** (420 Elbert Street, 303–688–1806), built in 1875 and one of the few stone depots built by that railroad.

STRASBURG

The effort to link the eastern and western sections of the Kansas Pacific Railroad became a race against time, as thousands of dusty workers cleared a roadbed across the plains and laid tracks. Every mile demanded 2,475 ties and 375 iron rails. Two crews, one working eastward from Denver and the other westward from Kansas City, laid ten-and-a-quarter miles of track in less than ten hours, hammering the final spike on August 15, 1870, at **Commanche Crossing** (near Exit 310 on Route 70, just east of Strasburg). Strasburg makes a persuasive claim that the first truly transcontinental rail line dates to this record-setting feat. It is generally accepted that the first transcontinental line was completed in May 1869 when the Union Pacific and Central Pacific railroads met in Promontory Point, Utah. However, a plaque at the Strasburg site notes, with admirable precision: "For the first time it was possible to cross this continent on rail unbroken by a river crossing over temporary track laid on ice or by ferry." The **Commanche Crossing Museum** (Colfax Avenue, 303–622–4668) exhibits seven historic buildings, including a homestead, a railroad depot, and a nineteenth-century wooden windmill, as well as a Union Pacific caboose, Indian artifacts, fossils, and early printing equipment.

SOUTHERN COLORADO

OPPOSITE: *The ruins of the Cliff Palace, the largest known pueblo in Mesa Verde National Park. Built between* A.D. *1073 and 1273, it was once inhabited by some four hundred Indians.*

T he first Europeans to explore Colorado approached not from the east but from the south. The Spaniards in Mexico had heard tales of cities where "the doors to the houses are studded with jewels and whole streets are lined with the shops of goldsmiths." To find these riches, in 1540 the viceroy of New Spain organized a northward expedition under Francisco Coronado. The explorers brought back nothing except the first description of the "hump-backed cow," or buffalo. It is probable that Coronado and his party became the first Europeans to set their boots in Colorado, during their homeward journey in 1541. After the Spanish colonization of New Mexico in 1598, Indians escaped enslavement by moving northward into Colorado territory, often to a place called El Cuartelejo, about a hundred miles east of today's Pueblo. Spanish soldiers pursued them, and on such an expedition in 1706, Juan de Ulibarri and his party saw signs of French incursions from the Mississippi, which prompted him to claim the land for Spain.

Increasingly alarmed by the westward push of French trappers and traders, the Spanish sent Pedro de Villasur into eastern Colorado in 1720 to check on their activities. The 100-man expedition was wiped out by Indians in what is today Nebraska, putting an end to Spanish attempts to occupy eastern Colorado. In 1739 a French expedition under the Mallet brothers passed through the present site of Trinidad, heading toward Santa Fe. The next Spanish effort in this area was in 1765, when Juan María de Rivera led an unsuccessful prospecting expedition into the San Juan Mountains. Then, in 1776, two Franciscan friars, Francisco Silvestre Vélez de Escalante and Francisco Atanasio Domínguez, crossed western Colorado in search of an overland route toward the California missions. Escalante kept a meticulous journal, full of useful observations of this region.

After the Louisiana Purchase, in 1803, Spain contested the border of the new American territory, asserting that Spanish claims stretched north to the Arkansas River. When Zebulon Pike, the first American to explore Colorado, camped in the San Luis Valley with his men in 1807, the Spaniards took him prisoner as a trespasser, but later released him in Mexico. Pike wrote a book in 1810 that helped attract trappers and traders to Colorado. The Glenn-Fowler party erected a log house at present-day Pueblo in 1822; Antoine Robidoux later built a trading post near today's city of Delta; and other posts were erected along the South Platte and Arkansas rivers. Thirsty for adventure, adept at staying alive, the fur traders roamed up the rivers and trails of Colorado during the 1820s and 1830s.

The Mexican copy of the Treaty of Guadalupe Hidalgo, which established American sovereignty over the territory that is now Colorado in 1848.

Mountain men such as Jim Bridger and Tom "Broken Hand" Fitzpatrick thrived despite bad weather, scarce food, high altitude, and occasionally hostile Indians. The trappers sought beaver pelts, in high demand in New York and London, and congregated at such trading posts as Fort Vasquez and Bent's Fort, an adobe bulwark near present-day La Junta. From 1831 to 1842, Kit Carson found work there as a hunter, earning a dollar a day furnishing buffalo meat. Carson guided Lieutenant John C. Frémont on an exploration that helped open the wilderness and make it more appealing to future American settlers. U.S. territory grew in one great leap with the Treaty of Guadelupe Hidalgo in 1848, by which Mexico ceded lands that included the rest of Colorado. Yet few Americans settled there. By then the fur trade had died, most of the mountain men had departed, and Colorado was essentially a wilderness.

After the beaver trade died out, mountain men hunted buffalo for robes that could be carried by wagons over the Santa Fe Trail. Along the Mountain Branch of this route, Charles and William Bent and Ceran St. Vrain began building Bent's Fort in the early 1830s

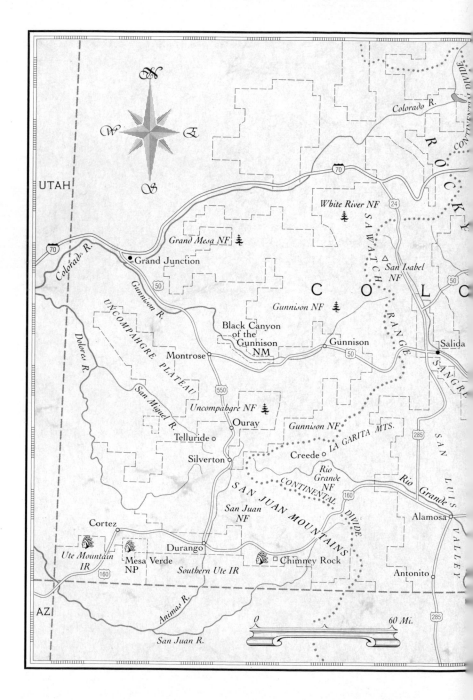

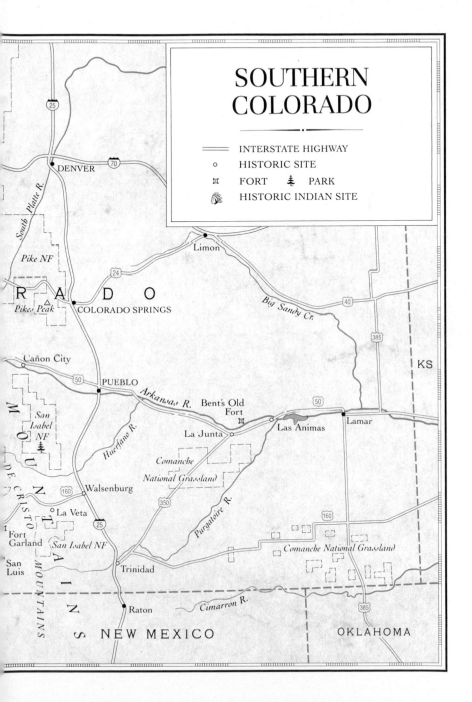

SOUTHERN COLORADO

═══ INTERSTATE HIGHWAY
○ HISTORIC SITE
⊠ FORT   🌲 PARK
  HISTORIC INDIAN SITE

DENVER

South Platte R.

Pike NF

Limon

R   A   D   O

Pikes Peak

COLORADO SPRINGS

Big Sandy Cr.

KS

Cañon City

PUEBLO

Arkansas R.   Bent's Old
Fort

La Junta   Las Animas   Lamar

San
Isabel
NF

Huerfano R.

Comanche
National Grassland

Purgatoire R.

Walsenburg

La Veta

Fort
Garland   San Isabel NF

San
Luis

Trinidad

Comanche National Grassland

Raton   Cimarron R.

NEW MEXICO   OKLAHOMA

DE CRISTO MOUNTAINS

near present-day La Junta. Seventeen years later, it was taken over by
the U.S. government as a military storehouse and hospital during
the Mexican War of 1846, serving the "Army of the West" under
General Stephen Kearny. Two years later, Mexico ceded all land
south of the Arkansas River and west of its source, about two-thirds
of the future state, to the United States.

The first permanent settlements in Colorado took shape in the
southern San Luis Valley on Mexican land grants, which were
honored by the U.S. government. San Luis on the Culebra River was
begun in 1851, and soon there were adobe villages harvesting crops
of corn and beans and ringing with Spanish guitar music. To protect
the villages from Indian raids, a U.S. military post, Fort
Massachusetts, was built in 1852. But the Indians continued to
attack. American forces, guided by Kit Carson, mounted a massive
campaign against them, and at last the Ute asked for peace. In 1858
soldiers moved into Fort Garland, of which several adobe structures
survive. As late as the early 1850s, however, settlers were few, and
southern Colorado was almost as empty as the cliff dwellings on
Mesa Verde abandoned by the Anasazi, or "ancient ones." Only after
gold and silver were found in the San Juan Mountains in the early
1870s did the area lure prospectors, who settled and created such
towns as Silverton. Railroad companies laid tracks across the
southern region in the 1880s, and eventually modern highways
linked such commercial centers as La Junta and Trinidad, where the
fur trade had once followed the Santa Fe Trail.

As miners spread out over the Continental Divide, the Ute
voiced their objections to incursions into the lands they had been
granted by the government. After a period of tension and skirmishes
including one at Milk Creek in 1879 and the Meeker massacre at the
White River Indian Agency, the Ute were removed to Utah and a
narrow strip of southwestern Colorado. The western slope was now
available for settlement, and the towns of Grand Junction, Delta, and
Montrose sprang to life on the vacated hunting grounds. Coal fields
were developed to fuel the railroads and smelters, and Colorado
mines poured out as much as $20 million in silver annually. But in
1893, when the federal government repealed the Sherman Act that
had subsidized the price of silver, mines shut down, and the

OPPOSITE: *Steam locomotives, which played an important role in the development of*
Colorado's mines, continue to carry passengers. OVERLEAF: *The Great Sand Dunes*
National Monument in the San Luis Valley along the base of the Sangre de Cristo
Mountains contains the highest dunes in the Western hemisphere.

economy declined. Only a fabulous new gold strike at Cripple Creek saved the state, creating such overnight millionaires as Winfield S. Stratton, whose philanthropies included giving a new bicycle and basket to every laundry woman in Colorado Springs.

Around the turn of the century, Colorado launched its sugar beet industry and a series of irrigation projects. A six-mile tunnel was built through solid rock to divert water from the Black Canyon of the Gunnison to the Uncompahgre Valley. Colorado farmers developed Rocky Ford cantaloupes and variegated carnations. At the same time, citizens began to think of the state's forests and mountains as attractions for tourists. After President Theodore Roosevelt visited the state in the early 1900s, he urged the preservation of Colorado's forests and proclaimed Mesa Verde a national park. Tourists came to Colorado, visiting Estes Park's white clapboard Stanley Hotel, which was built in 1909 and filled up with visitors as fast as Freelan Stanley could cart them up the mountain aboard his inventions, the Stanley Steamer automobiles. Spencer Penrose, a mining magnate, built a road to the 14,110-foot summit of Pikes Peak, promoted a hill-climb auto race, and built the elegant Broadmoor Hotel in Colorado Springs. After World War I Colorado celebrated engineering feats: The Moffat Tunnel was opened in 1928 as the nation's longest railroad tunnel; in 1929, the world's highest suspension bridge was built across the Royal Gorge of the Arkansas River. Then, during World War II, Camp Carson took shape near Colorado Springs, and Camp Hale near Leadville became a center for training mountain infantrymen on skis.

This chapter begins in the southeastern region and moves westward along the Arkansas River, from Las Animas to Canon City; then starting again farther south at Trinidad it moves westward to Antonito, then in a rough circle from Creede to Silverton; finally it moves south to Cortez, Durango, and Chimney Rock.

LAS ANIMAS

Kit Carson spent his last years in a cabin at Fort Lyon, across the Arkansas River from Las Animas. Born in 1809, he was perhaps the West's most famous scout, mountain man, and Indian agent. At age 17 he left Missouri on a wagon train for New Mexico, where he learned Spanish and worked as a saddler and teamster. For eight years he roamed the trails and passes of the Colorado mountains as a trapper. For about three years in the early 1840s Carson lived at

Bent's Fort, earning a dollar a day hunting buffalo and other animals for food. But the frontiersman became restless, and even after marrying a pretty Mexican bride in 1843, he guided most of the expeditions of John C. Frémont and John W. Gunnison. He served General Stephen Kearny as chief of scouts, and he drove a herd of 6,500 sheep to California. As the government's Indian agent at Taos, his understanding of Indians (he had been married to two) led to his appointment as chief mediator for the Southwest tribes, and he became Colorado's superintendent of Indian affairs in 1867. A brave, truehearted, and modest figure, he died the next year while quietly smoking his pipe. The **Kit Carson Museum** (425 Carson, 719–456–2005) displays blankets, arrowheads, and ceremonial items of the Sioux, Comanche, and Kiowa; also exhibited are local artifacts and various historic buildings.

LA JUNTA

The **Koshare Indian Museum** (115 West 18th, 719–384–4801) shows a collection of Southwest Indian arts, including kachinas and basketry. From mid-June to mid-August, the Hopi Snake Dance and other Indian dances are reenacted in the museum's round ceremonial room by specially trained Boy Scout troops.

Bent's Old Fort National Historic Site

As Matthew Field wrote in 1840, Bent's Fort was a sight "such as to strike the wanderer with the liveliest surprise, as though an 'air-built castle' had dropped to earth before him in the midst of the vast desert." The most important way station along the Santa Fe Trail, the fort was completed in 1833 by two Saint Louis brothers, William and Charles Bent, and a Missourian named Ceran St. Vrain. Partners in the fur trade, they picked this site on the Arkansas River for its strategic location. This was the hunting ground of the Cheyenne, Arapaho, and other tribes, who traded buffalo robes at the fort. In addition, American manufactured goods being hauled overland from Missouri and Mexican shipments coming north from Santa Fe passed this way. The fort was also a way station for mountain men, who swapped beaver pelts for supplies.

The adobe structure measured 135 by 180 feet, with walls 15 feet high, some planted on top with cactuses to discourage night visitors. Two corner bastions had openings for cannons and muskets, and

there was one main gate. In many ways the fortress resembled a medieval city gone Wild West, its fortifications enclosing living quarters, an Indian council room, a billiard room, warehouses, workshops, a trade room, and a dining room. A staple meal was dried buffalo meat with water biscuits, which a Comanche chief, Old Wolf, said were good only "to fuel a smoke-fire for coloring buckskins." The fort was a lively place, populated by trappers in buckskin, busy clerks and traders, Indian women padding on moccasined feet, Mexican residents, and travelers of all types who stopped for accommodation. At times the lodges of visiting tribes surrounded the fort for miles. The Bents knew very well how to get along with the Indians and encouraged friendly relations among rival tribes (warring could interrupt business). In 1837 William Bent married Owl Woman, daughter of a Cheyenne medicine man named Gray Thunder, further solidifying the fort's relations with the Indians. Bent also refused to trade much in whiskey and enforced a policy of fair bartering among his clerks—what historian Bernard DeVoto called "an elsewhere unheard-of standard of honor in dealing."

Historic figures passed through the fort, such as mountain men "Uncle Dick" Wootton and Bill Williams; Kit Carson, who was employed here as a hunter for three years; and John C. Frémont, who resupplied his exploring party in 1845. After war broke out with Mexico in the next year, the American army used the fort as the advance post for General Kearny's invasion of New Mexico. With the increased army population, the surrounding area was overgrazed by government cattle; watering places were fouled and the buffalo scared off. Disgusted and disillusioned when the federal government refused to purchase the fort, William Bent moved out in 1849. He packed all his goods—except powder kegs—and blew the fort to dust. Bent later built a second fort thirty miles down the river. The 1833 fort, known as Bent's Old Fort, has been reconstructed at the original site to reflect life in the mid 1840s; there are self-guided tours. During the summer season, guides in period clothing give talks and conduct demonstrations.

LOCATION: 35110 Route 194 East, 8 miles east of La Junta. HOURS: Memorial Day through Labor Day: 8–6. Daily; Labor Day through Memorial Day: 8–4:30 Daily. FEE: Yes. TELEPHONE: 719-384-2596.

OPPOSITE: *Bent's Old Fort had fifteen-foot walls to thwart nighttime attempts to scale them. A further protection was afforded by thickly planted cactuses that the Bents cultivated on top of certain walls.*

PUEBLO

Juan de Ulibarri chased fugitive Indians to this area from New Mexico in 1706. When Zebulon Pike came in 1806, he erected the state's first American structure, a breastwork of logs five feet high. The first private dwelling followed in 1822, when the trapper Jacob Fowler and his party built a three-room log cabin. By 1842 there was a crude adobe fort on the site of today's city. Frémont visited the next year, observing "a number of mountaineers who had married Spanish women in the valley of Taos, had collected together, and occupied themselves in farming." In 1846 Mormons set up a temporary colony nearby. "Uncle Dick" Wootton arrived in 1853 and went into the business of trading oxen with the emigrants who traveled through, taking three worn oxen in exchange for a single fresh one; then he rested the road-weary oxen and traded them again as fresh. At Christmas 1854 the Mexican inhabitants of the fort got drunk and invited the Indians inside, whereupon the latter attacked their hosts and left fifteen men dead, taking a woman and two boys as captives. Thereafter, Pueblo was virtually deserted; mountain men said it was haunted by the ghost of a headless woman. A new settlement was founded in 1860. With the arrival of the Denver & Rio Grande Western Railroad in 1872, followed by the Santa Fe in 1876, Pueblo blossomed into a smelting center thanks to the strategic availability of coal from the mines of Trinidad.

Rosemount Victorian House Museum

Among the features of this thirty-seven-room mansion of pink quarry stone are elaborately carved interior woodwork, stained-glass windows, and frescoes. Completed in 1893, the eclectic Richardsonian Romanesque house contains furnishings left by the family of its builder, the banker John Thatcher. The third-floor gallery houses a collection of objects—vases, paintings, birds, even a mummy—assembled on travels around the world by Andrew McClelland for the education of local children.

LOCATION: 419 West 14th Street. HOURS: June through August: 10–4 Monday–Saturday, Sunday 2–4; September through May: 1–4 Tuesday–Saturday, 2–4 Sunday. FEE: Yes. TELEPHONE: 719–545–5290.

OPPOSITE: *Rosemount's stairway features elaborate Golden Oak woodwork and a massive stained-glass window entitled* The Kingdoms of Nature.

El Pueblo Museum

A full-size reconstruction of the adobe fort as it was in 1842 is complete with corrals, storage, and adobe huts for about a dozen families. There are exhibits depicting the Anasazi culture of southwestern Colorado, along with artifacts relating to Pueblo's history. The museum also documents local steel production and narrow-gauge railroads.

> LOCATION: 905 South Prairie Avenue (behind Colorado State Fairgrounds). HOURS: Memorial Day through Labor Day: 10–5 Tuesday–Saturday; Labor Day through Memorial Day: 10–3 Wednesday–Saturday. FEE: Yes. TELEPHONE: 719–564–5274.

Other buildings of historic interest in Pueblo include the **Orman-Adams House** (102 West Orman Avenue) of 1890, which has been the home of two Colorado governors and a U.S. senator; the **Pueblo County Courthouse** (10th and Main streets) of 1912, a Neoclassical Revival building with massive Corinthian porticoes and a rotunda; the red sandstone **Union Depot** (B Street, private), built in 1889 and once one of Colorado's busiest passenger stations with fifty-five trains daily; and the **Quaker Flour Mill** (126 Oneida Street, private), built in 1869 of sandstone and brick, the oldest commercial building in Pueblo. **Pitkin Place** (even-numbered side of 300 block of Pitkin) is a street of fine old homes of Victorian, Queen Anne, and other styles. The **Fred E. Weisbrod Aircraft Museum** (Pueblo Airport, 719–948–3355) displays airplanes from World War II and after, as well as experimental vehicles.

CANON CITY

Canon City serves as the gateway for the Grand Canyon of the Arkansas River (*cañon* is Spanish for "canyon"). Ute camped on the site regularly, and Zebulon Pike's party stopped twice, but settlers did not arrive until after the Pikes Peak gold rush of 1859 when Canon City was established as a supply and layover center at the entrance to the mining areas. Along Main Street lies the **Canon City Downtown Historic Commercial District,** which extends from 3d to 9th streets and contains late nineteenth- and early twentieth-century commercial buildings. The **Hotel Saint Cloud** (631 Main) was home to Tom Mix when he was on location nearby. The cowboy movie star

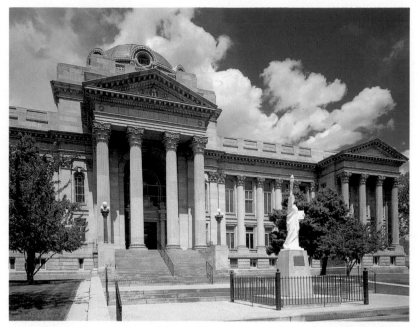

Liberty lifts her lamp in front of the Pueblo County Courthouse in this Western ver-sion of New York's famed statue, erected in 1950. OVERLEAF: *The Royal Gorge Suspension Bridge in Cañon City, which soars 1,053 feet above the Arkansas River, is the highest suspension bridge in the world.*

got his start in Canon City in about 1910, and for a period the city was a bustling film center. Built in the 1890s of pink lava stone is the third home of the **Fremont National Bank** (4th and Main streets), whose founder, long before federally insured bank accounts, secured deposits with "all the earthly possessions of Fred A. Raynolds."

Canon City Municipal Museum

The Canon City Municipal Museum exhibits big-game trophies bagged from Alaska to Africa by Dall DeWeese, an early nurseryman and land developer. (His unspliced log home at 1126 Elm Avenue, built in 1896, resembles a hunting lodge.) The museum also displays mineral specimens, mounted exotic birds, fossils, and memorabilia. Behind the museum stands the **Rudd Cabin,** built in 1860 by the pioneer Anson Rudd and his wife, who chose the area for its mild climate. A blacksmith, Rudd also served as the first county sheriff.

After living in the cabin for two decades, the Rudds built the adjacent **Rudd Stone Home,** which now contains a collection of period furnishings and cowboy equipment. A small log cabin, built in 1868 by a brick maker, W. C. Catlin, has also been reconstructed.

> LOCATION: 612 Royal Gorge Boulevard. HOURS: Mid-May through mid-September: 9–5 Monday–Saturday, 1–5 Sunday; mid-September through mid-May: 1–5 Daily. FEE: None. TELEPHONE: 719–269–9018.

Colorado Territorial Prison Museum and Park

When the citizens of Colorado Territory asked the government for a place to lock up hardened criminals, of which they had many, the result was a two-story cell house in 1871. The prison's most famous inmate, Alferd Packer, was jailed in 1886 for murder and cannibalizing. Part of his confession stated: "I killed Bell. Shot him. I covered the remains and took a large piece along." At his first trial, so the story goes, the Democratic judge said: "Packer, you so-and-so, there were seven Democrats in Hinsdale County and you ate five of them." Packer was released in 1901, but forty-five other inmates were hanged here over the years. The prison still operates, so it is not available for tours. The museum is housed in the adjacent women's cell block. There are displays of leg irons, striped suits worn by inmates, weapons used for escapes, and other sobering artifacts.

> LOCATION: 1st Street and Macon Avenue. HOURS: May through September: 9–5 Daily; October through April: 10–5 Wednesday–Sunday. FEE: Yes. TELEPHONE: 719–269–3015.

The world's highest suspension bridge (4218 Fremont County Road 3-A, 719–275–7507), 1,053 feet above the Arkansas River, spans the magnificent **Royal Gorge,** near Canon City. Built in 1929, the bridge stretches nearly one-quarter mile. An incline railway, the world's steepest, descends to the canyon floor at a forty-five-degree angle, and an aerial tramway glides 2,200 feet across the chasm.

TRINIDAD

Located on the Mountain Branch of the Santa Fe Trail, Trinidad was settled about 1859 by New Mexican sheepherders. Racial troubles between early Hispanic settlers and later Anglo arrivals led to rioting in 1867. Later some of the West's largest cattle companies operated here, and local coal fields were developed after the arrival of the Santa Fe railroad in 1878. The **Corazon de Trinidad Historic District** in the city center contains commercial, residential, and religious structures in various Victorian styles. The **Columbian Hotel** (Main and Commercial streets), built in 1880, has a plaque on the wall to mark the route of the old Santa Fe Trail..

Baca House, Bloom House, and Pioneer Museum

A two-story adobe home, the Baca House was built in Territorial style and furnished in the simple, handsome manner of a well-to-do Spanish-American family. It was owned by the rancher and freighter Don Felipe Baca, who gave the land for Trinidad's town site. An adobe outbuilding that once housed ranch hands has become the Pioneer Museum, with exhibits on the area's large ranches and displays of wagons and buggies used on the Santa Fe Trail. Nearby stands the three-story Bloom House, an ornate home in Second Empire style with a mansard roof edged with iron tracery. Frank G. Bloom, director of a cattle company, built the house in 1882. It is now restored and furnished in 1880s style with lace curtains, patterned wallpapers, and much china and silver; the grounds have been designed as a Victorian garden.

LOCATION: 300 East Main Street. HOURS: Memorial Day through Labor Day: 10–4 Monday–Saturday, 1–4 Sunday, and by appointment. FEE: Yes. TELEPHONE: 719–846–7217.

Also in the historic district, the **Trinidad Opera House** (100–116 West Main Street) is a two-story building built in 1883 of brick and sandstone in High Victorian Italianate style. The **A. R. Mitchell Memorial Museum of Western Art** (150 East Main Street, 719–846–4224) displays the work of its namesake artist and his contemporaries, including Harvey Dunn and Harold von Schmidt, along with early Hispanic religious folk art and Western artifacts.

A series of dioramas at the **Louden-Henritze Archaeology Museum** (Freudenthal Memorial Library at Trinidad State Junior College, 719–846–5508) shows the geology, fossils, and archaeology of the Trinidad area, including views of Trinchera Cave, a site near Trinidad once occupied by prehistoric peoples. The museum also houses a collection of Indian artifacts from the local area.

South of Pueblo, at milepost 59, Route 25 passes isolated **Huerfano Butte,** whose name is Spanish for "orphan." **Walsenburg** is the location of the **Huerfano County Courthouse and Jail** (400 Main Street), a limestone structure with Richardsonian Romanesque elements, built in 1904.

La Veta is located at the foot of the Spanish Peaks, where the rancher John Francisco built an adobe fort in 1863 to protect his huge land grant, which lay in the midst of Indian territory. As the first building in the area, the fort housed fourteen families. It now operates as the **Fort Francisco Museum** (300 block of Main Street), with rooms furnished in frontier style—parlor, kitchen, and so on—and there is a complex of other historic buildings with exhibits of Indian artifacts, furniture, buggies, and coal mining equipment.

FORT GARLAND

The first U.S. military post in Colorado, Fort Massachusetts, was built in 1852 but abandoned six years later as being too vulnerable to Indian attack. Its garrison moved to Fort Garland in 1858. The fort's main duty was to project military power without doing much fighting, in order to intimidate the Ute and protect San Luis Valley settlers. Adobe buildings enclosed a parade ground where infantrymen and riflemen mustered. Kit Carson commanded a volunteer regiment at the fort in 1866–1867. In 1880 the removal of the Ute from Colorado was completed, and Fort Garland was shut down three years later. The museum has re-created the commandant's quarters of Carson's time; there are exhibits of military life at the fort and Hispanic folk art from the San Luis Valley.

LOCATION: Off Route 160 on Route 159. HOURS: Memorial Day through Labor Day: 10–5 Monday–Saturday, 1–5 Sunday; September: By appointment. FEE: Yes. TELEPHONE: 719–379–3512.

In early 1806 Zebulon Pike and his men struggled over the snowbound Sangre de Cristo Range at Mosca Pass, traveled past the site of Alamosa, and reached the Conejos River, where they made camp five miles from the mouth. Here Pike built winter quarters,

OPPOSITE: *The Huerfano County Courthouse and Jail in Walsenburg was built by C. A. Henderson, an architect from Pueblo, for $35,000.*

now reconstructed as **Pike's Stockade** (twelve miles south of Alamosa via Routes 285 and 136 East). Made of cottonwood logs, the enclosure measured thirty-six feet square and twelve feet high, with projecting pickets and a moat as security against the Indians. It wasn't long before 100 Spanish troops came to inform Pike that he had strayed into Spanish territory and "invite" him to Santa Fe for questioning.

In **Alamosa** the **Luther Bean Museum** (Adams State College, 719–589–7121) displays pioneer clothing, Pueblo Indian pottery, Hispanic religious carvings called *santos,* and antique furniture and figurines from Europe and Asia.

ANTONITO

Two branches of the Denver & Rio Grande Western Railroad met here, and the narrow-gauge line running west toward Durango was for fifty years the most important means of transportation in this isolated section of the country. The line now operates as the **Cumbres & Toltec Scenic Railroad** (Route 285 at Route 17 West, 719–376–5483). From mid-June to mid-October, steam trains make a sixty-four-mile run to Chama, New Mexico, climbing over the Continental Divide at 10,022-foot Cumbres Pass, an opening in the San Juan Range that was once traveled by Indians and Spanish explorers.

At River Street and Pine stands the **Frank Warshauer Home** (private), a brown brick mansion with Oriental accents. In 1879, at the age of 20 and without any personal fortune, Warshauer emigrated to the West from Germany. He quickly became fluent in both English and Spanish and by 1902 had established a prosperous sheep and wool company in Antonito. The house was built in 1912 to replace a home on the same site that had burned down. Despite his outlay of $70,000 for "a home to suit his ideas of hospitality, comfort and general fitness of things" (in the words of the local paper), Warshauer committed suicide only a year later, after a period of poor health.

CREEDE

In 1890 Nicholas Creede, a prospector, stopped for lunch in the mountains above Wagon Wheel Gap. While idly poking at the ground, he detected some ore and exclaimed, "Holy Moses, I've struck it rich!" Creede's Holy Moses Mine launched a rush to the

After silver prices fell in 1893, Creede's population, which had climbed to 8,000 residents, declined rapidly.

area, and within a year miners had taken $6 million in silver from the hills. With a sheer canyon as its locale, the town of Creede flourished with a colorful cast of characters ranging from con man "Soapy" Smith to Bob Ford, the outlaw who shot Jesse James and was later gunned down in his own Creede saloon. The town's gambling, boozing, and brawling inspired newspaper editor Cy Warman to write the well-known lines: "It's day all day in the day-time / And there is no night in Creede."

GUNNISON

Founded in the mid-1870s, the town was named for John W. Gunnison (1812–1853), a West Point graduate who came to Colorado in 1853 to locate a westward route for a transcontinental railroad. He was killed by Indians in Utah the same year. The **Gunnison County Pioneer and Historical Society Museum** (110 South Adams, off Route 50 East, 303–641–0466) displays minerals, costumes, railroad artifacts, and historic buildings that include a log post office built in 1880, a Denver & Rio Grande Western Railroad depot from the 1880s, and a schoolhouse built in 1905.

MONTROSE

After the Ute were removed from the Uncompahgre Valley, the town of Montrose was founded in 1882 and named for a character from a novel by Sir Walter Scott, the Duchess of Montrose. With the arrival of the Denver & Rio Grande Western Railroad the same year, Montrose became a typical freighting town on the frontier. The area became arable following the construction of the Gunnison irrigation tunnel in 1909, and it produced a great many row crops, as well as hay, sheep, and cattle. The Denver & Rio Grande Western Railroad depot houses the **Montrose County Historical Museum** (West Main and Rio Grande streets, 303–249–2085), with an especially large collection of old farm machinery and implements.

Ute Indian Museum

The museum is located on the site of a farm that was the last residence of Chief Ouray (1833–1880) of the Southern Ute and his wife, Chipeta. As early as 1856, Ouray had learned some Spanish and English and worked as a government interpreter at a pay of $500 a year. The government favored Ouray's selection as the chief of all seven bands of Ute, for he was known as a peace maker who would sooner resort to diplomacy than to war in the struggle to save the Indians' homeland from the overwhelming American forces. In 1873 he helped negotiate the withdrawal of the Ute from the San Juan Mountains after rich minerals were discovered there, accepting an annual payment of $25,000 for his people. Ouray also influenced Northern Ute rebels to return the white captives taken after the Meeker massacre of 1879. The museum interprets the customs and ways of life of the Ute. There are galleries of traditional and ceremonial items collected as long ago as the 1880s, including dance skins, beadwork, feather bonnets, and leather garments, many of which belonged to Ouray and Chipeta (whose grave is near the museum). Personal objects of Buckskin Charley and Colorow, chiefs of other Ute bands, are also on display.

LOCATION: 17253 Chipeta Drive. HOURS: Mid-May through September: 10–5 Monday–Saturday, 1–5 Sunday. FEE: Yes. TELEPHONE: 303–249–3098.

OPPOSITE: *A portrait of the Ute Buckskin Charlie and his wife, in the collection of the Colorado Historical Society.*

In the words of the geologist Wallace R. Hansen, who mapped the **Black Canyon** region in 1950, "No other canyon in North America combines the depth, narrowness, sheerness, and somber countenance of the Black Canyon." Indeed, there was a lingering superstition among the Ute Indians and early settlers that anyone entering the inner gorge would not return alive. The river that carved this canyon is named for John W. Gunnison, who led a party to the upper reaches of the gorge in 1853. Daunted by the slow going and the difficulty of lowering equipment over the 2,000-foot cliffs, Gunnison withdrew without reaching the bottom of the gorge. In 1857 Lieutenant Joseph Christmas Ives, in a prefabricated steamboat, navigated the Colorado as far as the Black Canyon but did not penetrate into the gorge. The first detailed exploration of the Black Canyon was made in 1874 by Ferdinand V. Hayden, by then well known for his Yellowstone expeditions. In 1882 the Denver & Rio Grande Western Railroad paid for an exploration of the most inaccessible section of the canyon, in what is now the national monument area. Working for two months in winter, survey crews led by Byron H. Bryant made daily descents into the gorge, establishing that it would be impossible to lay track over the last thirty miles to Uncompahgre Valley. In 1901 A. L. Fellows and William Torrence navigated the Gunnison River through Black Canyon on rubber air mattresses. Their objective was to determine the feasibility of a remarkable engineering project achieved in 1909—the six-mile long Gunnison Diversion Tunnel, which burrows through solid rock to carry water from the Gunnison River to farms in the Uncompahgre Valley. **Black Canyon of the Gunnison National Monument Park** (Route 347, northeast of Montrose, 303–249–7036) protects an awesome twelve-mile stretch of the canyon.

OURAY

Ouray was the kind of place where an illiterate Irishman named Tom Walsh could get so rich from a gold mine that his daughter could buy the Hope Diamond. The town had started in 1875 with a silver strike that was called the Mineral Farm because its veins lay in neat rows. Ouray was so difficult to reach that only high-grade ore could be profitably shipped and staples were exorbitantly expensive. Cheaper freighting was the achievement of Otto Mears, the

OPPOSITE: *Black Canyon of the Gunnison National Monument preserves a 2,000-foot chasm cut through granite by the Gunnison River.*

Two engines were required to pull this Denver & Rio Grande train up the steep incline near Rockwood, Colorado, as shown in this 1880s photograph by W. H. Jackson.

"Pathfinder of the San Juans," who spent as much as $1,000 a foot to hack out a narrow "shelf road" over Red Mountain to Silverton. Today this is the breathtaking auto route known as the **Million Dollar Highway,** probably named for its surface of gold-bearing gravels. The decline of silver in 1893 hurt Ouray less than it did other camps, because Walsh's discovery of the legendary Camp Bird gold mine in 1896 kept the economy humming.

Ouray lies nestled among steep mountains, and the well-preserved town has been designated the **Ouray Historic District.** Among the buildings of note are the **Western Hotel** (220 Seventh Avenue), one of the town's few surviving all-wood buildings, with an elaborate false facade; Saint Joseph's Hospital, built in 1887, and now operating as the **Ouray County Historical Society Museum** (420 Sixth Avenue, 303–324–4576), with extensive exhibits on Ouray's mining history; the **Beaumont Hotel** (Fifth Avenue and Main Street, private), built in 1886 of brick and stone (this showplace of mountain resort architecture was visited by Theodore Roosevelt and the actress Lillie Langtry); and **Wright's Opera House** across the street, an eclectic structure of 1888 with a decorative iron front. The **Bachelor-Syracuse Mine Tour** (1222 County Road 14, 303–325–4500) takes visitors aboard a mine train into diggings that have been worked continuously since 1884.

The Durango & Silverton, shown here near Shelona Lake, is one of the last remaining narrow-gauge railroad lines in the Colorado mountains.

TELLURIDE

A year after gold was discovered in 1875, J. B. Ingram noticed that the neighboring Sheridan and Union claims seemed to exceed their legal limits, so he filed on the land between them. His well-named Smuggler Mine produced ore that held 18 ounces of gold and 800 ounces of silver per ton. More strikes were made, and a town was founded in 1878, soon to be named for tellurium, an element found in association with silver and gold. The first religious services were held in one of the town's three dozen around-the-clock saloons: A gambler prodded reluctant contributors to enrich the collection plate by making some "irreverent but persuasive remarks," according to the local historian Rose Weber, and "when the saloon reopened after the service, the parson often made a further attempt to add to church funds by buying a stack of chips with the collection money." Another man in search of increased funds, Butch Cassidy, held up his first bank in Telluride.

The economy was boosted after Otto Mears brought in the Rio Grande Southern Railroad in 1890 (the conductor typically hollered "To-hell-you-ride" upon arrival), and the population rose to 5,000. In 1888 L. L. Nunn installed the world's first long-distance alternating-current electrical system, invented by Nikola Tesla and

promoted by George Westinghouse, to power the Gold King Mine
and light the city. After the silver crash of 1893, Telluride citizens
took up gold mining. In the early 1900s, however, Telluride became
notorious for its mining strife, with battles between union and
nonunion miners and the murder of the manager of the Smuggler-
Union. To restore order the Colorado National Guard imposed
martial law. The **Telluride Historic District** includes the still-
operating **New Sheridan Hotel** (231 West Colorado Avenue,
303–728–4351) of 1895; though plain on the outside, it once rivaled
Denver's Brown Palace in cuisine and service. Atop a platform in
front William Jennings Bryan gave one of many deliveries of his
"Cross of Gold" speech in 1903. Next door the 200-seat **Sheridan
Opera House** of 1914 (now a movie theater) had a scene of Venice
painted on its curtain and presented such stars as Lillian Russell.

At the **San Miguel County Historical Society Museum** (317
North Fir, 303–728–3344) are exhibits of mining equipment and ore
samples, gambling equipment, railroad artifacts from the Rio
Grande Southern, Ute baskets, and various period rooms housed in
a miners' hospital built of sandstone in 1893.

SILVERTON

According to legend the town got its name when a miner remarked,
"We may not have gold, but we have silver by the ton." In fact, the
hills here have produced about a quarter of a billion dollars in ore,
including gold, silver, lead, copper, and zinc. The area was explored
tentatively by prospectors before the Ute formally ceded the San
Juans in 1873, and upon the signing of the treaty miners poured in.
Soon there was a town ·of 1,000, and Blair Street was blaring with
forty saloons. Wyatt Earp dealt cards at the Arlington Saloon, and
Bat Masterson came to town.

With the arrival of the Denver & Rio Grande Western Railroad
in 1882 and three more railroads soon afterward, the shipping of
ore became cheaper and mine production increased. The
Guggenheims bought mining interests, while citizens built a town of
consequence and permanence. Among the buildings still standing in
the **Silverton National Registered Historic District** are **Town Hall,**
built of native stone in 1908 and recently restored; the **San Juan
County Courthouse,** built in 1907 with a gold-painted dome clock
tower; and the **Grand Imperial Hotel** (1229 Greene Street,
303–387–5527) of 1882, whose Hub Saloon has a cherrywood back
bar that was shipped around Cape Horn and installed after 1900.

The **San Juan County Historical Society Museum** (1557 Greene Street, 303–387–5571/5671) was once the local jail and now exhibits its cells, as well as mining equipment, period rooms, and "Casey Jones," a rail bus made of an old Cadillac car body. The restored **Rio Grande Depot** of 1882 is used as ticket office for the Silverton terminus of the **Durango & Silverton Narrow Gauge Railroad.**

MESA VERDE NATIONAL PARK

Mesa Verde is a high tableland where about 1,400 years ago a group of Indians called the Anasazi, or "ancient ones," developed an accomplished and artistic culture. This can be divided into two major periods, the Basketmaker and the Pueblo (which includes the Cliff Dwellers). The Basketmakers near Mesa Verde learned how to grow corn and began to live a settled life in pit houses dug into the ground, at first in caves sheltered by the cliffs but later moving to the mesa tops. They made noteworthy coiled baskets and eventually

A chamber in the Mesa Verde pueblo, decorated with wall paintings in geometric designs. OVERLEAF: *The Cliff Palace Dwelling in Mesa Verde National Park comprises more than two hundred rooms for living, twenty-three kivas, and numerous storage rooms.*

developed pottery. By A.D. 750 they started building communal houses (*pueblos*) above ground; thus this culture is popularly known as the "Pueblo." Later they used sandstone blocks to build partitioned structures rising two or three stories.

Around 1200 the people of the pueblos moved into the canyons, where they built new masonry villages in eroded alcoves high on the rock walls, sites possibly chosen for reasons of defense. A large open terrace across the front of the communal pueblo was the scene of daily activities, such as making pottery or grinding corn; the earlier pit houses evolved into circular subterranean ceremonial chambers. Mesa Verde's golden age lasted only a hundred years, probably brought to an end by a period of drought or the depletion of farmland on the mesa tops. By 1300 the dwellers had abandoned the stone cities, probably joining similar peoples in today's Arizona and New Mexico and evolving into the modern Pueblo Indians.

Although the Anasazi had no alphabet, horses, wheels, or metal implements, the structures they built still survive after nearly seven centuries. The first to document them was pioneer photographer William H. Jackson, whose photos of Two-Story House astonished the world in 1874. Jackson observed that "the entire construction of this little human eyrie displays wonderful perseverence, ingenuity, and some taste," but he missed the most extensive ruins. In 1888 two cowboys, Richard Wetherill and Charles Mason, reached the rim of a canyon and gazed with astonishment at Cliff Palace—a complex of 200 rooms, with what looked like ruined towers and castles—under a massive brow of rock on the opposite rim. Ruins in the national park lie in two main areas, Wetherill Mesa and Chapin Mesa. The former includes Step House and Long House; the latter embraces Cliff Palace, Balcony House, and Spruce Tree House. An archaeological museum on Chapin Mesa interprets the life of the Anasazi.

LOCATION: Route 160, 10 miles east of Cortez, then 21 miles to ruins. HOURS: Park and museum open year-round; many ruins open only in summer. FEE: Yes. TELEPHONE: 303–529–4465.

Yucca House National Monument has two large but unexcavated mounds of rubble and earth. The larger contains the ruins of a

OPPOSITE: *Among the Anasazi objects found at Mesa Verde and displayed there today are a necklace, a large cache of sea shells, and a storage jar decorated with abstract designs. The shells indicate that the Anasazi carried on trade with coastal Indians.*

three- or four-story building; depressions in the ground suggest round rooms dating to the Pueblo culture of A.D. 1000–1300. (The undeveloped site is located eight-and-a-half miles from the intersection of Routes 160 and 666 in Cortez; turn west on County Road B to the junction of County Road 20.5, and follow that to the monument. It is a ten-minute trip from the highway to the mounds.)

UTE MOUNTAIN TRIBAL PARK

Outside Mesa Verde National Park is Ute Mountain Tribal Park, part of the Ute Mountain Ute Reservation, where an extensive archaeological district contains hundreds of Anasazi surface ruins and multistory cliff dwellings. The area contains some of the best-preserved remains of Anasazi culture in the Four Corners region. Trained Ute guides take visitors into canyons where ruins are in their primitive state and such artifacts as pots and corncobs are still to be seen. Ancient petroglyphs and Ute paintings adorn rock walls.

LOCATION: Route 666, 15 miles south of Cortez. HOURS: Tour at 8 A.M. Daily, reservations req. FEE: Yes. TELEPHONE: 303–565–3751.

The **Anasazi Heritage Center** (Route 184, two miles west of Dolores, 303–882–4811) tells the story of the Anasazi with a pit-house reconstruction and exhibits of jewelry and artifacts illustrative of daily life. Near the center to is the **Escalante Ruin,** a site from A.D. 900–1300 with nine rooms, a kiva (round room), and a midden. It was reported in 1776 by the Domínguez-Escalante expedition, making this the first recorded prehistoric site in Colorado.

HOVENWEEP NATIONAL MONUMENT

Some Anasazi moved to the heads of the canyons at Hovenweep, presumably to be near permanent springs where they built villages and towers of coursed-stone masonry. Six village sites survive on both sides of the Colorado-Utah border. Hovenweep means "deserted valley" in the Ute language, and to reach the ruins one must drive more than twenty miles on unpaved roads.

LOCATION: 43 miles west of Cortez. HOURS: Mid-April through October: 8 to sunset. FEE: None. TELEPHONE: 303–529–4461.

OPPOSITE: *The Hovenweep National Monument, which spans the Colorado–Utah border, preserves the ruins of distinctive masonry structures built here between A.D. 400 and 1300 by Anasazi Indians.*

The existence of a great kiva, or circular chamber, at the **Lowry Ruins** (off Route 666, thirty miles northwest of Cortez) seems to link this fifty-room pueblo to sites found farther south in New Mexico and Arizona. It was probably a ceremonial center around A.D. 1100.

DURANGO

Founded in 1880, Durango began to grow the next year when the Denver & Rio Grande Western Railroad arrived. Today the **Durango & Silverton Narrow Gauge Railroad** (479 Main Avenue, 303–247–2733) chugs through the wilderness of the San Juan National Forest on a forty-five-mile run to Silverton. Steam trains with 1880s coaches follow the Animas River through canyons, past waterfalls, and over trestles. An estimated $300 million in precious metals was hauled from the San Juans over this route. The train operates from May through October, departing from a depot built in 1882. In 1887 Henry Strater erected the red-brick **Strater Hotel** (699 Main Avenue, 303–247–4431), despite his want of money, a building permit, or any experience of running a hotel. It became the town's best hotel, although the fourth floor was notorious as the residence of chambermaids known to be friendly toward male guests. A liveried porter regularly went to the train station to tout the hotel, but once mistakenly shouted "Strater Hotel—best house in town! One clean meal and three square sheets every morning!" which became a staple of local humor. Over the years guests have included Will Rogers (who said of Durango, "It's out of the way and glad of it") and the Western writer Louis L'Amour, who wrote several novels in a suite he kept at the Strater. The **Animas Museum** of La Plata County Historical Society (31st Street and West Second Avenue, 303–259–2402) has exhibits on local history and archaeology.

CHIMNEY ROCK

Chimney Rock (Route 151, four miles south of Route 160) is an Anasazi site once occupied by perhaps 2,000 people. The ruins of their dwellings lie on a mesa. Only one chamber, about 200 feet long, has been excavated, but there are 100 mounds in the vicinity, which probably contain other structures.

OPPOSITE: *Sunlit aspen trees in front of Chimney Rock, once inhabited by the Anasazi. Many of their dwellings remain unexcavated.*

NORTHERN AND CENTRAL COLORADO

OPPOSITE: *The Shrine of the Sun, a memorial to the humorist Will Rogers near Colorado Springs, is situated where the sun's rays light it from sunrise to sunset. Rogers was killed in a plane crash in Alaska in 1935.*

orthern Colorado has been segmented by nature into three zones. From east to west, these are the high plains, the mountains, and the high plateau country. And that is the order in which the forces of progress encountered the landscape. In the far northeastern corner of the state, the Union Pacific's tracks touched Colorado at Julesburg when they linked with the Central Pacific's in 1869. The next year another railway carried Nathan Meeker and fifty families of Union Colony farmers to settle what is now Greeley, commencing the agricultural use of a vast region.

Long before silver miners and cowboys appeared, 150 million years earlier than card sharks preyed on tenderfeet, real sharks roamed the ocean that covered today's Colorado. Dinosaurs lived in jungles and swamps, out of which the Rocky Mountains heaved to their present form. During this period super-heated steam enriched with gold and silver thrust up from far inside the earth and deposited the metals in rocky cracks. A slow process of erosion began 3 million years ago. Soil worn away from the mountains built the high plains of eastern Colorado. Erosion carved the western plateau into a zone of canyons and steplike mesas.

The last region in Colorado to be settled was the western slope. For centuries this had been the province of the Ute, although their realm was steadily encroached upon by the invading settlers. In the Grand Valley of the Colorado River, from which the Ute were expelled in 1881, emigrants seeking land rushed in so fast that they actually saw the last of the departing Indians ahead of them. Grand Junction sprang into being, the Denver & Rio Grande Western Railroad arrived, and irrigation canals made possible peach orchards. But in the state's northwest corner a wilderness remained in what is now Dinosaur National Monument: twisting canyons, cascading waters, and weird rock formations. With the dawn of the automobile age, tourists began to visit even this lost kingdom of the prehistoric reptiles.

This chapter treats the sites of northern Colorado in two east–west journeys from plains to mountains to western plateau. The first touches sites north of Denver from Julesburg westward to the area of Meeker. The second moves from Cripple Creek westward to Grand Junction.

OPPOSITE: *When the Union Pacific Railroad opened a line to Denver in 1869, it advertised specifically to miners.* PAGES 116-17: *The Garden of the Gods near Pikes Peak, a region of red sandstone formations from the late Paleozoic era.*

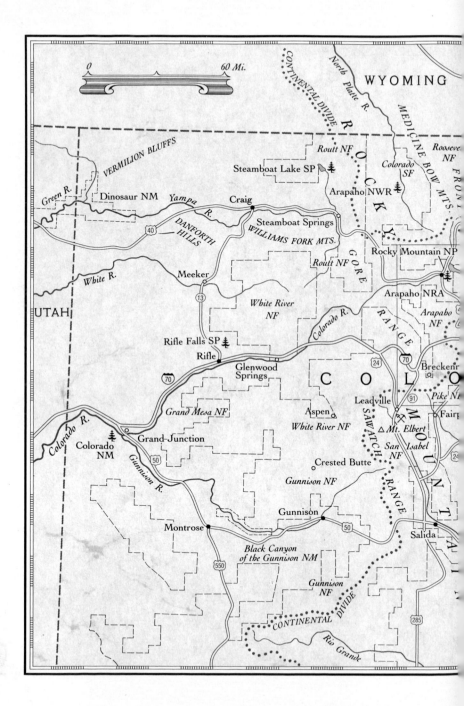

0 60 Mi.

WYOMING

North Platte R.

CONTINENTAL DIVIDE

VERMILION BLUFFS

ROCKY

MEDICINE BOW MTS.

FRON

Routt NF

Roosevelt NF

Steamboat Lake SP

Colorado SF

Dinosaur NM

Yampa R.

Craig

Arapaho NWR

Green R.

Steamboat Springs

40

DANFORTH HILLS

WILLIAMS FORK MTS.

Rocky Mountain NP

GORE

Routt NF

White R.

Meeker

Arapaho NRA

UTAH

13

White River NF

Colorado R.

RANGE

Arapaho NF

Rifle Falls SP

70

Rifle

Glenwood Springs

COLO

24

70

Breckenr

Grand Mesa NF

Aspen

Leadville

91

Pike N

MOUNTAIN

SAWATCH

Fairj

White River NF

△ Mt. Elbert

Colorado R.

Gunnison R.

Grand Junction

50

Colorado NM

Crested Butte

San Isabel NF

24

Gunnison NF

RANGE

Montrose

Gunnison

50

Salida

550

Black Canyon of the Gunnison NM

Gunnison NF

CONTINENTAL DIVIDE

285

Rio Grande

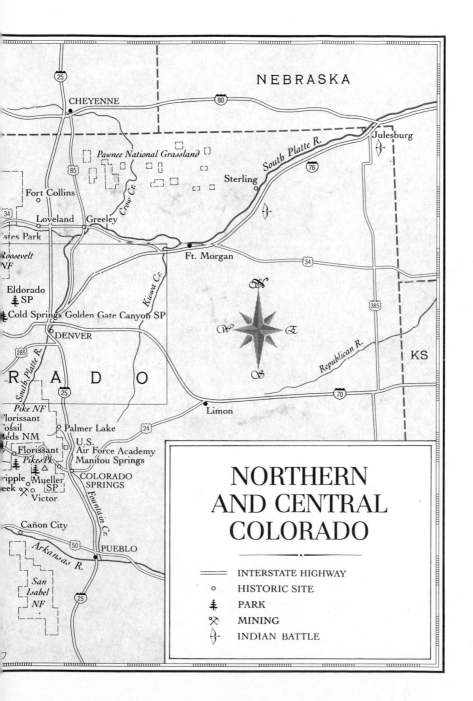

NEBRASKA

CHEYENNE

Julesburg

Pawnee National Grassland

South Platte R.

Sterling

Fort Collins

Loveland   Greeley

Estes Park

Roosevelt
NF

Ft. Morgan

Eldorado
SP

Cold Springs Golden Gate Canyon SP

DENVER

COLORADO

KS

Pike NF
Florissant
Fossil
Beds NM

Florissant

Pikes Pk

Cripple
Creek Mueller
Victor   SP

Limon

Palmer Lake

U.S.
Air Force Academy
Manitou Springs

COLORADO
SPRINGS

Cañon City

Arkansas R.

PUEBLO

San
Isabel
NF

NORTHERN
AND CENTRAL
COLORADO

═══	INTERSTATE HIGHWAY
○	HISTORIC SITE
⚘	PARK
✗	MINING
⚔	INDIAN BATTLE

JULESBURG

In 1860 Colorado's first U.S. mail service started by stagecoach between Denver and Julesburg, a settlement on the Oregon and Overland trails. Around the time Buffalo Bill Cody signed on as a Pony Express rider here, a hell-bent bunch of desperadoes rode into town. Stationmaster Jules Beni and his gang allegedly joined with marauding Indians to attack ore-laden wagon trains. When the stage line fired Beni, he emptied a shotgun into his replacement, Jack Slade, who miraculously lived. The local legend that Slade vowed to kill Beni, cut off his ears, and wear them as watch fobs is just that, a legend. A thousand Indians sacked and burned Old Julesburg in 1865 to avenge the massacre of peaceful Cheyenne and Arapaho at Sand Creek the previous November. Today's town was platted near the old one in 1884 to serve passengers on the transcontinental Union Pacific, the only stop in Colorado. The UP station, built in 1929, now houses the **Fort Sedgwick Depot Museum** (200 West 1st Street, 303–474–2264), with exhibits on local history, agriculture, minerals, and transportation.

STERLING

A product of railroads and irrigation canals, Sterling was laid out in 1881 and became a center for agriculture, grazing, and business. On the edge of town is the **Overland Trail Museum** (junction of Routes 76 and 6, 303–522–3895), which exhibits Indian artifacts, stagecoach memorabilia, rifles, and household furnishings. Outdoors are replantings of some of the grasses that have sustained grazing animals on the plains.

Colorado's last fight between the Plains Indians and U.S. soldiers took place in 1869 at **Summit Springs Battlefield** (south of Sterling, off Route 76 at exit 115). The Fifth U.S. Cavalry and 150 Pawnee scouts, having pursued a band of Cheyenne raiders from Kansas, made a surprise attack on their camp at Summit Springs. Among the fifty-two warriors killed was Tall Bull, chief of the Dog Soldiers, the most renowned of the Cheyenne soldier societies.

GREELEY

Of Colorado's various experiments in colonization, the most productive was at the site of today's Greeley. Union Colony was established in 1870 by Nathan Meeker, agricultural editor of the *New York Tribune,* and was named for his boss, Horace Greeley, who judged this area near the junction of the South Platte and Cache la Poudre rivers as being particularly amenable to irrigation. Indeed, within two months after the arrival of the colonists, they had dug an irrigation ditch nine miles long and six feet wide. Water was important in other ways; one of the abstemious colony's commandments read: "Thou shalt not sell liquid damnation within the lines of Union Colony." By mid-1870 the sober, industrious colonists had built more than 200 houses and business structures.

Meeker Home Museum

Built in the vernacular Italianate style in 1870, Nathan Meeker's home now serves as a museum, with about a third of the furnishings original to the house and the Meeker family. Exhibited are family books—Meeker had been a poet and novelist in New York City's Greenwich Village—and a dress made of an army blanket, worn by Meeker's daughter Josephine when she was held captive by the Ute Indians following the massacre in the town of Meeker.

LOCATION: 1324 Ninth Avenue. HOURS: 10–5 Tuesday–Saturday. FEE: Yes. TELEPHONE: 303–350–9220.

The **Centennial Village Museum** (1475 A Street, 303–350–9224) has arranged thirty-four homes and buildings in chronological fashion, beginning with an Indian tepee and log courthouse of 1861; other exhibits are a one-room schoolhouse, a train depot, later commercial buildings, and a typical workingman's home from Union Colony. The **Greeley Municipal Museum** (919 7th Street, 303–350–9220) is a local archive of Horace Greeley's correspondence and other documents; changing exhibitions illustrate the history of the town.

FORT COLLINS

To guard the Overland Mail and protect travelers and settlers along the trail during a period of Indian raids, in 1862 two companies of the Kansas Volunteer Cavalry established a small military post called Camp Collins. After the camp was destroyed by a flood in 1864, a larger and supposedly permanent fort replaced it on the site of the present city. Three years later, the new fort was abandoned. With a decline in Indian attacks and the return of federal troops to the frontier after the Civil War, the fort had outlived its function, and the site was taken over by a town company hoping to emulate the Union Colony at Greeley. In 1873 the Larimer County Land Improvement Company hired Franklin C. Avery to survey the town and lay out the streets of Fort Collins. Avery, a young farmer and surveyor from New York State, had done the same for the town site of Greeley in 1870. He returned to New York in 1876 to marry and then settled in Fort Collins to raise a family and establish a career as a builder, rancher, banker, and city and county official. The **Avery House** (328 West Mountain Avenue, 303–221–4448), where Franklin and Sara Avery lived with their three children, was built in 1879 of native red sandstone. The Averys' son, Edgar, resided in the house until he died in 1961.

The restored historic district of **Old Town** had its beginnings as an extension of the fort and was the business center of Fort Collins through the 1870s. The **Avery Block** (Mountain and College avenues), built of native red sandstone, was completed in 1897 for the First National Bank, which Franklin Avery had established in 1880. Also noteworthy is the **Miller Block** (162 Linden), with its original cast-iron columns and grillwork.

Housed in the old Carnegie Library, the **Fort Collins Museum** (200 Mathews Street, 303–221–6738) exhibits a model of the fort and preserves its only surviving building, a private cabin built in 1864 and used as an officers' mess. The city's only remaining trolley car, **Birney Car 21,** has been restored and operates on Mountain Avenue from April through October.

LOVELAND

When W. A. H. Loveland's Colorado Central Railroad came to this settlement in 1877, appreciative residents named their town after him. A number of failed prospectors grew rich in Loveland as farmers because their produce could be sold in Denver at inflated prices. Their crops of sugar beets led to the building of eastern Colorado's first sugar mill in 1901. The **Loveland Museum and Gallery** (5th and Lincoln streets, 303–667–6070) portrays life in northern Colorado and Loveland at the turn of the century, with Victorian interiors and building exhibits including a blacksmith forge, general store, and dentist's office. The art gallery features local, regional, and national art exhibitions.

The blacksmith shop at the MacGregor Ranch Museum was originally part of the MacGregor Hotel, established in 1874 on the family's ranch. It was converted into the ranch's blacksmith shop at the turn of the century.

ESTES PARK

The genesis of the splendid **Stanley Hotel** (333 Wonderview Avenue, 303–586–3371) involved an almost ridiculously mixed cast of characters. Isabella Bird, an intrepid English writer who wore Turkish pants and rode alone through the mountains, rhapsodized in *A Lady's Life in the Rocky Mountains* about her visit to Estes Park in 1873 and her dalliance in a "bower of evergreens" with handsome Rocky Mountain Jim ("desperado was written in large letters all over him"). Her descriptions of the landscape—Long's Peak was "heaven-piercing, pure in its pearly luster"—enticed the earl of Dunraven to buy large holdings and build a hunting lodge and hotel in 1878 on a site chosen for him by the painter Albert Bierstadt. At the turn of the century Freelan O. Stanley, co-inventor of the Stanley Steamer automobile, arrived from the East to recover his health in the mountain air. He took walks with Enos Mills, an ardent nature lover who hoped to attract tourists to the area by immersing them in the great outdoors. Stanley developed a steam car—the Stanley Steamer Mountain Wagon—bought Lord Dunraven's holdings, and spent $500,000 in 1909 to build the white clapboard Stanley Hotel. Like the inns of his native New England, it gleamed with lofty white columns, leaded glass windows, sweeping porches, and polished furniture—still to be seen today. John Philip Sousa and Theodore Roosevelt were guests. An original 1909 Stanley Steamer is on display at the **Estes Park Area Historical Museum** (200 South 4th Street, 303–586–6256), which focuses on regional history.

The **MacGregor Ranch Museum** (180 MacGregor Lane, off Devil's Gulch Road, 303–586–3749) is a working mountain ranch of the 1870s that still does haying and raises cattle without modern gasoline-powered machinery. The ranch house contains artifacts of three generations of the pioneering MacGregor family. Traversing **Rocky Mountain National Park** (303–879–0080) since 1935, **Trail Ridge Road** follows an old Ute path. It is the highest continuous highway in the United States, crossing the Continental Divide at 12,183 feet. The park headquarters and visitor center was designed by Edmond Thomas Casey, an architect of the Taliesin Fellowship (Frank Lloyd Wright Foundation) in Scottsdale, Arizona.

STEAMBOAT SPRINGS

Early fur trappers in this region were greeted by the sound of a "steamboat"—actually the noise of a small geyser puffing out gas every ten seconds—a phenomenon that apparently gave rise to the town's name. In 1875 James H. Crawford emigrated from Missouri to become the first homesteader, later building the stone **James H. Crawford House** (1184 Crawford Street, private). With more than 150 medicinal springs in its vicinity, the town attracted health seekers via the Denver, Pacific & Northwestern Railway. The **Steamboat Springs Depot** (13th Street and Stockbridge Road) dates to 1909.

Early home furnishings and artifacts illustrating the local history of Indian life, mining, and skiing can be found at the **Tread of Pioneers Historical Commission Museum** (8th and Oak streets, 303–879–2214). Exhibits include skis used in the late 1800s by the first skiing mailmen. Recreational skiing was brought to the area by the Norwegian stonemason Carl Howelsen, who had been performing ski jumps for the Barnum & Bailey Circus out of Chicago and came west in 1913.

HAHNS PEAK

The **Hahns Peak Schoolhouse** (Main Street off Route 129, 303–879–6781), built in 1912, is a preserved one-room educational center, complete with desks, library, and piano. An old horse barn and mining artifacts are also on the site. Next to it is the **Hahns Peak Historical Society,** which exhibits old mining equipment and photographs and artifacts illustrating the town's past.

MEEKER

The town named itself for Nathan Meeker, founder of Union Colony in Greeley, who had been appointed Indian agent at the White River Agency but was slain with all the post's men during a Ute Indian revolt in 1879. Meeker had tried to make farmers out of the hunting tribe and had seriously offended them with a series of denigrations of their traditions. The **White River Museum** (565 Park Street, 303–878–9982) is housed in the officers' quarters of the military post that was erected in 1888 after the Meeker massacre. Built of cottonwood logs, it contains a stagecoach and other artifacts from the locality.

Located in the vicinity of **Palmer Lake,** an early Colorado resort town, the **Ben Quick Ranch and Fort** (6695 West Plum Creek Road, private) is made up of an Italianate house built in 1885, a cabin dating from 1867, and the site of Fort Washington, which was built on Benjamin Quick's homestead in 1868 to defend the West Plum Creek valley.

COLORADO SPRINGS

Colorado Springs began as a dream—part financial, part romantic—in the mind of General William Jackson Palmer. Traveling west from Philadelphia after the Civil War, he conceived the notion of laying a north–south railroad along the eastern base of the Rockies. Palmer's Denver & Rio Grande Western Railroad introduced narrow-gauge tracks to the Colorado Rockies and reached the future site of Colorado Springs in 1871. The location was five miles from old Colorado City, a town that had petered out after its founding in 1859 as a supply center for the mines of South Park.

Palmer remained convinced that "this belt of country had special advantage in its location, climate, and natural resources," and his romantic side now came into play. To entice his New York fiancée to join him in the raw West, he would lay out a city, "the most attractive in the west for homes—a place for schools, colleges, literature, science, first-class newspapers, and everything the above implies" at the foot of Pikes Peak, surrounded by natural beauty. His resort, he believed, would grow as fashionable as such eastern spas as Saratoga Springs—from which he appropriated the word *springs*, although the closest ones were several miles away at Manitou. By the end of 1871, there were 800 settlers and 150 buildings. An influx of English citizens lent refinement and also earned the community the nickname "Little London." Among the American writers and artists who settled here was Helen Hunt Jackson, author of *Ramona*. The Antlers Hotel opened in 1882 with billiard rooms and Turkish baths.

When the nearby Cripple Creek mining district roared to life west of Pikes Peak in 1891, the gleam of gold also reflected on Colorado Springs. Winfield Scott Stratton, who had worked for $3 a day as a carpenter, became the "Midas of the Rockies." He built the town a trolley system at a cost of $2 million, then donated a large park. Mining magnate Spencer Penrose developed the **Broadmoor Hotel** (1 Lake Circle, 719–634–7711), a pinkish hotel in the Italian Renaissance style, set in a stunning location below Cheyenne Mountain. Incorporating a Georgian ballroom and frescoed ceilings, the hotel was designed by Warren & Wetmore, the New York architects whose buildings included New York's Grand Central Terminal and the Biltmore Hotel. After the Broadmoor's opening in 1918, Maxfield Parrish arrived to paint its picture. For the convenience of guests, the hotel included every amenity, from a stock market ticker to a fleet of Pierce Arrow touring cars for jaunts into the mountains.

Some of the early conveyances collected by Spencer Penrose are preserved at the hotel's **El Pomar Carriage House Museum** (719–634–7711, ext. 5353), the earliest being a brougham used in the inauguration of William Henry Harrison in 1841 (the new president caught pneumonia and died a month later). There are twenty-eight carriages with complete tack, a Conestoga wagon, and Buffalo Bill's Yellowstone Coach. Penrose was also an auto

OPPOSITE: *The Broadmoor Hotel, a lavish resort near Colorado Springs, was developed by Spencer Penrose and Charles Tutt, who intended to make it "permanent and perfect."*

enthusiast, so he built the Cheyenne Mountain Highway to broaden the appeal of the resort. On a knoll along this highway stands the **Will Rogers Shrine of the Sun Memorial,** named to honor the humorist (a friend of Penrose); the medieval-looking tower made of rose granite is the burial place of Penrose and his wife, Julia. In 1936 the Santa Fe artist Randall Davey decorated the interior with frescoes illustrating the history of Pikes Peak.

In downtown Colorado Springs, another creative talent from Santa Fe, John Gaw Meem, designed the Pueblo-style **Colorado Springs Fine Arts Center** (30 West Dale Street, 719–634–5581), which was the country's second free community center when it opened in 1936. Its collection includes Native American pieces, Hispanic colonial folk art, and American Western paintings and bronzes; there is a portrait of General Palmer's daughter by John Singer Sargent.

Colorado Springs Pioneers Museum

The El Paso County Courthouse was built in 1903 of rusticated stone with a clock tower and domed cupola. It now houses the Colorado Springs Pioneers Museum, where a steel birdcage elevator transports visitors to three reconstructed rooms from the home of the novelist Helen Hunt Jackson. Other galleries display Anasazi pottery, weapons, Indian artifacts, Van Briggle pottery, Victorian decorative items, jewelry, and period costumes from the Pikes Peak region.

LOCATION: 215 South Tejon Street. HOURS: 10–5 Monday–Saturday, 1–5 Sunday. FEE: None. TELEPHONE: 719–578–6650.

Several other museums in the area focus on special subjects. North of town near the U.S. Air Force Academy, the twenty-seven-acre **Western Museum of Mining and Industry** (125 Gleneagle Drive, exit 156 off Route 25, 719–598–8850) has an operating ten-stamp ore mill and a reconstructed hard-rock mine with working machinery, and it also offers instructions in blacksmithing, prospecting, and other skills. The **ProRodeo Hall of Fame and Museum of the American Cowboy** (101 Pro Rodeo Drive, 719–593–8840) displays saddles, boots, and other artifacts tracing rodeo history since 1865.

Downtown, the **Museum of the American Numismatic Association** (818 North Cascade Avenue, 719–632–2646) has the largest collection of coins, paper money, tokens, and medals west of

Two santos, carved and painted religious sculptures from New Mexico, in the collection of the Colorado Springs Fine Arts Center: Our Lady of the Immaculate Conception *by an anonymous carver known only as the Arroyo Hondo Carver, and José Rafael Aragón's* Our Lady of the Rosary.

the Smithsonian Institution. Collections focus on American coins and paper money, the gold rush era, and selected numismatic themes from ca. 600 B.C. to the present. On display in Antlers Park (Sierra Street, northern fringe of downtown area) is old **Denver & Rio Grande Engine Number 168,** a narrow-gauge "ten-wheeler" that saw hard service over Rocky Mountain passes.

McAllister House Museum

The first brick home in Colorado Springs, this Downing Gothic–style cottage was built in 1873 by Major Henry McAllister, director of Palmer's early colony. The twenty-inch-thick walls were designed to withstand chinook winds, which were sometimes violent enough to blow a narrow-gauge locomotive off its tracks. The museum's furnishings represent the way of life of the upper class of the city in the 1880s. (The Pearce-McAllister Cottage in Denver was also owned by Major McAllister.)

LOCATION: 423 North Cascade Avenue. HOURS: May through August: 10–4 Wednesday–Saturday, 12–4 Sunday; September through April: 10–4 Thursday–Saturday. FEE: Yes. TELEPHONE: 719–635–7925.

The Colorado Springs Pioneers Museum is housed in the 1903 El Paso County Courthouse, designed by A. J. Smith in the Renaissance Revival style.

White House Ranch Historic Site

At this historic site, interpreters in period clothing portray life in the Pikes Peak area from 1860 through 1910. Buildings and activities are emblematic of the site's progressive history as a homestead of the late 1860s, a working farm, and a turn-of-the-century country estate.

> LOCATION: East entrance of Garden of the Gods Park, off 30th Street. HOURS: June through August 10–4 Wednesday–Sunday; September through December: 10–4 Saturday–Sunday. FEE: Yes, for Orchard House. TELEPHONE: 719–578–6640.

Near Garden of the Gods Park is **Glen Eyrie** (3820 North 30th Street, 719–598–1212), General Palmer's sixty-seven-room Tudor castle. Set in the red-rock country, the turreted castle was built in 1904 of lichen-covered local stone and weathered red clay roof tiles (taken from an English church) to convey a feeling of age. Glen Eyrie was engineered with its own power plant, laundry, telephone system, central vacuuming system, ice-making machinery, greenhouses, dairy barn, bowling alley, three-story elevator, and fire-fighting equipment. The property now houses a retreat center of the

Navigators, a Christian ministry. The public may drive through or arrange a tour in advance.

The **Garden of the Gods** is a wildly beautiful realm of tilted slabs and sculpturesque shapes in red Fountain Formation sandstone. Helen Hunt Jackson described the place as "all motionless and silent, with a strange look of having been stopped and held back in the very climax of some supernatural catastrophe." It was created when sedimentary rocks were thrust up about 65 million years ago. It is said to have been given its present name during a conversation between two friends in 1859. When Melancthon Beach said that the setting would be a fine place for a beer garden, Rufus Cable replied reprovingly: "Beer garden? Why this is a fit place for a garden of the gods!" Picturesquely named formations include Indian Head, Kissing Camels, and Balanced Rock. The 1,350-acre city park is crossed by the old Indian trail to Ute Pass. Tours are available.

MANITOU SPRINGS

A fashionable resort from the 1870s until the era of the automobile, Manitou Springs was founded in 1872 by General Palmer and his friend Dr. William A. Bell, an Englishman. In 1875 a certain Dr. Solly wrote a lovingly phrased pamphlet claiming that the area's soda springs would cure just about any ailment from bronchial catarrh to

Balanced Rock, one of the most famous formations in the Garden of the Gods.

corpulence, and health seekers flocked in. "Manitou Ginger Champagne," a drink made from a special recipe, was shipped out by the millions of bottles.

When the mattress king Zalmon G. Simmons suffered a jarring mule ride to the summit of Pikes Peak, he decided to finance a railway to the top. First operated in 1891 and powered by little teapot steam engines, the **Manitou and Pikes Peak Cog Railway** (515 Ruxton Avenue, 719–685–5401) still climbs a path of steel to the mountain's 14,110-foot summit. It is the highest cog railway in the world, ascending to the windy province above the timberline, where the view sweeps from Denver to New Mexico.

At **Pikes Peak National Historic Landmark** in 1806, Zebulon Pike tried, but failed, to scale the peak that now bears his name. "I believe no human being could have ascended to its summit," he wrote. It was a chilly November and his men were dressed in summer uniforms. Fourteen years later, members of Major Stephen H. Long's party climbed the mountain. In 1893 a young Wellesley College professor named Katherine Lee Bates took a leisurely wagon trip up Pikes Peak and later wrote: "It was then and there, as I was looking out over the sealike expanse of fertile country spreading away so far under these ample skies, that the opening lines of the hymn floated into my mind." The hymn to which she referred was

Anasazi cliff dwellings, reconstructed in Manitou Springs as a tourist attraction in 1906. OPPOSITE: *In the 1880s before the cog railway was constructed, tourists wishing to see the view from Pikes Peak ascended in carriages for five-hours along twisting trails.*

The forty-six-room Miramont Castle was built in 1895 by a French priest who had moved to Manitou Springs for his health. He lived there for only five years.

her creation "America the Beautiful." By 1915 Spencer Penrose (developer of the Broadmoor Hotel) and his associates had built a zigzag auto road to the summit. The next year Penrose staged the first **Pikes Peak Auto Hill Climb** race (719–685–4400), an American classic that still takes place annually on the Sunday after July 4.

Other attractions in Manitou Springs include **Manitou Cliff Dwellings Museum** (Route 24 Bypass, 719–685–5242) in Phantom Cliff Canyon. The outdoor museum is made up of reconstructed cliff dwellings depicting the life of the Anasazi, whose culture flourished in southwestern Colorado from A.D. 550 to 1300. The stone structures, which can be explored room by room, were dismantled and brought here by promoters in 1906. There are also displays of Anasazi artifacts and Indian dance performances.

The cream of "Little London" society met at **Briarhurst** (404 Manitou Avenue, 719–685–1864), Dr. William Bell's Tudor Revival house, completed in 1888. Other guests included Ulysses S. Grant. Bell and his wife first built Briarhurst in 1872. When a fire destroyed the house in 1886, a second and more elaborate Briarhurst was built, complete with a schoolroom, conservatory, library, and cloister. The 1888 stone house now operates as a restaurant.

In 1895 a French priest named Jean-Baptiste Francolon, who was the administrator of several Indian missions, erected the eclectic forty-six-room edifice as a home for his mother, who came from France to live there. It now houses the **Miramont Castle Museum** (9 Capitol Hill, 719–685–1011). There are tours of restored rooms and exhibits of model railroads and toys.

CRIPPLE CREEK

"Free gold sticks out of the rock like raisins out of a fruit cake," said a reporter visiting Cripple Creek during its heyday. Legend has it that a drugstore clerk flung his hat aloft and dug where it hit the ground, discovering the Pharmacy Mine. Cresson Mine workers hit an underground chamber lined with nearly pure gold.

It all began in 1891 when a cowpoke named Bob Womack found gold on a cattle ranch. The hordes then rushed in, laying out a town they named Cripple Creek because cows had been lamed when they stumbled in a local stream bed. The town became a financial center for the mining district, whose outpouring of gold saved Colorado's economy after the decline of silver in 1893. Businesses boomed on Bennett Street, while Myers Street became one of the West's most notorious red-light districts. When a resident prostitute named Jennie LaRue got into a fight with her boyfriend and knocked over a stove, a fire was started that devastated the business district in 1896; another fire five days later leveled the rest of town.

Building this time with brick and stone, settlers raised an elegant new city, whose leading citizens included such men as Winfield Scott Stratton, a carpenter who became sole owner of the fabulous Independence Mine. By 1900 a pair of opera houses and 14 newspapers flourished; there were good hospitals and a stock exchange (as well as 139 saloons) to serve the town of 50,000; electric trolley cars rolled through downtown. Cripple Creek could well afford these civic improvements: About $500 million worth of gold was mined in the district.

Relics of the boom days are displayed at the **Cripple Creek District Museum** (head of Bennett Avenue, 719–689–2634), where the Midland Railroad Terminal Depot of 1896 has exhibits about the mining and social history of Cripple Creek; the Colorado Trading

Cripple Creek, which had a population of more than 25,000 in 1900, today only has some 650 inhabitants.

and Transfer Building displays historical photographs; and the Assay Office features geological exhibits and demonstrations of ore testing. Departing from the Midland terminal, the **Cripple Creek & Victor Narrow Gauge Railroad** (5th and Carr, 719–689–2640) operates four-mile trips past historic mines on trains pulled by an 0-4-0-type steam locomotive. Many turn-of-the-century buildings are standing. Victorian decor has been retained at the **Imperial Hotel** (123 North 3rd Street, 719–689–2713) of 1896, whose still-lively playhouse has been called "the Old Vic of modern melodrama." The **Old Homestead Museum** (353 Myers Avenue, 719–689–3090), a former brothel where such madams as Pearl de Vere drew the town's elite clientele, now displays original furnishings.

On tours of the **Mollie Kathleen Gold Mine** (Route 67, one mile north of Cripple Creek, 719–689–2465), visitors ride a miner's cage 1,000 feet below the surface to see gold veins and learn about mining tools and methods. On the road from Cripple Creek toward Mount Pisgah lies the **Mount Pisgah Cemetery,** whose most memorable tombstone is inscribed: "He called Bill Smith a liar."

VICTOR

Most of the miners from Cripple Creek lived in the less opulent town of Victor, seven miles distant, where the Portland Mine alone produced 3 million troy ounces and was Colorado's largest and most productive gold mine. The district declined around World War I, due to union disputes, lower gold prices, and higher production costs, but today some mines continue to operate.

A number of Victor's business blocks and other buildings remain; the town was rebuilt after a fire in 1899. At the **Victor Record Building** (118 South 4th Street), local resident Lowell Thomas got his start in journalism, becoming editor of the paper in 1911. **Lowell Thomas's boyhood home** is located at 225 South 6th Street; and the **Victor/Lowell Thomas Museum** (Victor Avenue and 3d Street, 719–689–3211) has displays on the wide-ranging reporter's life, as well as on mining, Cripple Creek millionaires, and other local history. Remains of the **Gold Coin Mine** are visible on Diamond Avenue; workers discovered this fabulously rich lode while they were digging the foundation for the Victor Hotel.

FLORISSANT FOSSIL BEDS NATIONAL MONUMENT

After visiting the Florissant area, an early fur trapper told a tale that common in Western mythology, all about a "petrified forest of petrified trees, full of petrified birds singing petrified songs." Indeed, when homesteader David Long arrived with his family in 1871, he settled on a piece of land that was covered with petrified sequoia trees. Scientists from Colorado Springs became interested when Long unearthed the skeleton of a mastodon.

The fossil beds are made up of Oligocene Epoch shales imprinted with images of dragonflies, beetles, spiders, fish, and birds that lived about 35 million years ago. Once part of ancient Lake Florissant, the shale forms the most extensive fossil record of its type in the world. Tree stumps include one of the largest known petrified sequoias, a *Sequoia affinis* measuring eleven feet tall and ten feet around.

LOCATION: 2.5 miles south of Florissant on Teller County Road 1. HOURS: Mid-September through mid-June: 8–4:30 Daily; mid-June through mid-September: 8–7 Daily. FEE: Yes. TELEPHONE: 719–748–3253.

FAIRPLAY

Fairplay was the center of activity in South Park, a 900-square-mile valley surrounded by the Mosquito and Park ranges. Captain John C. Frémont and Kit Carson passed through the site of Fairplay in 1844. In 1807 Zebulon M. Pike had heard a report from James Purcell about finding gold in South Park. By 1859 a group of prospectors, rankled by the way nearby Tarryall's settlers had staked all the good claims, started their own town, which they named Fairplay as a promise of equal treatment for all settlers. The idealistic period was short-lived, however. One city father, Jim Reynolds, became a highwayman who robbed gold shipments. A Methodist reform pastor had his horse shaved by the town toughs, and parties unknown attempted to steal his church. The Presbyterians' **Sheldon Jackson Memorial Chapel,** built in 1874, still stands, a delight in Carpenter Gothic style, as do a number of other buildings from the late 1800s.

A burro named Shorty and his faithful dog companion Bum are buried in the **Fairplay Cemetery.** Burros served miners as both helpers and companions, and the **Prunes Monument** near the center of town marks the grave of a 63-year-old burro who supposedly labored in every mine in the district.

South Park City Museum

An unusual suburb of Fairplay is this stretch of thirty-five historic buildings gathered from around South Park. The outdoor museum represents a typical Colorado mining town in the period from 1870–1900. Cabins and buildings have been refurnished with 50,000 authentic artifacts to illustrate home life and professions ranging from dentistry to pharmacy. Among the buildings are the **South Park Lager Beer Brewery,** built of stone in 1879 by Charles and Leonard Summer, and the **Summer Saloon,** a false-front building next door for imbibing the brewery's products.

LOCATION: 100 Front Street. HOURS: Mid-May through Memorial Day, and Labor Day through mid-October: 9–5 Daily; Memorial

BRECKENRIDGE

After building a fort in 1859 for protection from Indians, prospectors established Breckenridge in an area of rich placer and lode gold. It is said that silver mining began here in the late 1870s after a barber commented on the silver dust in a gold miner's hair. Starting in 1898, dredges mined the nearby rivers, cutting swaths up to 100 yards wide and 80 feet deep. Towering piles of rock and debris from these operations remain in the area. Various historic buildings still stand. **Breckenridge Mining Camp Museum** (115 North Main Street, 303–453–2342) displays mining machinery and household and office furnishings arranged in the county clerk's original office, built in 1870.

LEADVILLE

When Abe Lee looked at glittering nuggets in his gold pan in 1860 and exclaimed "Boys, I've got all California here in this pan," he named California Gulch and started a rush that yielded $10 million and started the town of Oro City. But the gold played out and the town nearly emptied, until a day in 1875 when two experienced prospectors, William Stevens and Alvinus Woods, opened one of the most remarkable chapters in Western history. While exploring

Leadville's Roman Catholic church was constructed in 1879 with the first load of brick to reach the town, commandeered by Father Robinson, who organized the parish.

abandoned claims, they decided to test the heavy sands that had hampered the gold miners. The test showed nearly pure lead carbonate imbued with silver; the news leaked out, and by 1878 a new town called Leadville was famous around the world for its overnight millionaires and its streets teeming with gunmen, shady ladies, bunco artists, and gamblers. Helen Hunt Jackson wrote: "[The street] looked all the time as if there had been a fire, and the people were just dispersing. . . . All the faces looked restless, eager, fierce. It was a Monaco gambling room emptied into a Colorado spruce clearing."

Thousands of dollars were paid for prospect holes; some claims changed hands many times in a single day. Men shot each other over trifles and died of exposure, for Leadville lies in a bleak spot above 10,000 feet, with short summers and raw winters. Graves were excavated in the frozen ground with dynamite, and at least one mine was discovered during a burial. In the overcrowded settlement, miners slept on saloon floors (tables were reserved for regular customers); one fellow made $1,000 a night renting bunks in a large circus tent. Real estate prices skyrocketed, and storekeepers turned scalpers, selling groceries at a 400 percent profit; even water cost fifty cents a barrel. David May started the May Company department stores in a tent on Harrison Avenue. A Swiss immigrant named Meyer Guggenheim launched the family fortune with the A. Y. and Minnie mines in 1880 and went on to build a smelting empire.

Another Leadville success story was that of Horace Austin Warner Tabor, whose life reads like a historical romance. In 1878 this storekeeper grubstaked two prospectors to $64 worth of groceries in exchange for a third interest if they struck pay dirt. They walked up Fryer Hill and hit a fabulous vein that became the Little Pittsburg mine, worth $20 million within a year. It seemed Tabor could not lose, even when he bought a "salted" hole from a fraud named Chicken Bill; rather than admit he had been cheated, Tabor dug twenty-five feet deeper and hit the massive Crysolite lode, where he mined about $1.5 million in ore. Buying and trading mines, he became wealthy enough to build the town's opera house, was elected lieutenant governor of the state, and slept in silk nightshirts with diamond buttons. In a café, while eating oysters, he met blue-eyed young "Baby Doe" McCourt, a divorced waitress who had come to

OPPOSITE: *The remains of a once-prosperous mine in Leadville.*

Red plush seats in Leadville's Opera House, the most lavish theater between St. Louis and San Francisco at the time of its construction. It was built by Horace Tabor in 1879.

Leadville to scout quietly for a new (preferably rich) mate. Abandoning his wife, Augusta, Tabor began a romance that scandalized Colorado; he married his mistress in 1883, in a wedding in Washington, DC attended by President Chester A. Arthur. By the time of his death in 1899, he was ruined, his fortune wiped out by bad investments and the silver crash of 1893. His dying words to Baby Doe were said to be, "Hold on to the Matchless," the last of his mines. She did, remaining loyal to his memory for thirty-six years and living in a cabin south of the Matchless shaft house, where her undernourished, frozen body was found in 1935.

Leadville's decline mirrored Horace Tabor's, with empty streets and silent mines after the turn of the century. Much of the town was torn down for firewood. During Prohibition many abandoned mine shafts were taken over by bootleggers, whose stills produced "Leadville moon," popular all over the West. The **Matchless Mine Museum** (two miles east of town on East 7th Street, 719–486–0371) cost Tabor $117,000 in 1881 and earned him $10 million. When Oscar Wilde visited Leadville, he descended a shaft at the mine and had dinner with the miners, "the first course being whiskey, the second whiskey, and the third whiskey." His hosts admired the foppish poet's immense capacity for hard liquor. The shack where Baby Doe spent her last years is open for tours.

The remains of other mines surround Leadville. A self-guided mine tour map is available at the Chamber of Commerce (809 Harrison Avenue, 719–486–3900). A thirty-minute historical film is shown at the church next door. Much of town has been designated as the **Leadville Historic District.** At the **Tabor Opera House** (308 Harrison Street, 719–486–1147), built in 1879, a self-guided tour covers the balcony, the backstage dressing rooms, and the stage itself, where Helena Modjeska, the actress, and Harry Houdini, the magician, entertained. Hand-painted scenery from the theater's early days is still in use. On his lecture tour of 1882, Oscar Wilde appeared in a black velvet suit and read to the miners from the autobiography of Benvenuto Cellini. "They seemed much delighted," he wrote later. "I was reproved by my hearers for not having brought him with me. I explained that he had been dead for some little time, which elicited the inquiry, 'Who shot him?'"

The simple frame **H. A. W. Tabor Home** (116 East 5th Street, 719–486–0551) was built in 1877 and was the residence of Horace Tabor and his first wife, Augusta, until 1881. The rooms contain artifacts of the time. Named for its stained-glass "eye"—a small window in an attic roof—the **House with the Eye** (127 West 4th Street, 719–486–0860) was built in 1879 by the French architect Eugène Robitaille. The gingerbread-fronted house now contains a museum displaying carriages, guns, antique bottles, and mining tools.

Tours of Colorado's last operating hot-lead daily newspaper are given at the **Herald Democrat Newspaper Museum** (717 Harrison, 719–486–0641), which exhibits turn-of-the-century typesetting equipment, a flatbed press, and historic newspaper issues. **The National Mining Hall of Fame and Museum** (120 West 9th Street, 719–486–1229) presents the history of the American mining industry. Leadville memorabilia, Victorian furniture, and mining dioramas are displayed at the **Heritage Museum** (102 East 9th Street, 719–486–1878). Departing from Leadville's depot, built in 1884, the **Leadville, Colorado & Southern Railroad Train Ride** (326 East 7th Street, 719–486–3936) chugs past an old roundhouse and a water tower along the headwaters of the Arkansas River, a two-and-a-half-hour round trip.

Healy House and Dexter Cabin

The clapboard **Healy House** was built for the mining engineer August Meyer in 1878 and became a social hub in the young city. Daniel Healy purchased it in 1881 and operated it as a boardinghouse. Today costumed guides play the roles of Victorian boarders. **Dexter Cabin** appears from the outside to be a simple log structure, but inside it reflects the flamboyant tastes of the banker and mining magnate James V. Dexter, who built it in 1879 and furnished it expensively—not for his family, but for his poker pals, who gathered here as a kind of private club.

LOCATION: 912 Harrison Avenue. HOURS: June through August: 10–4:30 Monday–Saturday, 1–4:30 Sunday; September through May: By appointment. FEE: Yes. TELEPHONE: 719–486–0487.

TWIN LAKES

A designated **historic district** (private) along both sides of Route 82, Twin Lakes began as a mining community but became a summer resort for people attracted to the area after the Leadville boom of 1878. Much of the late-nineteenth-century character remains. East of Twin Lakes lies the old **Interlaken Resort District** (private), which began with the opening of a lodge in 1879 and operated until the mid-twentieth century. Structures that survive from the once-extensive complex include the log hotel, barns, and a cabin.

ASPEN

The prospectors who spread out from Leadville and swarmed west over the Continental Divide found silver in the Roaring Fork Valley, where they established Aspen in 1880. Out of the ground came great riches. The Smuggler Mine, for example, produced the largest silver nugget in the world, weighing 2,060 pounds. Because of the town's isolation, ore-freighting costs were high, so Aspen developed slowly.

Jerome B. Wheeler, a partner in Macy's department store in New York, moved west in 1883 seeking a better climate for his wife, who suffered from a respiratory illness, and came to play an important role in the development of this young community. He invested in

OPPOSITE: *Leadville's Healy House was built by August Meyer, who lived in it for only two years before moving on to Kansas City. In the 1890s it served as a boarding house occupied largely by teachers.*

The Interlaken Resort near Twin Lakes, which became a summer vacation spot after it was discovered by those attracted to the Leadville silver rush of 1879.

the sorely underfinanced SPAR and Galena mines, completed work on a half-constructed smelter, and started an ore-shipping company. Wheeler was influential in extending the Colorado Railroad line into Aspen. He also built the town's first bank, the Wheeler Opera House, and the Hotel Jerome in an effort to create a more substantial community.

Although the mines were spewing ore, it often was left piled in drifts around town awaiting shipment by wagon over Independence Pass. When the Denver & Rio Grande Western Railroad reached town in 1887, followed the next year by the Colorado Midland, Aspen's fortunes soared. Silver production reached $6 million a year, better than Leadville's at the time. Unlike Leadville, however, Aspen built ten churches during the 1880s, and its red-light district occupied only a two-block strip of Durant Avenue. Millionaires built their houses on Hallam Street, called Bullion Row. The house built in 1888, with a French mansard roof, at **232 East Hallam** once belonged to Fred Glidden, better known as Luke Short, the author of many Western novels. Jerome B. Wheeler's Queen Anne–style house of the same year, now the **Wheeler-Stallard House Museum** (620 West Bleeker, 303–925–3721), preserves furniture, photographs, garments, and other local memorabilia. Wheeler lost the house after the silver crash and the failure of his bank.

Wheeler also lost the **Wheeler Opera House** (330 East Hyman, 303–920–2268), his "perfect bijou of a theatre," which was Aspen's cultural center in the boom days. It cost $80,000 to erect the Renaissance Revival structure of stone and brick in 1889. On opening night lavishly gowned ladies received programs made of scented satin. Spectators sat in gilded boxes under a star-spangled dome and watched the touring companies that played the western "silver circuit." Farce was popular with Aspen audiences, although Shakespeare was not. In 1912 the opera house burned, but it has been restored to its nineteenth-century grandeur and operates year-round with local and national productions, including the Aspen Music Festival opera productions. Wheeler's other civic monument, the brick-and-sandstone **Hotel Jerome** (Main and Mill streets, 303–920–1000), cost $160,000 to build in 1889 and boasted one of the West's first elevators and a greenhouse to supply fresh vegetables. It opened with a gala Thanksgiving ball that drew guests from New York and Paris. With its subtle Eastlake decor, the Jerome has been the hub of Aspen's social life since then—particularly the bar, which has hardly changed in 100 years.

Other notable buildings include the **Pitkin County Courthouse** (506 East Main Street) of 1891, the **Armory Hall** (130 South Galena Street), which was built in 1892 and now houses Aspen's City Hall, and the imposing red sandstone **Aspen Community United Methodist Church** (200 East Bleeker Street, 303–925–1571). **Pioneer Park** (422 West Bleeker Street), with its mansard roof and bay windows, was built in 1885 by Aspen's first mayor, who was accused of murdering his wife with strychnine. The house was later bought by Walter Paepcke, who founded the Aspen Institute for Humanistic Studies in 1949 and is credited with spurring Aspen's revival as a center of summer culture and winter sports. During the Goethe Bicentennial, and on his only visit to the United States, Albert Schweitzer was lodged in the carriage house.

Aspen, a silver mining boom town in the late 1880s, has boomed again with winter skiing and summer cultural activities. OPPOSITE: *The stage curtain at the Wheeler Opera House in Aspen features the Brooklyn Bridge.*

Ten miles up Castle Creek, just west of Aspen, is the ghost town of **Ashcroft,** once a rowdy mining center. It was visited by Bob Ford, the man who shot Jesse James, and by Leadville's Horace Tabor, who built a home there after he bought the Tam O'Shanter mine in 1881. When his bride, Baby Doe, came to visit, Tabor decreed a holiday and stood the whole town to drinks. A number of weathered ruins have been stabilized in an alpine meadow alongside Castle Creek. Gooseberry bushes still grow beside vanished doorsteps.

Another ghost town, **Independence,** lies east of Aspen along Route 82. Gold was discovered on July 4, 1879, launching the mining boom in the region. Ruins stand on two adjacent sites—the old town and the mill.

REDSTONE

John C. Osgood discovered large coal deposits and started the Colorado Fuel Company in 1884. He was an idealist who believed in good wages and working conditions, so he built a most unusual company town—forty pastel cottages, each of a different style and

The Vermont Marble Company opened quarries in the town called Marble in 1905.
Colorado Yule marble from these quarries was used in the Lincoln Memorial in
Washington, DC, and in many public buildings in New York and San Francisco.

color, and a luxurious inn for workers and visitors. Today the inn,
with a clock tower, is open for lodging and meals as the **Redstone
Inn** (Route 133, 303–963–2526). A mile from the model
workingmen's town stands Osgood's own $2.5 million Tudor Revival
country estate, Cleveholm Manor, now commonly called **Redstone
Castle** (0058 Redstone Boulevard, 303–963–3463). Operating as a
bed-and-breakfast inn, with tours available, it is a stone-and-timber
manor house in which the magnate installed gold-leafed ceilings,
Italian marble fireplaces, a library fitted out in Moroccan leather,
and a lavish gaming room.

MARBLE

The pure white Colorado "yule marble," discovered in 1873 by the
geologist Sylvester Richardson along the Crystal River, found a
commercial outlet in 1906, when rail service began. The town that
grew up here had its streets paved in marble, and local quarries
supplied the stone for projects all over the country; a notable

example is the Tomb of the Unknown Soldier, cut from a fifty-six-ton slab that took twelve men over a year to quarry. There is a quarry above town, as well as an old mill, located on the rough road to Crystal. The **Marble Historical Society** (412 West Main Street, 303–945–2824) is housed in a schoolhouse of 1910 and displays artifacts of Marble's past.

CRESTED BUTTE

Crested Butte produced $350,000 worth of gold from Washington Gulch, then settled down as a way station for passengers en route from Aspen to Gunnison. (To cross over Pearl Pass from Aspen, drivers sometimes had to take their stagecoaches apart, lower them as much as 100 feet down cliffs, and reassemble them.) In the late 1870s came a coal boom—3 anthracite and 3 bituminous mines and 150 coke ovens—and a town whose architecture stands as a fine example of the mining-camp style. With many Carpenter Gothic buildings, the town has been designated the **Crested Butte National Historic District.** Notable buildings include the Denver & Rio Grande Western Railroad depot of 1881, the restored Kochevar House, the Old Town Hall of 1883 with its Eastern European touches, and the Old Rock Schoolhouse, built of fieldstone in 1883 as the community's first school. In answer to the deep snows of winter, area residents invented the two-story outhouse—first floor for summer, top floor for winter when the snow piled up outside; an example can be seen in the alley behind the Company Store.

GLENWOOD SPRINGS

Well known to Ute Indians, who used the mineral springs to cure their sick, the area took shape as a white settler's town in 1882, after the Indians were removed to Utah. A 600-foot-long swimming pool was built by a British investment company in 1891, anchoring the resort, and two years later mining engineer Walter Devereux spent $850,000 to erect the **Hotel Colorado** (526 Pine Street, 303–945–6511) in the style of the Roman Renaissance. The elegant hotel had its own polo field and a railroad siding with space for sixteen private cars. Servants were brought from Boston, and local residents were forbidden to enter the building. Theodore Roosevelt was a frequent guest.

John Henry Holliday, a dentist suffering from tuberculosis, came to town to restore his health but died in 1887. "Doc" Holliday, remembered better as a card wizard and gunfighter than as a dentist, is buried in the Glenwood Springs cemetery. Holliday, who died of natural causes, had been one of the participants in the Gunfight at the O.K. Corral in Tombstone, Arizona, in 1881. He and the Earp brothers killed three men in that much-romanticized encounter, actually just a shoot-out between rival gangs of thieves.

GRAND JUNCTION

At the junction of the Gunnison and Colorado rivers, George A. Crawford laid out Grand Junction. Crawford was an avid town-site promoter and had been elected governor of Kansas, although he never served in that office because his election violated the state's constitution. Grand Junction was incorporated in 1882, and its future was brightened by the arrival of the Denver & Rio Grande Western Railroad the same year. Settlers dug irrigation canals and planted fruit trees and vines.

The **Museum of Western Colorado** (4th and Ute streets, 303–242–0971) focuses on the history of western Colorado after 1880, with a time line, weapons collection, and exhibits on farming, regional culture, railroading, and mining. The associated **Dinosaur Valley Museum** (4th and Main streets, 303–243–3466) is devoted to local fossil heritage. The region has yielded more than fifty dinosaur species, including the smallest and one of the largest known dinosaurs in the world. A working paleontological laboratory is open for observation, and information is available for a self-guided tour of turn-of-the-century dinosaur quarries at nearby Dinosaur Hill and Riggs Hill.

Also operated by the Museum of Western Colorado is the **Cross Orchards Living History Farm** (3073 F "Patterson" Road, 303–434–9814). From 1896 to 1923 Isabelle Cross, heiress to the Red Cross Shoe Company of Massachusetts, owned the orchards, which included over 22,000 apple trees and also produced pears and peaches on 243 acres. The site operates as an outdoor museum with costumed guides, restored buildings and equipment, apple orchards, and living-history demonstrations.

OPPOSITE: *Crested Butte's 1883 City Hall, one of the earliest structures in the town, saw double duty as the firehouse. The large doors on the ground floor accommodated the horse-drawn fire engine.*

CHAPTER FOUR

SOUTHERN
WYOMING

W yoming has been called the "Lonesome Land." Arid, lofty, cold, and remote, it supports nearly 1.4 million cattle but only a third as many people. Among the fifty states its population ranks smallest. As Wyoming is the ninth-largest state in area, this disparity says something about its terrain and its capacity to sustain human life. John Gunther described the landscape as "America high, naked and exposed." At an altitude of 5,000 to 6,000 feet, grasslands extend over the eastern third of the state, which is almost treeless and too arid for farming without irrigation. Dominated by short grass and sagebrush, this vastness gave Wyoming its name, derived from the Delaware Indian term *maughwau wama,* meaning "big plains." To the west of the Great Plains lie the silent snows and peaks of the Rocky Mountains. The Absaroka, Wind River, Teton, Gros Ventre, and Sierra Madre ranges trace the Continental Divide from the state's northwestern corner to the center of the southern border. Down from the mountains tumble Wyoming's rivers—too small to navigate, which probably accounts for the lack of major commercial centers along their courses. But the names of these streams resonate with the romance of the West: Wind River, Big Horn, Green, and Yellowstone, the Powder, North Platte, Sweetwater, and Snake. The southwestern part of Wyoming is an extension of the Great Basin to the south, which features the Bad Lands Hills, Alkali Flat, the Red Desert, and the Great Divide Basin. Salt sage, mountain spurs, and a few fretful creeks compose the landscape—not the sort of place to lure settlers.

It is important to pay attention to the land here, because as Neil Morgan remarked in *Westward Tilt,* "Except for Alaska there is no American state on which the passage of time and man has left so small an imprint as Wyoming." Indeed, most have seen the region as a place for passage. Fur trappers during the period 1810 to 1840 took beaver pelts and then drifted away. The scene that greeted emigrants crossing southern and central Wyoming on the Oregon Trail was pretty much as Daniel Webster described it in 1844, when he opined that Wyoming "was not worth a cent . . . a region of savages, wild beasts, shifting sands, whirlwinds of dust, cactus, and prairie dogs." The covered wagons just kept rolling toward the green valleys of Oregon and the gold fields of California.

When the Union Pacific laid the transcontinental railroad across Wyoming in 1867–1868, rowdy settlements along the tracks ballooned and then deflated as the construction workers passed by with their attendant group of ruffians and drifters, all part of a transient

Alfred Jacob Miller sketched the busy scene inside Fort William, the predecessor to Fort Laramie, in 1837. The Indians have come to the fort to trade pelts.

culture known as "Hell on Wheels." Cowboys too drove their longhorns right through Wyoming as they headed north on the Texas Trail. Yet these two forces—rails and cattle—brought permanent settlement to the Lonesome Land. Cheyenne and Laramie started as railroad towns. Ranching became a major industry once there were trains to ship cattle to eastern markets.

Ancient hunters came into these empty lands at least 12,000 years ago. Near Worland they slaughtered mammoths and left stacks of bones, stone knives, and projectile points. And at the "Spanish Diggings," near Guernsey, they operated primitive quarries, splitting quartzite to make tools and weapons. (When first rediscovered, the area seemed to suggest that the hunters had left last week, not 10,000 years ago: Wedges were discovered protruding from cracks in the rock, ready to be hammered.)

By the end of the eighteenth century mounted Indians roved the plains, although Wyoming supported no more than about 10,000 of them, because intertribal wars and a sparsity of buffalo kept the population down. At first, the Shoshoni controlled the region in the west; to the north lived the Crow; and in the southeast roamed the Arapaho and Cheyenne. The latter two tribes joined with the Sioux,

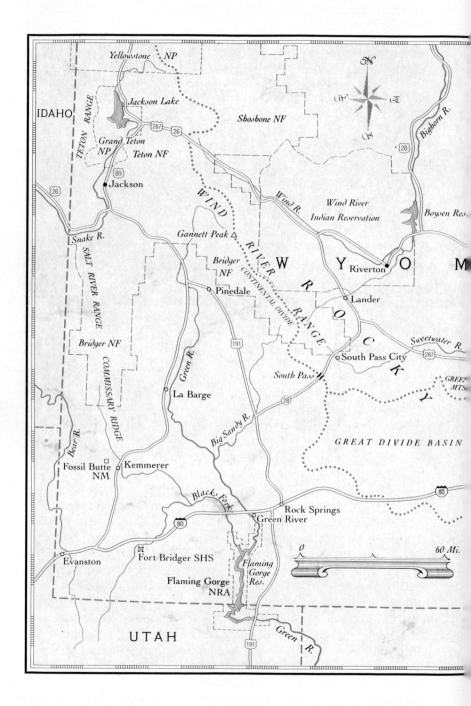

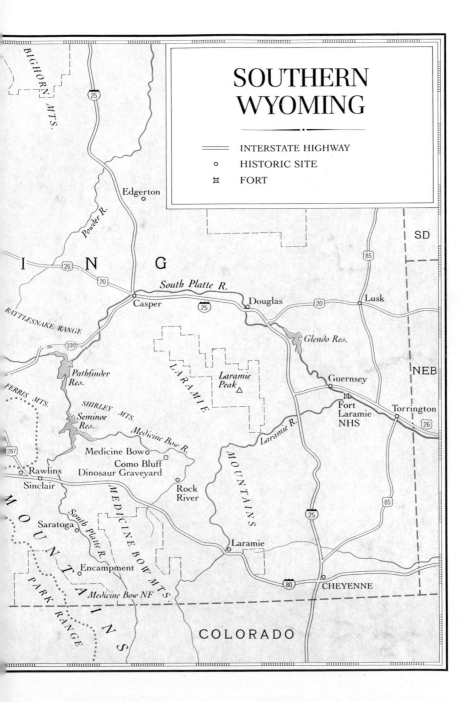

SOUTHERN WYOMING

——— INTERSTATE HIGHWAY

o   HISTORIC SITE

⊟   FORT

who came from the east in about 1830 and pushed the Crow and
Shoshoni into the western mountains. That left the eastern plains in
the control of these more aggressive tribes, who later opposed the
tide of emigrant homeseekers and miners that spread across
Wyoming. The culture of the Plains Indians revolved around more
than hunting and fighting. Children played with tops or rawhide
toboggans; young people married with an exchange of gifts between
families. Social life had an intriguing complexity: The Cheyenne
ascribed magical powers to a warrior society that was known as "con-
traries" because they said "no" when they meant "yes."

No one knows which European was the first to come to
Wyoming. A blade that might be part of a seventeenth-century
Spanish rapier was found near the Tongue River at Dayton. And
Indians in nearby Montana spoke of mounted, "iron-covered" men
whom arrows could not kill. But there is no sure record of a visit by
Spaniards or anyone else until two French Canadians named
François and Louis Joseph Vérendrye wrote a description indicating
they had seen the Big Horn Mountains in 1743. They spoke of high
mountains toward which they traveled through "magnificent
prairies" where "wild animals" roamed. The Vérendryes were seeking a route to the Pacific and—like so many later visitors—viewed
Wyoming as a place to travel through on the way to somewhere else.
Frightened of the Snake (Shoshoni) Indians, however, they turned
around and headed home. No other white visitors came until the
next century.

In 1806 John Colter asked permission to leave his $5-a-month
position as a private with the returning Lewis and Clark expedition
(which did not pass through Wyoming) to trap in the wilderness.
With a fur trader named Manuel Lisa, he crossed into Wyoming the
following year, where one of the epic events of Western history took
place: A party of Blackfoot captured Colter in 1808, stripped him,
and asked if he was a good runner, to which he shrewdly answered
no. They gave him a chance to run for his life, and he soon out-
paced the Indians (except one whom he killed), then hid for hours
in a chilly river. Naked, eating roots to stay alive, he made a 300-mile
walk over rocky ground to Manuel Lisa's trading post. Colter's explorations of the Big Horn Basin and the Jackson Hole region helped
open the era of the Wyoming fur trade. In 1812 Robert Stuart, the
young and inexperienced leader of the returning party of Astorians,
traveled east on a new route that would become famous as the
Oregon Trail. En route Stuart crossed near (or perhaps through)

South Pass, a gentle opening through the Continental Divide that was vital to the later emigrants. That winter Stuart and his men erected Wyoming's first building, a rough cabin on Poison Spider Creek.

In 1822 William Ashley placed a famous advertisement in a Saint Louis newspaper, seeking 100 "Enterprising Young Men" for the fur trade. Jedediah Smith and Jim Bridger were among those who answered the ad, joining other mountain men to trap beavers along the Green River. In this country Ashley organized the annual "rendezvous," at which trappers, traders, and Indians gathered for a few weeks to swap furs for such supplies as whiskey, ammunition, coffee, sugar, and flour. After a lonely year in the wilderness the trappers found companions with whom to drink, fight, race, gamble, and tell tall tales. (One of Jim Bridger's classic stories was about the Yellowstone River, where a man could catch a fish in the stream, flip it over his shoulder, and cook it in a boiling pool.) Ashley profited greatly by the rendezvous system: In 1825, the year of the first gathering, he took pelts to Saint Louis worth $48,500, and in only two years he retired a wealthy man.

Jim Bridger, "King of the Mountain Men," began his travels though the Great Plains in the 1820s, when he was in his teens. He was the first white man known to have visited Great Salt Lake, and was the most famous guide of his time. He died in 1881.

Thomas Moran's 1879 painting of Green River, Wyoming *depicts a group of armed*

For the convenience of trader and Indian alike, a few trading posts were built, the best known being Fort Laramie, erected in 1834 by William Sublette and Robert Campbell near the confluence of the Laramie and North Platte rivers. It was Wyoming's first permanent white settlement. The fur trade began to decline in the mid-1830s when silk replaced beaver for fashionable hats and the supply of pelts waned. The last rendezvous was held in 1840. Over the years only a few hundred mountain men had worked in Wyoming, and they left almost no physical mark—but they did blaze the way for the pioneers over South Pass. The first few emigrants actually joined the trappers and their supply caravans. These men were missionaries heading to the Far West—Jason Lee in 1834, followed by Marcus Whitman and Samuel Parker in 1835. At Hoback Canyon Parker gave what was probably the first Protestant sermon heard in the Rockies. In 1840 Pierre-Jean De Smet, a Catholic priest, joined the American Fur Company's expedition on the way to the last rendezvous, meeting a band of Indians of whom he said, "Our meeting

Utes returning to their encampment (detail).

was . . . like that of children who run to meet their father after a long absence." On De Smet's return trip, however, a Crow chief commented after a sermon that he knew of only two men in the entire Crow nation who had "never killed or stolen nor been guilty of the excesses you speak of. I *may* be mistaken about them, and in that case we will all go to hell together."

As the number of emigrants began to increase, John C. Frémont was sent on the first scientific expedition through Wyoming in 1842 to evaluate the route. His party paused at Fort Laramie, where Frémont heard of the mounting anger among the Sioux and Cheyenne over the white invasion of their lands. To protect emigrants on the Oregon Trail, Frémont recommended that the government take over Fort Laramie as an army post. His published account of the trip excited potential emigrants and offered valuable advice for the journey west. Meanwhile, exaggerated tales about the glories of Oregon and California drifted eastward. One pioneer reported that in Oregon "the pigs are running around . . . already cooked, with knives and forks sticking out of them so you can cut off a slice whenever you're hungry!" California was a sunny paradise that cured ills with its climate alone. Almost no one wanted to settle in arid, raw Wyoming. A traveler about to cross South Pass in 1846 wrote: "This is a country that may captivate mad poets, but I swear I see nothing but big rocks . . . high mountains and wild sage. It is a miserable country."

Between 350,000 and 400,000 pioneers traveled the great highway west from 1840 to 1868. With the dangers of bad weather, wild animals, disease, and stampedes, one out of every seventeen emigrants died along the way, and every mile of the Oregon Trail was scarred with an average of ten graves. Freighters and Pony Express riders also followed the route, and Ben Holladay ran the Overland stage line there until a rise in Indian hostilities prompted him to move his operations south in 1862. His new Overland Trail, crossing the Laramie Plains and Bridger's Pass, carried tens of thousands of emigrants. The flood of travelers caused further strain between whites and Indians, especially because the pioneer traffic depleted the grass and buffalo on which the Indians depended.

Anticipating trouble, the army had followed Frémont's advice, buying Fort Laramie in 1849 and installing a garrison. In 1851 the government met with a council of almost 10,000 Plains Indians at the fort to sign a treaty exchanging annual trade goods for the right to establish roads and military posts. But within a few years there were hostilities, including the Grattan Massacre of 1854, in which the Sioux wiped out a military detachment that had overreacted to a minor treaty infraction. Chief Washakie of the Shoshoni tribe signed a treaty in 1863. But the Sioux, Arapaho, and Cheyenne decided to fight to protect their hunting lands. In 1865 the Platte Bridge Station Battle, near today's Casper, killed twenty-six soldiers. The next year the army built Fort Reno and Fort Phil Kearny along the Bozeman Trail to the Montana mines, arousing Indian resentment that led to the Fetterman Battle and the Wagon Box Fight. An 1868 treaty ended hostilities for a while, ceding the land north of the Platte River to the Indians and closing the forts along the Bozeman Trail; in exchange, the Indians gave up land south of the river and agreed to allow a railroad and leave military posts in peace.

At this point the only real settlements in Wyoming were army posts, such as Fort Laramie and Fort Bridger, manned with soldiers to protect the passing emigrants. In 1853, near Fort Bridger, the Mormons had established an agricultural mission known as Fort

Supply, to serve travelers on the church's route to Utah. But only the transcontinental railway brought more permanent residents to Wyoming. After crossing the Rockies in 1835, the missionary Samuel Parker had predicted a railroad, saying, "The time may not be very far distant when trips will be made across the continent as they have been made to Niagara Falls, to see Nature's wonders." Within thirty years it was clear that the expanding West and the industrialized East needed such a rail link. In 1867 a cheering crowd greeted the first Union Pacific train to chug into Cheyenne—which, in four months of waiting for the train, had grown from an empty place on the prairie to a community of canvas and board-frame buildings with 4,000 people. During 1868 tracks were laid across Wyoming, and a string of towns popped up along the route. The coming of the railroad determined the course of Wyoming's development by providing a way to mine and ship the territory's large coal deposits. Miners also flocked to isolated mining camps such as South Pass City, site of an 1867 gold rush. Cattle ranchers began to realize that the endless grasslands of the eastern prairies offered free grazing, while the railroad gave access to eastern markets. As Wyoming grew, it gained businesses, people, and contact with the outside world. The frontier era began to wane.

The time had come to introduce some government to what was still officially part of the Dakota Territory. The Dakota legislature had no interest in trying to govern the wild newcomers that the railroad brought to Wyoming. Furthermore, Indian lands separated the two regions and made communication almost impossible. In 1868 parts of the Dakota, Utah, and Idaho territories were fitted together to form the new Wyoming Territory. In its first session the following year, the Wyoming legislature made history by passing a law that gave women equal rights to vote and hold office—something no American or European government had yet done. In the next year, women served on a grand jury, and Wyoming appointed the nation's first female justice of the peace. Remarkably, this social progress occurred in a territory populated almost entirely by men. Today, Wyoming is known by two nicknames that reflect this paradox: the Cowboy State and the Equality State.

During these years cowboys were pouring into Wyoming, especially after the first big cattle drive organized by Nelson Story in 1866. Within two years the Texas Trail blew with the dust of 300,000 steers annually. The trail drives not only became part of Western legend but also established cattle raising as a major industry. The years

A federal negotiating team led by General William T. Sherman discusses peace terms with Sioux leaders at Fort Laramie in 1868. Since the army had failed to subdue the Indians, the government had to agree to abandon forts on the Bozeman Trail.

from 1876 to 1886 brought huge profits that lured investors from the East Coast and Britain. In ten years, the "cattle king," Alexander Swan, built a herd of 3,000 head into an operation that was sold to Scottish investors for nearly $4 million. During his career Swan brought Herefords into Wyoming, controlled half a million acres, and ran cattle under so many brands that he had to publish a reference book for his cowboys. The cattle business encountered problems, however; there was overcrowding on the range, drought, and the severe winter of 1886–1887, during which the *Cheyenne Sun* remarked on "the most prolonged windstorm ever known in Cheyenne. . . . It began four months ago and has continued ever since from sunrise to sunset." Perhaps 400,000 cattle died. Some ranches went under, and others reduced their operations, firing many of their cowboys. These men often became homesteaders and acquired herds of their own—sometimes by claiming the unbranded calves (mavericks) of the bigger ranches. Rustlers had always been active in Wyoming, and the stockmen themselves also committed thievery. When they drove a huge herd past a small homestead, they could easily add its cattle and move on, thereby ruining the small rancher. Homesteaders who farmed often built fences across the open range—hazardous to cows and annoying to cattle drivers. As anger grew between the two sides, ranchers hired stock detectives and formed vigilante squads to combat rustling, and in 1889 they lynched two homesteaders who had filed in the middle of federal rangeland. No convictions were won against the ranchers, since all four witnesses mysteriously vanished.

In 1892 the so-called Johnson County War—an invasion of suspected rustler territory by cattle ranchers and hired killers—left two men dead but no one prosecuted. Soon the big cattle ranchers had a new enemy—sheep ranchers, whose flocks were said to ruin the land by cropping the grass too short. The ranchers clubbed, shot, and dynamited the sheep and hired such men as Tom Horn, a "range detective" who probably killed a dozen men before being hanged for murdering the 14-year-old son of a sheepman. The 1903 execution of this hired exterminator, who reportedly earned $300 for each killing, marked the end of the outlaw period in Wyoming. For the previous forty years, gangs of outlaws had robbed banks, stagecoaches, and trains. Butch Cassidy and the Sundance Kid hightailed it to safety at Hole-in-the-Wall, a hideout difficult for pursuers to enter because the few entrances could be easily defended. It lies among rocky ledges near today's Kaycee. It then lay conveniently near large stock herds and the Cheyenne–Deadwood stage line. To combat outlaws, citizens formed "vigilance committees" to mete out their own justice.

In this time of lawlessness and growth, statehood began to look like a good proposition to leaders of Wyoming. As a state, Wyoming would be more attractive to settlers by offering better law enforcement, and it would also be able to control its own water, grazing land, and mineral resources. In a mere twenty-five days, a constitutional convention cobbled together a working document by borrowing passages from the constitutions of at least a dozen other states, adding innovative provisions for women's suffrage and state control over water rights. Representative Joseph Carey introduced the statehood bill to Congress, estimating Wyoming's population at 125,000 (about double its actual figure) to enhance its allure. In 1890 Wyoming became one of the United States. Coal fired the state's economy during these days—Wyoming lies over the nation's largest deposit—as such towns as Rock Springs and Cambria produced fuel for the railroads and industry. Oil boomed, particularly at the Salt Creek Field, and Casper grew as a refinery and oil-headquarters town. Copper, iron, soda, silver, and bentonite mines opened. Even a massive "diamond field" lured investors including the Rothschilds and Horace Greeley—until it turned out that the promoters had scattered commercial gems around a field as a lure.

In the 1890s dry farming began to find boosters. One wry editor noted: "The soil is quite coarse, and the agriculturist . . . must run his farm through a stamp-mill in order to make it sufficiently mellow. . . . Again the early frosts make close connection with the late spring blizzards, so that there is only time for a hurried lunch between. Aside from these little drawbacks and the fact that nothing grows without irrigation . . . the prospect for the agricultural future of Wyoming is indeed gratifying in the extreme." Irrigation projects did follow, producing agricultural communities in the Wheatland and Torrington areas, the Eden Valley, and Star Valley. Wyoming's first dam was completed on the Shoshone River in 1910.

The federal government established the world's first national park in Wyoming in 1872, protecting the geysers and paint pots of Yellowstone. But a trip to the park still had its risks: During the 1877 Nez Percé War, Chief Joseph's warriors met two parties of tourists riding horseback and took them hostage. And as late as 1914, a pair of outlaws held up sixteen tourist stagecoaches in a single hour at Old Faithful. Across south-central Wyoming stretched the great highway west—the Oregon Trail. It ran along the south bank of the North Platte River to the Sweetwater River and then over South Pass. A wide, level opening in the Rockies merely 7,550 feet above sea level, South Pass offered the easiest route over the Continental Divide—so gentle that missionary Father Pierre-Jean De Smet described the pass as "almost imperceptible"—and it was negotiable by wheeled vehicle. When fur traders began to use it regularly in the 1820s, they might as well have shouted to the future: "Get those wagons rolling!" Over the trail more than 350,000 emigrants toiled. (About 60,000 members of the Church of Jesus Christ of Latter-day Saints also traveled along the northern bank of the Platte on what is now called the Mormon Trail.)

This period of emigration from 1840 to 1868 was one of the few times Wyoming was not lonesome. "The road, from morning to night, is crowded like . . . Broadway," reported one traveler in 1850, a year when 53,000 pioneers thronged the trail. Dust choked the air, and the route became a three-mile-wide trash heap as people discarded possessions to lighten the wagons and relieve their exhausted oxen. One diarist described "piles of bacon and hard bread thrown by the side of the road . . . trunks, clothes . . . boots . . . spades, picks,

guns." The travelers, who entered Wyoming near today's
Torrington, took three to five weeks to plod more than 400 miles to
Idaho or Utah. They marked their progress by the landmarks they
passed: Fort Laramie, a haven at the one-third point on the entire
trail from Missouri; Laramie Peak, visible from as far as 100 miles
away; Register Cliff, a soft limestone formation where emigrants
carved their names and dates of passage; Warm Springs, a natural
laundry; the Platte River crossing, by ferry or bridge; Independence
Rock, again used for leaving autographs; Ice Slough, grass-thatched
ground under which winter ice stayed frozen until July, useful for
chilling drinks or making ice cream; and Fort Bridger, a trading post
built by Jim Bridger and later taken over by the army. The travelers
missed Wyoming's more interesting northern scenery—Yellowstone,
the Tetons, Devils Tower. For them this stretch of the Oregon Trail
was, in the words of an emigrant in 1858, "a cheerless picture, made
still more so by the numerous human graves." A list of travelers'
tribulations compiled by historian Taft A. Larson includes "wind,
dust, blowing sand, cracked lips, mosquitoes, hail, cold, snow, no
grass, bad water, no fuel, quarrels, fatigue, dead draft animals, bro-
ken-down wagons, illness, accidents, Indian attacks and death."

This forbidding region was opened to mail delivery by stagecoach in 1850, and freighting followed under the firm of Russell,
Majors, and Waddell, which at one time ran 6,250 Conestoga wagons
and 75,000 oxen. The company made history with the Pony Express,
which operated through Wyoming on the Oregon Trail for a year
and a half starting in April 1860. Dressed in little more than buckskins, the riders braved blizzards and rode as fast as twenty-five miles
an hour between Saint Joseph, Missouri, and Sacramento,
California, often narrowly escaping Indians and bandits. Buffalo Bill
Cody joined up in his teens; once, when assaulted by robbers who
wanted the mail pouch, he threw a fake bag and fired his gun, then
rode off at top speed. Pony Express couriers rode 650,000 miles with
only one man killed by Indians, one schedule not completed, and
one mail bag lost. They kept the West informed—a service that was
particularly important at the outbreak of the Civil War. But the Pony
Express died with the birth of the nation's first transcontinental telegraph line in October 1861. On their final rides couriers galloped
past the new telegraph poles.

The "talking wires" became a sore point with Indians, who had
observed that military troops followed the lines, so they set the poles
on fire and attacked the telegraph stations along the "Great

In 1859 Albert Bierstadt traveled with the Lander expedition on its exploration of the West and painted this group portrait of Indians near Fort Laramie. Bierstadt wrote that "now is the time to paint them, for they are rapidly passing away."

Medicine Road." But the revolution in communications could not be stopped. The Union Pacific Railroad laid out a route for its transcontinental tracks in 1867. After considering the Oregon Trail, chief engineer Grenville Dodge picked a shorter southern route, parallel to the Overland Trail, for its proximity to coal deposits and timber. During 1867–1868, the work proceeded at an average of two miles a day, despite constant harassment by Indians and such logistical problems as hauling water to construction gangs sixty miles ahead. The workers ranged from Civil War veterans to former convicts, gamblers, and assorted roughnecks. To provide services wherever the tracks happened to terminate temporarily, movable "end-of-track" towns popped up, with tents purveying booze and gambling. Robbery and murder were commonplace. From town to new town, the "Hell-on-Wheels" transients floated along like scum on a stream, but their settlements often dried up overnight; two months after the track moved past Benton, all that was left of a town of 3,000 people were a hundred graves and a few barrel hoops in the dust. But at a few places citizens stayed—Cheyenne, Laramie, Rawlins, Rock Springs, and Green River among them. The increased population and activity brought by the Union Pacific wrought tremendous changes in isolated Wyoming. As Governor John Campbell noted in his inaugural address to the first legislature: "For the first time in the history of our country, the organization of a territorial government was rendered necessary by the building of a railroad. Heretofore the railroad has been the follower instead of the pioneer of civilization."

Today roads parallel the early routes: the first railroad by Route 30 (which began as a narrow dirt road called the Lincoln Highway in 1913). Motorists can also trace the Oregon Trail by following Route 26 from Torrington west to Casper; then taking Route 220 to Muddy Gap Junction; following Route 287 to Lander; and then Route 28 through South Pass. From there the trail went to Fort Bridger, now on Route I-80.

This chapter begins in the southeast in Cheyenne, moving west to Laramie, Saratoga, and Savery; then to Rock River and Rawlins; and on to Rock Springs and Evanston. Then it moves north to Kemmerer; and finally loops east to South Pass City, Casper, and Torrington.

CHEYENNE

Velma Linford, a Wyoming historian, once said, "Building the Union Pacific railway was really the extending of an empire under government subsidy." It is no surprise that when the UP established a division point called Cheyenne in July 1867, the U.S. Army built Fort Russell nearby. America needed a railroad, and the railroad needed protection from Indian attacks and from the violent "Hell-on-Wheels" crew that roared into each new town on the line. Because the army's main job was to guard Union Pacific property, it drove squatters out of Cheyenne unless they agreed to buy lots from the Union Pacific Land Company. Tents and shacks sprouted everywhere, and during that first summer perhaps 300 businesses, from lawyers offices to gambling halls, opened their "doors" of canvas and board. The first hint of Wyoming's winter winds, however, quickly inspired citizens to rebuild with pine, adobe, stone, and brick. By November, when the railroad tracks arrived, Cheyenne was a town of 4,000 people and the price of land had multiplied more than fifteen-fold. An Episcopal churchman wrote, "The amount that has been done here is wonderful, the activity of the place surprising and the wickedness is unimaginable and appalling. This is the great center for gamblers of all shades, and roughs."

From the start, law and order was a problem. In its very first week of publication in 1867, the *Cheyenne Leader* reported various robberies, a sergeant who cracked a drunken soldier's skull and shot himself by mistake, pistols and blankets stolen from tents, a dogfight on the street with a hundred enthusiastic spectators, assorted fights and maulings, men creating a "muss" at a whorehouse, and a man fined for trying "to run things at a saloon." To buttress law enforcement, vigilantes banished or lynched undesirables. Mayor Luke Murrin enforced the law in his own fashion, by adding twenty-five cents to every fine, explaining that his was "dry work" requiring "stimulants necessary to efficient administration of justice."

In the spring of 1868, the transients moved down the tracks, leaving only 1,500 citizens in Cheyenne. Local government was weak, and there were complaints about corruption, inefficiency, and the condition of city streets, which were full of wandering hogs, mud, and even dead animals. But the future looked brighter after the Union Pacific located its railway shops in Cheyenne and announced the building of a spur line to Denver. As Wyoming's largest town, Cheyenne was declared the territorial capital in 1869. The next year Cheyenne began loading cattle onto trains for shipment east, and within a few years the city was the hub of Wyoming's ranching industry. At the elegant Cheyenne Club—which had a mansard roof and nineteen hitching posts outside—ranchers hobnobbed with visiting foreigners and Easterners, ate well, and conducted cow business. A strict code of conduct prohibited cheating at cards and other ungentlemanly behavior; one member was suspended when he used his .45 to ventilate an oil painting on the club's wall. Club dances were social events, with men in dress clothes whose white shirtfronts earned them the nickname "Herefords."

The Black Hills gold rush of 1877 further promoted Cheyenne's growth as a stop for stagecoach and freight traffic heading north. The local newspaper boasted: "Cheyenne resembles ancient Rome—all roads lead to it." Theaters and entertainment abounded: Sarah Bernhardt appeared at the opera house, Buffalo Bill Cody used Cheyenne as a staging place for his Wild West Show, and 1897 marked the start of summer's Frontier Days rodeos and celebrations. Wealthy Cheyenne ranchers erected mansions on "Millionaires' Row" along Carey Avenue, replacing the unpainted and tattered frame buildings of early days. By 1890 Cheyenne had become the state capital in a celebration accompanied by speeches, parades, "clanging bells, shrieking whistles, incessant yelling." Everyone knew that statehood would draw more people and prosperity to Cheyenne. The city was one of the first in America to use electric lights; its airfield became a stop on the transcontinental air mail run; and Cheyenne grew into a center of government and commerce. Although the grizzled bull-whackers, rustlers, and gambling dandies have disappeared, Cheyenne's streets still bob with Stetson hats, and the hard heels of cowboy boots make the streets echo with history.

The **Historic Governor's Mansion** (300 East 21st Street, 307–777–7878) was the home of Wyoming's chief executives from 1904 until 1976. A Georgian Revival brick residence with a Corinthian portico, it received such famous guests as Theodore Roosevelt and Buffalo Bill Cody. But the mansion's true distinction is that it was the first in the nation to be occupied by a woman governor, Nellie Tayloe Ross, who was elected to serve the remainder of her late husband's term, from 1925 to 1927. **Saint Mary's Catholic Church** (2107 Capitol Avenue), an example of Gothic Revival architecture, was built of Wyoming gray sandstone in 1909. At 1908

The Wyoming Historic Governor's Mansion, built by the state in 1907 to house its governors. The Georgian-Revival residence was transformed into a house museum in 1967.

Central Avenue stands **Saint Mark's Episcopal Church,** a stone structure built in 1888 with Gothic Revival elements, pointed-arch windows, and a stained-glass window signed by Tiffany and Company. Saint Mark's was the religious, cultural, and social center of early Cheyenne. Formal ballroom dances were held in the parish hall at the turn of the century. The **First United Methodist Church** (18th Street and Central Avenue) is the second home of this congregation. The first was famous as the site of an 1876 wedding that joined Wild Bill Hickok and a lady circus rider; the minister noted in his records: "Don't think they meant it." The present red sandstone church, with elements of both Romanesque and Gothic Revival styles, replaced the original in 1894.

Wyoming State Museum

In a chronology of Wyoming life, exhibits begin with Plains Indian beadwork and feather headdresses, as well as a display about the buffalo on which the tribes depended (and which were virtually wiped out by white commercial hunters between 1830 and 1880). Among displays on wagon trains and army garrisons is an array of frontier medical instruments employed during a time when "amputation was a common surgical technique used in cases of gunshot and arrow wounds, frost-bite and fractures." The contrasts of the frontier economy emerge in comparing a cowboy's crude line shack with a cattle baron's opulent parlor. Other exhibits chronicle pioneer women, the Union Pacific (called "the largest single-purpose industrial effort ever mounted," requiring 21 million hammer blows to lay rails across the nation), rustling ("one way to get started in the ranching business"), and Old West violence ('self-defense' was so common a plea in shootings that it came to be regarded as less dangerous to kill a man than to steal a horse").

> LOCATION: 24th Street and Central Avenue. HOURS: September through May: 8:30–5 Monday–Friday, 10:30–2:30 Saturday; June through August: 8:30–5 Monday–Friday, 9–5 Saturday, 1–5 Sunday. FEE: None. TELEPHONE: 307–777–7024.

Across the street stands the **Wyoming State Capitol** (24th Street and Capitol Avenue, 307–777–7220), the seat of first the territorial and then the state government since 1888. Dominated by a central section with Corinthian columned pavilions and a gold-leafed dome,

The Wyoming State Capitol at Cheyenne was designed by D. W. Gibbs in 1887, three years before the territory achieved statehood.

the building acquired wings in 1890 and 1917. The interior is embellished with murals depicting Wyoming history, stained-glass ceilings, and polished cherrywood. In front of the main entrance stands a **statue of Esther Hobart Morris,** the world's first woman justice of the peace, who served in South Pass City in 1870 and is a symbolic figure in the Equality State. Tours of the capitol are available.

The **Nagle-Warren Mansion** (222 East 17th Street, private), one of Cheyenne's most elegant residences, was built in 1888 as the home of Wyoming businessman, governor, and U.S. senator Francis E. Warren. The **Atlas Theater** building (213 West 16th Street, 307–635–0199), of 1887, which originally contained offices and a tea shop, was remodeled in 1908 as a theater with an attached penny arcade and soda shop. The molded tin ceiling in the lobby and the asbestos stage curtain are original features. A symbol of Cheyenne's birth and growth, the **Union Pacific Depot** of 1887 (121 West 15th Street) was built of rough-hewn red and gray sandstone and topped with a clock tower that complements the capitol dome up the street. Additions made in 1922 to the Richardsonian Romanesque structure include a dining room and passenger concourse.

Now located in Holiday Park at 16th Street and Morrie Avenue, the **Big Boy Locomotive** chuffed its way through the end of the steam era. This mammoth 4-8-8-4 locomotive, weighing nearly 600 tons, was built in 1941 for a single purpose—to haul huge amounts of freight over the Wasatch Mountains from Ogden, Utah, to Green River. Later the engine regularly pulled its maximum 3,200 tons of freight between Cheyenne and Laramie, steaming up Sherman Hill at ten miles an hour—an effort that required 30,000 gallons of water and at least half its twenty-eight tons of coal. Number 4004 was retired in 1959, when the UP gave up steam locomotives.

On a smaller scale are the displays at **The National First Day Cover Museum** (702 Randall Boulevard, 307–634–5911), which is dedicated to displaying the first editions of postage stamps, including the *first* first day cover, issued in Britain in 1840 when postage stamps were invented by Sir Rowland Hill. The collection is valued at more than $1 million. Displayed at the **Cheyenne Frontier Days Old West Museum** (North Carey Avenue, Frontier Park, 307–778–7290) are more than forty vehicles, from an Overland stagecoach of 1860 to a Mercer touring car of 1923. One highlight is a Cheyenne–Deadwood stage, a type regularly held up by desperadoes. There are also Indian artifacts, a replica of an early railroad depot, a drugstore with vintage remedies, a Victorian parlor, and memorabilia of the Cheyenne Frontier Days dating from the earliest celebrations in 1897.

On the western edge of town lies **F. E. Warren Air Force Base** (Route I-25 and Randall Avenue), established in 1867 as Fort D. A. Russell to protect the transcontinental railroad. At the close of the Indian wars, the government decided to make the fort a permanent post, in 1885 replacing the original frame and log structures with red-brick buildings of Colonial Revival style. The air force took over the fort in 1947, and in 1958 it became the nation's first intercontinental ballistic missile (ICBM) base. About ninety structures survive from the period from 1885 to 1911. The post headquarters houses the **F. E. Warren Military Museum** (Room 210/211, 307–775–2980), with displays of uniforms, period rooms depicting army life, model airplanes, and military equipment dating back to 1854.

OPPOSITE: *Saint Mark's Episcopal Church in Cheyenne, established by the Reverend Joseph W. Cooke in 1868.*

Five miles east of Cheyenne lies the **Wyoming Hereford Ranch** (off Route I-80, 307–634–1905), once owned by cattle king Alexander Swan, who in 1878 brought the first Hereford cattle to Wyoming. The headquarters still has old wooden barns and a bunkhouse; signs identify some buildings at the still-operating ranch.

LARAMIE

Although no one knows much about French-Canadian fur trapper Jacques Laramie, or La Ramée, except that he was probably killed by Arapaho somewhere along the Laramie River in 1820, his musical-sounding name has outlived his lost deeds: The city of Laramie lies on the Laramie River, near towering Laramie Peak, at the edge of the Laramie Plains. (A fort and a county also are named for him.)

Three miles south of today's Laramie, the U.S. Army in 1866 built Fort Sanders to guard the Denver–Salt Lake stage line. Two years later the fort was expanded to protect the Union Pacific railroad crew from Indian raids. Before the tracks reached Laramie, future citizens erected about 500 structures of canvas, old wagon boxes, and discarded railroad ties. Newcomers who arrived with the first train in May 1868 included gamblers, land sharks, harlots, and the keepers of movable shops and saloons. Although a temporary government was established, outlaws overran the town, and within a month government officials abandoned any effort to maintain order. Vigilantes fought the desperadoes, lynching one known as "the Kid," and teaching a lesson in "triggernometry" that left several outlaws dead at the Belle of the West saloon and ended in the hanging of four more. Even Jesse James spent some time in the local jail. Finally the federal courts took jurisdiction over the city. In March 1870 the court called the first women jurors in U.S. history, garnering world-wide publicity. After the women heard cases involving murder, cattle theft, and disturbance of the peace, the judge remarked that he had never seen "any more faithful, intelligent and resolutely honest" jurors. Today a stone **tablet** (1st Street and University Avenue) marks the first woman jury.

A successor toa number of failed associations, the Wyoming Stock Growers Association was started in Laramie in 1879, after the "grass bonanza" of the Laramie Plains had attracted cattlemen who ran huge herds. The town also made its mark in journalism with the *Boomerang*, a wry newspaper founded by Bill Nye. "The paper was published in the loft of a livery stable," he explained. "That is the reason they called it a stock company." His mule, Boomerang, became the paper's namesake, and a sign at the foot of the office stairs read, "Twist the gray mule's tail and take the elevator." Nye went on to national fame as a humorist with the *New York World*. By the mid-1880s Laramie was humming with industries, among them a rolling mill, a tannery, and a cigar factory that rolled "Woman's Rights" perfectos.

In 1887 the **University of Wyoming** (9th Street and Ivinson Avenue) opened with forty-two students and seven teachers. Instruction took place in **Old Main,** which still stands. The university's **Geological Museum** (307–766–4218) has exhibits of minerals (including Wyoming diamonds), rocks, and fossils, all dwarfed by the seventy-foot-long skeleton of an *Apatosaurus* that once roamed the floodplains of Wyoming. The specimen was discovered in 1901 about fifty miles north of Laramie. The university's **Anthropology Museum** (307–766–5136) displays artifacts of the Northwest Plains Indians and the skeletons of primates and humans. Among 30,000 relics of local history, the **Laramie Plains Museum** (603 Ivinson Avenue, 307–742–4448) displays the cookware, buggies, tools, and furniture of pioneer families. These fill the **Ivinson Mansion,** a stone-and-shingle house designed in the Queen Anne style and built in 1892 for Edward Ivinson, a banker and philanthropist who became mayor of Laramie at age 88. His wife, Jane, founded Laramie's first public school and Sunday school. The Ivinsons contributed the steeple, clock, and chimes to **Saint Mathew's Episcopal Cathedral** (3d Street and Ivinson Avenue), an English Gothic church completed in 1896 using local limestone.

Just south of Laramie on Route 287, the **Fort Sanders Monument** stands where Fort John Buford, later renamed Fort Sanders, was built in 1866. The captain in charge noted: "The post is built with special reference to strength, durability, regularity, convenience, and economy in structure. The officers of the post are attentive, efficient, temperate, and have no unfit associations." With the coming of the railroad, the log fort was expanded to house six companies of soldiers. By 1882, however, the threat of Indian hostilities and other dangers had decreased, and the fort was abandoned. Fires and the removal of buildings to town left little but ruins, now marked with a stone memorial.

The **Wyoming Territorial Penitentiary** (intersection of Routes I-80 and 130/230) was Wild West all the way—even to the cornerstone

laid with a bottle of bourbon inside. The original 1872 and 1889 cell blocks, made of limestone walls two feet thick, are still standing. Although prisoners made bricks, quarried rocks, and made brooms and furniture, their labors did not always earn back their room and board, so on occasion in the late 1870s and 1880s Wyoming boarded its prisoners out of state. The most famous of the many dangerous outlaws who did time in the prison were Butch Cassidy and "Big Nose" George Parrott. When a new prison was built in Rawlins in the early 1900s, the University of Wyoming began using the old penitentiary and grounds as an experimental livestock farm, later remodeling the cells as stables for dairy cows—no doubt the mildest-mannered denizens ever to live there. The prison, now fully restored, is planned to be the highlight of a Wyoming and Western history theme park currently under construction. The stone **Bath Home** (Route I-80 at the Herrick Lane exit, twelve miles west of Laramie, private) was built in 1875 by Henry Bath, a German immigrant who was one of the first cattle ranchers on the Laramie Plains.

Cummins City (four miles south of Woods Landing on Route 10), a ghost town also known as **Old Jelm,** is what remains of a confidence scheme. The con man was John Cummins, who flashed ore samples he claimed to have found here in the Medicine Bow Range. Prospectors and investors created a small boom, sinking shafts and selling mine stocks, but they found only rock. Cummins probably had salted the ground with ore. During the fever a town site with 170 blocks was laid out, and perhaps two dozen structures were built. Visible from the highway is what's left of Cummins City—a few homes, a bar and a stable, a school, and the ruined post office.

CENTENNIAL

The site of a gold boomlet, Centennial was settled in 1876, the nation's hundredth year. One of four local mines was owned by Colonel Stephen Downey, who turned down $100,000 for his claim only to have the vein of gold dwindle, never to be located again. The "Lost Centennial Lode" has become part of Wyoming lore. Around 1900 a Boston syndicate invested heavily in Centennial, anticipating a rediscovery of the gold. It built a railroad, although when the

OPPOSITE: *The ruins of Fort Sanders, originally Fort Buford, which was established in 1866 to provide military protection for the Overland Trail.*

tracks reached Centennial all the gold to be found could be transported in a teaspoon, so the tracks for transporting coal, lumber,
and livestock were rerouted elsewhere. Regional history is presented
in the 1907 Union Pacific railroad depot at the **Nici Self Museum**
(Route 130, 307–742–7158/634–4955), whose exhibits include artifacts from the logging and lumber industries such as portable saws
and a beehive burner for sawdust, as well as tools for gold mining
and ranching.

COMO BLUFF DINOSAUR GRAVEYARD

Located on Route 30/287, ten miles northwest of Rock River, this
was the site of the world's first major discovery of dinosaur remains,
unearthed in 1877. The Indians nicknamed paleontologist O. C.
Marsh the "Big Bone Chief." Among the big bones that he and
other scientists removed from this ridge were those of the armored
Stegosaurus and a complete skeleton of the *Allosaurus*—a predator
whose teeth marks were found in remains of the plant-eating
Apatosaurus (formerly known as *Brontosaurus).* Scientists also located
two complete skeletons of *Diplodocus,* which measured eighty feet,
the longest dinosaur of all. The huge beasts roamed Wyoming when
it was a floodplain during the Mesozoic era; their bones were
entombed in the shales and sandstones of the Morrison formation.
In the early 1900s, geology students digging fossils here reportedly
also looked for caches of gold, said to have been buried by train robbers. Nearly all the bones from Como Bluff were taken to major eastern museums. The bluff is visible from the highway, but the old
quarries are located on the north side. Nearby is a private house
built mainly of dinosaur bones—which, in a sense, makes it the oldest building in the world.

MEDICINE BOW

Describing Medicine Bow in 1902 in his novel *The Virginian,* Owen
Wister compares it to other towns that littered the frontier like
"soiled packs of cards. Each was similar to the next, as one old five-
spot of clubs resembles another. Houses, empty bottles and garbage.
. . . They seemed to have been strewn there by the wind and to be
waiting till the wind should come again and blow them away. Yet
serene above their foulness swam a pure and quiet light . . . they
might be bathing in the air of creation's first morning." Wister was a
Philadelphian educated in music and law at Harvard. Bad health

prompted his trips west, and in Wyoming he became intrigued with cowboy life, riding with a cattle outfit called the Two Bar. Despite his unflattering portrayal, the town erected the **Owen Wister Monument** of petrified wood. It stands across the street from **The Historic Virginian Hotel** (404 Lincoln Highway, 307–379–2377), which was built in 1911 of brick and appears as solid in character as its namesake Western hero. On the grounds of the **Medicine Bow Museum** (405 Lincoln Highway, 307–379–2383) is the Owen Wister cabin, which was brought from Moose, Wyoming. The museum collections occupy the wooden Union Pacific depot of 1913 and present the history of Medicine Bow: childhood memorabilia from the early 1900s; blacksmithing tools, branding irons, and hand implements for ranching; saws for ice harvesting; a homesteader's cook stove and hutch; artifacts of the Union Pacific, including a caboose and telegraph; stereoscopes and a hand-turned record player; and a gas-powered beacon from the early days of air mail in the 1920s.

Fort Fred Steele (fifteen miles east of Rawlins, two miles north of the Fort Steele exit off Route I-80) was established in 1868 where the Union Pacific's transcontinental line crossed the North Platte River. Designed to protect railroad work crews and settlers, it also became a supply depot for troops fighting the Plains Indians and helped enforce the law during the rough-and-tumble territorial period. In 1879, when Nathan Meeker faced an uprising at Colorado's White River Agency and sent for help, Major Thomas Thornburgh left the fort with two companies, but the Ute ambushed and killed him and some of his men. As the Indian wars ended, the fort was no longer needed. Troops left in 1886, although civilians stayed on. Fort Steele's stone powderhouse has survived, but most of the frame and log buildings burned down. The old bridge tender's house serves as a summer visitor center, and there are interpretive signs.

SARATOGA

First known as Warm Springs in 1878, this town later changed its name in an effort to attain the gentility of elegant Saratoga Springs, New York. Said to be not only warm and medicinal but also odorless, the waters bubble from the ground at 114 degrees F. In 1921 the wife of Governor Robert Carey bet a federal judge six pairs of gloves that she could get back on track a bill for state purchase of the springs. She succeeded, creating a 420-acre state park. In 1947 it was said that

"Radio Activity" water from the springs was "a tonic for many ailments." The town also became a center of stock raising and mining in the Platte River valley. Boosters claimed that nearby Gold Hill was three-fourths gold, but it did not produce the predicted bonanza. In 1905 the Saratoga and Encampment Railroad was founded to help develop mines in the Grand Encampment region, but that boom died by the time the railroad was finished three years later. The **Saratoga Museum** (106 Constitution Avenue, 307–326–5511) occupies the wooden Union Pacific depot of 1890 and displays memorabilia of the old spur line to Encampment, a UP caboose, arrowheads, and relics of local history. The brick **Hotel Wolf** (101 East Bridge Street, 307–326–5525) was built in 1893 for miners, lumbermen, and tourists and became a local stagecoach stop. It still serves guests.

About ten miles north of Saratoga, now across private lands, the **Overland Trail** crossed the North Platte River at **Overland Crossing.** A stage station stood nearby, and because there was a good supply of water, wood, and forage, this was a well-known camping spot. A ferry was established, but business declined when the Union Pacific laid its tracks a few miles north in 1868. A commemorative **marker** stands near a small pioneers' cemetery.

ENCAMPMENT

The area known as Grand Encampment was a spot in the Sierra Madre where trappers and Indians gathered during the heyday of the fur trade. A large copper discovery in 1897 led to the building of the town of Grand Encampment and an early marvel of western engineering, a sixteen-mile aerial tramway that carried ore from the Ferris-Haggarty mine over the Continental Divide at an elevation of more than 10,000 feet, arriving at the Encampment smelter. The tramway's cables were supported by 375 wooden towers, and each bucket held 700 pounds of ore. With the falling price of ore and the third fire at the smelter in as many years, Grand Encampment's boom went bust in 1908. Three tram towers strung with cables and ore buckets have been preserved at the **Grand Encampment Museum** (7th Street and Barnett Avenue, 307–327–5310). There are thirteen restored buildings, including a livery barn, cabins, a two-

OPPOSITE: *The Grand Encampment Museum preserves a number of buildings from the 1890s copper-mining town of Encampment.*

story outhouse (designed for deep snow), a bakery, a sod-roofed
stage station, and a blacksmith shop. Among a large collection of
U.S. Forest Service memorabilia are uniforms, snow scales, and a
complete fire lookout tower. Collections include copies of the *Grand
Encampment Herald* dating from 1898 to 1912, homemade furniture,
pioneer clothing, old medicines and groceries, books, songs, and
poetry written by Grand Encampment pioneers, and Indian artifacts.

SINCLAIR

"The Wonder Town of Wyoming" sprang up all at once in 1923, created by the Producers and Refiners Corporation to complement its
oil refinery with a showplace company town. Houses and buildings
shared the gracious Spanish Mission style of architecture—"a pleas-
ing change for the visitor from the general, unartistic appearance of
towns," a newspaper commented. Designed for 1,500 people, the
settlement's name first was Parco (an acronym for the company's
name), but that was changed in 1934 when the Sinclair Oil Company
bought the property.

RAWLINS

In 1867 General John Rawlins's party, while exploring a route for the
transcontinental railroad, came upon a spring that Rawlins called
"the most gracious and acceptable of anything" found in the region.
Because it was located on the dry plain of the Great Basin, the water
succored the parched crews laying tracks the following year. Both the
spring and a settlement that grew up around it were named after
General Rawlins. A wild "end-of-track" town, the settlement grew to
2,000 people. A contemporary observer noted that "bad characters,
masculine and feminine, from the entire west had been drawn there
as by some great magnet. No day passed without a cutting, shooting,
or robbery by force or fraud." Outlaws were locked up at the
Wyoming Frontier Prison (5th and Walnut streets, 307–324–4111), a
stone facility completed in 1901 with a turreted Romanesque cell
block. In 1914 a wall and towers were added to prevent the escape of
prisoners, who repeatedly tore down the barbed-wire enclosure.
Nine prisoners were hanged here, and summer tours visit the old
gallows and gas chamber, as well as the cell blocks. There is also a

OPPOSITE: *The Wyoming Frontier Prison in Rawlins was constructed of locally quarried*
granite. It served as a prison until 1981 and now is open as a historic site.

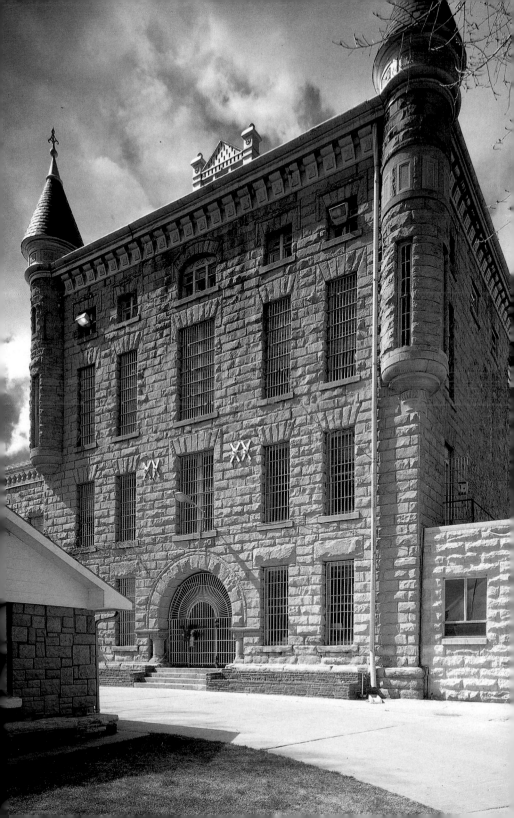

small museum. The notorious outlaw "Big Nose" George Parrott tried to break out of the Rawlins city jail in 1881, only to be lynched by vigilantes. "As a warning to those who might consider future troublemaking in Rawlins," citizens skinned Parrott and tanned his hide. A pair of shoes worn by a future Wyoming governor was made from his skin. This footwear is now on display at the **Carbon County Museum** (904 West Walnut Street, 307–324–9611), which also focuses on more savory moments of local history, including Rawlins's role as the hub of a large wool-growing region. A sheepherder's-wagon exhibit explains that a Rawlins citizen named James Candlish invented the house-on-wheels in 1884, giving herders relief from sleeping on the cold ground. The museum also displays an American LaFrance fire truck of 1919.

The Queen Anne–style **Ferris Mansion** (607 West Maple, private) was built in 1903 for George Ferris, a figure in the early mining industry. A sheep rancher built the Victorian Italianate **Blake House** (3d and Cedar streets, private) in 1881. Across the street stands the **France Memorial Presbyterian Church,** built in 1882 of sandstone in the Gothic Revival style to serve a congregation that was organized in 1869 by the Reverend Sheldon Jackson.

SAVERY

The **Jim Baker Cabin** was built in 1873 by the well-known trapper and scout who began his western career in 1838 with Jim Bridger in the American Fur Company and later guided John C. Frémont. Originally standing on Savery Creek near Dixon, the two-story fortlike cabin has been reconstructed using the original logs and was moved to Savery in 1976 in a ceremony attended by about twenty of Baker's descendants wearing mountain-man outfits.

Tumbling from the Medicine Bow Range, Rock Creek was an obstacle to travelers on the Overland Trail. In the early 1860s, a toll bridge and stagecoach depot were built at **Rock Creek Crossing and Stage Station** (Arlington exit of Route I-80), around which the hamlet of **Arlington** grew. A number of original wooden structures survive, including what may be the original stage station, various barns, and a blacksmith shop-saloon-dance hall.

OPPOSITE: *The Queen Anne style Ferris Mansion, built in Rawlins by a miner in 1903.*

ROCK SPRINGS

The site of Rock Springs was visited in 1825 by the fur trader William Ashley and later in 1849 by Captain Howard Stansbury. Stansbury, led by the mountain man Jim Bridger, was exploring the route that became known as the Overland Trail. In 1866 two Scottish brothers named Blair built a bridge and cabin near the spring and started mining a seam of coal for the approaching Union Pacific trains, which reached the site two years later. The UP's land also had large coal deposits, and Rock Springs developed, becoming the melting pot of Wyoming as laborers of many nationalities—Chinese, British, Irish, Greek, Scandinavian, Slavic, and Japanese—came to work the mines. With the increasing power of labor unions, Wyoming's first big strike took place at the mines in 1875. Chinese strikebreakers were brought in, creating racial prejudice that exploded ten years later in the so-called Chinese Massacre and Riot, in which whites killed twenty-eight Chinese, wounded fifteen, and burned Chinatown, driving out hundreds. A witness noted: "Two thousand or more shots were fired while the burning houses roared in the night. Men . . . were paid $20 for each dead Oriental that they found." No one was indicted. Later the United States paid a claim for Chinese property losses of more than $147,000. The Union Pacific brought back many Chinese workers, and a new Chinatown was built. To keep the peace, troops were maintained at **Camp Pilot Butte** (624 Bridger Avenue); this post was abandoned in 1899, and in 1951 the barracks became a Catholic school, while a mine superintendent's house became a convent. The **Rock Springs Stage Station Monument** (Spring Street, south of Route I-80) commemorates a stop on the Overland Trail; pioneers inscribed their names on a rock wall located near the stone monument that marks the site of the original spring.

South of Route I-80, twenty-five miles east of Rock Springs, the **Point of Rocks Stage Station** was built in 1862 to accommodate travelers on Ben Holladay's Overland stage line. Because the station was constructed of sandstone, Indians failed in their attempts to burn it. After 1868 the station served as the junction of the Overland Trail and the transcontinental Union Pacific line. It has been restored.

GREEN RIVER

Although it lies along the Union Pacific tracks, Green River was not begun by the railroad but by the mayor of Cheyenne, who led a group of squatters here. When the rails arrived there were already 2,000 people in a city of adobe buildings and relative peace. But the UP disputed the squatters' claims to the land and passed Green River without constructing the hoped-for roundhouses and machine shops. The town dwindled until the railroad later saw the value of the site and returned to make Green River a division point. Without much of the usual railroad-town crime, it was always relatively civilized. In 1868 Wyoming's first book was published here, a twenty-four-page pamphlet entitled *A Vocabulary of the Snake, or Sho-Sho-Nay Dialect*. Located in the courthouse, the **Sweetwater County Historical Museum** (80 West Flaming Gorge Way, 307-875-2611, ext. 263) displays pioneer artifacts such as furniture and toys, as well as ranching equipment, Chinese mementoes (gongs, opium pipes), and a dinosaur's footprint. The city's **Expedition Island Park** is situated where Major John Wesley Powell, the one-armed adventurer, set off on the first explorations of the Green and Colorado rivers and the Grand Canyon, embarking with a crew and boats in 1871. He made an earlier journey in 1869 that departed from an unknown point nearby. Powell's expeditions opened the last large unexplored region in the continental United States.

GRANGER

Before the Union Pacific's arrival created this town in 1868, the **Granger Stage Station** was already operating near the junction of the Oregon and Overland trails. Built in the early 1860s, the sandstone building replaced Ham's Fork Station, a dugout structure that Sir Richard Burton, the British anthropologist, once characterized as "a disgrace," commenting on its "squalor and filth" and the flies that "darkened the table and covered everything put upon it." The station was a Pony Express stop in 1860–1861, a depot for Ben Holladay's stagecoach traffic after 1862, and a telegraph station.

OVERLEAF: *A temporary wooden bridge carries the rails of the Union Pacific over the Green River as a crew constructs a permanent stone bridge alongside it.*

Fort Bridger, the second permanent white settlement in Wyoming, was established by the legendary Jim Bridger in 1842. A traveler on the Oregon Trail in 1845 who camped near the fort described it as being "built of poles and daubed with mud . . . a shabby concern." OPPOSITE: *The restored fort's officers quarters.*

In 1847 Mormons led by Brigham Young paused on the Oregon Trail at **Church Buttes** (off Route 30, ten miles southwest of Granger) to conduct religious services. The eroded sandstone cliffs, in the words of traveler Levancia Bent in 1882, "are the most wonderful formations . . . . They represent my ideal of old country architecture; churches and castles with dormer and bay windows, French roofs, projecting cornices and deep entrances." She mused that the Salt Lake tabernacle was "a perfect copy of one of these architectural mountains."

FORT BRIDGER

In the late 1830s, Jim Bridger watched the swelling tide of emigrants traveling through country that trappers like himself had opened up. Bridger was the frontiersman who had come to the Rockies at the age of 18 and was probably the first white man to view the Great Salt Lake. Now, as the fur trade declined, he observed that travelers on

the Oregon Trail were "generally well supplied with money, but . . . in want of all kinds of supplies. Horses, provisions, smith work, etc., bring ready cash." So in 1842 he and his partner, Louis Vasquez, built a trading post on Black's Fork of the Green River, squarely on the emigrant route west. A few years later, a traveler named Orson Pratt recorded that "Bridger's post consists of two adjoining log houses, dirt roofs, and a small picket yard of logs set in the ground, about eight feet high. The number of men, squaws, and half-breed children in these houses and lodges may be about fifty or sixty." Another emigrant called it "a shabby concern." Jim Bridger's tall tales were famous: One yarn concerned his attempt to leap a gorge in a petrified forest; it was too wide, and only the petrified air saved him from falling to his death.

The fort was a good business proposition; it attracted the attention of Brigham Young and the Mormons, who established Fort Supply south of it in 1853 to serve Mormon emigrants to Salt Lake. That year the Mormons also took over Fort Bridger. The mountain man claimed they had run him out; the Mormons claimed to have paid $6,000 for it. They made improvements and built a cobblestone wall around the fort (a portion of which has been reconstructed). But, by 1857, during the federal government's campaign in Utah, they abandoned and burned both of their forts and fled to Salt Lake. The federal commander—later Confederate general—Colonel Albert Sidney Johnston declared Fort Bridger a military reservation, building barracks and other structures of stone, logs, and rough lumber. The post sutler, Judge William A. Carter, became the fort's most influential citizen, erecting a store stocked with everything from bacon to cologne, establishing farmlands and herds, serving as judge and justice of the peace, and dispensing lavish hospitality. One visitor recalled Carter's insistence on serving him a drink. "Being under military order, I, of course, complied. Before I had the glass empty he had a bottle in my overcoat pocket and as I was starting he insisted that I didn't balance properly and he crammed one into the pocket on the other side." Carter was a friend of Shoshoni chief Washakie, who signed the treaty of 1868, allowing the railroad right-of-way through Shoshoni lands, at the fort. Carter also had a Steinway piano and a fine library that established an unusual level of traditional culture at his remote outpost. In the early 1860s he built Wyoming's first schoolhouse at the fort; the structure was fully restored in 1989.

During this time the post was very active, being an important station for the Pony Express, the Overland stage line, and the transcontinental telegraph. In 1868 Union Pacific construction crews passed nine miles north, and troops ranged over the trails to protect them and other travelers. By 1890, though, frontier threats had diminished and the soldiers were withdrawn from Fort Bridger; after the post was abandoned, many of the buildings were sold at public auction. A number of structures have been restored at the fort, including the two-story commanding officer's quarters, commissary, guardhouse, Pony Express barn, schoolhouse, icehouse, and Carter's store. There is also a reconstruction of Bridger's original log fort, with blacksmith's and carpenter's shops and goods for sale similar to those the emigrants and Indians bought or traded for. The barracks contain a museum whose displays span the nineteenth century and represent all the fort's various occupants and eras—from the Indians are an elk-dewclaw necklace, travois, bows and arrows; from the mountain men, trade beads and Jim Bridger's powder horn; there

Charcoal to fuel Utah smelters was made in these beehive shaped kilns, constructed in 1869, using the abundant local timber.

are emigrants' candle molds and mule shoes. In addition there is a
mailbag replica from the Pony Express; railroad dishes and oil cans
and musket balls and uniforms from the military, while civilian life at
the turn of the century is conveyed by a parlor display and collections of toys and clothing. The era of the cowboy is represented by
chuck wagons and saddles. During the summer there is living-history
interpretation by costumed frontier characters.

> LOCATION: Off Route I-80 at exit 34. HOURS: Mid-April through mid-
> October: 9–5 Daily; mid-October through mid-April: 9–4:30
> Saturday and Sunday. FEE: None. TELEPHONE: 307–782–3842.

Fifteen miles southwest of Fort Bridger stand the three remaining
Piedmont Charcoal Kilns (Leroy Road exit off Route I-80, three
miles south on a graded road), built in 1869 by Moses Byrne in a
location chosen for its abundant timber and available rail transportation to mining smelters in Utah. The conical limestone kilns are thirty feet across and thirty feet high. In this region there were forty
such kilns, said to produce more than 100,000 bushels of charcoal
per month.

EVANSTON

Evanston took shape when the Union Pacific tracks arrived in 1868,
bringing 600 persons; but soon the railroad decided to establish its
division headquarters farther west, and within a day Evanston emptied, leaving only two citizens. The next summer the railroad
changed its mind again, the headquarters returned, and settlement
really began. A sizable contingent of Chinese grew vegetables,
washed laundry, and operated shops and opium dens. Housed in the
1906 Carnegie Library, the **Uinta County Museum** (36 10th Street,
307–789–2757) displays Chinese items, relics of gambling and boot-
leg whiskey, Indian artifacts, a parlor of 1880, ranching items, and
early modes of transportation, including a covered wagon.

KEMMERER

In the coal town of Kemmerer, everyone bought on credit at the
company store. James Cash Penney had a different idea when he
opened the **First J. C. Penney Store** (Pine and Main streets), then
called the Golden Rule Store, in 1902. Operating on a strictly cash-

OPPOSITE: *The restored dining room of the J. C. Penney house in Kemmerer.*

and-carry basis, he sold $29,000 worth of varied goods the first year; by the time he died in 1971 he had more than 1,900 stores and a huge catalog business. A block away, **J. C. Penney's Home** (Main Street and J. C. Penney Drive, 307–877–4501) is a clapboard house where he moved his family after living in the store building; the house is open to visitors in summer and contains turn-of-the-century furnishings, some of which belonged to the Penney family. Across the street from the store, the **Kemmerer City Museum** (Triangle Park, 307–877–9761) is a log cabin that contains artifacts of the early coal era; from the wagon trains there are oxen yokes and a human skull with a bullet hole. Also on exhibit are memorabilia of America's first convicted woman rustler, and a display of fossils.

Ten miles west of Kemmerer, **Fossil Butte National Monument** (Route 30, 307–877–3450) contains a rare deposit of fossilized fish and other aquatic animals that lived about 50 million years ago, when a vast lake covered this region. The fossils were first noted along the Green River in 1856 and include fish up to five feet long, insects, an alligator, a chickenlike bird, snails, and various other fish and plants. Found mainly in limestone of the Green River forma-tion, located from 30 to 300 feet below the ground, the fish fossils make up one of the densest and rarest such deposits in the world. The fish are well preserved and show details down to tail rays and scales. The visitor center offers guided walks, and a signposted trail leads to the site of the old quarries, where some fossil fragments may still be visible. Five miles south of La Barge on Route 189, the cliffs of **Names Hill** rise beside the Green River. A formation of soft lime-stone with the carved names and dates of travelers along the Oregon Trail, it boasts the earliest pioneer inscription in Wyoming (1822) and the signature of "James Bridger" carved in 1844—although Bridger reportedly did not know how to read or write.

DANIEL

On a rise above the Green River, the **Father De Smet Prairie Mass Site** (one mile east of Daniel) marks where the tireless Belgian priest Father Pierre-Jean De Smet celebrated Wyoming's first Catholic

OPPOSITE: *A small chapel constructed by the Knights of Columbus commemorates the site of the first mass in the region that is now Wyoming, which was celebrated by Father Pierre De Smet.* OVERLEAF: *Wyoming's geography records many events in the geologic history of the world. These limestone cliffs formed in the Eocene epoch sur-vive at Fossil Butte National Monument.*

mass. It was held on July 5, 1840, before an altar of boughs decorated with flowers and bows and arrows. De Smet spoke in French and English but also addressed the Indians, who called him "Blackrobe." Today a small chapel of wood and rock commemorates this early religious service.

PINEDALE

In 1878 settlers came to this area because the meadows in the Pinedale region produced good hay for winter cattle feeding; it is still a ranching center. The **Museum of the Mountain Men** (700 East Hennick Street, 307–367–4101) emphasizes the fur trade and mountain men through artifacts such as Jim Bridger's rifle and bullet molds. Western exploration, the Plains Indians, and western Wyoming settlement are also represented by collections containing a rare sheep-horn bow, war shirts, pipes, saddles, and guns.

TRAPPER'S POINT

Six miles west of Pinedale at Cora Junction, a monument overlooks the beautiful river valley where the raucous fur traders' rendezvous was held six times from 1833 to 1840. "The first day is devoted to 'High Jinks,' a species of Saturnalia in which feasting, drinking, and gambling form prominent parts," wrote artist Alfred Jacob Miller, who traveled with Sir William Drummond Stewart and spent a month at the rendezvous of 1837. "The following days exhibit the strongest contrast to this. The Fur Company's great tent is raised; the Indians erect their picturesque white lodges; the accumulated furs of the hunting season are brought forth, and the Company's tent is a besieged and busy place." A beaver pelt garnered $5 to $8 worth of supplies carried by pack train from Saint Louis. In 1825 William Ashley instituted the rendezvous as a system for Indians and independent trappers to buy supplies and sell pelts to traders, who could avoid the expense of maintaining a year-round trading post. The rendezvous was attended by such frontiersmen as Jedediah Smith and Kit Carson. At the 1835 gathering, Jim Bridger had an arrowhead removed from his back by Dr. Marcus Whitman, and two years later he was presented a full English suit of armor by Sir William Drummond Stewart. In 1835 Whitman and Dr. Samuel Parker varied the daily carnival of cursing, wrestling, racing, and drinking by introducing religious sermons. But Joe Meek recalled that when a herd of buffalo appeared in the valley during the first service, the trappers took off on horseback with their guns, leaving Parker talking to the breeze. Gambling was more to the trappers' taste, as George F. Ruxton recalled: "The stakes are 'beaver,' which here is current coin; and when the fur is gone . . . daring gamblers make the rounds of the camp, challenging each other to play for the trapper's highest stake—his horse, his squaw (if he has one), and, as once happened, his scalp." During the 1836 gathering, which drew 300 trappers and more than 2,000 Indians, Narcissa Whitman and Eliza Spalding added refinement as the first white females at a rendezvous. The 1840 rendezvous was the last, because of the overtrapping of animals, a change in fashion from beaver hats, and a shift toward trading posts. The Green River valley remains nearly unchanged since the days of the rendezvous.

SOUTH PASS CITY

Miners returning from California looked for gold all over the Rockies, and in 1867 the rich Carissa lode in Wyoming's Sweetwater district prompted a gold rush. The rushers swelled South Pass City to 2,000 citizens within a year. Prospectors reveled at a beer garden and thirteen saloons and had their pockets vacuumed clean by gamblers and harlots; stamp mills pounded; even the town's two doctors

An old wagon in South Pass City, a ghost town from the Wyoming gold rush of the 1860s. The town was established in October 1867, by 1870 it had 4,000 inhabitants, and by the end of 1873 it was deserted.

moonlighted as miners. Streets were laid over the rough terrain in a casual manner, and local government was equally casual. An attorney recalled: "We did not know the laws . . . and paid no attention to them . . . we lived the life of primitive man . . . and really got along very well." Soon after Wyoming became a territory in 1869, the town took its place in legal history when representative William Bright, a local saloon keeper, introduced a successful bill for women's suffrage—the first in the nation. The next year Esther Morris became America's first female justice of the peace. (Legend claims that the six-foot-tall Mrs. Morris collared Bright at a tea party and extracted a promise that, if elected, he would introduce the suffrage bill.)

By the 1870s the city had a long main street with good shops. "The ladies liked to have the latest Paris hats then just like they do now," an old-timer recalled. "Only in those days it took a lot longer to get the hats out here. But then they stayed in style a lot longer, too." Despite the substantial appearance of South Pass City, with its school, stage lines, newspaper, and business buildings, the foundations were beginning to slip. Rich ore veins proved hard to find and develop, and eventually the miners moved on. By 1875 South Pass City was virtually a ghost town. Twenty-four original buildings make up the **South Pass City State Historic Site** (off Route 28, 307–332–3684), including miners' cabins, a livery stable, a dugout cellar once used to store perishable foods, the South Pass Hotel of 1868, the Carissa Saloon, the Masonic lodge of 1868 and subsequently rebuilt, a stamp mill, and the oldest standing jail in Wyoming, built in 1870. A visitor center presents displays on mining technology, social history, and the Oregon Trail.

The **South Pass Overlook** (Route 28, fourteen miles southwest of South Pass City) offers a view of the historic twenty-five-mile-wide pass whose gradual incline made it possible for wagons to cross the Continental Divide. It was probably first crossed by Robert Stuart's Astorians in 1812, and after Jedediah Smith and Thomas Fitzpatrick used South Pass twelve years later, it would take its place in history: From 1840 to 1868, between 350,000 and 400,000 emigrants crossed the Rockies via this 7,550-foot-high pass.

During the rush to South Pass City, miners spilled over and found gold in Atlantic Ledge in 1868. Within two years **Atlantic City** had 500 citizens. A few of the town's log and frame structures sur-

OPPOSITE: *An abandoned gold mine in South Pass City.*

vive. As historian Lambert Florin notes, "There is a 'boardwalk' in Atlantic City, Wyoming, also"—referring to the wooden sidewalks in front of the old buildings.

LANDER

After a gold strike in 1868, miners came into the Wind River region. Lander was founded on the site of old Camp Augur, which had been established to protect Indians on the Wind River Reservation. The town was named for Colonel Frederick Lander, who in 1857 surveyed and improved the Lander Cut-Off from the Oregon Trail, which left the main route at South Pass and headed west toward Fort Hall in Idaho. The **Fremont County Pioneer Museum** (630 Lincoln Street, 307–332–4137) began in 1913 with an unusual first exhibit— Harvey Morgan's skull, which, at the hands of Indians, had suffered an encounter with a wagon hammer, still embedded. This and other artifacts are displayed in nine rooms, including a saddle shop and a chapel; exhibits also include rocks and minerals, Plains Indian dioramas, and memorabilia of Lander's One-Shot Antelope Hunt.

Devil's Gate, above, a four-hundred-yard-long gorge through which the Sweetwater River passes. Wagon trains often were ambushed by Indians here. OPPOSITE: *A restored saddle shop in the Fremont County Pioneer Museum in Lander.*

Independence Rock, where nineteenth-century travelers left their signatures carved in granite, was named by the trapper and trader William Sublette, who celebrated Independence Day there in 1829.

Southwest of Independence Rock is another Oregon Trail landmark, **Devils Gate,** a cleft in a 330-foot-high cliff through which the Sweetwater River runs. Since 1872 it has been part of the **Tom Sun Ranch,** one of Wyoming's earliest open-range ranches, started by a French-Canadian trapper named Thomas Soleil; the original log building still stands. Both sites are visible from Route 220.

   Independence Rock (off Route 220, eighteen miles southwest of Alcova) was a major landmark for travelers along the Oregon Trail, rising 193 feet above the plain and located where the trail first approaches the Sweetwater River. This granite dome, with joints and exfoliations along its sides, received its name on July 4, 1830, from a party of mountain men celebrating Independence Day. In 1840 Father De Smet called the rock "the great registry of the desert," because, as explorer John C. Frémont later said, "everywhere within six or eight feet from the ground, where the surface was sufficiently smooth, and in some places sixty or eighty feet above, the Rock was inscribed with the names of travelers." (By 1855 Mormons were charging travelers up to $5 a name to do the engraving for them.) Alfred Jacob Miller found the names of fur traders Sublette and Wyeth; he also noted that "a man by the cognomen of Nelson had carved his name, and to insure *him* immortality we added to it, 'Of the Nile!'" (Many earlier names have fallen away with layers of rock.)

   In 1812, near **Bessemer Bend** (off Route 220, ten miles southwest of Casper), the returning Astorians under Robert Stuart built winter quarters where Poison Spider Creek enters the North Platte. Wyoming's first European-American building was the rough cabin they sheathed with buffalo hides and nicknamed the "Chateau of Indolence." Then, fearing trouble from Arapaho, Stuart's party decided "to extricate ourselves out of the paws of our rascally neighbors by going a very considerable distance." They had been the first white men to travel through the Platte River valley, and their route, later known as the Oregon Trail, became the major corridor of westward expansion. Oregon Trail emigrants who wanted to avoid tolls and ferry fees often crossed at Bessemer Bend. On a nearby ridge stood the Red Buttes station of the Overland stage line and the Pony Express. According to legend, this was the start and return point of a 322-mile ride to Rocky Ridge station completed by Buffalo Bill in twenty-four hours and forty minutes.

CASPER

The first settlers in the Casper region were Mormons. In 1847 they operated a ferry at the Upper Platte River Crossing on the Oregon Trail. Later, soldiers came to Fort Caspar, and J. M. Carey established a cattle-ranch operation in 1876. But the town of Casper itself did not start until the railroad arrived in 1888 and a land company sold lots. In 1890 Casper lost a contest for county seat but was awarded the title because of irregularities in the election—rival Bessemer City had cast more than 700 votes for itself but was observed to have fewer than 100 citizens. Black gold entered Casper history with the first strike at the bountiful Salt Creek Field in 1890, which produced oil so fine that financiers insisted on independent testing to eliminate the chance of fraud. In 1895 Casper built Wyoming's first refinery, and later the automobile and World War I created a tremendous oil boom, with two pipelines running to the city from Salt Creek. Workers and speculators slept in shifts at hotels or paid outrageous rents to live in shacks and tents. The trading of oil stocks accelerated at a frenetic pace, with auctioneers in the lobby of the Henning (Midwest) Hotel standing atop desks and shrieking prices to crowds that included businessmen, housewives, ministers, and other assorted traders. It was also a time of claim jumping and legal shenanigans, prompting one land office clerk to observe that Wyoming had a "whole herd" of promoters. "Once in a while to protect themselves from the Post Office Department they do a little drilling, but their chief aim is to sell stock." Ambitious oil developers also became embroiled in the Teapot Dome scandal. The region north of Casper produced more than 400 million barrels of oil, and by 1925 the city had grown to a substantial community of 30,000 people. The **Natrona County Pioneer Museum** (1014 South David Street, 307–237–7514), housed in Saint Mark's Episcopal Church of 1891, displays Indian artifacts such as a beaded bag and gloves as well as guns, saddles, and gold-dust pans belonging to early settlers.

Fort Caspar

After Brigham Young and the first 149 Mormon emigrants departed from the Upper Crossing of the North Platte in 1847, they left a contingent of men to operate a wooden ferry and began charging "gentile" travelers a crossing fee, payable in staples such as flour and bacon. Each autumn the Mormons sank the ferry to prevent its theft, then raised it the following spring for business. When trouble arose between the federal government and the Mormons in 1858, U.S. soldiers arrived to keep order and guard the Oregon Trail. The next year Louis Guinard built a trading post and a toll bridge at the crossing; he hiked prices as the river rose and fording became more dangerous for emigrant wagons. The post also served as a station for stagecoaches, the Pony Express, and the telegraph.

As a focal point of white activity, the bridge attracted the enmity of the Sioux and Cheyenne who were massing under Red Cloud and Dull Knife in 1865, determined to end the traffic westward. When young Lieutenant Caspar Collins and twenty-five men were assigned to ride out from Platte Bridge Station to meet an arriving wagon train, they had no sooner crossed the bridge than they were set upon by thousands of Indians. Collins died during the battle, and in his honor the post was renamed Caspar. (Later, one of history's typographical errors changed the spelling of the town's name from *a* to *e*.) Fort Caspar was abandoned in 1867. Today the log fort has been reconstructed to its appearance in 1862, with officers' quarters, commissary, telegraph office, squad room, and mess hall furnished in the style of the time. The **Fort Caspar Museum** has exhibits about military life, Indians, and the development of the city of Casper.

LOCATION: 4001 Fort Caspar Road (Rancho Road exit from Route I-25). HOURS: Mid-May through mid-September: 9–6 Monday–Friday, 9–5 Saturday, 12–5 Sunday; mid-September through mid-May: 9–5 Monday–Friday, 2–5 Sunday. FEE: None. TELEPHONE: 307–235–8462.

To the north, **Teapot Dome** (visible from Route 259, twelve miles south of Edgerton) has weathered so much that it no longer resembles a teapot, but it does prompt memories of the Teapot Dome scandal of the 1920s. Albert Fall, secretary of the interior for President Warren Harding, took a $400,000 bribe from Harry Sinclair, the oil producer, in exchange for granting a lease on a vast underground oil reserve (or "dome") here without competitive bidding. The scandal ended with Fall being fined and jailed; but Sinclair's company did gain rights to the oil. The phrase *Teapot Dome* became a synonym for corruption.

Fort Fetterman (ten miles west of Douglas, off Route 93, 307–358–2864) was established in 1867 as a supply post for the army's operations against the Indians. That year the commander's report noted that "officers and men were found under canvas exposed on a bleak plain to violent and almost constant gales and very uncomfortable." Thus, Fort Fetterman was considered a hardship post and had a high desertion rate; even after log buildings were erected, the fort lacked fresh food and basic supplies. Its most historic moments came in the mid-1870s, when three of General George Crook's Powder River expeditions departed from the fort. (Calamity Jane was one of his teamsters.) As the Plains Indians were conquered, however, Fort Fetterman lost purpose and was abandoned in 1882. A wild civilian community then developed at the post to sell supplies to nearby ranches and passing wagon trains. (Fetterman City appeared in Owen Wister's novel *The Virginian* as "Drybone.") The city emptied when nearby Douglas was founded in 1886. Only the restored officers' quarters and an ordnance warehouse survive from the original fort; a **museum** contains exhibits about early days on the post.

DOUGLAS

Douglas got its start in 1886 as Tent Town—three canvas "buildings" that housed a store, a restaurant, and a saloon. (That year the saloon doubled as a church, with a poker table as an altar.) The town was almost immediately moved by wagon ten miles east, in order to locate where a spur railroad had announced its imminent arrival. In three days about $100,000 worth of lots were sold, and 1,000 citizens started to build. Douglas became a center for cattle ranchers and homesteaders, as well as the site of the Wyoming State Fair. At the fairgrounds the **Wyoming Pioneer Memorial Museum** (307–358–9288) displays historical relics such as guns, saddles, military equipment, and vehicles, including an army escort wagon of the 1860s; a barroom with old roulette wheels; Indian artifacts; and dolls. An outdoor railroad collection includes a locomotive, diner, and sleeper of the 1940s and a caboose of 1884.

LUSK

When Lusk got its start in 1886 along the tracks of the Fremont, Elkhorn & Missouri Valley Railroad, the first issue of the local newspaper proclaimed: "Lusk has a future. It is located in the midst of the best agricultural land in Wyoming." Dry farming was a great success in the region, producing wheat, potatoes, and vegetables, and ranching was also successful; five miles east of town the Texas Trail swarmed with cattle—800,000 head in 1894 alone. Farm products and stock were shipped out by rail, and a brief oil boom in 1918 swelled the town. The **Stagecoach Museum** (322 South Main Street, 307–334–3444) features county historical items, including a stagecoach of the Cheyenne–Black Hills Stage and Express line, which carried passengers and gold between Cheyenne and Deadwood and was robbed regularly by road agents. Also on display are pioneer furnishings, rocks, wagons, and a 1900s schoolhouse.

About thirteen miles north of Lusk stands a lone log building—the **Hat Creek Stage Station** (three miles off Route 85). The Hat Creek Ranch stood on the Cheyenne–Deadwood Stage Road, on the edge of the most dangerous section of the entire stage route, where many Indian raids and stage holdups occurred. A traveler in 1876 described it as typical of road-ranches along such trails: "There are hotels, bar-rooms, and stores for general merchandise, all combined in one . . . a traveler can purchase almost anything, from a glass of whiskey to a four-horse team, but the former article is usually the staple of demand." Attached to the ranch in its heyday were a telegraph office and post office, blacksmith shop, brewery, bakery, and butcher shop. The ranch was established in 1876 by John Bowman after an earlier building had burned. The two-story stage station dates to the early 1880s.

TORRINGTON

When Robert Stuart's party of eastward-bound Astorians stopped just east of today's Torrington in 1812, they set up their second winter camp in a wooded region with plenty of buffalo nearby. The Oregon Trail they blazed enters Wyoming just eight miles southeast of town. Items from Torrington's settlement period are on display at the **Homesteaders Museum** (South Main Street, 307–532–5612), including furniture, dishes, and other household articles brought west on wagon trains and prized on the remote frontier; also, ranching artifacts, paleo-Indian bird-bone tools and stone scrapers, and military items housed in the Union Pacific depot (1926).

GUERNSEY

Just south of Guernsey is the **Oregon Trail Ruts,** a section of the emigrant trail where the rough terrain forced travelers to follow a single set of tracks across a relatively soft sandstone formation. The endlessly passing wagon wheels carved ruts so deep that the wheel hubs also cut into the stone. In the soft sandstone-limestone formation called

At the Oregon Trail Ruts National Historical Monument, the track left by the wagons that carried 350,000 emigrants traveling along the Oregon Trail are preserved in the soft limestone. Few of these travelers stayed in Wyoming.

A few of the seven hundred names inscribed on Register Cliff. Some names inscribed on

Register Cliff (three miles south of Guernsey), fur traders, emigrants, soldiers, and pioneer ranchers carved their names and dates during the nineteenth century. The site lies eleven miles, or a day's travel, from Fort Laramie and so it made a natural camping place, particularly with broad river bottoms for campsites and good pasturage. Because emigrant travel involved so much hardship and illness, such layovers were important for recuperation; graves beside the cliff hint at the large numbers who died along the trail. In 1860–1861 a Pony Express station stood in the meadow west of the cliff at a site now marked with a **plaque.**

FORT LARAMIE NATIONAL HISTORIC SITE

Near the confluence of the North Platte and Laramie rivers stands one of the West's most important forts. The earliest permanent white settlement in Wyoming, the first Fort Laramie (known officially as Fort William) was built in 1834 by William Sublette and Robert Campbell as a fur trading post. The American Fur Company bought

the cliff show up on gravestones farther west on the Oregon Trail,

the operation in 1836 and replaced the rotting log structure with one of adobe which included bastions and other fortifications; it called the site Fort John on the Laramie (soon shortened to Fort Laramie). During the 1840s the trading post also became an important stop on the Oregon Trail, marking the route's one-third point and the first contact with civilization in more than 300 miles. Largely to protect and resupply the emigrants, the federal government acquired the fort in 1849. Around a parade ground, soldiers built quarters, stables, and other buildings for the troops assigned there. Indians came to the fort regularly, and up to 100 lodges were sometimes erected nearby. The fort was an important spot for peace councils, beginning in 1851 when almost 10,000 Plains Indians gathered for the signing of a treaty with a white delegation that included government officials from Washington, DC and such frontiersmen as Jim Bridger and Tom "Broken Hand" Fitzpatrick. Later the fort would become the jumping-off place' for campaigns to subdue the Northern Plains Indians. Fort Laramie served as a station for the Cheyenne–Deadwood stage line, the Pony Express, and the transcontinental telegraph. The sutler's store was a busy place, described by a

Alfred Jacob Miller's visited Fort Laramie, then named for Fort William, in 1837, and recorded his impressions in this painting, now in the Thomas Gilcrease Institute in Tulsa, Oklahoma (detail). OPPOSITE: *The ruins of Fort Laramie today.*

woman traveler in 1866 as "a scene of seeming confusion not surpassed in any popular, overcrowded store of Omaha itself . . . soldiers . . . teamsters, emigrants, speculators, half-breeds, and interpreters. Here, cups of rice, sugar, coffee, or flour were being emptied into the looped-up skirts or blankets of a squaw; and there, some tall warrior was grimacing delightfully as he . . . sucked his long sticks of peppermint candy."

With the fort's abandonment in 1890, some buildings were dismantled for lumber by local ranchers and farmers, while homesteaders moved into others. Eleven structures have been restored to their historic appearance, including the sutler's store, the surgeon's quarters, and the cavalry barracks. "Old Bedlam," the post headquarters and bachelor officers' quarters, is Wyoming's oldest standing military building, erected in 1849; the name arose from the noisy, bibulous parties given here by the young officers. Fort Laramie was never completely surrounded by a palisade because of lack of funds, and in its later years it looked less like a fort than a town, complete with gaslights and streets lined with houses and boardwalks. Self-guided tours of the grounds and buildings explain life at the fort, and there is a visitor center in the old commissary building.

LOCATION: Off Route 26, 3 miles southwest of the town of Fort Laramie on Route 160. HOURS: *Visitor Center:* September through April: 8–4:30 Daily; May: 8–6 Daily; June through August: 8–7 Daily. *Grounds:* 7–Dusk Daily. FEE: Yes. TELEPHONE: 307–837–2221.

NORTHERN WYOMING

OPPOSITE: *Travertine formations in Yellowstone Park's Mammoth Hot Springs, where the steaming water deposits up to two feet of new limestone annually.*

At an altitude of about 10,000 feet in the Big Horn Mountains lies the Medicine Wheel. An almost perfect circle of white stones, measuring seventy-five feet in diameter, it has twenty-eight spokes radiating from a hub of rock. No one alive today knows who built it, when they built it, or what it signifies. To deepen the mystery, more rocks form a fifty-eight-foot-long arrow near Meeteetse—more than fifty miles away—and the Great Arrow points directly at the Medicine Wheel. Of the theories advanced to explain the Medicine Wheel, perhaps the most powerful comes from the Crow, who say that the Sun laid out the stone circle to teach the tribe how to make a tepee. This myth reveals something of the intimate relationship between the Plains Indians and their natural surroundings of sun and earth. It was a bond the Indians did not share with all the white men who came to their country. In 1805 a French-Canadian fur trader, François Antoine Larocque, and his party rode up the Powder River and then on to the Big Horn. Along the way they acquired beaver pelts—"a great many more than we needed," in the opinion of the local Indians, who did not like slaughtering beaver for money. Some of the Indians, Larocque noted, "seemed to desire that I go away." The trader moved on, but other white men arrived, and stayed.

In 1806 John Colter left the returning Lewis and Clark expedition to trap beaver and later discovered Colter's Hell (a region of thermal activity near today's Cody), Jackson Hole, and the Big Horn Basin. He was the first white man to view Yellowstone, returning to Saint Louis in 1810 full of stories of smoking ground and boiling springs. The public dismissed his tales, although Colter's achievements were memorialized when "Colter's Route" was added to the official map of the Lewis and Clark expedition.

Colter helped open the fur trade era, which in turn opened Wyoming and brought more whites into contact with Native Americans. When Wilson Price Hunt led a party of Astorian trappers over the Big Horn Mountains in 1811, Indians directed him toward peaks that he called the Pilot Knobs—later renamed by French trappers as *les trois tetons* (three breasts). On meeting the tall, vain Crow, Price remarked: "Even the children do not go afoot. These Indians are such good horsemen that they climb and descend the mountains and rocks as though they were galloping in a riding school." Although peaceful toward the whites, the Crow enjoyed stealing horses. They "spare no chance to rob us," observed trapper William Gordon, "but never kill. This they frankly explain by telling us that if they killed, we would not come back, and they could not rob us."

Golden Gate, Yellowstone National Park, *painted in 1893 by Thomas Moran, who had first visited the region with Dr. F. V. Hayden's expedition in 1871. Moran's illustrations of Hayden's subsequent article in* Scribner's *helped convince Congress to establish the first national park there.*

It seems probable that fur trappers regularly visited Jackson Hole and the Big Horn Basin. By 1828 Antonio Mateo had built Wyoming's first trading post, the log Portuguese Houses, on the Powder River. As more whites entered Wyoming—emigrants, soldiers, prospectors, freighters—the Sioux, Arapaho, and Cheyenne became convinced that they would have to fight to protect their hunting lands, especially after 1864, when the Bozeman Trail opened to serve miners rushing north to Montana boomtowns. In 1865 Brigadier General Patrick E. Connor launched the Powder River expedition to crush the tribes and "kill all male Indians over the age of twelve," but the federal government halted the campaign. Colonel Henry Carrington's men built three forts along the Bozeman Trail, where regular skirmishes occurred—the Sioux made fifty-one attacks on Fort Phil Kearny in the last five months of 1866 alone. About a third of the fort's garrison was wiped out in one engagement when warriors under Red Cloud and Crazy Horse attacked a woodcutting detail and the force sent out under Captain William Fetterman to protect it. A thousand arrows per minute

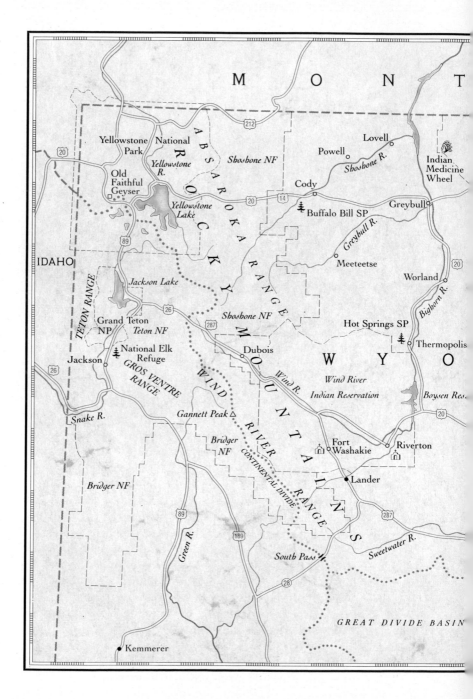

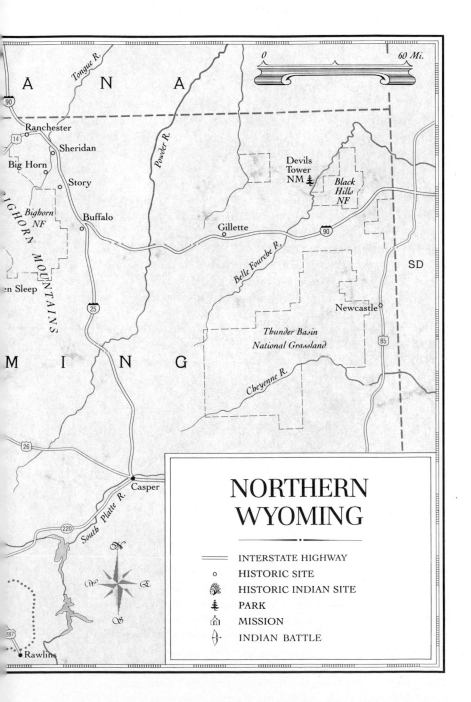

A   N   A

Tongue R.

Ranchester

Sheridan

Big Horn

Story

Powder R.

Devils
Tower
NM

Black
Hills
NF

Bighorn
NF

Buffalo

Gillette

BIGHORN MOUNTAINS

Belle Fourche R.

SD

en Sleep

Newcastle

Thunder Basin
National Grassland

M   I   N   G

Cheyenne R.

Casper

South Platte R.

Rawlins

0   60 Mi.

NORTHERN
WYOMING

————— INTERSTATE HIGHWAY
   ○   HISTORIC SITE
         HISTORIC INDIAN SITE
   🌲   PARK
   ⌂   MISSION
  ⊣|⊢   INDIAN BATTLE

rained down on the troops, killing all eighty-one men. Now overconfident, Red Cloud sent his warriors against Major J. N. Powell in the Wagon Box Fight of August 1867 but found that the soldiers had new Springfield breech-loading rifles, whose constant fire inflicted heavy casualties. Red Cloud decided to negotiate with the encroaching whites, giving up major concessions in an 1868 treaty that also guaranteed the Powder River country to the Indians and closed the Bozeman Trail and its forts. As troops abandoned Fort Phil Kearny and rode away, the exuberant Sioux torched it.

Whites kept finding new reasons to come through Wyoming. In 1866 an Ohioan named Nelson Story made the first great cattle drive into the region, disobeying army orders to stop in Indian territory near Fort Phil Kearny. Instead, he headed for Montana. The Texas Trail he blazed became a major artery for moving livestock, and in 1886 a million cattle raised dust along it. Wyoming cowmen established vast ranches but were annoyed to find that small ranchers and homesteaders also wanted to use the public lands, and some were not above rustling animals to add to their herds. Eventually, a group of stockmen concocted a plan to invade Johnson County and wipe out their competition, but the campaign ended after the invaders murdered two men.

Wyoming also developed a coal industry, and in 1888 the Cambria mine opened with an adjacent company town where miners lived in decent bunkhouses and even had an opera house. Farmers benefited from Wyoming's first important dam, started in 1899 on the Shoshone River to irrigate nearly 100,000 acres west of Cody. In the early 1900s the Chicago, Burlington & Quincy Railroad laid tracks to the ranching town of Sheridan and other northern communities. By then the world the Plains Indians had known was almost gone. Tribal myths repeated for centuries around night fires faded in the dawn of progress. Buffalo Bill Cody, who had been a genuine hero of the frontier, sat on the porch of the Sheridan Inn and interviewed Indians as potential cast members for his touring Wild West spectacle. By 1904 at Yellowstone National Park—the country of steaming ground and hissing waters where John Colter had wandered in 1807—tourists could sit on a second-story balcony at the Old Faithful Inn and sip drinks while watching the geyser rush toward the sky.

This chapter begins in the northwest corner of the state at Yellowstone National Park. The route then travels south to Jackson be-

fore turning east to Dubois and Riverton. It next explores central
Wyoming up to the Montana border, from Thermopolis to Cody to
Lovell. Finally the chapter moves east, from Ranchester to Devils
Tower National Monument.

YELLOWSTONE NATIONAL PARK

With 10,000 hot springs and two-thirds of all the geysers in the
world, to say nothing of bubbling paint pots, thundering waterfalls,
and petrified forests, Yellowstone inspires awe. Indians knew about
this wonderland of volcanism, of course, before John Colter became
the first white man to discover some of its wonders in 1807–1808 (he
did not see the extensive geyser basins). His accounts seemed out-
landish to those in the East and were generally derided. In 1829 Joe
Meek looked over a mountain "and behold! the whole country
beyond was smoking with vapor from boiling springs, and burning
with gases issuing from small craters." In 1834 an educated young
fellow named Warren Ferris, traveling with some Pend d'Oreille, saw
"from the surface of a rocky plain or table, burst forth columns of

Old Faithful, named by members of the Washburn-Langford-Doane Expedition in
1870, erupts on a regular basis throughout the year. Each eruption is signaled by rum-
bling from deep in the earth followed by a cloud of steam.

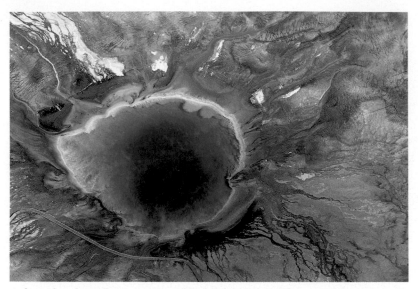

A thermal pool in Yellowstone National Park, where unusual thinness in the earth's crust allowed the formation of the largest concentration of thermal activity in the world.

water of various dimensions, projecting high into the air, accompanied by loud explosions and sulphurous vapors." Although he went close and touched the water, but the Indians "could not by any means be induced to approach them. They believed them to be supernatural. . . the production of the Evil Spirit. One of them remarked that hell, of which they had heard from the whites, must be in that vicinity."

In the mid-1830s Osborne Russell, a trapper, noted: "Some of the geyser cones are very serviceable to the hunter in preparing his dinner when hungry, for his kettle is always ready and boiling." Such odd phenomena inspired Jim Bridger, a notorious fabricator of tall tales, to make up stories only loosely based on fact. His yarn about a stream that cascaded downhill so fast it got hot on the bottom sounds much like the real Firehole River, which is heated by submerged hot springs. Yellowstone's petrified forests inspired Bridger to add petrified birds singing petrified songs.

In 1869 three men in the mining industry, David Folsom, C. W. Cook, and William Peterson, saddled up and headed for the area to see for themselves what was really there. The descriptive, and accurate, article they published in *Western Monthly Magazine* amazed the public. It encouraged exploration in 1870 by the surveyor general of

Montana Territory, Henry Washburn; army lieutenant G. C. Doane; and Nathaniel Langford, a bank examiner, who later journeyed east to spark interest in an official government expedition. A geologist, F. V. Hayden, led the federal scientific party in 1871, taking along the photographer William H. Jackson and the painter Thomas Moran, whose images of Yellowstone later publicized the area. These travels helped prove the existence of Yellowstone's wonders and finally influenced Congress to create the world's first national park in 1872. Termed a "pleasuring-ground for the benefit and enjoyment of the people," the park guaranteed the "preservation, from injury or spoilation, of all timber, mineral deposits, natural curiosities, or wonders within." According to a local historian, Donald Swain, "The concept of reserving lands from the public domain for use as parks and to preserve unique examples of natural beauty was a distinctly American idea. Many other nations later set up parks modeled after the national park system in the United States. The Yellowstone Act of 1872 therefore had great historical significance." The national park idea and its history are illustrated at the **Explorers' Museum** (Madison Junction). Information about all of Yellowstone's facilities is available from the National Park Service (307–344–7381).

The **Old Faithful Inn** (Grand Loop) stands beside the world's most famous geyser, Old Faithful, which erupts with a column of boiling water as high as 160 feet every 33 to 120 minutes. Playing for one-and-a-half to five minutes, the geyser was first reported and named by the Washburn-Langford expedition in 1870. The inn was built of rocks and lodgepole pines in Western Stick style and is probably the world's largest log building. Robert Reamer designed the three-story main building and wings, which was built from 1903 to 1928. The dramatic open lobby rises more than ninety feet, edged with natural branch railings and log staircases; a weight-and-pulley metal clock hanging down the immense stone fireplace was fashioned from Reamer's drawings.

After the park's creation, troubles arose as hunters, trappers, woodcutters, and vandals entered the area despite its protective covenant; and Yellowstone was large and difficult for the civilian staff to police or oversee. In 1886 the U.S. Army began to administer the area from Fort Sheridan at Mammoth Hot Springs. The cavalry—riding horses in summer and using skis in winter—caught poachers and established and enforced rules of behavior for a national park, such as preventing vandalism by souvenir hunters who broke off pieces from the mineral formations. It also fought fires and in 1891 built

Fort Yellowstone, which now houses park headquarters. One of the best-preserved late-nineteenth-century cavalry posts in the country, Fort Yellowstone still has most of its original buildings, including sandstone structures on officers row and original frame buildings. A summer walking tour explores bachelor officers' quarters, the guardhouse, barracks, stables, and other buildings. The **Albright Visitor Center** (Mammoth Hot Springs, 307–344–7381) examines the army's role in the park, showing uniforms, rifles, and skis, displays watercolors by Thomas Moran and photographs by William H. Jackson, and includes artifacts from historic Yellowstone expeditions, including personal effects such as Henry Washburn's medical kit.

The **Norris Soldier Station** (about a mile north of Norris Junction) was one of the log army posts maintained to administer the park. **Roosevelt Lodge National Historic District,** near Tower Junction, includes the main lodge and surrounding cabins of the 1920s, an example of an early automobile camp. These proto-motels made it possible for middle-income families, not only the wealthy, to visit natural wonders such as Yellowstone. At one time Yellowstone was the last place where bison roamed free, since they had become nearly extinct in the wild. **Lamar Buffalo Ranch National Historic District** (twelve miles east of Tower Junction on Route 212) operated as part of the effort to preserve bison in the West.

Just east of Yellowstone stands the **Pahaska Tepee** (two miles from park boundary on Route 14/16/20, 307–527–7701). *Pahaska,* or Longhair, was the Sioux name for William F. "Buffalo Bill" Cody; it was suggested for the lodge by his friend Iron Tail, known as the man on the Buffalo nickel. Located in the Absaroka Range, the log lodge was hewn with axes and adzes in 1904 to a high standard of craftsmanship. The two-story building—which looks like a cabin, not a tepee—served as a hunting lodge where Cody entertained well-known guests from the worlds of politics, the arts, and the military, including General Nelson Miles and the prince of Monaco. The lodge later accomodated tourists on the wagon road to Yellowstone National Park; it is now open to the public as a visitor center.

Six miles south of Moran stands the **Cunningham Cabin** (Route 26/89/191). Made of logs and roofed with sod in about 1889, this one-story cabin is a good example of the area's earliest European

OPPOSITE: *A petrified 50-million-year-old tree stump in the Specimen Ridge area of Yellowstone National Park.*

building style. Its builder, J. Pierce Cunningham, was a county rancher. When he offered two strangers a place to stay with their train of horses while he was away from his ranch for the winter of 1892, it was whispered in the valley that they were horse thieves. The following spring a group of men claiming to be an Idaho marshal and his deputies inquired about any horse thieves in the region and were led to Cunningham's cabin, where they shot the two men without letting them speak and rode away with their train of horses. It has been speculated that this may have been a case of mistaken identity, or even that the "posse" was really a group of horse thieves masquerading as lawmen.

MOOSE

Grand Teton National Park (307–733–2880), Wyoming's second national park, embraces almost the entire Teton Range. The park headquarters and visitor center are at Moose, a town named for the world's largest animal with antlers, which is seen here regularly. In Moose are several historic sites connected by a half-mile historic trail. The **Chapel of the Transfiguration** is a one-room log chapel built in 1925, well known for the view of the Tetons seen through the window behind the altar. Nearby is **Menor's Ferry,** established in 1894 by William D. Menor in one of the few spots where the Snake River kept to one navigable channel. Operating from spring until winter, the ferry was little more than a platform on pontoons, with room for a wagon and team or a good crowd of livestock. The ferry has been reconstructed. The site also includes Menor's homestead of log cabin construction, a root cellar, a smokehouse, and the **Maude Noble Cabin.** Maude Noble came west from Philadelphia and bought the ferry in 1918; five years later her cabin was the site of a meeting between Horace Albright, superintendent of Yellowstone Park, and a few conservation-minded valley residents to discuss the prospect of preserving the region as a national recreation area—not a national park, but a "museum of the hoof," with some grazing and dude ranching. After bitter battles in which ranchers and the U.S. Forest Service opposed the National Park Service and environmentalists, Grand Teton National Park was created in 1929. But it protected only the Tetons and a swath of land at their feet. Jackson Hole, which has been called "the natural foreground of the Teton Range," was left out because of local opposition. In the meantime Albright had enlisted the help of John D. Rockefeller, Jr., who visited the Tetons on vacation. When the philanthropist saw telephone lines, crumbling gas stations, tourist cabins, and a billboard for a future "Hollywood Cowboys Home" blighting the view of the mountains, he formed the Snake River Land Company and bought about 35,000 acres. This land was included in Jackson Hole National Monument of 1943, and by 1950 it had became part of an expanded Grand Teton National Park.

The **Colter Bay Indian Arts Museum** (forty miles north of Jackson, 307–543–2467) displays artifacts of the Plains Indian culture: pipe bags and pipes, shields, moccasins, leggings, toys, dolls, clubs known as "skull crackers," and other items of warfare. There are also some Southwestern items such as Navajo belts. This was the collection of David T. Vernon, who started with arrowheads at age 13 and continued collecting all his life.

JACKSON

A green valley nearly fifty miles long, Jackson Hole is surrounded by the Grand Tetons, the Wind River Range, and the Gros Ventre Mountains. It has sheltered all sorts of Western characters, from fur trappers to rustlers and outlaws. ("Hole" was trappers' lingo for a protected valley.) First explored in 1807 by the intrepid John Colter, it was entered by mountain men in the 1820s—most notably by the expeditions of William Ashley. One of his crew, David E. Jackson, joined with William Sublette and Jedediah Smith in 1826 to buy Ashley's fur company, and it is for Jackson that the region is named. Settlers had arrived by the early 1880s and started large ranches. The remote valley also made a perfect hideout for cattle rustlers. The town of Jackson was laid out in 1897 on a patch of sagebrush, becoming a ranchers' supply town and later a dude ranch center. With log and false-front buildings and boardwalks, Jackson still reflects the Old West.

The **Jackson Hole Museum** (105 North Glenwood, 307–733–2414) displays fur trappers' weapons, tools, and traps; Plains Indian trade beads, a war bonnet, moccasins, and dance and ceremonial items; 10,000-year-old projectile points, soapstone dishes, and scrapers from the Jackson Lake area; and settlers' tools and cowboy gear. The **Teton County Historical Center** (105 Mercill,

OVERLEAF: *This rustic ranch in Jackson Hole, a four-hundred-square-mile valley named for the pioneer fur trader David Jackson, has a magnificent view of the Grand Tetons.*

307–733–9605) contains similar exhibits on the fur trade and Plains Indians. **Saint John's Episcopal Church** (North Cache Street) is a log church dating to the turn of the century.

The **National Elk Refuge** (Route 26/89/191, just north of Jackson, 307–733–9212) shelters up to 10,000 elk in winter; they can be seen east of the highway. The establishment of farms, ranches, and the town of Jackson had partially blocked elk from their usual winter feeding ranges, a state of affairs that, coupled with raw winters from 1909 to 1911, caused hundreds of the animals to starve. Some elk pilfered hay from ranchers, who were sympathetic but could not afford the loss. Residents of the area appealed for a federal refuge to feed and protect the animals, and by 1912 Congress acted to purchase the land and fund the refuge. From late December through April, the refuge offers tours by sleigh. Within the refuge stands the so-called **Miller Cabin,** really two cabins, located on Flat Creek property homesteaded in 1885 by Robert Miller, who laid out the town of Jackson. The one-room cabin was his home-office for administering the Teton Division of the Yellowstone Timberland Reserve, beginning in 1903. Miller used the larger, two-story building as headquarters for the elk refuge, which incorporated 2,000 acres of his land.

DUBOIS

In 1886 this settlement got a post office and applied for the name Never Sweat, a nickname Mrs. John Burlingham used to tease the men of the place about their aversion to hard work. The designation was rejected by postal officials, who suggested the more sober name of an Idaho senator. Dubois later grew into a cow town and a center for cutting railroad ties. The **Dubois Museum** (Route 26/287, 307–455–2284) has timbering artifacts from the tie-hack industry of 1914 to 1940, including broadaxes, two-man whipsaws, and horse-pulled sleds. Also on the premises are a schoolhouse of 1925, a furnished ranch bunkhouse built in 1920, a saddle shop, a U.S. Forest Service cabin, a meathouse, and a 1920s service station.

FORT WASHAKIE

The Shoshoni chief Washakie had early recognized the futility of opposing the invasion of Indian lands: "When we had bows, the whites had pistols, when we got pistols, the whites had rifles, and when we got rifles the whites had cannons." So he had always counseled peace, working to get the most for his people through negotiation. When the Fort Bridger treaty of 1868 established the Wind River Reservation for his tribe, Chief Washakie asked for protection, since the Shoshoni would be defenseless against their traditional foes. Only after the government built a fort did he move his people onto the reservation. During the height of the Indian wars, Washakie joined with the Crow to help the U.S. Army overcome tribal enemies—the Sioux, Arapaho, and Cheyenne—and in 1878 the fort was renamed for the Shoshoni chief. Decommissioned in 1909, the fort now serves as headquarters for the Wind River Indian Agency.

Washakie's Grave (Old Military Cemetery) is the final resting place of the man who ruled his people for more than half a century. Washakie's name means "rattler," a reference to a special buffalo-skin rattle, stuffed with rocks, that the chief carried in battle to drive his warriors, often singing an accompaniment. A government historian tells this anecdote about Washakie's mettle: "In 1869, when the Government was slow to fulfil treaty obligations, he heard young braves disputing as to what warrior should succeed him as chief. He rode eastward alone, says legend, and returned with seven Sioux scalps; hurling them on the ground before the disputants, he challenged any of them to duplicate his act." Another side of this leader is indicated by Washakie's conduct on receiving a silver saddle from President Ulysses S. Grant. Someone asked the chief to make a short statement of thanks. Washakie responded: "Do a kindness to a white man; he feels it in his head, and his tongue speaks. Do a kindness to an Indian, he feels it in his heart; the heart has no tongue." Although the Reverend John Roberts baptized Washakie, at the end of his life it was said that the chief was "troubled by the thought that he might go to the white man's heaven and be lost to his own people." Washakie died in 1900, the only Indian chief known to have received full military burial rites. His grave marker cites an 1804 birthdate, but he may have been born as early as 1796, indicating a life that touched three centuries.

The Shoshone Cemetery is the site of the **Grave of Sacajawea**—although many historians dispute this location, placing the grave site in South Dakota instead. She was a Shoshoni kidnapped by another tribe in her youth and later sold to a French-Canadian trapper as a wife. Also called the Bird Woman (her name more properly translates as Boat Pusher), Sacajawea traveled 3,000 miles with the Lewis and Clark expedition of 1805–1806, often acting as an interpreter. After these travels she returned to Indian life. One report indicated that she died in South Dakota in 1812 of "putrid fever," but the Reverend John Roberts identified an Indian woman who died on the Wind River Reservation in 1884 as Sacajawea. Next to the grave is a monument to Sacajawea's son Baptiste, who received an education through the auspices of William Clark and even traveled to Europe after Prince Paul of Württemberg took an interest in him.

The **Saint Stephen's Episcopal Mission** (three miles southwest of Fort Washakie on Moccasin Lake Road, 307–856–6797) was founded by the Reverend John Roberts. He built a girls' boarding school on 160 acres beside Trout Creek donated by Chief Washakie, who said "our hope is in the children and the young people, the old people can't hear." The red-brick school building was built in 1890 and now serves as mission headquarters; other structures include a turn-of-the-century log chapel, the log home of the Arapaho churchman Sherman Coolidge, and the frame Church of the Redeemer, built in 1885 and moved to this site from the Wind River Agency.

ETHETE

When the Episcopal missionary church established **Saint Michael's Mission** with the Arapaho around 1887, those gathered sanctioned the plan by saying *Ethete*, or "Good." Present buildings include homes and the log **Church of Our Father's House,** all built from 1910 to 1917 under the guidance of Arapaho minister Sherman Coolidge. The **Arapaho Museum** in Ethete (307–332–2660) has tribal artifacts and exhibits on Arapaho history. Also here are the painted skins that once decorated the door of the mission church.

RIVERTON

When a treaty in 1905 removed the future site of Riverton from the Wind River Indian Reservation, it spurred a land rush. White settlers filed on plots in town, but claim jumpers arrived from Lander and tore up the stakes. This led the original settlers to pick up rifles and reassert their titles, even after troops were called in from Fort Washakie. After the building of a federally funded irrigation system, the windswept, dusty environs turned green, and Riverton became a

OPPOSITE: *Saint Stephen's Mission was founded by a Jesuit missionary from Philadelphia. When his letter to Bishop O'Connor was published in a Philadelphia newspaper, Catherine Drexel donated $5,000 to found the mission.*

Sandstone formations in Castle Garden near Moneta in central Wyoming.

center for the cultivation of grain, corn, sugar beets, and livestock. The exhibits of the **Riverton Museum** (700 East Park Street, 307–856–2665) focus on the institutions of local history: a school, shoe shop, blacksmith shop, general store, saloon, bank, and the Atlantic City gold mine. Other exhibits include quilts and tatting, musical instruments, and Indian artifacts.

The **Wind River Reservation** was set aside for the Shoshoni in 1868. Ten years later the Northern Arapaho also were moved here to Wyoming's only Indian reservation, and although it was to be a temporary arrangement, they have remained ever since. On the reservation stands **Saint Stephen's Mission** (three miles south of Riverton off Route 789, 307–856–7806), which began in 1884 with a tent and altar erected by Father John Jutz to hold mass for Arapaho chief Black Coal and his family. The Jesuit missionary built permanent structures in 1887, including a convent that still exists, and also undertook farming. The church is painted inside and out with bright Arapaho geometric designs.

Petroglyphs at Castle Gardens are more precisely carved than other Wyoming examples.

Eighteen miles south of Moneta are the **Castle Garden Petroglyphs,** prehistoric drawings incised in sandstone cliffs in a rugged area where rock towers create the impression of a palace. The unknown artists may have belonged to a group that spread westward from the Mississippi and Missouri rivers—which may explain the pictures of nonnative water turtles. Other images depict buffalo, birds, and hunters. That there are no drawings of horses or other European elements dates the site to before the coming of the white man. These cliffs constitute perhaps the best and most extensive collection of Wyoming petroglyphs; their meaning, however, remains a mystery.

THERMOPOLIS

The town's name, unexpectedly erudite for the Wild West, is composed of Latin (*thermae,* hot baths or springs) and Greek (*polis,* city). Here are the largest hot springs in the world, gushing 18,600,000 gallons a day. Originally they were part of the Wind River Reservation,

but in 1896 the federal government bought the mineral springs and ten square miles of land, agreeing to Shoshoni chief Washakie's stipulation that some of the waters be reserved for free public use. **Hot Springs State Park** (Route 20, 307–864–2176) became Wyoming's first state park. The water of Big Horn Spring flows at 128 degrees F., and its overspill has created travertine terraces brightly colored with algae, visible from a walkway. Washakie once had a bathhouse at nearby Black Sulphur Spring. Bison graze in the park, which is divided by the Big Horn River.

The **Wyoming Pioneer Home** (5 Pioneer Drive, 307–864–3151), a state-run residence for the elderly, has a small museum of Indian artifacts and antiques. The most discussed exhibit at the **Hot Springs County Museum and Cultural Center** (700 Broadway, 307–864–5183) is the cherrywood bar from the Hole-in-the-Wall Saloon, once patronized by Butch Cassidy and the Sundance Kid and other members of the Wild Bunch. (Outlaws thrived in the area until the county was organized in 1913; the nearest law enforcement was a day's ride away.) The museum also has a main-street exhibit, gemstones, oil and farming artifacts, a country school, 8,500 Indian arrowheads, and a caboose. The **Downtown Thermopolis Historic District** encompasses a block and a half of Broadway, with buildings erected from the 1910s to the 1920s.

The **Legend Rock Petroglyph Site** (eight miles from Hamilton Dome) is made up of sandstone outcrops on which various cultures of the late prehistoric period incised drawings of people, mythical figures, and such animals as bears, rabbits, and birds; some images are four feet high.

MEETEETSE

One of the earliest settlements in the Big Horn Basin, Meeteetse takes its name from an interesting Shoshoni term that means "meeting place" or "nearby"; if this place was at a distance, the syllables were drawn out; if close, they were pronounced rapidly. First established near the present site in 1883, the hamlet was relocated on the Greybull River twelve years later. Only recently have churches out-

OPPOSITE: *The carved cherrywood bar from the notorious Hole-in-the-Wall Saloon, an outlaws' hangout, is preserved in the Hot Springs County Museum and Cultural Center in Thermopolis.*

numbered saloons in this wild and woolly town. In 1935 Amelia Earhart visited a ranch near the town and decided to build a cabin on an old mining claim. The first woman to fly across the Atlantic, she was lost on an around-the-world flight in 1937. Her cabin was never finished; the remains can be found in the Shoshone National Forest thirty-seven miles southwest of Meeteetse, on the Wood River Road to the old mining town of Kirwin. There is a stone **memorial** to her on Route 120 at Meeteetse. The **Meeteetse Museum** occupies two sites: The **Bank Museum** (1033 Park, 307–868–2423) houses the town archives and old newspapers in a restored 1901 bank; the **Hall Museum** (942 Mondell, 307–868–2334) displays clothing from early families, a church pew and organ, an old school, and household rooms; it occupies the Masonic hall built in 1900 and later used as town hall and general social center.

CODY

John Colter passed the future site of Cody in 1807, observing what was then an active thermal area later called **Colter's Hell** (two miles west of Cody, near Route 14/16/20); the term is often mistakenly applied to the Yellowstone region, but it properly refers to this site along the Shoshone River, now almost inactive but marked by old geyser cones and craters. After the Carey Act of 1894 opened the way for federal support of land reclamation, George Beck and his partners decided to organize a development company and invited Buffalo Bill Cody to look at the area in 1894. The frontiersman became an enthusiastic partner, and in 1896 the company laid out a town site for which Cody's name was proposed. Because Cody was, in Beck's words, "probably the best advertised man in the world," the glitter of his name lured homesteaders to the region; the company also actively recruited settlers and advertised the town in Cody's Wild West Show. The Chicago, Burlington & Quincy Railroad began serving the town in 1901, its cars filled with tourists bound for Yellowstone and the big-game-hunting region near Cody. The city grew and became county seat eight years later.

Buffalo Bill Historical Center

This complex embraces one of the nation's finest collections of western Americana, with four major museums and a great amount of material relating to William F. "Buffalo Bill" Cody. The frame clap-

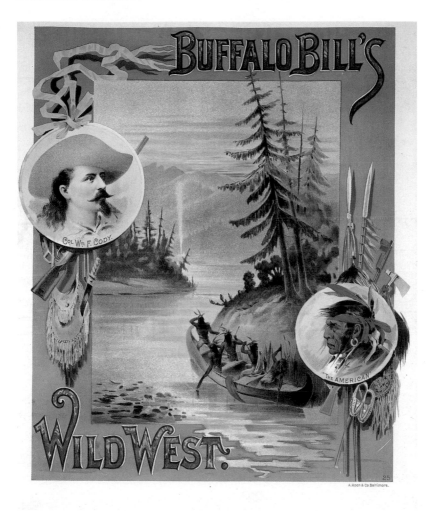

An 1890s poster for Buffalo Bill's Wild West show.

board **Buffalo Bill Boyhood Home,** in which Cody lived as a child in LeClaire, Iowa, was built in 1841 and moved to Cody in 1933. In 1922–1923 Gertrude Vanderbilt Whitney sculpted her **Buffalo Bill Statue;** she worked in New York, and for models she brought a cowboy and Cody's horse all the way from Wyoming by train. The bronze statue depicts Cody as a mounted army scout with a Winchester rifle held aloft; it rests on a granite representation of Cedar Mountain, which is visible in the distance behind.

The studio of the famed Western artist Frederic Remington at the Buffalo Bill Historical Center in Cody.

The **Buffalo Bill Museum** contains 5,000 items in its biographical and Western collections, including Cody's Congressional Medal of Honor earned in 1872 for Indian fighting, gifts of jewelry from Grand Duke Alexis of Russia and Queen Victoria, a stagecoach used in the Wild West Show, billboard-size lithographs that made Cody's face one of the most recognized in the world, two stuffed buffalos, saddles, Annie Oakley's firearms and gloves, and James Butler "Wild Bill" Hickok's handgun. In the vast collections of the **Plains Indian Museum** are Ghost Dance materials, such as buckskin dresses adorned with images of birds and stars, used during an Indian religious movement in the late 1880s; spectacular necklaces made from the claws of the Plains grizzly bear, a huge species extinct by the 1850s; a rare buffalo-hide tepee; tepee furnishings such as backrests; family clothing; bows, arrows, and quivers; tobacco bags; and a large exhibit of beaded and quill-work moccasins. The collection concentrates on the Northern Plains Indians, but all twenty-seven Plains tribes are represented.

About 1,500 firearms are displayed at the **Winchester Arms Museum,** a study collection that shows the technology and aesthetics of firearms, with representatives from the entire history of projectile arms from crossbows to modern automatic weapons. The collection includes "hand cannon," matchlocks, flintlocks, and other early firearms. There is a complete collection of Winchester guns, including such predecessors as the Volcanic (the first practical lever-action firearm) and the Henry (an 1860s rifle popular with frontiersmen). Some are highly embellished and were made for presentation to presidents and other public figures. The collection numbers about 8,000, of which 1,500 guns are on display.

The **Whitney Gallery of Western Art** houses a collection of paintings and sculptures by artists that include George Catlin, Albert Bierstadt, Thomas Moran, Frederic Remington, and Charles M. Russell. About a dozen of the paintings came from the collection of Buffalo Bill. The gallery also exhibits reconstructions of Remington's and W. H. D. Koerner's original studies.

LOCATION: 720 Sheridan Avenue. HOURS: March and November: 10–3 Tuesday–Sunday; April: 8–5 Tuesday–Sunday; May and September: 8–8 Daily; June through August: 7–10 Daily; October: 8–5 Daily. FEE: Yes. TELEPHONE: 307–587–4771.

In 1902, after the railroad was built to Cody and a wagon road from Cody to Yellowstone was under construction, Buffalo Bill built his famous **Irma Hotel** (1192 Sheridan Avenue, 307–587–4221) to accommodate well-heeled big-game hunters, Yellowstone Park sightseers, and the affluent ranchers who came to town. He named the luxurious hostelry for one of his four children. Built of rock-faced stone and brick, the two-story edifice is adorned with a red-stone buffalo head above the corner entrance. Cody had the enormous carved cherrywood back bar imported from France, shipped by rail to Red Lodge, Montana, and brought by wagon to Cody. The lobby fireplace incorporates stones embedded with fossils; Remington and

In Old Trail Town, near Cody, an enormous pile of antlers, which are shed annually,
has been collected over many years.

Russell paintings once hung on the wall. The hotel, always a social
center, opened with a formal-dress party for businessmen and
Indians, politicians and cowboys, ranchers and artists. Retaining
much of its early-1900s look, the hotel still accommodates guests.
Housed in the Latter-day Saints church, the **Historic Cody Murals**
Information Center (1719 Wyoming Avenue, 307–587–3290/3659)
depicts the history of the Mormon church through murals by
Edward Grigware and includes exhibits on local history and the early
settlement of the Big Horn Basin.

   Old Trail Town (one mile west of Cody off Route 14/16/20) is
an assemblage of historic buildings, most of them unimproved
except for stabilization. They include a trapper's cabin, a trading
post, a stage station, and a saloon arranged along a sagebrush

"street." Some were brought from the old stage road between Fort Washakie and Red Lodge. Also on display are a Yellowstone stagecoach of the 1880s, a buckboard, freight wagons, and other vehicles. The grave of the mountain man John Johnson (called "Jeremiah" in the film about this character) was moved to the site in 1974.

Buffalo Bill Dam (five miles west of Cody off Route 14/16/20) was Wyoming's first major dam, started in 1905 but not finished until 1910 because of flooding, high winds, freezing weather, and its location between the granite walls of two mountains. The 328-foot-high dam was built to impound the Shoshone River and irrigate 94,000 acres. When constructed it was the highest concrete dam in the world—it is a National Historic Civil Engineering Landmark.

About thirty-two miles west of Cody stands the **Wapiti Ranger Station** (one-half mile north of Route 14/16/20), the nation's oldest ranger station, erected in 1903 for the Shoshone Division of the Yellowstone Timberland Reserve. *Wapiti* is an Indian term for elk.

POWELL

Just after the turn of the century, the Department of the Interior laid out Camp Colter as headquarters for the Shoshone Reclamation Project. It was later renamed for John Wesley Powell, who was known as the "father of reclamation," and became the center of a successful farm district after about 1910. The **Homesteaders Museum** (1st and Clark streets, 307–754–9481) displays memorabilia, horse-drawn machinery, cookware, washtubs, and other items used by early Powell homesteaders.

The **ML Ranch** (fourteen miles east of Lovell, off Route 14-A, 307–548–2251) was started in 1879 by Henry Lovell. He had carried mail on wagon trains, a dangerous occupation in which he was shot three times. His ML Ranch (owned in partnership with Anthony Mason of Kansas City) ran 20,000 beef cattle, one of the biggest outfits in the region. After the cattle operation dissolved, a post office was established here from 1894 to 1908. The headquarters of the old ranch is represented by a few well-weathered log cabins, including the tack room and stables.

Indians have said that the mysterious **Medicine Wheel** (thirty-five miles east of Lovell, off Route 14-A) was built "before the light came"—so long ago that no tales about it survive. Located on the highest spot on the western peak of Medicine Mountain, this circle of limestone rocks measures seventy-five feet across, with a rock hub (perhaps symbolizing the sun) from which radiate twenty-eight spokes (possibly indicating the lunar month). The Crow named the six oblong stone cairns arrayed around the wheel "medicine tepees." Because no one knows the original purpose of the Medicine Wheel, theories abound: sun worshiping center; ceremonial site; astronomical calendar; and link to ancient Egyptians, Druids, Aztecs, and even the Masons. It probably had some religious significance, for many Indians visited the site—the area is laced with the timeworn trails of travois. White men first saw the Medicine Wheel in the 1880s. The state archaeological society has said that the stone circle was probably constructed around 1770 as a monument to a chief. All such theories remain unproved.

Eight miles west of the town of Emblem, the **Bridger Road Dry Creek Crossing** offers a place to see double-track ruts on a surviving stretch of the dirt road laid out in 1864 by Jim Bridger and members of his wagon train. The road led northwest from the Oregon Trail at Fort Caspar and across the Big Horn Basin on its way to the gold fields of Montana. Bridger, a mountain man whose grasp of geography was so complete and unerring that Bernard De Voto called him "an atlas of the West," developed the trail to avoid the Indian country east of the Big Horns, where white traffic along the Bozeman Trail violated agreements and provoked Indian hostilities.

Greybull stands in a vicinity of vast fossil beds, whose products are displayed at **The Greybull Museum** (325 Greybull Avenue, 307–765–2444), including one of the world's largest ammonites; rocks and minerals are also on exhibit. The town was founded in 1909 and named for a legendary albino buffalo that was sacred to the Indians. Greybull became a center of oil and bentonite development. To the south, on Medicine Lodge Creek, Indians once camped where the warm springs never froze in winter. Their legacy is the pictographs (paintings) and petroglyphs (carvings) on the sandstone of the **Medicine Lodge Creek Site** (five miles northeast of Hyattville). They depict men in buffalo headdresses and animals shot with arrows. Artifacts from 8000 B.C. to A.D. 300 indicate that this residence along the canyon floor offered early hunters all the required amenities: water, fish and game, and shelter under the rock ledge.

WORLAND

A genial man named C. H. "Dad" Worland set up camp along the Bridger Trail to the Montana gold country in about 1900, building a post office and stage station; the settlement that grew here was called Camp Worland. In his account of the town, D. Ray Wilson wrote: "Worland was originally on the west side of the Big Horn River. The Burlington railroad came down the east side of the river, much to the dismay of Worland residents. During the winter, when the river was frozen over, the settlers packed up and moved across the river to the railroad." The self-proclaimed "Town That Skated on the Ice" became a farm center, with the state's oldest sugar mill. The **Washakie County Museum and Cultural Center** (1115 Obie Sue Avenue, 307–347–4102) displays the bones of mammoths and has changing exhibitions that often include pioneer artifacts and local archaeological relics. The **Worland House** (520 Culbertson Avenue, private) is a bungalow-style house built in 1917. It belonged to Charlie Worland (Dad's son) and his wife, Sadie.

TEN SLEEP

According to Indian time, this spot lay "ten sleeps," or a ten-day journey, from three important places—Fort Laramie, Yellowstone, and the Stillwater Indian Agency in Montana. The town grew from one cabin erected in 1882. According to Mae Urbanek, a local historian, a teetotaler ran the post office and sold candy: "A salesman sold her some Rock N' Rye cough syrup; all the cowboys in the vicinity soon developed bad coughs." During the struggle between cattle and sheep ranchers from 1897 to 1909, the Ten Sleep area was the site of a notorious raid when masked night riders swooped down on a sheep camp on Spring Creek. Although it was customary practice during this feud for cowmen to club, dynamite, shoot, or "rimrock" sheep by running them off cliffs, this night in 1909 they killed two sheep owners and a herder, then set fire to a wagon to incinerate the bodies.The **Sheepmen Burial Site** (seven-and-a-half miles south of Ten Sleep on Route 434, follow the signs to Spring Creek) is the location of a marker and the graves from the raid. With sponsorship from the National Wool Growers Association, the prosecution of the case led to jail sentences, and one remorseful witness committed suicide. After these somber events, compromise took the place of violence between the factions. The **Ten Sleep Museum** (Vista Park on 2d Street, 307–366–2265) displays local artifacts, fossils, rocks, pioneer clothing, and farm and household equipment. **Ten Sleep Hardware** (2d and Pine streets, 307–366–2324) is one of the town's original business buildings from the early 1900s.

BUFFALO

Although some say this town's Main Street occupies an old buffalo trail (or possibly a cow trail), the town is named for Buffalo, New York—not because of any real connection, but because five settlers dropped names into a hat and the winner was submitted by an immigrant from Buffalo. The town was established in 1879 by cattle ranchers and farmers; the former sought to graze their herds on the open range, the latter to fence the land. Since rustlers also opposed the big ranchers, they became natural allies of the farmers and small cattle ranchers, who were suspected of rustling or of picking up strays. Suspicions repeatedly flared into violence. In 1892 a group of big ranchers decided to settle accounts by organizing an armed invasion of Johnson County and Buffalo. With about twenty mercenaries, they set off from Cheyenne aboard a train full of supplies and ammunition. In Casper they loaded wagons and continued north, stopping fifty miles south of Buffalo at the KC Ranch. At a cabin here, they pumped twenty-eight bullets into one "rustler" and shot another, pinning a card reading "Cattle Thieves, Beware" to one of the corpses. The men of Buffalo organized a posse and intercepted the invaders at the **TA Ranch** (fourteen miles south of Buffalo off Route I-25). After a two-day skirmish, federal troops from Fort McKinney arrived to capture the invaders. All charges against them were dismissed, however, even after one gunman confessed that they had a hit list of men in Johnson County and had been promised $50 per "rustler" killed. The "Johnson County War" is portrayed in a diorama at the **Jim Gatchell Memorial Museum** (10 Fort Street, 307–684–9331), along with scenes of the Wagon Box Fight and of the town's main street as it was in 1882. Jim Gatchell had lived among Indians, learned their languages, and collected their artifacts; among 5,000 items on display are a chuck wagon and other vehicles, coins, military items, and rocks.

At 10 North Main Street stands the **Occidental Hotel** (closed), where the hero overcame the desperado Trampas in Owen Wister's *The Virginian*. **Fort McKinney** (two miles west of Buffalo off Route 16,

The Fetterman Battle Site monument commemorates the deaths of eighty-one soldiers from Fort Phil Kearny, killed in battle by Sioux and Cheyenne warriors led by chiefs Red Cloud and Crazy Horse. Fetterman had previously claimed that he could defeat all the Indians on the Plains with eighty men.

307–684–5511), now the Veterans Home of Wyoming, still has a few buildings from the time when the fort was an active military post, established at this site in 1878. Its soldiers were involved in Indian fighting and the capture of the mercenaries during the "Johnson County War" of 1892.

The **Fetterman Battle Site** (about four miles northeast of Story off Route I-90) has a stone monument to mark where eighty-one men from Fort Phil Kearny died in 1866 when their leader, Captain William J. Fetterman, disobeyed strict orders to "not engage or pursue Indians at any expense" and thereby fell for one of the oldest Indian strategies. Sent to rescue a woodcutting detail under attack, he chased a small party of Indian decoys into an ambush, where an army of warriors waited. Fetterman's command was annihilated. Crazy Horse, who was then a young warrior, led the Sioux decoys; Red Cloud reigned as war chief. That night John "Portugee" Phillips left Fort Phil Kearny on the most famous ride in Wyoming history—four days and nights across the frozen landscape to Fort Laramie to obtain reinforcements. Arriving at the fort after the 236-mile ride, Phillips, numb from the cold, broke in upon a Christmas party and told his tale. The **Wagon Box Fight Site** (about one mile south of Story) is where the situation was reversed the next year when the same Indian leaders attacked soldiers guarding Fort Phil Kearny's woodcutting detail. Captain J. N. Powell took fourteen wagon boxes off their wheels and arranged them in a makeshift oval "fort." With 32 men armed with breech-loading rifles that let the soldiers fire more shots without reloading, he fought off perhaps 1,500 Indians. The new weapons thwarted the Indians' usual tactic of drawing fire and then rushing the soldiers while they reloaded. A few warriors charged within five feet of the corralled wagons, but after facing steady gunfire for perhaps four hours the Indians departed, leaving behind either six dead (Indians' estimate) or sixty dead (Powell's estimate in the official report). A monument in a meadow marks the battle site.

The **Fort Phil Kearny Site** lies between Sheridan and Buffalo, two miles off Route I-90. Founded in 1866 on Little Piney Creek, the fort was one of three posts established by Colonel Henry Carrington along the Bozeman Trail. Gold had been discovered in Montana, and hopeful miners poured across the Wyoming hunting grounds guaranteed to the Indians. After the Sioux killed a number of civilian travelers on the road, the forts were built. "Fort Phil" had a heavy pine stockade with two blockhouses at opposite corners, fortifications that were kept under constant attack by Red Cloud and the Sioux. In 1868, after the Fetterman Battle and the Wagon Box Fight, the fort was abandoned by treaty. While the departing soldiers were still within sight, the Sioux burned Fort Phil Kearny to the ground. The **Fort Phil Kearny Museum** (307–684–7629) provides exhibits and information.

BIG HORN

Wyoming's largest collection of original false-front buildings is located in the **Downtown Big Horn National Historic District.** About two miles southwest of Big Horn, the **Bradford Brinton Memorial Museum and Ranch** (307–672–3173) offers the best of the West: a setting among trees along Little Goose Creek, below the Big Horn Mountains, and a ranch house filled with collections of Western painting and sculpture (Frederic Remington, Charles M. Russell, Ed Borein, Frank Tenney Johnson), Indian artifacts, antiques, and books (including rarities by Samuel Johnson and Robert Louis Stevenson). The Quarter Circle A Ranch was founded by a Scotsman, William Moncreiffe, who built his house in 1893. In 1923 an Illinois businessman and sportsman named Bradford Brinton bought the spread, expanding the house to twenty rooms and installing his collections. The ranch reflects the life of a wealthy rancher in this century. There are a number of well-preserved frame and log buildings at the ranch headquarters.

SHERIDAN

The Sheridan Valley remained an area set aside for the Indians until 1877, when it was opened for settlement by whites. A year later Jim Mason, a trapper, heralded the future city of Sheridan by building a one-room cabin on the site. Within a few years the structure had evolved into a post office and store, where J. D. Loucks laid out a plat map for Sheridan on a sheet of brown wrapping paper. Upon the town's incorporation in 1883, Loucks became mayor of what turned out to be a peaceful settlement; in the first two years there was only one arrest. This case was decided by a judge who lived across Goose Creek. High water prevented the constable and prisoner from crossing the creek, so after the prisoner pleaded guilty, "the

The 1892 Sheridan Inn was conceived by the General Manager of the Chicago, Burlington & Quincy Railroad, George Holdredge, who realized that the completion of the rail line to Sheridan presented a business opportunity.

The Trail End Historic Center, housed in a Flemish-style mansion of 1913.

justice shouted back above the roar of the stream the first legal decision in the Sheridan Municipal Court," a $5 fine. There were two
newspapers in town by 1887, both good-humored and reflecting the
cow-town character of Sheridan. And it was in Sheridan, Martha
Cannary Burk claimed in her outlandishly inaccurate autobiography,
that she got the nickname "Calamity Jane"—supposedly bestowed by
an army captain whose life she saved during battle.

The arrival of the Chicago, Burlington & Quincy Railroad in
1892 led to the building the next year of the **Sheridan Inn**
(Broadway and 5th Street, 307–672–5825), a gambrel-roofed hotel
with so many dormers that it has been called the "House of 69
Gables." It is said that Thomas Kimball, its architect, modeled his
design on a Scottish country inn. The hotel greeted such diverse
guests as the artist Charles M. Russell, Calamity Jane, President
Theodore Roosevelt, Will Rogers, and the novelist Mary Roberts
Rinehart. But its most famous habitué, and its owner from 1894 to
1896, was Buffalo Bill Cody. Then at the height of his success as a
showman, he would be seen sitting on the inn's porch meeting with
cowboy and Indian candidates for his Wild West Show. In 1964 the
inn was saved from demolition and subsequently renovated.

A story of personal drive and ability lies behind the **Trail End Historic Center** (400 Clarendon Avenue, 307–674–4589). John B. Kendrick drove a herd of cattle from Texas to Wyoming in 1879, then educated himself at night while the other cowboys drank and gambled. While working as a ranch foreman, he built up his own herd and married his employer's daughter. His own spread grew to 200,000 acres, and after becoming a millionaire, he entered politics. He became governor in 1915 and later a three-term U.S. senator who asked the Senate to investigate the Teapot Dome controversy. His house offers concentrated evidence of the riches to be earned in cattle country. The brick mansion, built in the Flemish style with curvilinear window gables, was completed in 1913 after five years of construction. Golden oak and mahogany paneling shipped by rail filled thirty-six boxcars. The eighteen-room house boasted stained glass, an elevator, a central vacuuming system, eight bathrooms, a third-floor ballroom, and an English Gothic library. Heating the house in winter required up to a ton of coal per day. The house is now operated as a museum, with furnishings typical of the turn of the century.

RANCHESTER

What is now Ranchester City Park (off Route 14 West) was in 1865 the **Connor Battlefield,** site of a major engagement of the Powder River expedition. This campaign was an attempt by Brigadier General Patrick Connor to secure the Bozeman Trail and, in Connor's words, "to kill all male Indians over the age of 12" in retaliation for defeats inflicted on the U.S. Army. He and Colonel J. J. Kidd led their troops in the Battle of Tongue River, a surprise raid against the Arapaho village of Black Bear and Old David. Connor claimed thirty-five warriors slain, all 200 lodges destroyed, and 500 horses captured, with only eight soldiers lost. But the Powder River expedition was hampered by inefficient guides, by the difficulty of coordinating the columns in strange country, and by a late-summer snowfall. Connor was recalled, and the federal government turned to negotiation by 1866.

GILLETTE

Any settlement called Donkey Town would soon change its name—although not necessarily to Rocky Pile, as this one did. Finally, upon the arrival of the Chicago, Burlington & Quincy Railroad in 1891, the town was renamed again for railway surveyor

Weston Gillette. It became a center for shipping livestock; at times the yards contained more than 50,000 sheep and cattle. In 1911 a pilot brought an airplane to Gillette by train, reassembled it, and made Wyoming's first airplane flight. The oil and coal fields near Gillette have boosted the town's growth. At the **Campbell County Rockpile Museum** (1000 West 2d Street, 307–682–5723) are Indian artifacts, a mammoth's tooth, guns, cowboy gear, a sheep wagon, homestead relics, farm machinery, and a newspaper print shop.

DEVILS TOWER NATIONAL MONUMENT

At this site the core of an ancient volcano thrusts up 1,267 feet above the Belle Fourche River, exerting a power that causes many to fall silent before it. The formation has also spawned many legends among the Indians. They called it *Mateo Tipi*, or bear lodge, and told the story of seven maidens fleeing a bear. To rescue them, the rock rose higher and higher, while the bear's claws scored the sides of the tower with fluting that is still visible. Another explanation is that the formation was created when a flow of magma 60 million years ago pushed up into a layer of sedimentary rock, where it cooled and shrank, separating into columns, or flutes; millions of years of erosion exposed the volcanic mass of igneous rock that forms today's tower. In 1875 Colonel Richard Dodge named the formation, adapting the Indian term, Bad God's Tower. On July 4, 1893, two local men made the first climb to the top; today more than 1,000 climbers reach the summit annually, using more than eighty different routes. In 1906 President Theodore Roosevelt declared Devils Tower the nation's first national monument. A museum contains exhibits on the area's history, geology, and animals.

LOCATION: 6 miles north of the town of Devils Tower off Route 24. HOURS: Always open. FEE: Yes. TELEPHONE: 307–467–5370.

NEWCASTLE

A railroad town founded in 1889, Newcastle is the "Western Gateway to the Black Hills." Local history is presented at the **Anna Miller Museum** (401 Delaware Avenue, 307–746–4188), housed in a former cavalry barn of the army's National Guard, built in the 1930s of native sandstone. The complex includes the Green Mountain School of 1888, horse-drawn wagons, a hand-pulled fire truck, fossils (including bones of the *Tyrannosaurus rex*), Indian artifacts, and coal

The spectacular Devils Tower, the core of a long-dead volcano.

miners' lamps and equipment from the old mining town of Cambria. Also on the premises is the **Jenney Stockade,** built in 1875 as a supply center for a Black Hills expedition to assess the worth and size of gold deposits in the area. The party of geologists and miners was led by Professor Walter P. Jenney and accompanied by a sizable army detail from Fort Laramie. Although Jenney found gold, he reported that "the richness of the gravel has been greatly exaggerated." Nonetheless, goldseekers flooded in and were soon using the post as a stopover. By 1877 the stockade had become a stagecoach stop on the Cheyenne–Deadwood run. Part of the old structure was moved to Newcastle in 1928. The original site was near Route 16, four miles east of where it crosses Route 85.

The **Flying V Cambria Inn** (eight miles north of Newcastle on Route 85, 307–746–2096) offers the surprise of a Tudor estate in Wyoming. Constructed with sandstone and immense beams (some of them old mine timbers), it was built as a memorial and recreation site for workers in the anthracite coal industry. The mines were in Cambria, a now extinct town two miles distant. The complex, built in 1928, includes a former museum, with stained-glass windows depicting mining scenes; a stable; and a stone bathhouse.

SOUTHERN IDAHO

OPPOSITE: *McGown Peak in the Sawtooth Range, part of the Sawtooth National Recreation Area.*

During most of its history, Idaho has been remote, sequestered, insular. Although Indians have lived here for perhaps 15,000 years, by 1800 not a single outsider had set foot in Idaho. It was the last of the fifty states to be visited by white men. Idaho lay too far from the theaters of exploration where Spain, France, and England acted out their dramas in the New World. Lewis and Clark, the first white explorers to arrive, looked back on their entire round trip from the Great Plains to the Pacific Ocean in 1805–1806 and declared that the worst obstacles had been Idaho's mountains. The Bitterroot Range rises to almost 10,000 feet along the eastern border, while the center of Idaho contains a wilderness of ridges and pinnacles, from the Sawtooth Range to the Clearwater Mountains, where even today hardly a Jeep road penetrates. Yet these forbidding mountains lured many trappers and prospectors, men whose quests into the wilderness opened the way for settlement.

Emigrants on the Oregon Trail traveled roughly parallel to the Snake River, which crosses the entire state, making a thousand-mile arc from Wyoming to Oregon and Washington. The mountains establish natural barriers that divide Idaho into regions, as do social orientations developed during the past century and more. In this "house divided," the northern Panhandle considers Spokane, Washington the commercial and cultural hub; the Mormon farms and towns of the southeast look toward Salt Lake City; and the southwest generally focuses on the capital city of Boise, although its desert wastes seem linked to neighboring Nevada. Idaho's borders, which touch on six other states and British Columbia, seem to pull the state apart rather than hold it together. Only the spirit and pride of its people have assembled an identity for this oddly shaped piece of a jigsaw puzzle.

Before outsiders arrived in Idaho, their influence had ridden on ahead. The horse, which was brought to New Mexico by the Spaniards, reached the distant tribes of Idaho early in the eighteenth century. In southern Idaho the Shoshoni were the first to mount up; soon horses spread to the associated Bannock, and then to the more northerly Nez Percé, Coeur d'Alene, Pend d'Oreille, and Kutenai. With mounts, Indian life changed forever.

The eastern Shoshoni and the northern groups became roving hunters and followed the buffalo onto the plains. Here they made contact with Plains Indians and began to adopt a new culture. The

The Great Seal of the State of Idaho, painted in 1893 by Emma Edwards Green, includes figures of a miner and Justice, and horns of plenty. It was the first state seal created by a woman.

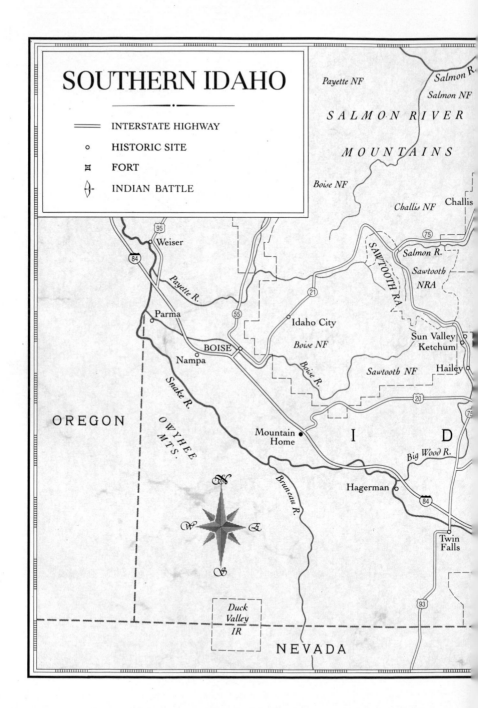

SOUTHERN IDAHO

═══ INTERSTATE HIGHWAY

○ HISTORIC SITE

⌷ FORT

☖ INDIAN BATTLE

Payette NF

Salmon R.

Salmon NF

SALMON RIVER

MOUNTAINS

Boise NF

Challis NF Challis

95 Weiser

84

Payette R.

Parma

55

BOISE

Nampa

Snake R.

O W Y H E E

M T S.

OREGON

75

SAWTOOTH RA.

Salmon R.

Sawtooth NRA

21

Idaho City

Boise NF

Boise R.

Sun Valley
Ketchum

Sawtooth NF Hailey

20

Mountain
Home

I

D

Big Wood R.

Bruneau R.

Hagerman

84

Twin
Falls

*Duck
Valley
IR*

93

NEVADA

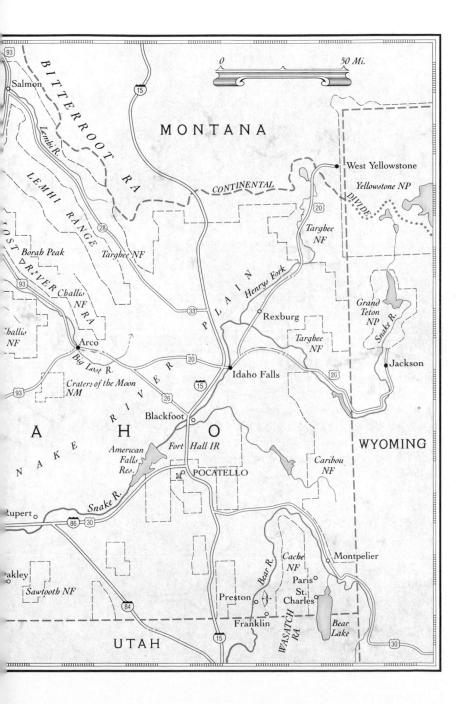

eminently portable teepee, the feather headdress, the "jerking" of meat to preserve it, the ceremonial dance—all were imported into Idaho with the returning hunters. Perhaps more important, Idaho tribes adopted the Plains model of organizing themselves into bands for hunting and defense. These were led by chieftains all roughly equal in power, for the tribes never accepted the authority of one "big Indian chief," an idea introduced by white men.

In many ways this period at the end of the eighteenth century was a golden age for Idaho's native peoples, with more food and convenience than they had ever enjoyed. But trouble from the white man arrived even before he did: When Blackfoot Indians began raiding and stealing horses from Shoshoni and Nez Percé villages, they had an advantage obtained from British fur traders in Canada—guns. Idaho's first direct contact between Indian and white was peaceful, however. Lewis and Clark's 1805–1806 expedition met a friendly reception from the Shoshoni and Nez Percé in northern Idaho. After their epic journey, the two explorers spent eight years preparing their journals for publication. With less regard for literary perfection, a member of their party named Sergeant Patrick Gass had a book in print within a year. His diary pages fired the American imagination. Among the readers set aflame was John Jacob Astor, who sent out trapping parties in hopes of monopolizing the Northwest fur industry. Although the effort failed, it did result in important explorations of southern Idaho. In October 1811 a party of Astorians under Wilson Hunt loaded fifteen dugout canoes with five tons of supplies, traps, and trade goods and set off down the Snake River, singing heartily in the face of winter. Below American Falls they passed miraculously through a maelstrom, only to reach a gorge that grew ever narrower and deeper as they proceeded. Near Twin Falls the canoe carrying most of the provisions flipped over, drowning one man. At this point the party scouted from the canyon rim and saw that the rest of the Snake was impassable. They had to proceed to Oregon on foot.

In 1816 a former Astorian leader named Donald Mackenzie returned to Idaho. A man who loomed large in the fur trade—he weighed nearly 300 pounds—Mackenzie organized the annual Snake-country expeditions that opened the interior of Idaho. The Hudson's Bay Company took over Mackenzie's outfit in 1821, only to face a new challenge three years later when its fur fiefdom was invaded by Jedediah Strong Smith and other mountain men from Missouri. Only 25 years old, Smith was probably the youngest captain in fur-trade history and a tough competitor. The "Knight in Buckskin" already had survived such frontier hazards as finding his head inside the mouth of an enraged grizzly bear. The British company decided on a strategy of trapping out the Snake country to create a "fur desert," an unprofitably barren zone that would hold the Americans back. In 1832 the annual rendezvous came to Pierre's Hole—today's Teton Valley—with 200 lodges of Indians and 200 mountain men in an alcohol-drenched holiday of celebration and trading. Washington Irving wrote of "the motley populace connected with the fur trade . . . traders, trappers, hunters, and half-breeds, assembled from all quarters, awaiting their yearly supplies, and their orders to start off in new directions." Two years later Nathaniel Wyeth, a businessman from Boston, built the first permanent American outpost beyond the Continental Divide. Called Fort Hall, it stood at the junction of the Snake and the Portneuf rivers and goaded the competitive Hudson's Bay Company to erect Fort Boise in the western region.

The decline in the beaver population because of trapping was followed by a decline in the trapper population. But then came the missionaries. In 1834 one of Wyeth's party at Fort Hall conducted Idaho's first religious service; after the sermon there was a horse race. When a French-Canadian trapper was killed during the contest, he received three funerals—Catholic, Protestant, and Indian. (As Wyeth commented, he was "well buried.") The emblematic event signaled the start of a prolonged competition among proselytizers in Idaho. The missionaries engaged in rivalries that would only confuse and discourage the Indians. And the goodwill and brotherhood preached in church stood in ironic contrast to the white man's general behavior—drinking, gambling, fighting, subjection of the Indians by rough-handed soldiers, and broken treaties.

Emigrants followed the missionaries. Much of the route across southern Idaho that was blazed by Hunt and later by Wyeth became known as the Oregon Trail. With Kit Carson as guide, John C. Frémont mapped the Oregon Trail in 1843, and his published account assured would-be pioneers that wagons could negotiate the rough terrain. Soon clouds of dust and the cries of bawling cattle filled the air as emigrants in white-topped wagons passed the sites of today's Montpelier and Soda Springs, arriving at last at Fort Hall,

OVERLEAF: *The lazy loops of the East Fork of the Owyhee River flow between lofty walls of volcanic rock.*

where they rested; but the summer dryness of southern Idaho did not tempt the pioneers to linger. Along the way some would branch off and turn south on the California Trail, as half of the pioneering Bidwell-Bartleson party did first in 1840. The rest went on to the haven of Old Fort Boise, no doubt cursing the Snake River, which had cut deep, rocky canyons they sometimes had to clamber down into to obtain fresh water. Idaho, a traveler named Albert Richardson once remarked, was the "barest and most desolate of all our Territories, with vast wastes of lava, sand, and sagebrush."

The emigrants' passage did have an important effect: As thousands settled in Oregon, a boundary agreement was reached between Great Britain and the United States in 1846, making Idaho U.S. territory. But, except for a few remaining trappers and missionaries, Idaho at this point still belonged to the Indians. Then, in 1860, two groups arrived who effected fundamental change: Mormons and prospectors. A Mormon party moved north from Utah to establish Franklin, Idaho's first town—although the colonists did not realize they had crossed the border and thought they were still in Utah. Within a few years, other farming communities became extensions of the Mormon domain. But it was gold, not gospel, that settled Idaho and also ended traditional Indian life there. After gold strikes in the north, a Bannock had advised that if the prospectors wanted yellow metal, they should try Boise Basin. A week after the first strike there in 1862, the leader of one party met with an ambush and his friends hurriedly buried him in a prospect hole. Mere violence did not stop thousands more miners from working the basin, which produced more than $24 million in gold in four years and led to the development of Boise as a supply center.

The expanding gold rush caused a shift of population and influence in the Washington Territory, of which Idaho was then still a part. Politicians in Olympia grew fearful of losing power to the Idaho mining region, and so in 1863 they pushed to have it separated as Idaho Territory. The territorial boundaries also included Montana and most of Wyoming—a total area bigger than Texas. This configuration proved to be somewhat unwieldy, however, when Montana legislators making the 300-mile trip home from Lewiston in February 1864 were blocked by winter snows and had to make a detour through Portland, San Francisco, and Salt Lake City—about 2,000 miles out of their way.

Congress soon separated the northeastern region as Montana Territory, and when Wyoming was established four years later,

Albert Bierstadt depicts the Great Migration in his dramatic painting The Oregon
Trail *(detail).*

Idaho's boundaries were fixed. But the lines were quite illogical. The
division between northern Idaho and Washington had been drawn
through a naturally cohesive region that should never have been
split. Northern and southern Idaho, though divided by mountains
and with few common interests, were yoked together. Northern citizens tried unsuccessfully for two decades to somehow separate themselves from the south.

Boise Basin took the lead in population and mining production,
thanks largely to a boom at Idaho City. By 1864 that town had 6,000
residents and hundreds of buildings, supplanting Portland as the
Northwest's biggest metropolis—if not its most respectable. One citizen griped that "the priest and the saloon-keeper jostle each other
on the sidewalks, and the gentleman's wife must walk around the
trail of the courtesan who lives next door." Nearby Bogus Basin got
its name because some of the more crooked residents were in the
habit of mixing their gold dust with brass filings before selling it.

Boise developed into an agricultural and supply center for the
mining towns, and its assay office was said to have handled more
than $75 million worth of gold and silver bullion. South of Boise, in
the Owyhee Mountains, miners uncovered such lodes as the
Poorman, which produced more than $500,000 worth of ore in just

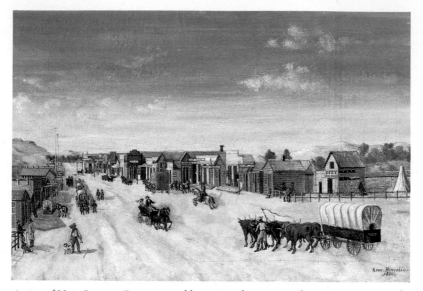

A view of Main Street in Boise, painted by A. Hincelin in 1864. The City Brewery at right was one of the prominent landmarks of the time.

six frenzied days. Ruby City, whose streets "looked like they were laid out by a blind cow," faded away when all its buildings were moved to Silver City, a mile closer to the precious mines. In the boomtowns populations ebbed and flowed. As historian H. H. Bancroft noted: "The miners of Idaho were like quicksilver. A mass of them dropped in any locality, broke up into individual globules, and ran off after any atom of gold in the vicinity. They stayed nowhere longer than the gold attracted them." Some mining areas were played out by 1870, at which time more than half of Idaho's miners were Chinese, who patiently worked over placer claims abandoned by the whites. Racial prejudice was rampant, with Chinese miners and prostitutes paying special taxes of $4 a month just to live in the territory. Racial violence cost the lives of more than a hundred Chinese.

On a lighter note, the territorial government of Idaho provided a diverting spectacle for the rest of the nation. The comedy started when Congress established the territory in 1863 but failed to provide any funds. As a backwater, Idaho did not attract the highest caliber of office seeker, and of sixteen territorial governors appointed, only eight spent a year or more in the job; some never even bothered to show up. Caleb Lyon was a flamboyant egotist who spent more time lecturing on his world travels than governing. He and the legislature removed the capital from Lewiston to Boise, which caused a Lewiston judge to declare the legislature illegal. Lyon left town on the pretense of going duck hunting. The next governor stole the territorial seal and archives and hied off to Boise. Another sterling leader, Horace Gilson, was characterized as "a small gambling bar tender" of "dubious Moral antecedents." He promptly took the entire territorial treasury of more than $40,000 and absconded to Hong Kong and Paris. Even if he had been indicted, Idaho's criminal laws remained somewhat mysterious, because no one had paid the printing bill on the law books, and they were being held in San Francisco. In addition, Idaho's legislature was dominated by Confederate Democrats, but its federally appointed governors were Republicans. One wry observer commented on the territory's affliction as a "quadrennial shower of Egyptian frogs."

The government may have had its internal conflicts, but another more serious and tragic confrontation also developed in Idaho—a battle between red and white. Under steady pressure after 1855, most of Idaho's Indians "agreed" to move onto reservations, such as Fort Hall for the Shoshoni. From an Indian perspective, whites seemed to be everywhere, and this incursion led to the 1863 Battle of Bear River, in which Colonel Connor's California volunteers massacred 400 Shoshoni warriors, women, and children. Settlers were even grazing hogs on the camas prairie, where Native Americans traditionally dug lily bulbs for food. Unhappy about this situation and about conditions on the Fort Hall Reservation, in 1878 the Bannock went on the warpath, cutting a swath of terror across southwestern Idaho. Their leader, Buffalo Horn, led his braves toward Oregon, hoping to find allies, but a battle at South Mountain with militiamen from Silver City ended the thrust. Buffalo Horn was wounded and was a casualty of the battle. After 1879 the "Indian problem" had been solved. The territory was now open for rapid expansion.

The first railroad, the Utah & Northern, arrived in 1874 and spurred Mormon settlement in southeastern Idaho. In 1882 the Oregon Short Line completed tracks that ran 500 miles from Wyoming to Oregon, roughly along the Oregon Trail. A transportation revolution was occurring: The trip from Omaha to Portland now took just five days, a journey that had taken Lewis and Clark a year and a half. But the railroads' major contribution was to the advancement of mining—hauling in heavy equipment, shipping ore to smelters, and developing the state's hard-rock lodes. Ketchum and Hailey boomed in the Wood River area, and that region became the most progressive in Idaho, with the state's first telephone system and electric light plants. In the 1880s new towns, such as Pocatello, American Falls, Mountain Home, and Caldwell, sprang up along the tracks. By 1883 Charles Walgamott had developed a tourist trade among train passengers at Shoshone Falls, a natural attraction whose cascade drops a greater distance than Niagara's. Walgamott's hostelry was not a five-star operation. Although he played host to forty travelers at a time, he had only enough bedding for a dozen, so in a pinch he rented hammocks. "The tourists did not take kindly to these hammocks at a dollar a night," he wrote, "but my partner was a good storyteller, and every night before bedtime he would tell stories of rattlesnakes crawling into people's beds. A few stories usually created a demand for hammocks."

In Boise new buildings rose, French Second Empire mansions, Romanesque Revival banks, and a Moorish Revival natatorium. Meanwhile, the Mormons came to southeast Idaho in search of more room, and established their largest center outside the Great Basin. Rexburg and many more of their settlements dotted the upper Snake River valley. It was rail service and the influx of Mormons that led to the development of irrigated farmland, and irrigation changed the face of southern Idaho from tracts of scrubby desert to fertile fields. Mormon canals in the upper valley of the Snake were so efficiently constructed that at Rexburg water flowed in the town canal the same day digging started in 1883. But the group's presence led to a strong anti-Mormon political backlash, primarily due to the Latter-day Saints' plural marriages and their tendency to vote as a bloc. In 1882 a series of political maneuverings disqualified the Mormons from voting or holding office. During Idaho's statehood movement, anti-Mormon provisions were incorporated into the constitution.

Idaho now had a large enough population to qualify for statehood, and the process of admission presented the only case in U.S. history of a long-established territory faced with the choice of being abolished. In a move to grab southern Idaho's resources, Nevada had been suggesting annexation. Northern Idaho would probably have separated by itself or joined Washington. For Idaho to become a state, though, both halves had to stay together. To placate the northern region, the statehood convention picked Moscow for a university site, and so without much wrangling Idaho became the nation's forty-third state in 1890.

Disputes among ranchers marred the following decade. Cattle ranchers who had brought vast herds to Idaho as early as the 1860s now came into conflict with sheep raisers. Merle Wells, a local historian, records that "a notorious fracas—generally interpreted as an incident in a sheep and cattle war—led to the trial, conviction, and pardon of a cattleman, 'Diamondfield' Jack Davis, who was charged with getting rid of some sheepherders simply by shooting them."

But Idaho's affairs were generally peaceful after 1900, with major reclamation projects creating a vast farming industry that boosted the state's famous potatoes. In the Boise valley, problems with a major canal system helped prompt the 1894 Carey Act, allying state governments with private enterprise to develop the vast reclamation projects in dry western lands. After the Reclamation Act of 1902, farm expansion took place even more rapidly. New settlements sprang up over the irrigated regions. Twin Falls was founded in 1904, and within four years all of Idaho's major urban centers were on the map. The commercial timber industry surpassed mining in Idaho's economy—although by 1906 a conservation movement succeeded in placing great tracts of timberland under U.S. Forest Service management. Potlatch Forests and Boise Cascade became Idaho's leading forest products companies. And during this period a young logger named Jim Stevens collected tall tales for his book that would introduce a new figure to American folklore—Paul Bunyan.

Engineering projects also came to the fore in the twentieth century. Arrowrock Dam was the nation's highest when it was built in 1915 to serve the Boise reclamation district. In 1926 a student in Rigby named Philo Farnsworth was developing a working model of a television set. By 1938 one of the state's lingering problems had been eased by the construction of a paved highway that linked the southern region with the isolated north. But even today roads cannot penetrate the mountains of central Idaho. To travel from Idaho Falls to Coeur d'Alene requires skirting the wilderness and driving some of the way on a slight detour—through Montana.

This chapter commences in southeastern Idaho with Saint Charles and proceeds in an arching route north to Rexburg; then it restarts in the southeast at Franklin and heads west to Murphy, next to Boise, moving west to Nampa and Parma, and finally looping east and south through Idaho City, Ketchum, and Hailey.

SAINT CHARLES

Founded by Mormons as a center for commercial gardening in 1864, Saint Charles was the birthplace three years later of artist Gutzon Borglum, best known for sculpting Mount Rushmore. It is thought that the log hut where he spent his first year was incorporated in the later **Wilhelmina Nelson House and Cabins** (Route 89, private), a typical homestead of southeastern Idaho between 1870 and 1899.

PARIS

After the Mormons' success in settling Franklin, Brigham Young asked other Utah pioneers to pull up their roots and colonize valleys in southeastern Idaho. The earliest settlement in the Bear Lake valley was Paris, founded in 1863 on land granted by a Shoshoni chief in exchange for a share of the Mormons' crops. (The settlers would soon break their bargain.) Paris was platted in 1864 by Frederick Perris, whom the town commemorates by misspelling his name.

The town's pride is the **Paris Idaho Stake Tabernacle** (Main Street, 208–945–2112), a masterpiece of communal construction. Emigrants hauled blocks of red sandstone almost twenty miles, some-

The Stake Tabernacle in Paris was completed in 1889 after four years of construction. (In Mormon terminology, a "stake" denoted a regional cluster of congregations.) The interior, above, could accommodate 1,500 worshippers. OPPOSITE: *The Romanesque Revival exterior of the tabernacle, which was designed by one of Brigham Young's sons, Joseph D. C. Young. The tower is eighty feet tall.*

times sledding them over the frozen lake; Swiss converts cut the stone; a shipbuilder carved elaborate wooden ceilings; Mormons from other settlements helped with the four-year construction process; Brigham Young's son served as architect. In 1889 the tabernacle was completed—a five-story bell tower, buttresses, seating for 1,500 people, a slanting floor so those in the rear could see the front—a jewel of eclectic architecture, primarily in Romanesque Revival style. The tabernacle has a visitors center and offers summer tours, during which it is explained that a Mormon stake is a collection of local congregations and that a stake tabernacle served as a community center for its region.

A collection of fine buildings survives from pioneer days. The first building in the valley, dating from 1863, is the tiny **Thomas Sleight Cabin** (South Main Street), which was partitioned to house two couples. Frame houses, whose lumber was sawed by an 1870s mill on Paris Creek, stand on South East Second. An ironic feature of the 1885 **Bear Lake County Courthouse** (Center and Main streets) is the widow's walk, used in the late 1880s by the polygamous Mormons as a watchtower for antipolygamy raids. **Adobe houses** on South First West are Paris's oldest brick buildings (now sheathed in siding). Town founder Charles Rich built them to replace the five log cabins where he housed his five wives. Fathering fifty-one children, Rich just about populated Paris all by himself.

MONTPELIER

Settled by Mormons in 1864 and named by Brigham Young for the capital of his home state of Vermont, Montpelier became a rail shipping center and stockyard town after 1882, attracting so many outsiders that tensions between "gentile" railroad employees and Mormons led to the building of a fence between their two parts of town. Montpelier's most exciting event occurred in 1896, when George L. Parker—also known as Butch Cassidy—robbed the bank.

The **Daughters of Utah Pioneers Relic Hall** (430 Clay Street, 208–847–1069) is housed in the Mormon church's 1895 tithing office. (One-tenth of a Mormon's labor and income was given as tithes to the church.) The sandstone building displays pioneer clothing and artifacts that include spinning wheels, candle molds, handmade matches, a pump organ, and household irons that were filled with hot coals; it also has many pioneer photographs. A noteworthy building is the Queen Anne–style **John Bagley House** (155 5th Street, private), built in 1890 by the state attorney general.

A bartender in Pocatello pours a beer with great concentration. His establishment promoted Pabst beer and the undoubtedly fragrant "Dramatic Bouquet" cigars.

POCATELLO

Pocatello, built on land purchased from the Shoshoni and Bannock tribes, was named for a Shoshoni chief, *Po-Ca-Ta-Ro*. It took shape in 1882 as a tent camp at a railway crossroads. The Mormon-built Utah & Northern had come up from Ogden on the way to Montana's mines, while the Oregon Short Line crossed Idaho from east to west. Because of its fortunate location, Pocatello became one of the biggest rail centers west of the Mississippi and is now the second-largest city in Idaho. The railroads brought many non-Mormon workers, including some of Idaho's first black Americans and Chinese, into a strongly Mormon region.

Rail passengers arrived at the **Oregon Short Line Depot** (end of West Bonneville Street), a three-story station built in 1915, and often crossed the street to stay at the **Yellowstone Hotel,** erected a year later of wine-colored bricks with terra-cotta trim. One owner of the hotel was Drew Standrod, a leading citizen and banker whose **Standrod House** (648 North Garfield Avenue, 208–234–6184) was built of rusticated stone in 1901 and is considered by some to be Idaho's best example of Victorian architecture. Its style is vaguely that of a chateau on the Loire, with Queen Anne elements, incorporating an elaborate front verandah and a round corner tower. It had central heating and the first electric plug in any house in Pocatello. The house has been restored by the city and is open to visitors.

On the campus of Idaho State University, the **Idaho Museum of Natural History** (5th and Dillon streets, 208–236–3168) displays Shoshoni-Bannock weapons, basketry, and beadwork, as well as prehistoric projectile points and basic tools used 14,000 years ago by unknown hunters on the Snake River plain. A special exhibit features animated robotic dinosaurs.

Bannock County Historical Museum

Not surprisingly for a museum in a railroad-junction city, the focus here is on train history: narrow-gauge and standard rails, lanterns, brass buttons, and even the primitive wooden sign from the "Paymaster Tree" that stood on Monida Pass; railway workers who could not come to town to pick up their monthly paychecks met the paymaster under its boughs. Other displays include a hand-carved wooden Indian that stood in front of a drugstore on Main Street; household items such as washing machines; and Shoshoni and Bannock baskets, beadwork, and moccasins. The museum occupies the 1907 Carnegie Library, Pocatello's first example of classical design, built of beige brick and sandstone on a cruciform plan.

LOCATION: 105 South Garfield Avenue. HOURS: 2–5 Tuesday –Saturday. FEE: None. TELEPHONE: 208–233–0434.

Fort Hall Replica

The first permanent post to fly the Stars and Stripes west of the Continental Divide, Fort Hall resulted from a broken promise. At the annual fur-trade rendezvous in 1834, Nathaniel Wyeth arrived with $3,000 worth of goods that the Rocky Mountain Fur Company had agreed to buy. But the company had already made purchases from an earlier arrival, leaving Wyeth stuck. He declared to the Rocky Mountain partners: "Gentlemen, I will roll a stone into your garden that you will never be able to get out," and built Fort Hall as an outlet for trading his goods to the friendly Bannock and Shoshoni.

OPPOSITE: *The restored Standrod House in Pocatello, a solid bastion of stone built for a banker in 1901.*

Located where the Oregon Trail met the Snake River, the fort was a stockade measuring eighty feet square and fifteen feet high, built of heavy cottonwood logs. That first season, the isolated post was not much to look at, but, as Wyeth said, it was functional: "Its bastions stand a terror to the skulking Indians and a beacon of safety to the fugitive hunter. It is manned by 12 men and has constantly loaded in the bastions 100 guns and rifles." Wyeth's venture also brought a Methodist missionary, Jason Lee, who conducted Idaho's first religious services at the fort in 1834. "The Indians sat upon the ground like statues," reported one observer. "Although not one of them could understand a word that was said, they nevertheless maintained a most strict and decorous silence, kneeling when the preacher kneeled, and rising when he rose, evidently with a view of paying him and us a suitable respect."

To compete with Wyeth, the Hudson's Bay Company built Fort Boise, undercut his prices, and like any successful monopoly, forced him out of business. The company took over Fort Hall cheaply in 1836, added adobe and whitewash to the walls, and flew a red flag lettered H.B.C.—which, said waggish trappers, meant "Here Before Christ." After 1840 Fort Hall was a major stop for emigrant wagon trains, the only inhabited place on the lonely plains between Fort Laramie and Fort Boise. Here the California Trail branched off from the Oregon Trail, so agents from both regions regularly visited the fort to sign up settlers. But by 1855 Indian uprisings caused by the heavy pioneer traffic were interfering with access to the upper Snake country. The Hudson's Bay Company abandoned Fort Hall in 1856, and eight years later a flood demolished it.

This replica, located eleven miles from the actual site, was built from the original plans. Exhibits evoke early life at the fort, and Indian artifacts are on display.

LOCATION: Ross Park, upper level, South 4th Street. HOURS: April through May: 10–2 Tuesday–Friday; June through mid–September: 9–8 Daily. FEE: Yes. TELEPHONE: 208–234–6233.

The original site of Fort Hall lies eight miles north of Pocatello within the **Fort Hall Indian Reservation** (Exit 80, Route 15, 208–238–3700). Tours of the site leave from the **Shoshone-Bannock Tribal Museum,** which displays beaded clothing, war bonnets, and other artifacts.

BLACKFOOT

In 1878 citizens named this town for the Blackfoot River. It became the seat of Idaho's top potato county and in 1885 the site of Idaho's first insane asylum. Local heritage is on display at the **Bingham County Historical Museum** (190 North Shilling Avenue, 208–785–8065), which occupies a restored house of the early 1900s and contains rooms furnished appropriately—a parlor with piano, a kitchen with butter churns and molds, and a basement with farm tools. Also of interest are the 1921 **Mormon Tabernacle** (East Judicial and South Shilling avenues), a semicircular building with Neo-Georgian details, and the stone **Blackfoot Railway Depot** (North Main Street), completed in 1913 to serve the Oregon Short Line.

For the world's first nuclear power plant, scientists looked for a place no one wanted, without population or earthquake history. That described the open desert between Arco and Idaho Falls, where in 1951 the federal government first operated **Experimental Breeder Reactor Number 1** (Route 20, eighteen miles east of Arco, 208–526–0050). The first reactor to produce electricity by atomic

A locomotive of the Utah & Northern Railroad pauses on a bridge at Eagle Rock, near Blackfoot. The two-man crew seems to have full confidence in the frail-looking span as they stand patiently for the camera.

energy, it also demonstrated that nonfissionable uranium could be transmuted into fissionable. This facility, now decommissioned, is part of the 890-square-mile **Idaho National Engineering Laboratory,** whose facilities have trained operators for reactors to propel nuclear submarines. The fuel rods, reactor, and other components of EBR-1 are on display as well as two nuclear engines designed to power a nuclear airplane. No such plane was ever built, and after the development program was ended in 1961, the Smithsonian Institution acquired the engines. They are displayed here because they weigh too much and are too large to ship to Washington, DC.

The hub of religion, civic life, and education in a Mormon town such as **Iona** was the meetinghouse. The one-story **Iona Meetinghouse** (3670 North Main Street) was built of sandstone in 1888, with a second section added in 1894; it is now an art gallery.

REXBURG

As with many Mormon communities, Rexburg's tribute to its planning is its graciously wide streets (including the widest Main Street in Idaho). It is remarkable that the streets are straight, as when surveyors laid out the town in 1883 a foot of snow covered the ground. Industrious citizens took only a year to raise all the funds for the 1911 Rexburg Stake Tabernacle, built of gray stone in a generally Italianate design with Mission-style elements. Too small for the area's growing Mormon congregation, the tabernacle now houses the **Teton Flood Museum** (51 North Center Street, 208–356–9101), which focuses on the Teton Dam flood disaster of 1976, when the dam broke and spilled 80 billion gallons of water into the town and neighboring Sugar City. The museum also displays old farm equipment, quilts, furniture, radios, televisions, license plates, and 317 pairs of salt- and-pepper shakers.

FRANKLIN

Idaho's first permanent community was settled by Mormons who thought they were in Utah. When Thomas Smart led a small group of pioneers north through the Cache Valley in 1860 to found the town of Franklin, no one realized that they had crossed the border about a mile back. Picking a site near the Cub River (a tributary of the Bear), the Mormons soon built a fort, a corral, mills for lumber and flour, and a creamery, all for communal use. They also built

The simple stone facade of the Hatch House, Franklin, is embellished with a carved cornice and quoins—large blocks marking the corners.

Idaho's first school for white children. In 1861 Brigham Young ordered a steam engine for the Franklin sawmill to be shipped overland—a remarkable feat, considering that it weighed 10,000 pounds and had to travel hundreds of miles over rough terrain by wagon and team. Abandoned to rust in pieces, the engine now rests at Franklin's **Relic Hall** (2d East and Main Street), which also displays photographs, furniture, and farm implements dating back to pioneer days. The Relic Hall is housed partially in a stone cooperative store built in 1895. The town's first cooperative store was established in 1868 by Lorenzo Hill Hatch, a church bishop and Idaho's first Mormon legislator. His 1874 **Hatch House** (127 East Main Street, private) is one of the finest Greek Revival residences in the state and one of the last to be built in America. It is built of stone, with fine proportions, classical details rendered in wood, and a gable end facing the street.

PRESTON

The Battle of Bear River, which took place on January 29, 1863, northwest of Preston, was the most costly defeat suffered by Native Americans in war with the European-Americans. In retaliation for white encroachment on their lands, several tribes had begun to attack wagon trains in the early 1860s. To protect the settlers, Colonel Patrick Edward Connor and his California volunteers headed for Shoshoni country, shooting unarmed Indians on the way and executing hostages for unproved crimes. The Shoshoni set up a line at Bear River, promising to kill any white seen on the north bank.

When, after many raids and incidents of cattle-stealing, several white miners were killed while trying to cross the river at Richmond, just across the border in the Utah Territory, Connor decided to move against the Shoshoni. He marched 225 men 120 miles in six days through deep snow, and on a freezing January morning they found the Indian encampment at the mouth of Beaver Creek. The Shoshoni were ready to fight, and baited the soldiers across the river. Fourteen soldiers were killed in the first volley, but in the ensuing battle the troops flanked the ravine and trapped the Indians, raking them mercilessly with gunfire. The following morning civilians from Franklin returned to the site to search for survivors and counted 364 Shoshoni lying dead, stacked up to eight deep—two-thirds of them women and children. According to one witness, "You could walk on dead Indians for quite a distance without touching ground." Others had been thrown into Bear River for burial; the band was nearly annihilated, and the Shoshoni regarded the battle as a massacre. Two months later Colonel Connor was promoted to the rank of brigadier general. The causes of the battle were summarized by Indian Agent James Doty as a lack of game and the white takeover of fertile land, which forced the destitute Indians to plunder. "It is not to be expected that wild and warlike people will tamely submit to the occupation of their country by another race," he wrote, "and to starvation as a consequence thereof." Many of the Mormon settlers in the Cache Valley had found the Indians "a source of great annoyance" and saw Connor's action as "intervention of the Almighty," but others were sympathetic toward the Indians. The next summer Connor induced various Shoshoni groups to sign treaties. The **Bear River Battleground** lies three miles northwest of Preston. There is a **monument** on the east side of Route 91. To reach the actual site, take the gravel road located across the highway from the monument and drive 300 yards, then turn right at the fork for a third of a mile along the edge of what is now known as the Battle Creek ravine.

From about 7,000 years ago until the nineteenth century, the **Weston Rock Shelter** (four miles northwest of Weston, on the north side of

Weston Canyon Road) was occupied by various cultures known by regional, rather than historical, names: the Archaic Great Basin, northwestern Great Plains, and Rocky Mountain. All were hunters of mountain sheep and other large game.

Ten miles southwest of **American Falls** lies **Massacre Rocks State Park** (Exit 28 off Route I-86, 208–548–2672), which encompasses the site of an 1862 Indian attack. Three wagon trains were heading west through bleak sagebrush country on the Oregon Trail when the first two were set upon by Indian warriors, who stole their stock and clothing, killed nine emigrants, and scalped six. About two miles west of park headquarters stands **Register Rock** (Route I-86), where Oregon Trail travelers carved their names or painted them in axle grease. Similar rocks along the Trail chronicle their passage. Also in the vicinity are undisturbed ruts from wagons on the trail.

ALMO

From a distance, the granite spires of the **Silent City of Rocks** (six miles southwest of Almo on a graded dirt road) indeed appear to be a metropolis. Fantastic shapes—pinnacles, mushrooms, dragons' heads, temples—have raised themselves in strange, picturesque formations. The Twin Sisters tower sixty-two stories above the nearby California Trail. Emigrants on that trail left one of the great chronicles of overland travel—their names and dates written in axle grease on **Register Rock** and **Camp Rock**, along with messages for travelers

Frederic Remington's 1891 painting of Register Rock. OVERLEAF: *The Silent City of Rocks, near Almo.*

yet to come. A mile and a half south of the Twin Sisters, the California Trail met the Salt Lake Cutoff, and there are still traces of an old stage station. Hudspeth's Cutoff also passes through the "city." In 1856 an emigrant named Carpenter reached the Silent City of Rocks and wrote in his diary: "We were so spellbound with the beauty and strangeness of it all, that no thought of Indians entered our heads." But travelers had good reason to worry about Shoshoni ambushes in such irregular terrain. An 1862 Nevada newspaper mentioned an emigrant party that passed through the Silent City of Rocks and arrived in Humboldt with wagons "whose sides and covers were transformed into magnified nutmeg-graters by Indian bullets." In 1878 a lone-wolf bandit who robbed an Overland stage near Oakley was captured in the City of Rocks, and ever after searchers have looked for the $150,000 in gold he is assumed to have hidden there.

At **Granite Pass** (just north of the Utah border, southeast of the California Trail–Salt Lake Cutoff junction), there is a relatively undisturbed stretch of the California Trail with visible wagon ruts.

RUPERT

When Congress passed the Newlands Act of 1902, giving federal money to reclamation projects, it had a greening effect on distant Idaho. With the 1909 completion of the **Minidoka Dam and Power Plant** (ten miles northeast of Rupert off Route 24, on County Highway 400), about 120,000 acres were opened to farmers, with canals, pumping stations, and enough extra power to sell to local customers. It was the second federal power project in the Northwest, and·a model that served to spur congressional approval of the Tennessee Valley Authority. Visitors are permitted at the power house. Also here is **Walcott Park,** with interesting rockwork done by the Civilian Conservation Corps in the 1930s. In Rupert the **Minidoka County Historical Museum** (100 East Baseline Road, 208–436–0336) displays local historical artifacts, from a 1920s permanent-wave machine to hand-pumped washing machines and washboards; also farm machinery, man-powered fire carts of the late 1800s, and such oddities as a wood-rimmed bicycle wheel.

OAKLEY

Mormon settlers founded Oakley in 1878 as an agricultural center, and farmers were able to reclaim arid land here after the building of the 1911 Oakley Dam, for a time the world's largest. Idaho quartzite is quarried in the vicinity, and in the **Oakley Historic District,** the mineral's multiple hues decorate the outside of the town's first bank, on Main Street. Next door at Main and Center streets is the 1883 **Oakley Co-op Store.** The former Worthington Hotel on Main Street now houses the **Oakley Pioneer Museum** (208–862–3626), which displays antique furniture and clothing, rocks, arrowheads, and photographs. At Blaine and Poplar stands the 1909 **Howell Residence** (private), a judge's brick house sporting two levels of round porches topped by a turret.

A range war between cattle and sheep ranchers erupted near Oakley in 1895. John Sparks, a cattleman who became governor of Nevada, enlisted "Diamondfield" Jack Davis as an armed cowboy to hold back the sheep, and Davis winged one of the herders. The next year, when two sheepherders were killed in their wagons, Davis was the suspect. His colorful trial ended in a death sentence for Davis, but he was acquitted when two other men confessed to the shootings. Diamondfield was once incarcerated in a jail cell that is now in the Oakley city park, and the **Church Street cemetery** is the final resting place of the two sheepherders who were killed.

Two miles east of the town of **Murtaugh** lies the most southerly point on the Snake River and the site of **Caldron Linn** (3425 North Road). In 1811 a canoe full of Astorian fur trappers under Wilson Hunt overturned nearby, drowning one member of the party. Scouting downstream, the rest of the group was frightened by the sight of Caldron Linn, a narrow section of the canyon where the churning water is compressed in a rock chute, and decided to leave the river and travel overland to Oregon. Robert Stuart returned to the site to pick up cached equipment and later wrote of the violent rush of water: "Hecate's caldron was never half so agitated when vomiting even the most diabolical spells." In the 1930s some old guns and traps found in the river were judged to be those from the party's overturned canoe of more than a century earlier.

TWIN FALLS

For farming, the rich silts and lava soils around Twin Falls lacked just one thing—water. But this arid valley became the "Magic Valley" after the Carey Act of 1894 spurred Idaho's first large reclamation projects. Milner Dam was built, about 60,000 acres of farms were irrigated, and the desert bloomed. The town began in the early 1900s, growing in a few years from a collection of shacks to a substantial community with a courthouse, hotel, and school. Three corners of the city park (Sixth Avenue North and Shoshone Street) are occupied by **churches** dating from 1909–1929: Catholic (Renaissance Revival), First Christian (Classic Revival), and Methodist (Tudor Gothic). The **Justamere Inn** (Fourth Avenue North and Second Avenue North), built in 1911, is a fine example of Mission-style design, and is now restored for offices.

The **Herrett Museum** (315 Falls Avenue, College of Southern Idaho campus, 208–733–9554) contains a remarkable collection of 6,000 artifacts from the pre-Columbian cultures of the Americas. A range of changing exhibits includes Mayan jade pendants and beads, Inca capes and other South American textiles, and various objects from Peru's pre-Inca cultures, the west coast of Mexico, the Pacific Northwest, and the southeastern United States. The **Twin Falls County Historical Society Museum** (Route 30, 208–734–5547) is a pioneer museum featuring home furnishings, clothing, farming implements, and wagons used to haul ice and lumber.

Shoshone Falls (off Route 93, five miles north of Twin Falls) was called by the Shoshoni *Pah-Chu-Laka,* which translates as "hurling waters leaping." The first white man to see it was Wilson Price Hunt, leading a party of trappers in 1811. At 212 feet high, the falls are greater than Niagara's, and they were Idaho's primary tourist attraction for pioneers on the Oregon Trail. An early writer said, "Never anywhere else was there such a scene; never anywhere else so beautiful a picture hung in so rude a frame." In 1905 Harry Wilson became the first person to go over the rim on purpose, and according to the Twin Falls *Daily News,* "he swam to a rock and calmly awaited the arrival of his clothing, which had been removed before making the leap." Today power plants and the impounding of irrigation water upstream have marred this natural treasure, but the sight is still splendid from December through April, when water is not held back.

The **Idaho Heritage Museum** (off Route 93, twenty-seven miles south of Twin Falls) displays 10,000 Indian artifacts such as scrapers and arrowheads, mainly from the Shoshoni-Bannock; about 300 mounted animals found in a geographical range between the arctic tundra and the Grand Canyon; and a collection of firearms.

OPPOSITE: *Shoshone Falls on the Snake River, 212 feet high.*

Founded in the 1860s, the mining town of Silver City still sprawls across a hollow in the Owyhee Mountains, its buildings linked by a twisted network of dirt roads.

HAGERMAN

In the Hagerman area, prehistoric horses wandered into what was then a boggy landscape. Probably they came to drink; their bones were found among the remains of fish and aquatic animals such as turtles and frogs. In the 1930s Smithsonian scientists excavated the **Hagerman Fossil Beds** (about five miles southwest of Hagerman off Route 30). Amid the world's largest deposit of fossil horses, they unearthed more than a dozen skeletons of a previously unknown zebralike horse called *Plesippus shoshonensis Gidley,* which lived prior to Pleistocene times—the oldest type ever found in North America. (This predecessor of the horse had become extinct by the time humans arrived in North America; the horse was re-introduced to the continent by Europeans.) Also uncovered here were the bones of cats, camels, and peccaries. When the quarry caved in and scientists had to dynamite, the blast tossed the skull of a mastodon right out of the upper rock layer. On the way to the town of Hagerman from the fossil beds is the **Archie Teater House** (Old Highway 30 west of the Malad River bridge, private). The low stone house is Frank Lloyd Wright's only work in Idaho.

A gathering of Silver City's miners, with only a few smiles in evidence, sometime around the turn of the century.

In the town itself, the **Hagerman Valley Historical Society Museum** (Main and State streets, 208–837–6288) displays a cast replica of a prehistoric horse and a mural depicting the savannalike environs when the horses roamed. Also on display are Indian artifacts, household items and clothing, and an old saddle from a rider who drowned while trying to ford the Snake River.

SILVER CITY

The patriarch of Idaho historic mining towns, Silver City lies in the Owyhee Mountains, where prospectors came after hearing one of the West's ubiquitous "Blue Bucket" legends. (Oregon-bound emigrants were supposed to have picked up nuggets from a creek and used them as fishing sinkers, storing them in a blue bucket. Eventually someone realized the nuggets were gold—but no one could ever find that special creek again.) In 1863 a party of gold seekers did find placer deposits on Jordan Creek, and the next year a silver and gold rush followed rich discoveries on War Eagle Mountain. The Oro Fino and Morning Star mines earned their owners $1 million the first year, while the Poorman produced a stunning quarter-ton mass of solid ruby-silver crystals.

Over the years Silver City sprawled across a gulch, and what now remains is designated the **Silver City Historic District.** The city comprised an assay office, several stamp mills, drugstores, a barbershop (whose advertisements offered the special lure of baths—"Call and be convinced"), the first telegraph service in Idaho Territory, "Dead Man's Alley" (where several shootings took place), a Wells Fargo office, and a courthouse whose surviving stone arches still stand like Roman ruins in the sagebrush. Most of these buildings exist today in a state of picturesque dilapidation. One noteworthy site is the office of the *Owyhee Avalanche*, the territory's first daily newspaper and surely its most humorous. In 1866 it reported a man's trial for shooting another during a poker game, noting that he was acquitted by the jury on the theory that "five queens are too many for one hand."

In 1868 Silver City made national news when miners working in the Golden Chariot broke through to Ida Elmore's tunnel. The miners began to shoot it out in the drifts and stopes, and soon the two mining companies recruited thugs for an underground war. A marshal and ninety-six soldiers restored order, but a week later one of the mine owners was shot and killed in front of the Idaho Hotel. Silver City's social center, stagecoach stop, and finest hostelry, the fifty-room **Idaho Hotel** (Jordan Street) was built in 1863 by New Englander Hosea Eastman. Over the years the hotel was remodeled and expanded—most notably after one memorable Fourth of July when some locals shot off a cannon and blew out a third of the hotel's windows. It contains a small museum.

Idaho's mining communities were devastated by the failure of the Bank of California in 1875. When the county seat moved in 1935, Silver City—the hub of a district that had produced $60 million in gold and silver—became a derelict. Today the roughly forty surviving buildings are privately owned by people who come for summer vacations or to work their own mining claims; it is not a true "ghost town." Some property owners have ancestors in the town's four cemeteries, and the stories behind pioneer names on the headstones can be traced at the **Old Schoolhouse Museum** (Morning Star Mill Street, 208–337–4239). On the hill beyond it stands the **Stoddard House** (private), built in 1870 by Jack Stoddard, who married his wife after a longhorn cattle drive, and perhaps as an antidote to the trail, decorated their bedroom with wallpaper roses, cupids, and garlands.

OPPOSITE: *The remains of the Silver City jail, which once housed veterans of the town's gambling and mining wars.*

A view of the Boise skyline, with the dome of the state capitol visible above the treetops.

The hamlet of **Murphy** is the seat of a county with nearly 5 million acres but only two principal roads and fewer than 10,000 people. It is also the home of the **Owyhee County Historical Museum** (one block off Route 78, 208–495–2319), whose exhibits include cowboy gear, minerals, Indian artifacts, and an old schoolhouse.

BOISE

It is said that the Boise River got its name from French-Canadian fur trappers remarking on the trees nearby—*bois* being French for "woods." But the trappers may have been translating a previous English designation, since by 1812 the Astorian Robert Stuart had referred to the "wooded river." The Boise Valley was well known to later travelers on the Oregon Trail, who had less trouble with nomenclature than with Indians. After a number of skirmishes and two massacres along the trail, the army established **Fort Boise** in 1863 to protect the emigrants. The city's oldest buildings—except for a few preserved settlers' cabins from 1863—stand on the fort grounds. The army chose a strategic spot on the Boise River, next to

the trail that linked the gold camps of the Boise Basin with those in the Owyhees to the south. At the same time a party of civilians laid out on 442 acres of sagebrush what they hoped would become a supply town beside the post. Soon the settlement grew, and Ben Holladay's Overland Stage Company was bringing passengers all the way from Kansas. By 1864 the governor had designated Boise to replace Lewiston as territorial capital. When Lewiston balked at the shift of power, the territorial governor stole the government's archives and seal and smuggled them to Boise.

Within a few years the capital was the hub of an agricultural district supplying the mining camps and the soldiers. By the end of the 1860s, Boise had about 1,000 citizens and 400 buildings. True to its name, it became a city of trees; the town's first nursery began importing stock in 1870, the trees being shipped more than 200 miles via stagecoach. Entertainment and theater flourished, and in 1879 *H.M.S. Pinafore* was presented just a year after the musical's London premiere. In an early case of truth in advertising, the Naked Truth Saloon announced the sale of "liquid fire" guaranteed to cre-

The Idaho State Capitol, above, was built in 1905 of local sandstone. It strongly resembles the U.S. Capitol in Washington, DC in the proportions and arrangement of its three domes. OPPOSITE: *The ceiling of the capitol's lofty rotunda with an oculum decorated with stars.*

ate "drunkards, paupers, and beggars for the sober, industrious and respectable portion of the community to support." Silver City's Hosea Eastman took over the Overland House, a pioneer hotel that became a mecca for miners, farmers, and emigrants and was called "the political caldron of Idaho Territory."

The Idaho Central Railroad linked Boise to the Oregon Short Line in 1887. When Eastman and his partners tapped the local hot springs in 1890, at the end of what would become Warm Springs Avenue, Boise became the first town in America to use this source of energy for residential heating. Farm acreage increased along with the population of farmers after the completion of a dam and the New York Canal in 1908. Buildings in Gothic Revival and other early styles were replaced by Romanesque Revival structures, French Second Empire houses, and other signs that modern life had come to the old sagebrush town. Perhaps this change is best symbolized by the 1905 **Idaho State Capitol** (8th and Jefferson streets), which replaced an 1886 territorial capitol that in turn had replaced makeshift quarters in various hotels, lodge halls, and rented stores. The state bought a quarry at nearby Table Rock and used sandstone

from it to build this Classic Revival structure, whose Corinthian columns and dome echo those of the national capitol in Washington, DC. The rotunda rises four stories. On the second floor stands an 1869 gilded statue called "George Washington and Horse," which was carved by an Austrian immigrant, Charles Ostner, from a single pine tree; his model for Washington was an image of the president on a postage stamp.

Across Jefferson Street is a **statue of Frank Steunenberg,** Idaho's fourth governor, who was assassinated in 1905 in the aftermath of a mining labor dispute in northern Idaho. Down State Street the **Alexander House** (304 West State Street) is a white Queen Anne residence built in 1897 by Moses Alexander, mayor of Boise and later the first Jewish governor in the United States. Now housing the Idaho Commission on the Arts and Humanities, it is open to visitors.

Northwest of the capitol is the 1892 **GAR Hall** (714 West State Street). A brick structure with decorative bargeboards, it was once the meeting place of the Grand Army of the Republic, made up of Union veterans of the Civil War. **Saint Michael's Episcopal Cathedral** (518 North 8th Street), built in 1899 in English Gothic style, incorporates a stained-glass window signed by Tiffany Studios of New York. Dating to 1895, **Congregation Beth Israel** (1102 West State Street) is the oldest synagogue west of the Mississippi that is still used by descendants of the original congregation. Organized by Moses Alexander and David Falk, it has the shape of a basilica and incorporates a rose window. At 1020 West Franklin stands the picturesque 1892 **Bush Mansion,** with a copper and slate roof; it now contains offices. Southeast is **Saint John's Cathedral** (804 North 8th Street), a Romanesque Revival structure begun in 1906 and completed in 1921.

Nearby is **Old Fort Boise** (5th and Fort streets), established in 1863 to protect emigrants, settlers, and gold miners from Indian hostilities. The earliest structures—the quartermaster's building and two houses on officers' row—date to 1864 and were built of sandstone. After 1879, Boise Barracks—as the fort was known—became a community center with band concerts, theatrical performances, Christmas parties, and friendly competitions between soldiers and Boise residents. After cavalry troops introduced polo in 1909, games against civilians became social events, and Boise was known as the polo capital of the Northwest. One of the oldest structures in Boise is the **O'Farrell Cabin** (4th and Fort streets), which dates to 1863. Built by John O'Farrell for his 17-year-old bride, the one-room cabin was the site of Boise's first Catholic mass and its first school.

On the other side of the capitol from the fort area lies **Old Boise,** now the site of considerable urban renewal. The 1864 **Cyrus Jacobs House** (607 Grove Street, 208–386–9394), built by a store owner and located in a once-elegant neighborhood with shady trees, was one of the first brick houses in Boise. It later became a boardinghouse for Basque immigrants and now contains the **Idaho Basque Museum and Cultural Center,** with a boardinghouse dining area, kitchen, and bedrooms circa 1910. The museum is devoted to the Basque community, which came to Idaho from northwest Spain in the 1890s to herd sheep and has contributed much to local culture with its dances and heritage. At 609 Main Street stands the 1899 **Telephone Building,** home of an early exchange that reserved the easiest phone number for itself: "1." An exotic landmark from the golden age of movies, the **Egyptian (Ada) Theater** (Main Street and Capitol Boulevard, 208–342–0090) reflects the fascination with Egypt that swept the country after Tutankhamen's tomb was opened. Built in 1927, the theater features winged scarabs, lotus columns, sphinx statues, and Egyptian icons. The 1901 **Idanha Hotel** (928 Main Street, 208–342–3611) reflects the eclectic taste at the turn of the century, with its castellated mansard roof and corner turrets. The first elevator in Idaho whisked such guests as Theodore Roosevelt a full six stories into the sky, and the brick hostelry was a gathering spot for Boise society.

Down Main Street is a doorway through which passed more than $75 million in gold and silver bullion—the **Assay Office** (210 Main Street), built in 1871 in Renaissance Revival style. For obvious reasons, the stone walls are two feet thick. The assay office determined what percentage of ore was precious metal, bought raw silver and gold, and melted it in furnaces for bullion. The facility went out of business in 1933 and is now an office building.

The **Warm Springs Avenue Historical District** begins three blocks east, a mile-long stretch of fine homes in what became Boise's most elegant neighborhood after about 1890. The avenue's showplace is the 1892 **Moore-Cunningham House** (1109 Warm Springs Avenue, private), a three-story mansion that was the first residence in America to use natural hot water for heating. Owner C. W. Moore was president of the Boise Artesian Hot and Cold Water Company and used his home to prove that the new heating source was practical. Moore and Hosea Eastman also harnessed this 171- degree water for the natatorium, a Moorish-style plunge whose four floors included baths, a restaurant, a music hall, card and billiard parlors, and—when the vast swimming pool was floored over—a venue for the governors' inaugural balls. After 1891 streetcars took riders out Warm Springs Avenue to the "Nat" for a nickel.

Old Idaho Penitentiary

About a mile east of the Warm Springs Avenue mansions is another kind of big house. The Old Idaho Penitentiary, a walled complex of sandstone buildings, was established in 1870 to lodge horse thieves, rustlers, stage robbers, and other garden-variety outlaws who plagued Idaho settlers. A self-guided tour goes inside the cell houses—including "Siberia" (the solitary-confinement block) and cells with one-way mirrors that allowed guards to make secret security checks. Visitors see the separately walled women's ward (215 out of the 13,000 convicts who served time here were women); the scars of a riot; the "Deadline" (a dirt perimeter around the compound, so called because convicts would be shot if they set foot there); death row; and the gallows. A **museum** displays captured contraband weapons, a ball and chain, and material on tunnels and escape attempts. The former prison shirt factory now houses the **Idaho Transportation Museum,** which exhibits buggies, a stagecoach, and other vehicles, as well as a reproduction of a print shop. Another building contains the **History of Electricity in Idaho Museum.**

LOCATION: 2445 Old Penitentiary Road. HOURS: 12–4 Daily. FEE: Yes. TELEPHONE: 208–334–2844.

Idaho Historical Museum

Re-creating the past through historical interiors, this museum includes the saloon from the old Overland House hotel, furnished in the style of 1885 and complete with a faro layout for gamblers and a parlor stove for heated political gatherings. There are exhibits on pioneer and Indian life, with a display on Idaho's Chinese miners, who by 1870 outnumbered white miners and went on to become farmers, vegetable peddlers, laundrymen, and restaurateurs. In the adjacent **Pioneer Village** stand two 1863 cabins that are among

OPPOSITE: *The Idanha Hotel in Boise. When it opened in 1901 the Idanha boasted the state's first elevator.*

Idaho's earliest surviving homes. The Coston Cabin was cobbled together with driftwood from the Boise River and fastened with pegs. In its original location about seven miles upriver, it was a gathering spot for Indians, miners, and freighters. The Pearce Cabin was once a blacksmith shop and then the home of a Chinese family. The Thomas E. Logan House dates to 1865 and is the only unaltered adobe house in the city; its 1870s furnishings reflect the era when Logan was Boise's mayor. The simple Richard C. Adelmann House is a frame residence of the period 1870–1890, while the board-and-batten Colson Homestead Shack of 1909 is typical of modest housing on the sagebrush plains of southern Idaho.

LOCATION: 610 North Julia Davis Drive. HOURS: 9–5 Monday –Saturday, 1–5 Sunday. FEE: Yes.. TELEPHONE: 208–334–2120.

At the south end of Capitol Boulevard, the **Union Pacific Mainline Depot** perches on the edge of a hill, its Spanish Colonial Revival tower a Boise landmark since 1925. The sandstone structure was built to serve passengers when the UP's Oregon Short Line arrived in Boise, putting the city on the main line after forty years on a mere spur from Nampa. The clapboard **Christ Chapel** (Boise State University, 1010 Campus Lane, private) was built in 1866 in the Greek Revival style with Gothic elements.

NAMPA

Some sources say that "Nampa" is Shoshoni for "moccasin print," others that it comes from Nampuh, an Indian leader so large that the vest of a 315-pound man was fifteen inches too small to go around him. Named by the Oregon Short Line in 1883, Nampa's original nucleus was a station house and water tank. The railroad spurred the growth of the town and the building of one of Idaho's most picturesque passenger stations—the 1903 **Nampa Depot** (Twelfth Avenue and Front Street South). Constructed of brick and sandstone, it is designed in an eclectic style with elements of Romanesque, Renaissance, and Baroque. Today the depot houses the **Canyon County Historical Museum** (208–467–7611), whose displays include household items, a model train, and a set of more than 100 mustache cups.

PARMA

In what is now the Parma region, the Hudson's Bay Company erected a permanent British trading post at the confluence of the Boise and Snake rivers in 1834. Made of sun-dried adobe, **Old Fort Boise** was meant to compete with Fort Hall, an American post farther east. A milestone in the history of western travel occurred at the fort in 1836, when Marcus Whitman arrived over what would later be called the Oregon Trail in a two-wheeled cart—or more accurately, the back half of his wagon, which had slowly shaken off parts during the journey. From 1835 to 1844, Fort Boise was managed by François Payette, a pleasant host who welcomed the "Great Migration" of emigrant wagons in September 1843 with a fiddle, banjo, and accordion dance in their honor. Payette served good food—everything from duck to salmon to buffalo, with fresh bread and butter—and he made the fort a refuge for weary travelers and mountain men. Emigrants on the Oregon Trail resupplied themselves here with staples for the final stretch of their journey, as this was the only supply depot between Fort Hall and The Dalles in Oregon.

Crossing the Snake River was a dilemma for Oregon-bound travelers; usually they just floated their wagons across like boats. In 1852 two entrepreneurs established a ferry, charging whatever the traffic would bear. One emigrant's party paid $16 for passage, and he noted: "This money was made by the ferryman in half an hour. This is the way to wring hard-earned money from the starving poor." Indian hostilities caused the ferry to be abandoned in 1854, but by 1863 Jonathan Keeney had built another one for regular service, charging $2.50 per wagon, seventy-five cents for a rider and horse, and a nickel per hog. The river also posed a problem for the adobe fort itself, washing away most of it in a flood in 1853. Two years later the Hudson's Bay Company closed down its remaining operation. A massive flood in 1862 took whatever was left, and because of the river's shifting channel, the site is now in the middle of the Snake, about five miles outside of town.

In Parma a **replica of Fort Boise** can be visited at Old Fort Boise City Park, on Grove Street on the east edge of town. Nothing from the original fort is displayed—it all ended up in the river—but the dimensions are correct, being 100 feet on a side, and the cinderblock construction is a reasonable facsimile of adobe. A museum displays local pioneer items, particularly farm implements. Information is available through the Parma City Hall (208–722–5138).

Cliffs of basalt loom over the Snake River south of Boise. This stretch of the river is part of a nature preserve that protects the habitat of hawks, eagles, and falcons.

IDAHO CITY

An Indian told Moses Splawn that glittering metal could be found south of the Salmon River, so, in the summer of 1862, Splawn led a party of prospectors into the Boise Basin, where they found rich placers. Just eighteen miles square, this region would yield more than $24 million in gold in the first four years. The basin's leading town was Idaho City, which surpassed Hog 'Em (Pioneerville) and other camps because it had water for a longer period each spring to operate sluices. (In saloons whiskey was sometimes cheaper than water.) There were eighty miles of ditches in place by the 1863 season, and Idaho City even outgrew Portland as the biggest town in the Pacific Northwest. Such street names as Wall and Commercial indicate Idaho City's position as a hub of territorial commerce.

While there was enough water to wash the ore, miners worked their claims around the clock. At night from Idaho City visitors could see more than thirty bonfires lighting up the scattered diggings, and they heard the ringing of countless shovels in eerie symphony. The town grew steadily, although four serious fires destroyed most of the early buildings. An eyewitness to the great fire of 1867 wrote: "Multitudes who had breakfasted that morning with bright and confiding hopes of a prosperous business season had no appetite for a dinner at noon—and no place to dine if they did." The town rebuilt itself in brick. Theaters presented Shakespeare and melodramas, and besides the usual businesses there were four breweries, a mattress factory, a photographer's studio, and two bowling alleys. Gambling halls, thirty-five saloons, and brothels galore gave some rest and recreation to the hardworking miners. On Sundays, according to one observer, "they purchase most of their supplies . . . and do up their drinking for the week."

After 1870 Chinese miners numbered half the population, but they were discriminated against in Idaho Territory with a Chinese miners' tax. A hearing was held in Idaho City in 1869, addressed by a marshal who explained that President Grant had sent him to end the racial persecution. After collecting $1,600 to finance a court battle, however, he pocketed the majority for his own costs and headed east.

When the Boise Basin's stream gravels had been worked over, hydraulic mining became widespread, using hoses to blast away the hillsides to recover the gold, and in 1898 dredging began. Miners

A group of Chinese miners and laundry workers on their day off in DeLamar, where a Danish immigrant, Joseph DeLamar, operated a silver mine that yielded millions of dollars in the 1880s and 1890s. OVERLEAF: *The Sawtooth Mountains reflected in Little Redfish Lake at dawn. Mount Heyburn, over 10,000 feet tall, is at left.*

were not kind to the land here, but over the years they recovered a total of 3 million ounces of gold from the basin. Not surprisingly, with that much treasure around, Idaho City suffered a plague of bad-men. One of the town's first buildings was a jail, occupying an acre and containing not only cell blocks but a cemetery. Lambert Florin, a historian of ghost towns, has noted: "This last handily received the victims of fast-moving justice and hangings, all of which were carried out on the premises." Vigilantes also met here to plan the less-offi-cially-sanctioned executions of scoundrels such as Ferd Patterson, who murdered a boat captain, scalped his former mistress, and, writes one historian, "climaxed his playfulness by slaying the sheriff of Idaho City." A fop who sported high-heeled boots and a silk vest adorned with a chain of California gold nuggets, Patterson was near-ly lynched but went free after his trial. Herman St. Clair was not so lucky; for his hanging in 1898, the sheriff sent invitations written in ornate script and marked "Not Transferable."

Idaho's first jail can be seen in the **Idaho City Historic District.** This 1864 **Idaho Territorial Penitentiary** (Wall Street) was moved from another location and now stands next to the 1865 **Masonic Hall,** the oldest still in use west of the Mississippi. Inside an 1865 brick building with iron fire shutters, the **Boise Basin Museum** (Montgomery Street, 208–392–4550) displays costumes, glass, and other items of local history. Other sites include the *Idaho World* **building** (Main Street), home of the town's newspaper; **Saint Joseph's Catholic Church** (High Street), built after the fire of 1867; and the 1864 **Pioneer Lodge Number 1** (High Street), the Odd Fellows' earliest shrine west of the Mississippi.

Evidence of hydraulic mining can be seen by driving north on Main Street (which becomes Elk Creek Road) to its end. **Pioneer Cemetery** lies out Centerville Road and contains 200 graves. An old-timer in the turbulent town once remarked that only 28 ot those buried here died of natural causes.

KETCHUM

In 1880 thousands of lusty souls poured into the Wood River valley after lead-silver mining started the previous year. One of the early arrivals was fur trapper David Ketchum, who built the first structure of the town that was later named for him. The community helped develop the area's mines with a large smelter, opened in 1882. Along with nearby Hailey, Ketchum was one of the first communities in Idaho to boast electric lights. Ketchum boomed a second time in 1936 with the construction of the nearby ski resort **Sun Valley**—site of the world's first chair lift, which was inspired by banana-loading machinery on tropical cargo ships. Ernest Hemingway arrived in 1939, and in Parlour Suite 206 at the Sun Valley Lodge, he wrote part of *For Whom the Bell Tolls*—"the part with all the snow in it," he later said. Hemingway committed suicide at his home in the Warm Springs area (not open to the public), and his grave is in the pioneer cemetery north of Ketchum. The **Hemingway Memorial,** a bronze bust, stands beside Trail Creek, on Sun Valley Road one-and-a-half miles east of the lodge. The Ketchum Community Library shows a short film of Hemingway shooting pheasant. For those who would honor Hemingway in his own style, with a raised glass, the former Alpine Club where "Papa" and his pals drank is now called Whiskey Jacques, on Ketchum's Main Street.

HAILEY

John Hailey laid out his namesake town on 440 acres he had bought for speculation in 1880; then he drew on a Union Pacific land development company for capital. The district's mines boomed, and the arrival of the Oregon Short Line in 1883 brought further prosperity. That year the town opened the first telephone system in Idaho Territory, and electric lights followed in 1889. A number of handsome old buildings survive, including the 1883 **Blaine County Courthouse** (First Avenue South and East Croy Street) and the **Emmanuel Episcopal Church** (Bullion Street and Second Avenue), built in 1885 in Gothic Revival style. The **Ezra Pound home** (Pine Street and Second Avenue South, private) is a simple frame house where the poet was born in 1885. There is a small collection of Pound material at the **Blaine County Historical Museum** (North Main and East Galena streets), housed in an 1882 adobe building, along with 5,000 political buttons and various antiques.

NORTHERN
IDAHO

OPPOSITE: *The Osborne Ranch in New Meadows, established in 1880. The surrounding area was an important cattle-raising center in the late nineteenth century.*

I n the great wilderness of northern Idaho, the Nez Percé traveled with the seasons. Each winter they returned to villages
made up of gabled houses covered with mats, villages they had
occupied for thousands of years. They congregated along the
streams for communal salmon fishing and in spring gathered to dig
camas lily bulbs. Their tepees stretched more than two miles across
the camas prairie at Weippe. It was there that the Nez Percé first
met white men.

A small advance party from the Lewis and Clark "Corps of
Discovery" entered Idaho on August 12, 1805, descended the western slope of the Rockies, and came upon a band of Shoshoni. Each
brave gave Lewis a bear hug. Together they smoked a pipe in friend-
ship. Then the Shoshoni agreed to come back over the pass with
extra horses to transport the expedition's heavy gear. In search of a
passage west, Clark scouted about fifty miles down the Salmon River,
but his Shoshoni guides warned him that the mountains ahead
"were not like those I had Seen but like the Side of a tree Streight
up," and that the mountains closed to a gorge where "the water runs
with great violence from one rock to the other on each Side foaming
& roreing thro rocks in every direction." Clark rightly concluded
that any canoe attempting passage would be dashed to sticks, and he
turned back. The party had to trade for Shoshoni horses and travel
160 miles north to the Lolo Trail, a rough track used by the Nez
Percé when traveling between Idaho's interior and the buffalo plains
of Montana. An early snow hampered the explorers, and a scarcity of
game reduced them to eating several colts.

Over the mountains at last, Clark first met the Nez Percé at the
Weippe prairie. The Indians were friendly and helpful, agreeing to
take care of the party's horses for the winter while the trailblazers
went on. Three days after launching their dugout canoes at the forks
of the Clearwater, the explorers arrived at the river's confluence with
the Snake, where the busy city of Lewiston now stands, and went on
to the Columbia and the Pacific. (Remarkably, Meriwether Lewis's
Newfoundland dog made the entire journey.) Although their route
across Idaho had not been the easiest or most practical, the explorers had established friendly relations with the Indians and had
blazed the trail for the mountain men.

During their journey Lewis and Clark observed that fur-bearing
animals were so plentiful that they actually got in each other's way. It
is no surprise, then, that a member of the expedition, John Colter,
returned to the Teton Valley in 1808 in search of beaver. The next

Jerome, a leader of the Nez Percé, and his horse outside his log cabin about 1890. In the 1880s the government began to compel the Nez Percé to adopt the customs of whites, such as owning land individually and living a settled life in cabins.

year a Briton, David Thompson, established the first trading post—Kullyspell (Kalispell) on Lake Pend Oreille—for the North West Company. At this point Idaho was disputed territory between the United States and Great Britain, so trappers from each side tried to outwit each other, gain Indian allies, steal each other's caches, and explore and control new parts of the territory.

By 1831 the Nez Percé, having been exposed to the ways of white explorers and mountain men, sent a small delegation to Saint Louis to visit William Clark (whom they called Red Hair) in order to learn more about the "big medicine" of churches and the Bible. All of the Indians died before returning to Idaho, but word of their visit stirred up missionary ferment. In 1836 the Reverend Henry Spalding and his wife, Eliza, had crossed the continent and founded a Presbyterian mission in the north at Lapwai. Next came the Catholics, led by Nicholas Point, a Jesuit priest who arrived among the Coeur d'Alene Indians in the Panhandle in 1842 and founded the Mission of the Sacred Heart. The mission had some success, although Father Point himself was dismayed by what he saw as his flock's dirtiness, idolatry, and "moral abandonment." By 1853 the "black robes" had built a second mission at Cataldo; today it is Idaho's oldest surviving building.

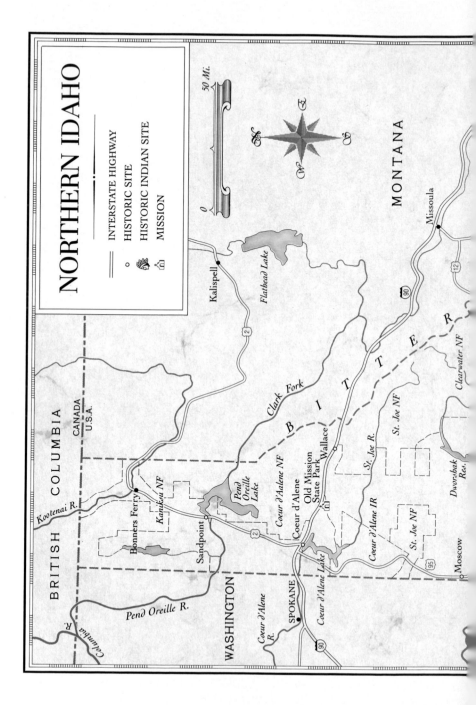

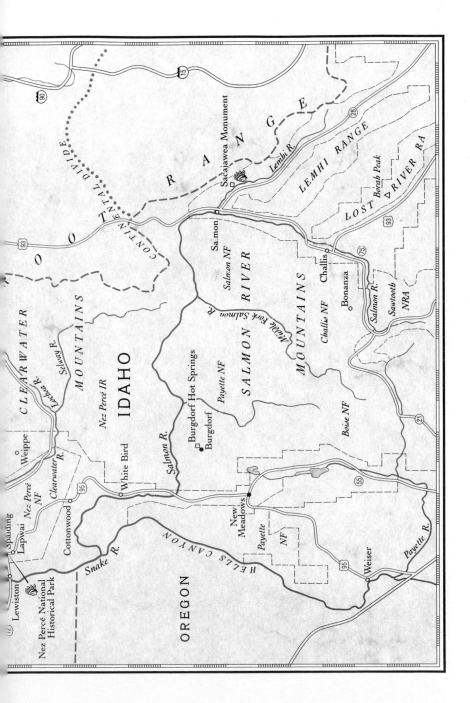

The next incursion of outsiders into Nez Percé country was entirely secular in its motives. In 1860 Elias D. Pierce, an Irish prospector disappointed in California, sneaked a small party of men onto Nez Percé treaty lands around the Clearwater. On Orofino Creek, he said, they "found gold in every place in the stream—I never saw a party of men so much excited; they made the hills and mountains ring with shouts of joy." By the end of the year, a rush of prospectors had established the town of Pierce. The accommodating Nez Percé—having observed that the newcomers just wanted to hike up isolated creeks and dig some gravel—agreed to let them work north of the Clearwater. Abusing this hospitality almost immediately, prospectors made strikes south of the river and started Elk City, then Florence, where one pan of dirt yielded $500 and a miner working in Baboon Gulch recovered $6,600 in a single day. By 1862 Florence bulged with 10,000 citizens—more than it would ever have again. Lewiston, located where the Snake meets the Clearwater, became a supply center for the mines even though it lay entirely on Nez Percé land. Representing another sort of western enterprise, outlaw Henry Plummer and his gang decided that guns were better prospecting tools than pans and picks, and they set off from Lewiston to rob miners across the district.

As a result of the gold lust, the Nez Percé found themselves outnumbered by whites on their own reservation. Some of the bands refused to sign an 1863 treaty trimming 7 million acres from the size of the land reserved as their exclusive domain by treaty in 1855. But in 1877, at the behest of white settlers, the government ordered "Non-Treaty Nez Percé" to move to the remaining 757,000 acres of the Lapwai reservation. The Nez Percé—a peaceful tribe who boasted that they had never killed a white man—agreed to move, even though it meant the loss of their hunting land. But when a few tense warriors from White Bird's band went out and killed four settlers in revenge for the murder of one of their fathers, it triggered the Nez Percé War of 1877. In the first engagement, Chief Joseph (known to his people as *Hin-mah-too-yah-lat-kekt,* or "Thunder Rolling Down from the Mountains") and other leaders routed a larger force of troops at White Bird Canyon. Then, pursued by 600 regulars under General Oliver. O. Howard, the Nez Percé headed for Montana.

OPPOSITE: *The Salmon River looking south from the area of Challis.*

The last of Idaho's Indian uprisings ended in 1879, and miners came north into the Coeur d'Alene country after A. J. Pritchard, a Montana "freethinker," struck gold in 1882 a few miles from today's Kellogg. He had tried to keep his little secret quiet, but the opportunistic Northern Pacific Railroad leafleted the nation with news of the glittering find in order to drum up traffic, and thereby promoted a stampede. But the real treasure of the Coeur d'Alenes had not even come to light yet—the largest lead-silver district in the United States, producing more than $2 billion in ore.

There were labor troubles at mines owned by distant capitalists, such as the Bunker Hill and Sullivan, in the 1890s. When about 100 masked miners dynamited the $250,000 concentrator at Wardner in 1899, Governor Frank Steunenberg declared martial law. Federal troops confined hundreds of miners in "bullpens," and peace eventually was restored. After an assassin killed Steunenberg with a bomb, in 1905 William Haywood, the organizer of the Western Federation of Miners, was named as a conspirator. His trial became a symbolic battle between management and labor, waged in the courtroom by prosecutor William E. Borah (later to be a six-time Idaho senator) and defense attorney Clarence Darrow. Darrow won, and Haywood was acquitted.

Mining was giving way to the timber industry in the state's economy. The most important lumber magnate was the German immigrant Frederick Weyerhaeuser, who, with his partners, bought up vast forest sections across northern Idaho starting in 1900. The Northern Pacific and other transcontinental railroads opened up outlets to the midwestern markets. Fortunately for the visitor, a great many of northern Idaho's woodlands are protected today in national forests. Such picturesque places as Coeur d'Alene Lake and Sandpoint draw travelers to their unspoiled wonders. In this sense, at least, northern Idaho remains what it was in the time of the Nez Percé—a place of timeless beauty.

This chapter begins where Lewis and Clark entered Idaho, at Lemhi Pass near Tendoy, and loops its way west across the state through Salmon, Challis, and Weiser; then moves north to Pierce; next it goes through Lewiston, heading north to Moscow, Cataldo, and Wallace; and finally moves to Coeur d'Alene and Sandpoint.

OPPOSITE: *A crane sorts a raft of logs by species into six groups on Coeur d'Alene Lake.*

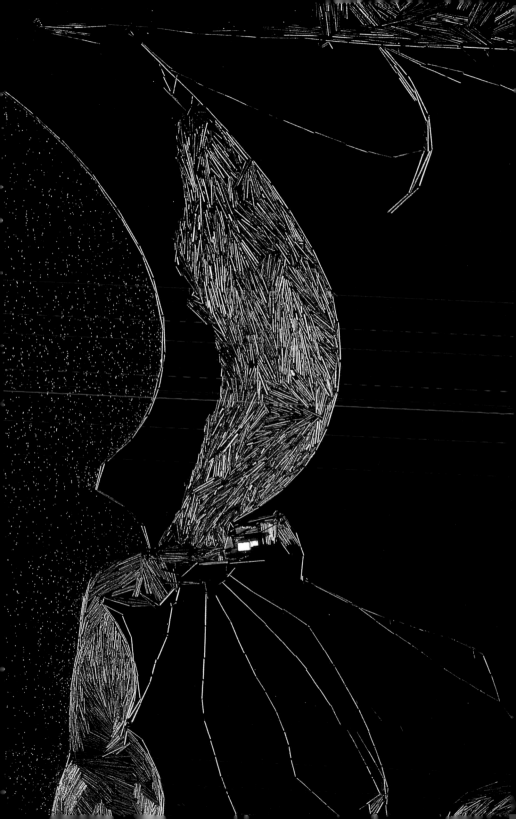

TENDOY

On August 12, 1805, at **Lemhi Pass** (twelve miles east of Tendoy on a dirt road), Meriwether Lewis attained one of his dreams. Here at 7,373 feet above sea level, he stood astride the Continental Divide. Behind him to the east the streams ran to the Mississippi, and before him the waters ran to the mighty Columbia. He had left the country clearly included in the Louisiana Purchase and trod now on land that belonged to no white man or government, though it was claimed by several.

Lewis realized that there would be no passage via water from Missouri to the outlet of the Columbia. He hiked down the steep western slope and located Indians whom he brought back to the main party to help with a portage over the pass. At this point a Shoshoni woman in the explorers' party became invaluable, and today she is honored with the **Sacajawea Monument** (Route 28, nine miles north of Tendoy). Sacajawea recognized the band of Indians returning with Lewis as her own people, from whom she had been stolen by the Crows five years earlier. In addition, their leader was her brother. This lucky reunion in 1805 cemented relations between the pathfinders and the Indians. The expedition then went on to success-ful explorations that strengthened the U.S. claim to the vast Oregon territory. (Sacajawea and her husband trekked with the expedition all the way to the Pacific and back carrying their newborn son.)

SALMON

Once over Lemhi Pass in 1805, Lewis and Clark's party descended to the Lemhi River and followed it northwest, along what is today Route 28, until they reached the Salmon River. Twenty-seven years later, trappers for the fur companies set up a winter camp near this confluence, with a roster of legendary mountain men that included Jim Bridger and Kit Carson. Miners came in the 1860s, and the town of Salmon was laid out as a supply center. It served the mining camp of Leesburg, and in 1867 an eighteen-mile toll trail was built between the two towns, with a crew of twelve men shoveling to open it for pack trains. Mining artifacts such as rockers and scales are dis-played at the **Salmon Museum** (210 Main Street, 208–756–3342), along with Shoshoni pipes, a headdress, and other Indian articles. There is also a fine gallery of Orientalia, collected in the 1920s.

About fifty-five miles south of Salmon stand the **Nicholia Charcoal Kilns** (off Route 28, six miles west on a marked road). From 1883 to 1889 these four domed ovens produced charcoal for the smelter at the nearby Viola lead mine. There were once sixteen kilns, each holding thirty-five cords of fir wood cut by immigrants from Ireland, China, and Italy; twelve kilns disappeared after the close of operations, when settlers scavenged the bricks.

CHALLIS

The **Challis Bison Jump** (north side of Route 75, just southwest of Route 93) is a combination of topography and ingenuity—a cliff that served the clever Lemhi Shoshoni better than spears or arrows. The Indians stampeded bison over the sixty-foot-high bluff and then butchered them at the bottom, where excavations have unearthed not only bison bones but also stone knives and glass beads from the late eighteenth to the early nineteenth centuries.

The Nicholia Charcoal Kilns, brick ovens built in the 1880s to provide fuel for the smelter of a lead mine.

From the main street of Challis an old toll road, the Custer Motorway, leads to the ghost town of **Custer,** founded in 1879. The thirty-five-mile trip once took teamsters five days over a route so steep they had to "snub down" their wagons by cinching ropes around trees. According to Lambert Florin, a local historian, the toll road brought civilizing change to the rough little town: "Married women joined their husbands and curtains went up on the windows." It also brought in such colorful characters as James McFadden, a toothless blacksmith who wanted to eat bear steaks and so hammered out a set of hinged steel choppers. There was also Godfrey Poquette de Lavallie, who had a lifelong obsession with inventing a perpetual-motion machine. One version was "a large wheel with pockets into which he dropped lead castings of varied weights. When the wheel stopped turning he would sigh and try again." The town, now a part of Challis National Forest, lay near the General Custer mill, where thirty stamps kept things noisy. A single shipment sent out by Wells Fargo was valued at $1 million. Today the 1900 schoolhouse contains the **Custer Museum** (Yankee Fork Road, 208–838–2201), which exhibits old school supplies, freighting equipment, and gold-rush mining gear such as picks and ore carts, including items used by Chinese miners.

Two miles south of Custer lies another ectoplasmic settlement, **Bonanza,** which started in 1878 with a collection of rough log structures. Among the earliest was a saloon, where to the strains of banjo and harmonica music Bonanza's first dance was held, hampered only slightly by the town's total lack of women. Half the men were issued red bandanas to tie around their arms, identifying them temporarily as ladies. "Any deficiencies caused by such man-to-man combat on the dance floor were overcome," it is reported, "after a few snorts of stingo from the bar." By 1879 Bonanza had nine saloons, as well as a Chinese laundry that advertised in the *Yankee Fork Herald*: "Charlie Bumboo, Prop. Shirts nicely starched and beautifully polished." The Bonanza **cemetery** (a half-mile west of town) contains pioneer graves, among them that of Agnes Elizabeth King, a woman of easy virtue who was shot in a dance hall. The good citizens had just established their brand new Boot Hill cemetery and did not want to inaugurate it with the likes of her, so they chose a grave site off in a corner and surrounded it with a high fence.

OPPOSITE: *An informal display of bottles and jars at the Custer Museum, Challis.*

Just north of Bonanza lies the **Yankee Fork Gold Dredge,** which went into business long after Bonanza and Custer were defunct. In 1938 investigations indicated that the bed of Yankee Fork might yield $16 million worth of gold, so the Silas Mason Company built the dredge on the site. It had seventy-two buckets and operated until 1952. Today a tour explains how such a contraption churns gravel to recover gold.

WEISER

Trapper Jacob Weiser prospected in Baboon Gulch, near Florence, in 1862, and in two days he collected $6,040 in gold. The next year he settled on a bend of the Snake River where the town of Weiser would grow up. Political clout came in due time. According to Cort Conley, an Idaho historian: "In 1879, through chicanery involving a generous jug of Snake River redeye and a lost ballot box, Weiser swiped the county seat." By 1890 the town boasted not only the usual stores and hotels but also six saloons. One customer, after an all-day drinking bout, went back to the Weiser Hotel and knocked over an oil lamp, starting a fire that razed the heart of the business district. A new town was soon established nearby.

Since 1914 Weiser has played host to fiddling competitions, and the third week in June is given over to the National Old-Time Fiddlers' Contest, which draws as many as 300 entrants, aged three to ninety-six. The **Fiddlers Hall of Fame** (10 East Idaho Street, 208–549–0450) has a collection of old-time instruments (including a miniature fiddle constructed of matchsticks) and contest mementoes. The **Intermountain Cultural Center and Washington County Museum** (2295 Paddock Avenue, 208–549–0205) displays household items, farm implements, tools, and tack. Exhibits explain irrigation in this part of the Snake River drainage and chronicle the extraordinary educational contribution of the Intermountain Institute, a trade school and high school for backwoods children of Idaho that operated from 1899 to 1933. The museum occupies the school's former administration building.

The town of Weiser offers a small turn-of-the-century architectural bonanza, the **Knights of Pythias Lodge Hall** (30 East Idaho Street, private), built in 1904 with a rusticated stone facade that transforms a western storefront into a castle with Tudor arched windows, a parapet, and two turrets—a sagebrush Camelot. Also of interest is the **Galloway House** (1120 East Second, private), built of brick in 1900 using proceeds that early settler Thomas Galloway earned from selling a herd of horses.

One of the oldest resorts in the state, **Burgdorf Hot Springs** (thirty miles northeast of McCall via minor roads) developed around natural hot springs in the 1860s, with a twenty-room hotel under the hospitality of Fred Burgdorf, a German immigrant. The gold rush to Thunder Mountain in the early twentieth century led to the enlargement of the resort, and a small number of buildings and cabins survive, mostly of log or frame construction.

WHITE BIRD

The first engagement of the Nez Percé War of 1877 took place on the hilly grassland at **White Bird Battlefield** (Route 95, fourteen miles south of Grangeville). Pamphlets for a self-guided tour of the battlefield area can be obtained at the Spalding headquarters of the Nez Percé National Historical Park. Word of raids by angry young men of the Non-Treaty Nez Percé had reached Fort Lapwai, where Captain David Perry set off with nearly 100 soldiers to round up the Indians and prevent them from reaching safety across the Salmon River. Aware that reprisals were coming, Chiefs Joseph and White Bird and their people camped warily at the bottom of White Bird Canyon. On the morning of June 17, 1877, Perry and his troops descended the slopes. The Indians may have tried to parley, but shots were fired. When Nez Percé bullets hit the company trumpeter, Perry was unable to broadcast clear orders on the battlefield and the troops were plunged into chaos. An Indian participant named Yellow Wolf later recalled: "The warriors charging up the west canyon struck that flank hard. Hanging on the side of their horses where not seen, they gave the soldiers a storm of bullets." The Nez Percé then sprang their trap, as hidden warriors emerged from buttes at the opening of the valley to flank the troops and send them running. Yellow Wolf said: "Two of my arrows struck soldiers only five steps away. . . . We drove them back across the mountain. . . . Then some of the chiefs commanded, 'Let the soldiers go! We have done them enough! No Indian killed!'" But Perry had lost a third of his men. The Nez Percé crossed to the west side of the Salmon River, which forestalled General Oliver. O. Howard from immediate pursuit with his 300 soldiers. On seeing that his quarry could choose any direction for retreat or face the soldiers if they tried to cross,

OVERLEAF: *The grassy, deeply ravined slopes of the White Bird Battlefield where the Nez Percé routed a cavalry force that had attacked them.*

A ferry lands four equine, five human, and one canine passenger on a rocky bank of the Salmon River. The ferry was pulled across the river by ropes.

Howard remarked admiringly, "No general could have chosen a safer position or one more likely to puzzle and obstruct a foe."

Neatly eluding their pursuers, the braves with their women, children, and all their possessions traveled over the difficult Lolo Trail, then fended off an attack by Colonel John Gibbon at Big Hole Basin in Montana. Clearly, the Nez Percé would find no peace, so they turned toward Canada, but Howard telegraphed ahead to General Nelson Miles to intercept them from the east. The Nez Percé fought well for six days against the soldiers, who used a cannon, until General Howard arrived with his troops. White Bird and more than 200 of his people managed to slip over the border to Canada at night, but Joseph and his band decided to avoid more bloodshed and go to the reservation in Idaho. It has been a 1,700-mile, four-month fighting retreat, and they were just 42 miles short of sanctuary. Contrary to government promises, the Nez Percé were sent to unhappy exile on reservations in Kansas and Oklahoma before being returned at last to the Northwest. Later, Nez Percé lands would be reduced by the Severalty Act to just 86,500 acres, an infinitesimal fraction of their original homeland.

COTTONWOOD

The **Cottonwood Skirmishes** (Route 95, two miles south of Cottonwood) took place after the battle at White Bird. Nez Percé warriors held off soldiers and volunteers, safely screening the movement of their people toward the Clearwater. During the 1880s Cottonwood was a hub for cattle roundups, and the region developed farming in wheat, barley, and peas—subjects of interest to visitors at the **Idaho County Farm and Ranch Museum** (Idaho County Fairground), which has an assemblage of reapers, threshers, seeders, and other early farming equipment.

Fascinating relics of Idaho County's past are displayed at **Saint Gertrude's Museum** (two miles west of Cottonwood via Main Street, 208–962–3224). There are personal items that belonged to the legendary "China Polly" Bemis, a tiny Asian woman who was virtually enslaved by a pimp known as Big Jim; after a man named Charlie Bemis won her in a poker game, she ran a boardinghouse for him. When Bemis was shot on the premises, she removed part of the bullet from his neck with a razor and crochet hook. Displays include books, Indian artifacts, and utensils crafted by a mountain man named Buckskin Bill. The 1925 **Convent of the Benedictine Sisters** next door was built of locally quarried blue porphyry in Romanesque style. The hand-carved high altar in the chapel is from Germany.

A remarkably cooperative enterprise, **Saint Joseph's Mission** (three miles south of Jacques on Route 95) was built on land given by Chief Slickpoo of the Nez Percé, with funds donated by Indians, whites, and Chinese. Erected in 1874 under the guiding hand of Father Joseph M. Cataldo, it was Idaho's first Catholic mission to the Nez Percé. It is now open as part of Nez Percé National Historical Park.

LAPWAI

For a while the federal government attempted to prevent prospectors and settlers from trespassing on Nez Percé lands, building **Fort Lapwai** (one block off Route 95, just south of Lapwai) in 1862. In later years, though, the fort protected the very settlers who had encroached. Fort Lapwai was Captain Perry's base when he galloped off with two cavalry companies in 1877, heading for defeat at White Bird in the first battle of the Nez Percé War. Today the site is largely occupied by the North Idaho Indian Agency, but the fort's duplex officers' quarters of 1883 still stand at the old parade ground.

NEZ PERCÉ NATIONAL HISTORICAL PARK

The park contains more than 12,000 acres with twenty-four sites interpreting the Nez Percé culture and the war of 1877, the Lewis and Clark expedition, the fur trade, missions, gold discoveries, and pioneer settlements. The **visitor center museum** contains a collection of Nez Percé artifacts that are extraordinarily fine—particularly the tanned-skin clothing adorned with elk teeth, porcupine quills, bear claws, shells, glass beads, and feathers; Chief Joseph's pipe bowl is also displayed. Exhibits explain the old Nez Percé way of life. The tribe called themselves *Ne-Mee-Poo*—the People—and spent a good part of each year on the move in quest of food. Fall was the time to fish for salmon, which was dried and stored for winter. Spring and summer were the seasons to gather roots, wild plants, and berries. Social life was organized by villages that sometimes associated in bands; these in

A group of Nez Percé horsemen in the early 1900s, when their fighting days were long past.

turn might join to form a confederacy. Within these units a hierarchy of councils and headmen made decisions for the group, but the decisions were not binding, and all were free to follow their own way of thinking. When white civilization invaded Nez Percé territory, there were perhaps 125 permanent villages and a population of 4,500.

The visitor center is adjacent to the **Spalding mission site.** Until 1897 this spot was known as Lapwai, a name that resonates because it was here in 1836 that Christianity arrived in Idaho in the person of Henry Harmon Spalding. With his wife, Eliza, he built the first mission house about two miles up Lapwai Creek from the Clearwater, but he soon realized that his evangelical seeds would take root only if the migratory Nez Percé would become settled farmers. The tireless missionary planted Idaho's first orchard and introduced the first irrigation for crops. Spalding also supplemented the gospel by constructing the first lumber mills and gristmills, teaching school, and

The Nez Percé were renowned horsemen.

importing the Northwest's first printing press to publish New Testament verses in Nez Percé translations. After two years mosquitoes and heat drove the Spaldings down to the banks of the Clearwater to build a new mission on this site at present park headquarters. Once comprising a house, school, wood house, granary, kitchen, shop, and wing for Indian students, the mission now exists only as a plot surrounded by a fence. The Spaldings are buried in the cemetery nearby. After 1860 the Nez Percé Indian Agency was based at the mission site, and the 1862 **Indian Agency Cabin** still stands. **Watson's Store,** opened in 1911, served whites and Nez Percé alike.

LOCATION: Route 95 at Spalding. HOURS: June through August: 8–6 Daily; September through May: 8–4.30 Daily. FEE: None. TELEPHONE: 208–843–2261.

Nez Percé mythology takes concrete form near Spalding, at the rock formation called **Ant and Yellowjacket** (just northeast of the junction of Routes 95 and 12). Here Coyote attempted to settle a battle between his two insect subjects, but when they ignored him Coyote magically turned them to stone, and they can be seen with their jaws locked. About five miles farther toward Lewiston on Route 12 is **Coyote's Fishnet,** where Coyote flung his net up one hill and Black Bear up the other, turning them to stone also.

LENORE

About 8000 B.C. the hunters known as Old Cordilleran lived at the **Lenore Archaeological Site** (Route 12, fifteen-and-a-half miles east of Spalding), one of the earliest places of human habitation in Nez Percé country. Interpretive signs at the roadside rest stop describe a long series of pit houses with village occupation dated circa 900 B.C. to A.D. 1300. The site was excavated from 1967 to 1971.

Twelve miles east of Lenore on Route 12, the **Canoe Camp** marks the site where Lewis and Clark shaped five canoes using the Indian method of burning out tree trunks. The explorers stayed here from September 26 to October 7, 1805, when they set off on the Clearwater River despite being hungry, ill, and poorly equipped. After the Canoe Camp they would make no more major stops until reaching the mouth of the Columbia in November 1805.

OPPOSITE: *A superbly crafted Nez Percé glove elaborately decorated with beads.*

A land agent, above at far left, allots white men a parcel of Indian land. Under the General Allotment Act of 1887, Nez Percé lands were divided into lots and distributed to the Indians; "surplus" lands were sold to whites. Today the Nez Percé hold only about 11 percent of the reservation set aside for them in 1863.

WEIPPE

On Weippe prairie William Clark and members of the "Corps of Discovery" came down out of the Bitterroot Mountains and met the Nez Percé at two villages a few miles south of Weippe and Route 11. It was September 20, 1805, and the friendly relations established that day on this wide upland plain would last more than seventy years. From the Indians Clark obtained three horse-loads of salmon and roots and dispatched them to the half-starved main expedition. Every August all the Nez Percé bands gathered on this prairie for a great fair to dig camas bulbs. On their return trip, Lewis and Clark would see the vast stretch of blue camas blossoms appearing like "lakes of fine, clear water." **Musselshell Meadow,** on the north side of Lolo Trail Road, fourteen miles east of Weippe, is the only place in Idaho where the Nez Percé still gather camas.

The **Lolo Trail** runs from near Weippe to the Lolo Pass—a 150-mile path where history walked. *Lolo* is Chinook for "carry," indicating that the route was a pack trail over which the mounted Nez Percé rode to and from the buffalo country to the east. On the way west in 1805 Lewis and Clark also traveled over the Lolo Pass. The trail was punishing—"excessively bad & thickly Strowed with falling timber. . . . Steep and Stony our men and horses much fatigued." With only two or three grouse to feed more than thirty hungry explorers, the party shot several colts to sustain themselves, and spirits plunged. On leaving the trail Lewis later wrote: ". . . the pleasure I now felt in having triumphed over the Rocky Mountains and descending once more to a level and fertile country where there was every rational hope of finding a comfortable subsistence for myself and party can be more readily conceived than expressed."

On their return eastward over the snowpacked trail in 1806, Lewis and Clark had to retreat for the first time during their journey, turning back to obtain Nez Percé guides. Lewis noted that without them, "I doubt much whether we . . . could find our way. . . . These fellows are most remarkable pilots." Another member of the party added: "It is but justice to say that the whole nation to which they belong are the most friendly, honest, and ingenious people that we have seen in the course of our voyage and travels."

In 1877 the Nez Percé had an unhappy reason for crossing the mountains. On July 11 General Oliver. O. Howard and his troops had come over the Clearwater and tried but failed to surprise the Indians. The ensuing skirmish ended with the withdrawal of 800 Nez Percé over Lolo Pass. They squeezed through the fallen timber, but the pursuing general had more difficulty making headway with his artillery, so he had fifty-two men with axes clear the route. (Cannonballs were found along the trail years afterward.) Today Route 12 parallels their route from Kooskia east to Montana. But much more congruent with the actual trail is Forest Service Road 500 (also called the Lolo Motorway), which is primitive and unsurfaced. Stretches of the true **Lolo Trail** and many of the historic sites en route are marked with signs, including a number of Lewis and Clark campsites. Travelers with sturdy vehicles wishing to sample a portion of the Lolo Trail can leave Route 12 east of Orofino at Forest Service Road 107, drive north to the Lolo Motorway (Forest Service Road 500), and turn east for a ten-mile stretch along the ridge, then return to Route 12 by turning south on Forest Service Road 569.

PIERCE

It was against federal law and contrary to a solemn treaty with the Nez Percé, but in 1860 E. D. Pierce went prospecting in the Clearwater country, camouflaging a gold-hunting jaunt as an expedition to trade with the Indians. After striking a little color, he returned with a party of men, found more gold, and platted a town. By the next spring, several thousand miners had poured into a new settlement of hewn logs called Pierce City, and the nearby slopes bustled with men, mules, and excited movement. One of the prospectors wrote home: "If all fools wore white hats, we should seem a flock of geese." Hardly had

Old Route 95 winds over hills to Lewiston where the Clearwater River joins the Snake.

gold been discovered at Pierce when it gave out, and after three years
the town dwindled to only about 500 people. As occurred elsewhere
in Idaho, patient Chinese miners worked over the "spent" mining
claims of the whites. The 1862 **Pierce Courthouse** (Court Street and
First Avenue West) was the first government building in Idaho, serving as the county courthouse and jail until 1885. At that time this two-
story frame structure with foot-square base timbers—built at a cost of
$3,700—was sold to a private party for the munificent sum of $50.

LEWISTON

When Lewis and Clark floated down the Clearwater River and
reached its confluence with the Snake in 1805, they noted: "The
Countrey about the forks is an open Plain on either side." Fifty-five
years later this spot seemed the logical place to disembark men and
supplies bound for the gold country at Pierce, since the plain was
the head of navigation on the Snake. Although the site was on Nez
Percé land—the tribe called it *She-me-ne-kem,* or "where the rivers
meet"—it soon blossomed with tents that gave rise to the nickname
Ragtown. The settlers had no legal right to the land, but they bought

lots and built on them, and by 1862 there were more than 2,000 squatters. A certain undesirable element crept in, the most notorious being Henry Plummer, who with his gang called the "Innocents" operated out of two nearby hideouts. Vigilantes forced him to move his business out of Lewiston in 1862, so the handsome, ingratiating Plummer moved on to Montana, where he became a lawman and was very likely the original model for a now-clichéd western-fiction character—the "honest" sheriff who secretly leads a band of outlaws.

When an 1863 treaty with the Nez Percé excluded the town from their reservation, it left the way clear to declare Lewiston capital of the territory. But the town lost power again when the northern region's mining population streamed south to the Boise Basin, and two years later Boise took over as the capital. Still, steamboats continued to churn into Lewiston with freight, the town hung on and grew slowly, and finally, in 1898—long after other communities had railroad service—the Northern Pacific arrived. Later, timber development and irrigation agriculture brought new solidity to the community, and after the turn of the century, the raucous mining supply town attempted to turn respectable with ordinances that forbade slot machines, vagrancy, "immoral plays," and cursing. On the site of the 1861 Luna House, Lewiston's first hotel, the **Luna House Museum** (3rd and C Streets, 208–743–2535) has many pioneer artifacts and a large collection of historic photographs. The **Lewiston Depot** (13th and Main Streets, private) is an eclectic brick building that contained ticket and telegraph offices and served the grain and fruit shippers of the region. The Northern Pacific and Union Pacific competed to serve Lewiston, then joined forces in creating the Camas Prairie Railroad, for which this depot was built in 1909. In Pioneer Park, near the 1904 **Carnegie Library,** stands an 1862 **log house** typical of Lewiston's transition from tent camp to town.

MOSCOW

Along Route 95 from Lewiston to Moscow, the traveler passes the world's most bountiful region for soft white wheat. Lying at the heart of this fertile Palouse country, Moscow had certain advantages from its founding in 1871, but it was hampered by isolation until a branch of the Union Pacific came to town in 1885. The University of Idaho

OVERLEAF: *A vivid field of flowering winter rape on a road near Cavendish.*

The administration building of the University of Idaho, built in 1906.

was established here in 1889 in a political trade-off by which Moscow agreed to stop backing a movement for northern Idaho to detach itself and meld into Washington as a new state.

In the **Fort Russell Historic District** (one block east of Main Street, from Jefferson to Monroe streets) there are a number of notable houses. The **Latah County Historical Society** (110 South Adams Street, 208–882–1004) occupies an Eastlake-style mansion built in 1886 by the state's first U.S. senator and third governor, William J. McConnell. The rooms are restored to the period of 1900, and there are changing exhibitions on Latah County history.

Two interesting downtown buildings, on opposite corners at 4th and Main streets, are the **Skattaboe Block,** a commercial structure in Richardsonian Romanesque style, and the red–brick **Hotel Moscow,** built in 1892 in the same general style. Also built of red brick is the **Moscow Post Office Building** (3rd and Washington streets), a 1911 structure in an eclectic Renaissance Revival style. The **Appaloosa Museum** (Moscow-Pullman Highway, 208–882–5578) exhibits paintings and artifacts related to the Appaloosa horse as well as early cowboy equipment and Nez Percé artifacts.

CATALDO

The spiritual inclinations of the Coeur d'Alene Indians were piqued by stories about the missionaries, "black robes" who were supposed to be powerful medicine men. Catholic Jesuit priests heard about this interest, and when Father Pierre De Smet visited the Indians in 1842, he promised them a mission. It was a hasty visit, so to save time he taught them translations of the Ten Commandments by having a group stand in a circle, each memorizing one commandment so that a communal recital would produce the entirety.

Old Mission of the Sacred Heart

De Smet sent Father Nicholas Point, who supervised the building of a log-cabin mission on the bank of the Saint Joe River and baptized the majority of the Indians. When he found that the site flooded every spring, the mission moved to the present grassy knoll in 1846. Overlooking the Coeur d'Alene River, it was a splendid setting for a fine work of architecture by Father Anthony Ravalli. A remarkable Italian who was a priest, physician, scientist, mechanic, artist, and sculptor, he radiated a strong personal magnetism in everything he worked on, and the Old Mission of the Sacred Heart remains affecting after nearly 140 years. The building is a treasure shop of Father Ravalli's arts and crafts, which raise the rustic to the sublime: European-style chandeliers made with tin from old cans; wallpaper made from East Coast newspapers painted white with floral designs; Hudson's Bay Company fabric to adorn the walls; pine altars painted to look like marble—a bit of Italy in the Old West.

The structure itself is built of huge logs that were latticed with saplings and woven with grass, then daubed with mud. Ravalli worked with a crew of Indians, his tools consisting of not much more than ropes, pulleys, an ax, and a pocketknife. No nails were used, only wooden pegs. The mission filled the Coeur d'Alene with awe, for it was the biggest, most complex structure they had ever seen. They called it the House of the Great Spirit. Because they liked to sit on the floor in their accustomed way, the mission had no pews.

A farming village had sprung up around the mission before it was complete in 1853. But by 1877 the federal government insisted that the Coeur d'Alene move to a reservation far south, and after some resistance they left their church and homes behind. After their departure Father Joseph Cataldo, who established several missions in

Idaho, made this one his headquarters, and it is often called the
Cataldo Mission. The 1887 parish house is the oldest standing building in Idaho. Each year on August 15, many Coeur d'Alene Indians
come to the mission to celebrate the Feast of the Assumption, moved
by strong feelings for the church their ancestors built.

> LOCATION: Old Mission State Park, 27 miles east of Coeur d'Alene
> off Route 90. HOURS: June through August: 8–6 Daily; September
> through May: 9–5 Daily. FEE: Yes. TELEPHONE: 208–682–3814.

WALLACE

In 1884 a man named Colonel W. R. Wallace (who was not a
colonel) bought eighty acres of swampy, cedar-clogged land with
Sioux scrip (which was not legal money) and established a town in
the gold-mining region of the Coeur d'Alene River valley. Because of
Wallace's questionable currency, his claim to the town site was
declared void in 1889, creating a frenzy of claim jumping and disputes as residents staked out and recorded lots all over town, leaving
Wallace with nothing. Others got rich, however, for in the meantime
the great Bunker Hill and Sullivan lode had been discovered nearby—found, as legend has it, when Noah Kellogg's jackass stood on a
huge outcrop of galena, a mineral that often accompanies silver.
With discovery of many other mines, the valley achieved the reputation of being the richest silver district in the United States, producing more than 1 billion ounces of silver. (In silver dollars this
amount would circle the globe at the equator.)

In the town of Wallace, the first saloon and first school opened
in 1886, and a narrow-gauge railroad arrived to haul out ore. The
next year Colonel Wallace went fishing on Placer Creek and caught
247 trout in a single day—the only bonanza he ever reported. But
businesses in Wallace continued to grow, catering to the often illiterate citizens by using signs whose shapes indicated the product or service offered, such as a shoe for shoe repairs. Saloons and faro tables,
horse races, and boxing matches entertained the townsfolk. After a
fire in 1890 razed the business district, citizens rebuilt more solidly,
using 400,000 bricks in a single summer.

OPPOSITE: *The Old Mission of the Sacred Heart in Cataldo, completed in 1853 in the Greek
Revival style, is the oldest building in Idaho. Its clapboards were added in the 1860s.*

Labor troubles erupted between the mine owners and the Central Miners Union in 1892 and the Western Federation of Miners in 1899, when the entire valley was placed under martial law for two years. Misfortune struck Wallace once more in 1910, when Idaho's devastating "great fire" swept through and burned a third of the town. Despite these disasters, enough of the old town survives to be listed as the **Wallace Historic District,** which has its hub at 6th and Bank streets. At this corner stands the **White and Bender Building** (524 Bank Street), a Queen Anne commercial structure with a pressed metal turret; it was the largest brick building to be erected the summer after the 1890 fire. Across the street to the east is the **Rossi Insurance Building** (1892), and to the north the **Smokehouse,** which served as the county courthouse from 1898 to 1905. At 509 Bank Street an old bakery now houses the **Wallace District Mining Museum** (208–753–7151), with its mine cars, mock-up tunnels, and the last steam-driven diamond drill in existence. There are models of underground workings, photographs, a mineral collection, and every-day artifacts such as miners' lunch buckets. Next door a tour departs to the **Sierra Silver Mine** (208–752–5151), a small underground hard-rock operation with working equipment.

The **Northern Pacific Depot Railroad Museum** (6th and Pine streets, 208–752–0111) occupies a 1901 depot with a three-story round tower. The first floor is built of rare Chinese bricks, while the second floor is stuccoed concrete that contains tailings from local mines. Inside, the museum re-creates a railway depot of 1900, with displays about the Union Pacific and the Railroad Express Agency and artifacts including a track drill, velocipede, and locomotive bell.

COEUR D'ALENE

It was beautiful scenery that gave rise to the city of Coeur d'Alene. When General William Tecumseh Sherman camped on the lakeshore during an inspection tour in 1877, he found the area so attractive that he mentioned it as a likely site for a fort. Fort Coeur d'Alene (later renamed for Sherman) was designed to protect railroad and telegraph crews, guard the U.S. border with Canada, keep the local Indians peaceful, and pave the way for settlement. General Sherman had traveled the Mullan Road, an east–west military route built by John Mullan, whose crews had passed through the area around 1859. (A portion of the road is now part of Sherman Avenue.) As people settled down to supply goods and services to the soldiers at Fort Sherman and mining boomed in the Coeur d'Alene area after 1883, a city grew up around the military base. By 1890 a number of steamboats served the community with freight and passenger service, and an electric railway brought excursionists from Spokane to board the steamers for Sunday outings. Of **Fort Sherman,** which once occupied a thousand acres next to Coeur d'Alene Lake and had fifty-two buildings, several buildings remain on and around the campus of North Idaho College. The **Fort Sherman Chapel** (Hubbard Street and Woodland Drive), of red clapboard with white trim, was the first church, school, and library for the fort and early settlers. The 1878 **Officers' Quarters** (West Garden Street) were part of officers' row and stand beside Barracks Company A. The 1885 stone powder magazine now houses the **Fort Sherman Museum** (College Drive, 208–664–3448), which contains exhibits and artifacts relating to the fort, as well as logging equipment and Forest Service artifacts.

The **Museum of North Idaho** (115 Northwest Boulevard, 208–664–3448) exhibits arrow points and mortars from the Coeur d'Alene Indians, rifles from explorers and trappers, a model of the *Amelia Wheaton* steamboat, built in 1880 with lumber from the sawmill at Fort Sherman, and logging artifacts such as crosscut saws (nicknamed "misery whips" or "Swedish fiddles").

SANDPOINT

Sandpoint got its start as a timber and mill town, its operations served by three railroads that arrived between 1880 and 1906. The gabled **Sandpoint Burlington Northern Railway Station** (Cedar Street at Sand Creek, private) was built by the Northern Pacific in 1916, partly in the Jacobean style. Another sort of transportation is enshrined at the **Vintage Wheel Museum** (Cedar Street and Third Avenue, 208–263–7173), which displays a collection of conveyances from the horse-drawn era (hearse, mail coach) to the dawn of the automotive age (1907 International Harvester Auto Buggy, 1923 Stanley Steamer) to the modern era (1962 Rolls-Royce). The museum emphasizes Fords, building its tours around Henry Ford and his contribution to the national culture and employing music, artwork, lighting, and special effects to tell the story of history on wheels. The **Bonner County Historical Museum** (609 Ella Avenue, Lakeview Park, 208–263–2344) has displays on Indians, logging, and milling.

C H A P T E R   E I G H T

WESTERN MONTANA

OPPOSITE: *Inside the rotunda of the Montana State Capitol in Helena are paintings of typical early pioneer characters. Shown here are the Cowboy and the Indian.*

To see Montana as others have seen it, simply look at the state's various booms: beaver pelts, buffalo hides, gold, silver, cattle, sheep, lumber, copper, wheat, petroleum, coal. Men have looked at Montana's wild, lovely landscape and seen mostly profit: Here was a place to extract riches as fast as possible—anything that could be trapped, shot, mined, herded, or farmed and shipped out. Montana even nicknamed itself the Treasure State.

Geography itself created these bonanzas—rivers swarming with beavers, mountains veined with ore, plains of waving grass for grazing. The western third of the state is a swath of more than twenty mountain ranges, which run from northwest to southeast and ally as the Rockies. The Continental Divide passes near Helena (which was founded on gold strikes at Last Chance Gulch) and proceeds to Butte (which grew around a single massive mountain of copper). Montana's very name derives from *montaña,* the Spanish word for mountain. From their lofty sources, Montana rivers flow eventually into three oceans—the Arctic, Pacific, and Atlantic (Gulf of Mexico)—a claim no other state can match.

Lewis and Clark, during their expedition of 1804–1806, stayed longer and covered more territory in Montana than they did anywhere else on their 8,000-mile journey. Their goals were established in a letter from President Thomas Jefferson after the United States paid France about three cents an acre for Louisiana in 1803. The expedition was to seek a water route to the Pacific by tracing the Missouri upstream, then making what was hoped to be a short portage, and finally following the Columbia westward. The explorers also were to amass scientific knowledge of the West's animals, plants, and minerals; to gauge the future of fur trading; to persuade the Indians to be peaceful and trade with the Americans rather than the British; and to affirm the U.S. claim over the Pacific Northwest, which was disputed by England, Spain, and Russia. To stop Lewis and Clark, Spain sent four separate expeditions, all of which ran into Indian trouble and had to turn back.

The two captains accomplished all their goals in nearly perfect fashion, living up to the name their party had been given: Corps of Discovery. They named more natural features in Montana than in any other state. (Some designations were later changed, however, since Westerners preferred such names as Big Hole, Beaverhead,

OPPOSITE: *While traveling through the territory that is now Montana, William Clark recorded his observations of a "Cock of the Plains, Heathcock' in his expedition journal on March 2, 1806.*

the feathers about it's head
pointed and stiff some he
the base of the beak. feath
fine and stiff about the ea
This is a faint likeness of t
of the plains or Heath
the first of those fo
we met with u
Missouri be
in the Neighb
of the Rock
and fun
which p
betwee
and Ra
Gange
an
m

use

it
oth
d eye.
Ne
Ne
ith
the
a
od
ntains
he Mountain
Columbea
Great falls
go in large
ngularly
e hide remarkably close when pursued.
e flights &c.

Large Black & White Pheasant is peculiar
at portion of the Rocky Mountains watered by
Columbia River. at least we did not see them until
eached the waters of that river, nor since we ha
those Mountains. they are about the size of
grown hen. the contour of the bird is mu
of the redish brown Pheasant common
ountry. the tail is proportionably as long and is

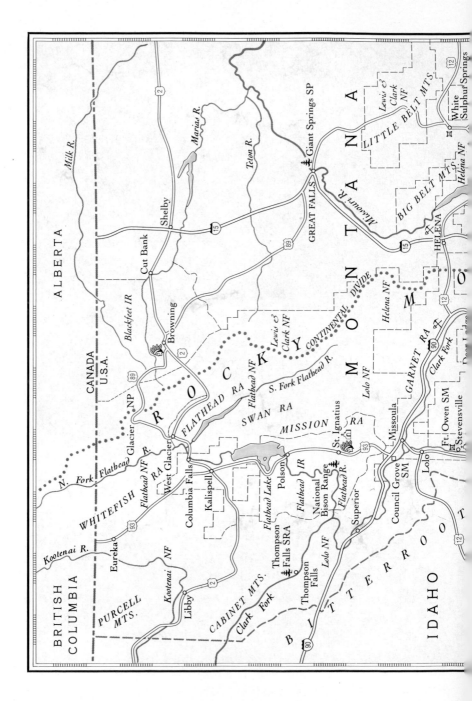

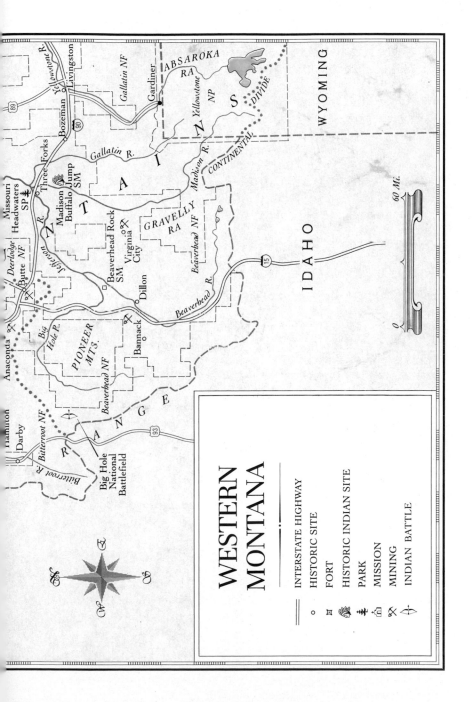

WESTERN MONTANA

INTERSTATE HIGHWAY

HISTORIC SITE

FORT

HISTORIC INDIAN SITE

PARK

MISSION

MINING

INDIAN BATTLE

WYOMING

IDAHO

60 Mi.

ABSAROKA RA

CONTINENTAL DIVIDE

Yellowstone NP

Gallatin NF

Gardiner

Livingston

Bozeman

Three Forks

Gallatin R.

Madison R.

Missouri Headwaters SP

Madison Buffalo Jump SM

GRAVELLY RA

Beaverhead NF

Beaverhead Rock SM

Virginia City

Deerlodge NF

Butte NF

Jefferson R.

Beaverhead R.

Dillon

Big Hole R.

PIONEER MTS.

Bannack

Beaverhead NF

Anaconda

Hamilton

Darby

Bitterroot NF

Bitterroot R.

Big Hole National Battlefield

R   A   N   G   E

and Ruby for their wild rivers instead of the explorers' Wisdom, Philosophy, and Philanthropy.) Adventuring up the Missouri in two pirogues and six canoes, the explorers soon came upon new animals. Before the expedition science knew nothing of the coyote, jackrabbit, prairie dog, or mountain goat—or of the dreaded grizzly bear. A grizzly came upon Lewis on open ground, charged him "open mouthed and full speed," and chased the explorer into a river. After firing at another bear, Clark observed that "not withstanding it was shot through the heart it ran at its usual pace near a quarter of a mile before it fell."

After struggling over Lolo Pass into Idaho, they went on to the Pacific. On the return journey through Montana, the party split in two in order to explore more territory. Lewis went up the Marias River, where the only hostile Indian encounter of the entire expedition left two Blackfoot braves dead and the explorers fleeing on horses day and night. Below the mouth of the Yellowstone River, Lewis rejoined Clark, who had explored the Gallatin Valley and then floated peacefully down the river. The explorers now returned to Saint Louis, their expedition a nearly perfect enterprise: The Corps of Discovery had explored and mapped a vast region, forced the abandonment of the hope of a northwest river passage, and established friendly relations with the Indians. (Portions of the route Lewis and Clark followed can be traced today by boat, foot, horseback, or car.)

Lewis and Clark also made an observation of special importance for the next phase of Montana history—that the upper Missouri was "richer in beaver and otter than any country on earth." The beaver trade developed because of a clothing trend thousands of miles away. When the beaver hat became fashionable in Europe, the rich flaunted their wealth with ever-taller headgear (incidentally giving rise to the term "high hat"). This fad created a demand that only the vast resources of North America could satisfy. From Canada the Hudson's Bay Company and the North West Company pushed toward Montana for the British. On the American side, the entrepreneur Manuel Lisa built Montana's first trading post in 1807 at the confluence of the Yellowstone and Bighorn rivers. To make contact with the Indians and invite them in to trade at Lisa's Fort, he hired John Colter, a member of the Lewis and Clark expedition. Colter was one of the rough-and-ready trappers who roamed the Rockies and in the process sustained another fashion trend—what the historian LeRoy Hafen called "perhaps the only original American costume—the fringed buckskin suit."

In 1808 the British established their own trading post near today's Libby in northwestern Montana, when David Thompson of the North West Company sent "Big Finan" McDonald to trade with the Kootenai Indians. The next year Thompson built Saleesh House, near present Thompson Falls. But John Jacob Astor's American Fur Company soon took the premier position on the upper Missouri. By 1828 the company's Kenneth McKenzie built a base of operations called Fort Union at the confluence of the Yellowstone and Missouri. Using every means fair or foul to overcome his rivals, Astor's men illegally distilled liquor at the fort for trade with the Indians and awed them with a "fireboat-that-walks-on-the-water," or steamboat.

In 1831 Astor's company even moved into the country of the Blackfoot, who had learned to be hostile to whites, erecting Fort Piegan near the mouth of the Marias, which the Indians burned as soon as the trappers left with a cargo of furs. It was immediately replaced with Fort McKenzie, built by a terrified crew who worked surrounded by thousands of curious, hostile Blackfoot. Foreseeing the end of the beaver market and the decline of the beaver population, Astor left the fur trade in 1834 and sold out to his managers. Alexander Culbertson took over Fort Union for the reorganized company and in 1846 built Fort Benton, an adobe post on the Missouri River.

Although the mountain men explored much of Montana, they left little of substance behind. The fur era did little more than strip Montana of a resource in exchange for profits made by a few men far away. The trappers did have an influence, though, by making the Indians aware of Christianity. After hearing of churchmen whose teachings could "enable [people] to live after death," the Flathead sent four parties to Saint Louis between 1831 and 1839 in quest of a "Black Robe" to bring the "white man's Book of Heaven." The Jesuit Pierre De Smet built Saint Mary's Mission in 1841 in the Bitterroot Valley; but when he offered the same powerful medicine to the enemy Blackfoot, the Flathead became disillusioned and the mission was temporarily abandoned in 1850.

Major John Owen paid $250 for the original Saint Mary's Mission, developing a trading post at the hub of a vast area. And it was John Owen who forged a link to the next stage of Montana history when he made the first documented mention of gold, a terse entry in his diary in February 1852: "Sunday, 15—Gold Hunting found some." Nothing developed, though, nor did any excitement

Montana artist Charles M. Russell painted this depiction of a buffalo hunt in 1912. The virtual elimination of the buffalo contributed to the rapid demise of the Indians living on the Plains (detail).

follow Francois Finlay's discovery of ore traces in the Deer Lodge Valley—probably because his employer, the Hudson's Bay Company, preferred to keep it quiet so as not to disrupt the fur trade with a gold rush. Montana got its gold boom, however, and it transformed the region from an almost unpopulated frontier to a U.S. territory. After a party of disappointed California prospectors made a small strike in the Deer Lodge Valley in 1858, "worn weary pilgrims in Search of the Auriferous Sands" poured into the area and soon pushed on to other parts of southwest Montana.

Fabulous strikes on Grasshopper Creek in 1862 created a camp called Bannack, which produced gold worth about $5 million the first year. This bonanza attracted the usual highwaymen, whores, and faro dealers and also inspired the citizens to rename their shack-and-tent hamlet with the grander title of Bannack City. A second rich find was made in Alder Gulch by a party of prospectors who were only trying to pan enough gold for tobacco money;

Virginia City took shape at the hub of a busy district. Then in 1864 a strike at Last Chance Gulch spawned the town of Helena. "In pronouncing the name, understand me well," said a popular jingle, "Strong emphasis should be laid on Hel." The town started out wild, but by the 1890s the more spectacularly rich prospectors lived in mansions, were driven about by liveried coachmen, and had butlers to serve them fancy foods that in no way resembled the bacon and beans of the early mining camp. Miners also flooded Confederate Gulch, where in a single day one claim yielded 700 pounds of gold.

Montana's landscape suffered as miners stripped the alder trees from Alder Gulch, gouged holes everywhere, and left mountains of dirt in city streets; one diarist reported that Virginia City looked "as if an enormous Hog had been uprooting the soil." A stench rose from outhouses, horse corrals, and smelters; mine tailings and rusting apparatus lay all over the land. Nor did men treat each other better than they had treated the earth. Although the murderous character of the early settlements has been exaggerated—in fact, Montana mining towns offered literary groups, social dancing, and French lessons—at such a distance from government authority, there was little to stop "road agents" and other brigands. Most notorious was Henry Plummer, who became county sheriff in Bannack in the 1860s, all the while secretly leading a gang of desperadoes. Vigilantes hanged all twenty-four members of the gang and eight more outlaws, often leaving the mysterious symbol "3-7-77" attached to the bodies.

Of all the mining camps, only Helena and Butte grew into substantial towns. Yet the gold rush contributed to Montana's growth and stability. The miners' demand for food created farming communities in the Gallatin, Bitterroot, and other valleys; financial transactions required banks and a legal system (even though one diarist sighed that "We had no need for law until the lawyers came"). Southern Montana boomtowns brought settlement to the northern part of the territory, as the mines needed timber and transportation, creating two industries. A network of roads soon tied the mining settlements to the rest of the territory and the world beyond: the Mullan Road to the Columbia River; James Fisk's overland routes from Minnesota; the Bozeman Trail from Casper, Wyoming; the Corinne–Virginia City Road to the transcontinental railroad line in Utah. Freighting companies did a huge business, requiring thousands of mules and oxen and hundreds of drovers and other employees. As hordes of miners took steamboats up the Missouri from Saint Louis at a $150 fare, Fort Benton became a thriving port.

Miners at the Montana Lead Mine at Rimini in 1889. This mining center near Helena received its unusual name after a traveling theatrical company performed the drama of

As Montana's population increased, so did the need for government. In 1864 Congress created Montana Territory, with its first capital at Bannack, switching the next year to Virginia City and later to Helena. Until about 1870 the government only hobbled along, as Washington sent Republican officials who were at odds with the territory's Democratic-controlled legislature. Some of the leaders were buffoons or simply did little constructive work. Acting governor Thomas F. Meagher, for example, ran up government bills of more than $1 million to fight a "Sioux invasion" he forecasted—incorrectly as it turned out.

Indian conflict was inevitable, though, as whites invaded Native American hunting grounds and homelands. Mountain men had introduced the destructive powers of liquor and guns, and in 1837 a Missouri River steamboat imported smallpox that killed 15,000 Indians of six nations. A trader came upon one Blackfoot camp where "hundreds of decaying forms of human beings, horses, and

Paulo and Francesca da Rimini here in the 1880s. OVERLEAF: *Bowman Lake in Glacier National Park lies at an altitude of 4,020 feet.*

dogs lay scattered everywhere among the lodges." All the while, treaties whittled away the territories of the Sioux, Gros Ventre, Assiniboine, Blackfoot, and Crow, in return for annual gifts of food and equipment. Other treaties set aside the Jocko Reservation for the Flathead, Pend d'Oreille, and Kootenai, and gave the Blackfoot a large territory north of the Missouri.

Whites had little understanding of Indian culture; many saw the tribes as murderous, lazy savages impeding progress in the West. The *Montana Post* said "We . . . know what an Indian is and . . . hate him and desire his death." The Indian agent to the Blackfoot suggested payment of their next annuity "in powder and ball from the mouth of a six-pounder." After a series of retaliatory raids by the Indians, General Philip Sheridan decided to "strike them hard," dispatching Major Eugene Baker from Fort Ellis in 1870. In a frozen dawn along the Marias River, troops attacked and burned a village and killed 173 slumbering Blackfoot, including more than 50

women and children; the camp turned out to be that of friendly chief. After this slaughter the Blackfoot relented and other tribes also went to reservations.

· With the growth of livestock and other industries and a greater population came the fulfillment of a twenty-five-year movement toward Montana statehood. A constitution was pasted together from the documents of other states, and in 1889 Montana became the forty-first state in the Union. In the ensuing struggle for political power, the issue of relocating the state capital in 1894 was typical of the time. In part, it was a battle between Montana's rival copper kings: on one side, the sociable, clever Marcus Daly, a red-cheeked Irishman who favored Anaconda, the town he created near his fabulous copper mines; and on the other, the ruthless William A. Clark, a "tight white starched little man" whose choice, Helena, won the election. Each man was hugely successful. In nine years the ambitious Daly extracted 36 million pounds of copper from the Anaconda, a mine so extensive that its continuing construction used up 40,000 board feet of timber a day. He also built an immense smelter, spewing arsenic smoke that "reportedly turned the wash green on the line," said historian Clark Spence, "and so impregnated grass that local cattle had copper-plated teeth." William Clark also grew rich from copper mines; the metal was coming into demand for use in electrical wires and motors, telegraph lines, and roofing materials.

During the 1920s the automobile brought tourism to Montana, and some failing cattle spreads were reborn as dude ranches. These offered a combination of outdoor life and ease that one resident hailed as "the West's soothing gift to a headachy world." And it's true: Montana's big skies and rugged scenery are among the few things no one has managed to haul away at a profit. They remain for the traveler to enjoy.

This chapter covers Montana's mountainous regions, begining in Great Falls and proceeding northward to Shelby. It then winds westward along the Canadian border to Libby, and then moves southward to Thompson Falls. Next it loops eastward to Polson and southwest to Superior; it continues southeast to Lolo and follows the Bitterroot River to Conner, proceeds northward to Drummond, and traces Route 90 eastward to Butte. After describing Helena, the chapter concludes in the southewestern region of the state

GREAT FALLS

In coming upon Great Falls on June 13, 1805, Meriwether Lewis stood in awe of "the grandest sight I ever beheld"—a series of five cataracts over which the Missouri River dropped 400 feet. He yearned for an artist's pen to render "this truly magnificent and sublimely grand object which has from the commencement of time been concealed from the view of civilized man." Then events went a bit sour. He was chased into the river by a grizzly bear and had run-ins with a mountain lion, a rattlesnake, and three menacing bull buffalo. And the price for the beauty of the cataracts was a her-culean labor. To carry their boats and cargo upstream past the falls, the party had to fashion crude carts, using sliced cottonwood trunks for wheels. The arduous eighteen-mile portage cost the corps about two weeks of slogging over gumbo mud, steep banks, and prickly pear cactus (the men's moccasined feet became bloody and torn), meanwhile enduring mosquitoes, rain, and hail. To lighten their moods, the explorers drank up almost all their remaining tipple to celebrate Montana's first Fourth of July, then danced and sang till ten at night. By July 15 they set off on the rest of their westward journey, and the next year Lewis returned east-ward by way of Great Falls.

Although the landscape of jagged rocks remains, dams have been built at the falls, with Ryan Dam at the "Great Falls." **Giant Springs Heritage State Park** (4600 Giant Springs Road, one-quarter mile north of the Great Falls city limits, 406–454–3441) is laid out on the site where the party discovered a "handsome cascade" of spring water, which Lewis called "the largest [spring] I ever beheld," later measured at an astounding flow of 338 million gal-lons a day. Called the Roe River, it runs only sixty-seven yards to the Missouri and may be the world's shortest officially named river. Civilization followed Lewis and Clark only in 1884, when Paris Gibson established what he hoped would be an industrial town. "Empire Builder" James J. Hill helped his old friend enlarge the settlement and gave it a future when he linked the Manitoba Railroad and the Montana Central at Great Falls. In the 1890s meat packing began, the Black Eagle Dam started generating power, and a copper smelter went into operation. After the turn of the century more hydroelectric plants and another railroad materialized, while Great Falls prospered further as an agricultural hub.

C. M. Russell Museum Complex

The cowboy painter and sculptor Charles Marion Russell (1865–1926) documented the romantic Wild West as it vanished around him. After arriving in Montana at age 15, Charlie Russell bunked in with a trapper, worked as a herder and range rider, dwelled with the Indians, and lived to complete more than 4,500 works depicting exactly what he saw. Having learned Indian sign language and having become friends with the tribes and seen them in full regalia (he was adopted by the Blood Indians, a Canadian branch of the Blackfoot), he was able to render the Plains Indians so accurately that he created a genuine historical record. He did the same with the cowboys. At first Russell gave away his works or sold them for almost nothing, but over time his talent was recognized and he exhibited paintings in New York ("this is one big settlement . . . tall tepees. I want to go back to God's Country") and London. Some of his pieces brought more than $20,000, which he said sounded like "dead man's prices," and today some Russell canvases command fifty times that. Despite his recognition and riches, Russell's studio was always open to his cowpoke pals, and he was a

Charles M. Russell with his wife in the company of Indians. OPPOSITE: *Russell sent a number of illustrated letters to his neighbor Trigg when he was traveling in the east. This description of a childhood hunt is from a letter dated November 10, 1903.*

stump or log so of corse he
cked the ammunition an don
he loding we were shooting in t
every thing in sight
I kept belly aking saying my tu
the big kid
rig youl get
rs an I did
when
I looded f
remem
ow the
jumped
of the b
he sher
or more to
the l

w handing the gun to me said t
t would kill a tiger an I think
ld if hed been on the same end

legendary storyteller. "I have always been what is called a good mixer," he said. "I had friends when I had nothing else." Will Rogers and Theodore Roosevelt were among them.

The museum contains the most extensive Russell collection anywhere, including watercolors, oils, bronzes, and illustrated letters; major canvases include *Jerkline*. Also in the complex are the artist's original 1903 **Log Cabin Studio** and the two-story frame **Russell Home,** furnished as it was from 1900 to 1926. Other collections include works by Russell's contemporaries, such as O. C. Seltzer and Joseph H. Sharp (who painted 200 of the Indians that fought Custer); also, photographs by Edward S. Curtis of Indian life. The collection of Browning firearms honors the achievements of John M. Browning, called "the greatest firearm inventor the world has ever known," with 128 patents.

> LOCATION: 400 13th Street North. HOURS: May through September: 9–6 Monday–Saturday, 1–5 Sunday; October through April: 10–5 Tuesday–Saturday, 1–5 Sunday. FEE: Yes. TELEPHONE:406–727–8787.

The **Cascade County Historical Museum and Archives** (1400 First Avenue North, 406–452–3462), housed in an 1895 school building, has changing exhibitions on the heritage of local homesteaders, farmers, miners, and railroaders. The archives holds the county immigration records and local newspapers from the 1880s forward. The **Cascade County Courthouse** (415 Second Avenue North), built in 1903, is a Tudor Revival structure of sandstone, capped with a copper dome. Old West artifacts can be found at the **Cowboys' Bar and Museum** (311 3d Street NW, 406–453–0651), a cocktail emporium whose collection includes saddles, hats, guns, and arrowheads, as well as Russell paintings and his hat, which were donated by the Montana Cowboys Association for display in this log bar from the 1930s.

Lewis and Clark made part of their 1805 portage across what is now the runway near the **Malmstrom Air Force Base Museum and Air Park** (east end of Second Avenue North, inside main gate, 406–731–2705). On the tarmac sit fighter planes, bombers, and other combat aircraft, while the museum exhibits a World War II barracks room, military models, and a flight-line diorama.

About ten miles east of Great Falls on Route 87 is **Mehmke's Steam Engine Museum** (406–452–6571), with a collection of about thirty operating steam-engine tractors, including the notable Case Number 110; also on display are gas tractors, Caterpillars, and old

Sunrise at Saint Mary Lake in Glacier National Park. Because the lake's surface is frequently disturbed by whitecapped waves, the Blackfoot believed it to be the home of the Wind Maker.

farm machinery. The **J. C. Adams Stone Barn** (sixteen miles northwest of Great Falls on Route 89, private) is notable for its great size (120 by 40 feet), its material (sandstone carved by Swedish stonecutters in 1885), and its history—it was headquarters for a pioneer freighting and livestock enterprise, and is the only barn of its kind west of the Mississippi.

During the years A.D. 650 to 1600, Indians used the **Ulm Buffalo Jump** (twelve miles southwest of Great Falls, off Route 15) to drive herds over a fifty-foot cliff, butchering the animals among the jumbled rocks at the base. Such a kill site is called a *pishkin*.

SHELBY

Shelby is said to have been founded when the Great Northern arrived during the winter of 1891 and shoved off a boxcar to shelter railroad crews, calling the spot where it landed Shelby Junction. The namesake of this impromptu station was the railroad's Montana manager—who promptly characterized the spot as a "mudhole." It became a roaring 1890s cow town, a turn-of-the-century homestead hub, and a 1920s oil burg. In 1923 what started as a public-relations venture—a championship heavyweight prizefight—did indeed take place here between Jack Dempsey and Tommy Gibbons. The town had a population of 500 but built an arena for 40,000—an economic disaster, since only about 7,000 paying customers attended. Dempsey-Gibbons fight memorabilia is displayed at the **Marias Museum of History and Art** (206 Twelfth Avenue North, 406–434–2551), along with dinosaur fossils, homestead artifacts, and oil-industry material.

In the oil and gas center of **Cut Bank**, the **Glacier County Historical Museum** (just north of Route 2, next to the Cut Bank Sports Complex, 406–873–4041) has a restored 1914 schoolhouse, Indian arrowheads, country-store and railroad-depot exhibits, a tack room, an oil-field diorama and tools, dinosaur bones, and railroad displays.

The headquarters for the Blackfeet Indian Reservation is the town of **Browning**. The **Museum of the Plains Indian** (junction of Routes 2 and 89 West, 406–338–2230) displays artifacts of the Northern Plains Indians—Blackfoot, Crow, Sioux, Assiniboine, Northern Cheyenne, and Chippewa-Cree—as well as Flathead items. Exhibits encompass warfare, clothing, household goods and containers, bead-and quillwork, painted hides, and a mural of a buffalo hunt. Changing exhibitions of arts and crafts interpret the cultural evolution of the American Indians.

GLACIER NATIONAL PARK

Congress created Glacier National Park (406–888–5441) in 1910, and soon the Great Northern Railway mounted a publicity campaign to boost tourism on its line. During the next decade, the railroad and others built a number of accommodations. In the backcountry is the rustic rock-and-timber **Granite Park Chalet and Sperry Chalet** (406–888–5511), built in 1914 and accessible by hiking or horseback only; **Lake McDonald Lodge** (near the north end of Lake McDonald, 406–226–5551) is an atmospheric hostelry, built in 1913, with a large stone fireplace whose petroglyphs may have been made by Charles Russell; west of Lake Sherburne is the **Many Glacier Hotel** (406–226–5551), which 400 workmen labored day and night to complete in the summers of 1914 and 1915. The fifty-mile **Going-to-the-Sun-Road,** opened in 1933, crosses the Continental Divide and is noteworthy for its scenery and difficult engineering.

OPPOSITE: *Artifacts from the Museum of the Plains Indian, clockwise from top left: a beaded bandolier from the Cree or Ojibway, a Sioux boy's vest decorated with quillwork, and moccasins from the northern plains.*

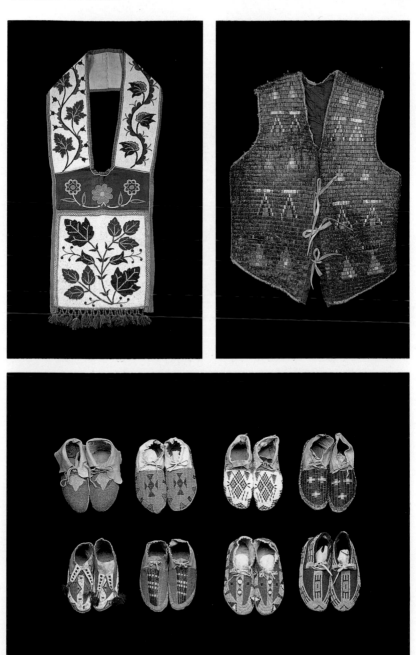

The Charles Edward Conrad Mansion in Kalispell, built in 1895 and designed by Kirtland Cutter, a prominent architect in Spokane, Washington.

KALISPELL

Started as a trading post in 1881, Kalispell got a boost ten years later from the arrival of the Northern Pacific, becoming a hub of farming and ranching. The **Conrad Mansion** (Woodland Avenue between 3d and 4th streets East, 406–755–2166) is a three-story, Shingle-style house, a twenty-three-room testimonial to Charles Edward Conrad. A native Virginian, Conrad came to Montana in 1868 at age 18 and worked for I. G. Baker's mercantile enterprises in Fort Benton. Like many "go-West" young men of the time, he profited mightily and brought Eastern civilization with him, building this elegant home in 1895. Many rooms retain their original furnishings; among them are a parlor that has not changed since Indian chiefs in full costume sat around the fire, bathrooms with imported-marble lavatories, and bedrooms with canopied four-poster beds. Among the house's original furnishings are a table and chairs in Chippendale style.

Perched on a hillside along the Tobacco River, **Eureka** is the home of the **Tobacco Valley Historical Village** (Main Street, 406–296–2122), a collection of buildings from the early 1900s—school, church, log

The Great Hall in the Conrad Mansion. Over the mantel are pieces of armor collected by Charles Conrad on his European travels.

cabin, general store, library, fire lookout tower, railroad depot—relocated and filled with appropriate artifacts. Located in the smelting town of **Columbia Falls** in the upper Flathead Valley, **Saint Richard's Church** (505 Fourth Avenue West) was built in 1891, making it one of Montana's earliest Catholic churches.

Because **Libby** lies in the middle of timber territory, it is no surprise that the **Heritage Museum** (Route 2 South, 406–293–7521) occupies a log building—but this one has twelve sides. Exhibits examine logging, mining, and pioneering from 1880 to 1920.

THOMPSON FALLS

A fur trader and an illustrious practical geographer, David Thompson, a Welshman, built an important fur post called Saleesh House in 1809 for the North West Company. Saleesh House stood on the Clark Fork near today's town of Thompson Falls. By 1883 the town had taken shape and the Northern Pacific had arrived, creating a boom as tens of thousands of hopeful prospectors passed the winter before heading to mining camps in Idaho. During this period of roaring saloonery, it is said that vigilantes sent written invitations to twenty-five outlaws requesting that they leave town. Today the **Old**

Jail Museum (Maiden Lane and South Madison Street, 406–827–3496), housed in a 1908 brick prison, displays its old cells along with Indian artifacts, antique toys, and settlers' belongings.

POLSON

Polson serves as a trading center for the farming region at the south end of Flathead Lake. The **Polson-Flathead Historic Museum** (708 Main Street and Eighth Avenue, 406–883–3049) recounts the history of the Flathead Valley through Indian artifacts, a stagecoach, steamboat-era exhibits, a print shop, homesteaders' buggies, and other memorabilia. The **Polson Feed Mill** (501 Main Street, 406–883–6817) was built in 1910 on Indian reservation land. The two-story wood-frame building with ship-lap siding has been fully restored and contains original equipment. At the **Miracle of America Story Museum** (one mile south of Polson on Route 93, 406–883–6804), artifacts and artwork depict America's progress in 200 years "from the walking plow to walking on the moon." In addition to complete carpenter's and blacksmith's shops, there are antique scales, a sheep-powered treadmill that runs a cream separator, snow vehicles ranging from a horse-drawn sleigh to an early snowmobile, early motorcycles, wooden boats built between 1868 and 1940, military articles from the Revolution to the Vietnam War, clothing, household items, and toys. Next door is the **Paul Bunyan Logging Tow,** a sixty-five-foot-long towboat built in Somers Mount in 1926 and used for twenty-five years to move logs on Flathead Lake.

One of the nation's oldest big-game reserves, the **National Bison Range** (Route 212 off Route 93, 406–644–2211), started in 1908, sprawls over almost 19,000 acres of grassland at the base of the Mission Range. About 350 to 500 bison live here, remnants of 60 million shaggy beasts that once roamed the continental United States. There is a nineteen-mile self-guided tour that climbs 2,000 feet through spectacular mountain scenery, populated by deer, elk, and bighorn sheep in addition to bison.

SAINT IGNATIUS

Saint Ignatius Mission (east of Route 93, 406–745–2768) dates to 1854, when Flathead Indians asked Jesuit priests to relocate an earlier mission from Washington State to their traditional homeland.

The Saint Ignatius Mission near the center of the Flathead Reservation.

Led by Father Adrian Hoecken, the Jesuits erected a cabin and several workshops, as well as a chapel that still stands. The Indians' response was remarkable: More than a thousand Flathead, Pend d'Oreille, and Kootenai presented themselves in 1855 for Easter rites, and the fathers baptized hundreds of new converts. Soon the mission was raising sheep, probably Montana's first flock, and in 1864 Indian workers put up a sawmill and a flour mill that still exists. The settlement reached its peak of importance from 1888 to 1896, when the mission's school for boys had 320 students. The present brick mission dates to 1891, a building of High Victorian Gothic style with the Mission Mountains for a backdrop. Brother Joseph Carignano painted the interior walls and ceilings with fifty-eight murals depicting the history of man according to the Bible. The church, with its 100-foot-high belfry, still ministers to the Indians of the Flathead Reservation.

The **Flathead Indian Museum** (Route 93, 406–745–2951) is a rarity—an Indian museum owned by an Indian family on an Indian reservation. Its extensive collection is drawn mostly from the Flathead and Kootenai peoples and includes clothing, weapons, ceremonial material, and healing items; there is also a sampling of artifacts from other U.S. and Canadian tribes, as well as a mounted animal collection.

The **Four Winds Historic Village** (three miles north of Saint Ignatius on Route 93, 406–745–4336) is a collection of historic buildings moved from the neighboring region: the Jocko Indian Agency, built in 1862 of logs by Major John Owen; the 1870 Duncan MacDonald home and trading post; the Ravalli depot, now housing a toy and train museum; and a "Sunday house" from the Saint Ignatius Mission, used by a family of settlers who came a long distance each Sunday for church services and had to stay overnight.

SUPERIOR

Although a post office was established here in 1871, after a decade "Superior City" consisted of exactly one house and a barn. Local industries—logging, mining, railroads, the U.S. Forest Service—are reflected in the collection of the **Mineral County Historical Museum** (301 East Second Avenue, 406–822–4078); there is also a display on Captain John Mullan and his trail from Fort Benton to Walla Walla.

The Missoula County Courthouse was designed by A. J. Gibson, a local architect, and completed in 1910.

MISSOULA

Meriwether Lewis camped at the site of Missoula in July 1806 before going into a nearby gorge that later trappers would name Hell Gate Canyon; the Blackfoot Indians ambushed other tribes at the entrance. The same area was surveyed for a railroad in 1853 by Isaac Stevens. He returned two years later to meet the Flathead, Kootenai, and Pend d'Oreille under the cottonwoods at what is now **Council Grove State Park** (seven miles west of Missoula on Route 263), where they negotiated a treaty that opened the region for white occupation. The first settler passed the winter in a log cabin in 1860; within three years the Mullan Road had been built through Hell Gate Canyon, and Idaho miners were swarming past the site of Missoula to Montana's gold camps. The town took shape in 1865 when Frank Worden and Captain C. P. Higgins erected lumber and flour mills. In 1877 the army established Fort Missoula for protection against the Indians.

With the establishment of a division point on the Northern Pacific line in 1883, the city's growth was ensured; the **Northern Pacific Depot** (Railroad Street and Higgins Avenue), built in 1889, is now restored as a restaurant and brewery. An economic boon also derived from the **University of Montana,** founded in 1893; the brick-and-stone **University Hall,** a Romanesque Revival building topped with a bell tower, was built in 1898. Further urban expansion came in 1908 with the arrival of the Chicago, Milwaukee, St. Paul & Pacific Railroad, whose **Milwaukee Road Depot,** now known as Milwaukee Station, has been restored as a restaurant and can be found just off Higgins Avenue, south of the Higgins Avenue Bridge over the Clark Fork River. In 1892 the **Saint Francis Xavier Church** (420 West Pine) opened; a brick structure on a foundation of rubble stone, it has notable stained-glass windows. The 1910 **Missoula County Courthouse** (220 West Broadway) blends sandstone walls with a copper-roofed clock tower; the design shows elements of Beaux-Arts and Classic Revival styles. Inside are eight murals of Montana history by Edgar S. Paxson (1852–1919), a New York transplant who painted the Western landscape, wildlife, and Indians, who gave him the name *Cot-lo-see* ("He Sees Everything").

Fort Missoula

In 1877 the army built Fort Missoula to protect Missoula settlers from the region's Flathead Indians. When Chief Joseph and his band were entering Montana during the Nez Percé War later that year, Captain Charles Rawn and his men rode out to build fortifications in Lolo Canyon—but the Indians easily detoured around them. About the only combat the troops saw was in the Battle of the Big Hole. Fort Missoula became home to two unusual military units—in 1888, an all-black infantry regiment (whose officers were white), and in 1896 the Twenty-fifth Infantry Bicycle Corps, which was established to test the military potential of the bicycle as a means of transporting troops in a mountainous country. The advantages of the bicycle over the horse, said the corps organizer, Lieutenant James Moss, were that "it doesn't require as much care. It needs no forage; it moves much faster over fair roads, it is not as conspicuous . . . it is noiseless and raises but little dust." The corps's journeys included a 1,900-mile trip to Saint Louis, whereupon the army voted down bicycles; the troops took the train back to Missoula.

Fort Missoula served as an army training center during World War I, a regional headquarters for the Civilian Conservation Corps (CCC's) in the 1930s, an alien detention center for 1,200 Italian merchant seamen and 650 men of Japanese descent during World War II, and a prison for U.S. court-martialed military personnel from 1945 until the post was closed in 1947.

Today the core area of the original 1877 fort is part of the **Historical Museum at Fort Missoula,** a 32-acre site which is headquartered in the 1911 quartermaster's warehouse. The museum contains exhibits on the history of Missoula County, Fort Missoula, as well as the history of forest management and timber production in western Montana. On the grounds are a number of historic structures: two original buildings from the 1877 fort—a log noncommissioned officers' quarters and a fieldstone powder magazine, both built in 1878; others, including the **root cellar** of 1908, date from the fort's later history; still others have been relocated to the museum from other sites, such as **Saint Michael's Church,** built in 1863, **Grant Creek Schoolhouse** of 1907, **Drummond Depot** of 1910, and Sliderock Lookout (a USFS lookout tower), built in 1933. A Willamette Shay-type locomotive is currently being restored on a logging spur on the grounds.

LOCATION: 322 South Avenue, west of Reserve Street. HOURS: Memorial Day through Labor Day: 10–5 Tuesday–Saturday, 12–5 Sunday; Labor Day through Memorial Day: 12–5 Tuesday–Sunday. FEE: None. TELEPHONE:406–728–3476.

OPPOSITE: *Saint Francis Xavier Church, built in 1891.*

The Queen Anne style Greenough Mansion in Missoula.

At Higgins Avenue and Main Street stands the 1889 **Higgins Block,** which has housed many financial and retail enterprises. Topped with a corner turret and cupola, it was built with granite, brick, clay tiles, and pressed metal to achieve the gingerbread effect of a Queen Anne house in commercial architecture. The **Greenough Mansion** (102 Ben Hogan Drive, 406–728–5132) was built of native tamarack wood in 1897 by Thomas Greenough, who grew rich acquiring and selling mines. Moved from its original location, the mansion now houses a clubhouse and restaurant.

A **marker** six miles west of **Lolo** on Route 12 indicates the site of a fort, built when a large band of Nez Percé, stung by broken treaties and determined not to be confined on a reservation, made their exodus from Idaho into Montana. To contain them, Captain Charles Rawn, the Seventh Infantry Regiment, and citizen volunteers left Fort Missoula in July 1877 for Lolo Canyon, where they erected a log-and-earth breastwork. The Indians wanted only safe passage either to Canada or to Crow territory. Although they outnumbered the defending force ten to one, they spent three days trying to negotiate a peaceful passage. Finally, they simply bypassed the barricade, climbing a steep ridge to the north, despite being encumbered with women and children, all their belongings, and a large herd of horses. They made their way without incident southward through the Bitterroot Valley, and residents nicknamed the useless barrier "Fort Fizzle." The last vestiges of the breastwork were destroyed by a wildfire in 1934.

STEVENSVILLE

Saint Mary's Mission (West 4th Street, 406–777–5734) is a descendant of the first Catholic mission in the Northwest. In 1841 Father Pierre De Smet established Saint Mary's Mission along the Bitterroot River, on the site where a dying Flathead child had had a vision of a "house of prayer." The Indians learned to farm after the tireless De Smet traveled 600 miles round trip to what is now Washington State to obtain seeds for wheat, potatoes, and oats. After taking baptism and instructions, the Flathead were soon playing accordions, a clarinet, a bass drum, and other instruments in a mission band. In 1845 Father Anthony Ravalli joined the mission, a

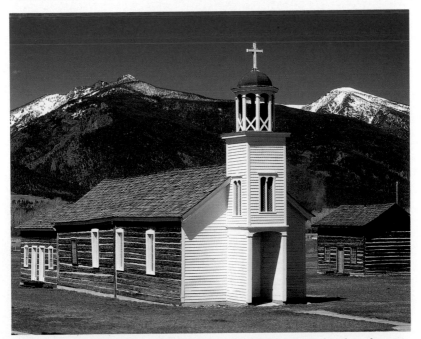

The second Saint Mary's Mission, established in 1866, was built using logs from the original structure. A clapboard facade added a modern touch.

European genius in the Western wilderness—physician, pharmacist, architect, artist, woodworker, and horticulturalist. Ravalli built a gristmill and erected a sawmill to build a larger church.

The motivation for "conversion" to Christianity is irrecoverable from records available to us; but when Father De Smet seemed to offer the same religious protection to the enemy Blackfoot, the Flathead attitude changed to anger. Relations deteriorated further when white trappers appeared, selling whiskey to the Indians, and there were also hostile attacks by Blackfoot. By 1850 the priests saw no choice but to accept defeat and abandon the mission. In 1866 Father Ravalli and other missionaries reestablished Saint Mary's Mission in present Stevensville, using logs from the original church and partially covering the building with clapboard. The complex includes the chapel and Father Ravalli's house and dispensing drugstore. Saint Mary's is the state's oldest church and first pharmacy.

Fort Owen (on Stevensville crossing road, just east of Route 93) was built when Major John Owen bought the abandoned site of Saint Mary's Mission in 1850, paying $250. This was the oldest white settlement in Montana and the site of its first irrigation, school, and cattle herd. Owen established a trading post, where he sold meat, flour, shirts, beads, guns, ammunition, whiskey, tobacco, playing cards, and other requisites of Western life. In 1857 Owen became Indian agent for the Flathead, using the fort as headquarters, and soon replaced the log palisade with a wall of 100,000 adobe bricks. By 1860 the fort had bastions, adobe buildings, a root cellar, and mills for flour and lumber. It was the hub of trade and travel in the Bitterroot Valley. One visitor remarked that Owen "seems to have lived like a prince here in the wilderness." But travel routes bypassed Fort Owen by the late 1860s, business declined, and the trading post was inactive by 1872. The east barracks still stand, with bedrooms and an office-library filled with interpretive exhibits.

HAMILTON

Founded in 1890, Hamilton owes its achievements to copper king Marcus Daly and to ticks. Daly purchased 22,000 acres for a horse farm and on one margin established the town. Here he built a summer home, the **Daly Mansion** (two miles northeast on Route 269, 406–363–6004). Known to the family as "Riverside," the imposing

OPPOSITE: *This ornately carved Italian-marble fireplace in the music room is one of seven in the Daly Mansion. The walls are covered in imported silk damask.*

Classic Revival mansion has forty-two rooms, seven Italian-marble fireplaces, much of the original furniture, and even a scale-model playhouse for Daly youngsters. The extensive grounds are planted with specimen trees. As for Hamilton's ticks, their infestation of parts of the Bitterroot Valley led scientists at the Rocky Mountain Laboratory of the U.S. Health Service to develop a vaccine for spotted fever in 1924. Exhibits on the study of tick-carried diseases can be found at the **Ravalli County Museum** (3d Street and Bedford Avenue, 406–363–3338), along with artifacts of the Flathead, an 1890s parlor, and a trapper-miner's cabin containing homemade furniture and equipment for each livelihood (men often trapped in winter and mined in summer). The museum occupies the stone-and-brick county courthouse, a modified Romanesque Revival building of 1900, whose interior has fine wood panelling. The **Charles Hoffman House** (807 South 3d Street, private) was built in 1914 in the Prairie style.

DARBY

A logging center on the Bitterroot River and a terminus of the Northern Pacific, Darby was established in 1889. The **Pioneer Memorial Museum** (103 East Tanner, off Route 93) displays community artifacts, including clothing and furniture. About ten miles south of Darby stands the **Medicine Tree** (Route 93), a 400-year-old Ponderosa pine whose place in a Salish Indian legend about Coyote and a ram has given it sacred significance. A ram's horn is embedded somewhere within the trunk; the tree has become a shrine where Indians still hang beads, cloth, ribbon, and other offerings.

The **Alta Ranger Station** (West Fork Road, twenty-eight miles south of Conner off Route 473, 406–821–3269), built in 1899, was the first ranger station in the nation. Erected by two forest rangers, the small log cabin served the Bitterroot Forest Reserve created two years earlier. An interpretive marker describes the history of the building.

BIG HOLE NATIONAL BATTLEFIELD

This is the site of a major engagement of the Nez Percé War of 1877. The nontreaty Nez Percé—those who had refused to sign an 1863 treaty reducing their reservation to one-fourth of its size—were fleeing from Idaho ahead of the U.S. Army and hoping to find a place to be left in peace. About 800 Indians under Chief Looking Glass and Chief Joseph had crossed Lolo Pass well ahead of the pursuing General Oliver O. Howard, then stopped to camp on the bank of the north fork of the Big Hole River. After erecting eighty-nine tepees, they sang and danced into the night, so sure of safety that Looking Glass posted no guards. But before daybreak on August 9, 1877, the Nez Percé were roused from sleep by the gunfire of General John Gibbon and the Seventh Infantry in a sneak attack. The troops fired at point-blank range, killing warriors, women, and children without discrimination. The drowsy Indians managed to scatter and establish sniper positions, shooting with such remarkable accuracy that Gibbon was forced to retreat back across the north fork of the Big Hole River, where his men were pinned down until the next day. Meanwhile, Chief Joseph assembled the tribe and its belongings and broke camp. A few sharpshooters stayed behind to harass the soldiers as the Indians withdrew to the south, then slipped away at dawn on the second day, ending the battle. Although the Indians had won, they lost forty women, children, and elderly, and thirty warriors, which reduced their fighting ability. Realizing that the army would never leave them alone, they eventually decided to retreat to Canada and avoid more bloodshed. In October, however, they were forced to surrender just south of the Canadian border. The site of the Nez Percé camp and the wooded scene of the twenty-four-hour siege can be reached by foot trails; the visitor center has museum exhibits dealing with the Nez Percé War of 1877 and the Battle of the Big Hole.

LOCATION: 10 miles west of Wisdom on Route 43. HOURS: Memorial Day through Labor Day: 8–8 Daily; Labor Day through Memorial Day: 8–5 Daily. FEE: Yes. TELEPHONE: 406–689–3155.

Up a treacherous dirt road from the town of Philipsburg lies **Granite**, a silver mining town of the 1880s. Before the bonanza came in, the mine's Eastern backers had decided the diggings had little potential and ordered the work stopped, but their telegram was delayed; the last powder detonation at the end of the last workday uncovered a fabulous lode. There were 1,310 residents on the 1890 census, but the silver crash of 1893 closed the Granite Mountain Mine and eventually the town emptied. Still standing is the stone-and-brick shell of the **Miner's Union Hall,** built in 1890, a three-story social center whose main room boasted a wooden "spring

floor" that made it reputedly the best dance floor west of the Mississippi. The **Superintendent's House** of 1888 is an imposing building of native granite, once occupied by progressive mine superintendent Thomas Weir, who also built a miners' hospital.

Another ghost town lies east of Missoula, at the end of an unsurfaced road. **Garnet** (Garnet Range Road, off Route 200, 406–329–3914), is the ghost of a gold camp that boomed in the 1860s. About fifty buildings survive, including the three-story **Wells Hotel**; most are of log construction. Also extant are the shafts and other structures of the rich Nancy Hanks mine, which produced $3 million in gold. One old tale says that during a snowbound winter when the food ran low in Garnet, a brave worker wearing a miner's lamp walked eleven miles through the dark, interconnecting tunnels of various mines to reach Beartown and arrange a supply shipment. Another story is that somewhere along the steep "China Grade" approaching Garnet, a Chinese miner put his fortune into a baking powder can and buried it.

DEER LODGE

Laid out in 1863, Deer Lodge was a stop on the Mullan Road, supplying travelers with beef and fresh vegetables. It also developed into a mining center. The history of the Deer Lodge Valley is recounted at the **Powell County Museum** (1193 Main Street, on the grounds of the Old Montana Prison, 406–846–3294); displays include dinosaur bones, mining and lumbering equipment, cowboy gear, and railroad memorabilia. The **Old Montana Prison** (1106 Main Street, 406–846–3111) was established in 1871. Convicts built a Romanesque sandstone wall that rises twenty-four feet and is buried four feet below ground level to prevent tunneling escapes. In 1912 they erected the present cell house; there were seven locked doors between a prisoner and the outside world. A law-enforcement museum displays iron boots designed to discourage prisoners from roaming and the handcuffs worn by Lee Harvey Oswald when he was shot. The "galloping gallows" was built in the 1920s as a portable facility, since Montana law required that a guilty party be hanged in the county where the crime was committed; it was used seven times. The copper king William A. Clark funded the prison theater, one of the first such facilities in the nation. Also at the prison is the **Towe**

OPPOSITE: *Twelve-pound Mountain Howitzer overlooking Big Hole National Battlefield. The Nez Percé captured the artillery piece and 2,000 rounds of ammunition after U.S. soldiers were able to fire only two rounds.*

Henry Ford's personal camper, built on a 1922 Lincoln chassis, was used by the "four vagabonds"—Henry Ford, Thomas Edison, John Burroughs, and Harvey Firestone—to travel in and camp out. The car is part of the collection in the Old Montana Prison, opposite.

Ford Museum (406–846–3111), which displays more than eighty Ford and Lincoln automobiles built from 1903 to the 1950s, including two of Henry Ford's own cars—one of them a camper, built on a Lincoln chassis and used as a "chuck wagon" stocked with fine china and silver. Across the street, **Yesterday's Playthings** (1017 Main Street, 406–846–1480) exhibits the Hostetter Collection of 1,000 dolls—Madame Alexander, ethnic, advertising, and Indian dolls among them—as well as toys up to a century old. The **Bielenberg Home** (801 Milwaukee Avenue), a Prairie-style house designed in 1910, was built by Nick Bielenberg, whose brother John developed a ranching empire with Conrad Kohrs.

The **Grant–Kohrs Ranch National Historic Site** (just north of Deer Lodge on the Route 90 frontage road, 406–846–2070) is a pioneering ranch complex started in 1862 by John Grant, the first major stockman in the Deer Lodge Valley. Married to a Bannock, Grant built a handsome two-story wooden home, which one newspaper said looked as if "it had been lifted by the chimneys from the banks of the St. Lawrence and dropped down in Deer Lodge Valley. It has twenty-eight windows, with green painted shutters, and looks very pretty." In 1866 Grant sold out to Conrad Kohrs, a German immigrant who had previously worked as a sailor, Mississippi rafts-man, sausage salesman, and California gold miner. By selling beef in mining settlements, Kohrs and his partner and half-brother John Bielenberg developed a large herd, and the ranch became their headquarters. Their cattle at one time spread over more than a million acres. Kohrs and Bielenberg are said to have shipped thirty trainloads of stock to the Chicago market in a single season. Today the ranch has been preserved to reflect the early cattle industry of the northern plains. Buildings include Grant's ranch house (to which Kohrs added a brick wing in 1890), shops, barns, a granary, an icehouse, and the bunkhouses where cowboys chewed tobacco and spun yarns around the stove.

ANACONDA

The copper king Marcus Daly chose the Anaconda region for its abundance of water, timber, and limestone, needed to build a huge smelter that would process the ore from Butte. There would also be a company town, and in 1883 Daly stood on a hill with his engineer, pointed to a cow, and said, "The main street will run north and south in a direct line from here to where that cow is standing." And so it did. Daly dubbed the settlement Copperopolis, but the post-master renamed it for Butte's Anaconda Mine. The town grew with the copper industry, and to bring copper ore from Butte, Daly built the Butte, Anaconda & Pacific Railway. He ardently wanted his town to become Montana's capital, but the election of 1894 retained Helena, the choice of William Clark.

Anaconda history is presented at the **visitor center** (306 East Park Street, 406–563–2400), housed in a replica train depot. The center displays a Pullman coach, ore car, and pusher engine, along with foundry molds and other smelter paraphernalia.

Marcus Daly's **Montana Hotel** (Main and Park streets) opened in 1889. Now revamped as Montana Square, the eclectic brick struc-ture was too big for the town—Daly apparently hoped it would fill up with legislators when Anaconda became the capital. The **Washoe Theater** (Main Street near Third) is a movie palace built in 1936 with Art Deco furnishings, murals, and ornamentation in silver, cop-per, and gold leaf. Tours are available. William Randolph Hearst's

The Washoe Theater with its intricate Art Deco ornamentation was built in 1936.

father, George, was one of the first to back Marcus Daly's copper-mining ventures; his mother, Phoebe, built the **Hearst Free Library** (401 Main Street) in 1898, a brick Classic Revival structure. Mrs. Marcus Daly donated the pipe organ for the **Saint Mark's Episcopal Church** (600 Main Street), built in 1891. The **Courthouse,** built at the south end of Main Street in 1900, features a lighted dome with art glass, circular staircases, and a dumbwaiter to carry books from the clerk's office to the court upstairs.

The **Copper Village Museum and Arts Center** (400 East Commercial Street, 406–563–2422) occupies part of the **City Hall** of 1895, a brick-and-granite building that is, naturally, trimmed in Anaconda copper. The center's historical museum has displays on Anaconda and county history, emphasizing the smelting process and town businesses, such as the Tuchscherer Drugstore with its original contents. The 585-foot-high **Washoe Smelter Smokestack** was built in 1918 to replace an earlier stack. Said to be the world's tallest free-standing masonry structure, it is the only remnant of what was once

the largest copper smelter in existence. The brick Victorian **Butte, Anaconda & Pacific Railway Depot** stands at 300 West Commercial Street; the **Roundhouse and Shops** are located along Route 1.

The preservation of ghost towns is the concern of the **National Ghost Town Hall of Fame Museum** (Fairmont Hot Springs Resort, eleven miles east of Anaconda off Route 90, 406–797–3241), which displays photographs of Montana mining camps and a few artifacts.

BUTTE

"The richest hill on earth" is riddled with more than 2,000 miles of underground tunnels, but mining in the area began with a simple prospect hole dug by an unknown person using elk horns. A gold camp was started here in 1864, with a silver boom ten years later—but the real riches had not been discovered yet. In 1880 Marcus Daly bought the Anaconda silver mine for $30,000 and struck a vein of fabulously rich copper that made Butte the greatest copper camp on earth. Meanwhile, Daly's arch-rival, William A. Clark, also was extracting a fortune in red ore.

By 1885 Butte had a population of 22,000, including Welshmen, Finns, Chinese, and many Irishmen. One character was rug merchant Mohammed Akara, who changed his name to Mohammed Murphy "for business reasons." Saloons such as the Graveyard and Pay Day roared around the clock. (If a Butte saloon was built with a door lock, on opening day the proprietor ceremoniously tossed the key into the privy.) The Atlantic Bar stretched a full block and had fifteen bartenders dispensing a reputed 12,000 glasses of beer on Saturday nights. The WPA book *Copper Camp* reports that "Jerry Buckley, a purveyor of moist goods, indignantly remarked to a stranger who ordered a glass of milk: 'Do you see any room in here for a cow?'" When not drinking, workers toiled in about 300 mines on Butte Hill; smelters spewed smoke and railroads hauled out ore. In 1887 more than 50 million pounds of copper came from the Anaconda mine alone.

Butte's famous "war of the copper kings" encompassed two decades beginning in 1888, when Marcus Daly scuttled William Clark's election as territorial delegate to Congress. Educated at the Columbia School of Mines, Clark was short, with a high voice and a

OPPOSITE: *The copper-plated tower of the Anaconda–Deer Lodge County Courthouse, built in 1898. Outlined in copper trim, the courthouse was the tallest building in town when it was first built, standing 110 feet high.*

face that has been compared to a ferret's. Daly was an uneducated but witty Irishman, popular with the miners and as intelligent and determined as Clark. But Clark and Daly met their match in the coal mining engineer F. Augustus Heinze, who came to Butte in 1889 and parlayed a stint as a mine surveyor into a complete knowledge of the tangled veins of copper inside Butte Hill. He applied the "Apex Law," which allowed the owner of land where ore came to the surface to follow the vein underground. Heinze gleefully pursued copper deposits from his own poor property into adjacent mines, where he hauled out ore day and night. Often he got court orders prohibiting the legitimate owners from working their own mines until the resulting lawsuits could be settled. The fact that Heinze had the county judge in his pocket ensured a long string of favorable decisions. Underground warfare sometimes broke out as Heinze looted the rich mines of the Amalgamated Copper Company, which Daly had created as a holding company for the Anaconda mines. Workers set off dynamite, blew smoke and noxious fumes through ventilating shafts, and wielded rifles. Frustrated by Heinze's thievery, Amalgamated finally shut down all its Montana operations. With 20,000 workers suddenly out of work, political pressure forced the governor to pass a law permitting plaintiffs such as Amalgamated to obtain a change of venue to avoid corrupt judges. Foreseeing the end of his capers, in 1906 Heinze accepted a $12 million settlement from Amalgamated in exchange for dismissing 110 cases in the courts. Amalgamated had already purchased control from Daly, and bought Clark's mining interests in 1910. The war of the copper kings was over. The company (once more called Anaconda) wielded enormous power; it was controlled by Eastern financiers, and the profits, as usual, left the state. Corporate mining stopped in the 1980s after a century during which $22 billion in copper, gold, and silver had come out of Butte Hill. Head frames scattered here and there indicate the sites of old mines, which sometimes penetrated as deep as a mile into the hill. The Butte Historical Society publishes a brochure for a self-guided tour of the mines.

The **Butte Historic Districts** include the residential West Side and the Uptown commercial core. Moving from north to south: At the **Original Mine** (corner of Wyoming and Quartz streets), an iron "gallows frame" marks the site of Butte's first diggings, later developed with a shaft. The **Copper King Mansion** (219 West Granite Street, 406–782–7580) was built in 1888 for William A. Clark. It is located atop a hill (to indicate the entrepreneur's position in Butte)

The rotunda of the Butte–Silver Bow City-County Courthouse, designed by the firm of Link and Haire and built in 1910, features a stained-glass dome and murals.

and designed in Victorian mode with a castellated roof (to make a lordly impression). The three-story red-brick mansion boasts thirty rooms, Tiffany windows, frescoed ceilings, marquetry floors, a sixty-two-foot-long ballroom, a billiard room, a chapel, and an 850-pipe organ. The house is preserved and furnished in the style of the 1880s; tours are available. Next door, the Italianate **Leonard Hotel** dates from the "war of the copper kings"; it is said that Marcus Daly had it built to obstruct Clark's view. The doors of the **Butte–Silver Bow City–County Courthouse** (155 West Granite Street, 406–723–8262) are made of copper; inside are murals, a stained-glass dome, and the capstan of the battleship *Maine*. A classical facade adorns the **Butte Water Company Building** (124 West Granite Street), whose appearance is said to suggest the style of eighteenth-century London. The **Hennessey Building** (East Granite and Main streets) of 1897 was designed to resemble a Renaissance palace, with terra-cotta embellishments of Italian style, and has housed offices of the Anaconda Copper Company. On opposite corners of Broadway and Idaho are the English Country Gothic **Saint John's Episcopal Church,** built in 1921, and the **First Presbyterian Church** of 1897.

A string of mansions of the 1880s occupies the 300 block of West Broadway; Spanish Revival at 321 and Italianate at 309 (the Tiffany window on the landing was freighted to Butte by wagon); Augustus Heinze's attorney once lived at 315, and Clarence Darrow was later a regular guest. The **Arts Chateau** (321 West Broadway, 406–723–7600) was built in 1898 for William A. Clark's son Charles. A single curving staircase ascends from the ground floor to the fourth-floor ballroom. The twenty-six-room Chateauesque mansion has stained and decorative glass, imported wood panelling, a Louis XVI salon, and a massive corner tower with iron balconies. Open to the public, it is now a community art gallery and period museum. The **Curtis Music Hall** (15 West Park) is a bit of ornate Victorian whimsy with a turret and tower, built of brick in 1892 and trimmed with stone. At Galena and Washington streets stands the 1904 **B'Nai Israel Synagogue,** the oldest operating synagogue in Montana. The **Mineral Museum** (Montana College of Mineral Science and Technology, 406–496–4101) displays 1,300 specimens from around the world, including fluorescent minerals and collections from Butte and other areas of Montana.

World Museum of Mining and Hell Roarin' Gulch

Located on the site of the Orphan Girl Mine, a former silver and zinc producer, the museum has twelve acres of displays. Inside the museum are early underground fire-fighting gear, gold scales, memorabilia of Butte's copper kings, mine models, and a Stanley steam engine. Outside the museum stands a towering steel head frame above the Orphan Girl shaft, which descends 3,200 feet; also exhibited are mine cages, ore wagons, and a 1928 LaSalle armored pay car. Hell Roarin' Gulch is a replica of a mining camp, containing such buildings as an assay office, Chinese laundry, millinery shop, sauerkraut factory, and saloon.

LOCATION: End of West Park Street. HOURS: Mid-June through Labor Day: 9–9 Daily; Labor Day through late November, April through mid-June: 10–5 Tuesday–Sunday. FEE: None. TELEPHONE:406–723–7211.

The museum entrance is the departure point for the **Neversweat & Washoe Railroad,** a motorized railcar built in 1925 to maintain the overhead trolley wires of the Butte, Anaconda & Pacific Railway, whose route it follows for six miles through the old mining district.

HELENA

In 1864 a party of prospectors whom history calls the "Four Georgians" had just about given up. Disheartened and low on supplies, they decided to give their luck one more try at Prickly Pear Valley—our "last chance," as one of them said. Soon they were so busy working their strike at Last Chance Gulch that for three months they did not even have time to plat a town. But they had the forethought to draft rules for locating and protecting claims. The town grew to 4,000 people by 1876, becoming a supply center for other mining camps. Helena brokered food grown in the Prickly Pear Valley and imported goods from Fort Benton, the head of navigation on the Missouri. Freighting became easier when the Northern Pacific arrived in 1883. Even as the placer gold started to dwindle, quartz deposits were developed. By the late 1880s, Helena rejoiced in the claim of having more millionaires per capita than any city in America—about fifty. Life was never as wild here as in other boomtowns. Helena had become territorial capital in 1875, temporary state capital in 1889, and, after a hot contest against Anaconda in 1894, it retained the title permanently. The silver crash of 1893 caused many of the city's millionaires to vacate their mansions on both sides of Last Chance Gulch and in the subdivisions of Lenox and Kenwood (whose advertising claimed "A Gold Mine on Every Lot"). Thereafter, Helena's fortunes rose or fell with those of the mining industry.

Last Chance Gulch was the center of the old mining excitement. The **Helena Historic District** stretches along the gulch from the Reeder's Alley area, heads north through small commercial buildings of the 1870s and 1880s, and ends downtown, where there are some remaining business blocks of the 1890s. Among many notable buildings are the **Power Block** (1888) and the Richardsonian Romanesque **Securities Building** of 1886, with its interesting carved thumb print between the arches on the first floor. Along **Reeder's Alley** are restored miners' houses of the 1860s,

1870s, and 1880s, many built of bricks brought by riverboat up the Missouri River. Today the alley contains shops and restaurants. At the alley's lower end stands the **Pioneer Cabin** (208 South Park Avenue, 406–443–7641), built of logs in 1864 and decorated with period furnishings to depict pioneer life. The Norwest Bank **Gold Collection** (350 North Last Chance Gulch, 406–447–2000) displays gold dust, nuggets, and leaf, rare "wire gold," and gold coins.

On the east side of Last Chance Gulch are a number of historic structures: Because three fires had raged through Helena's business district by 1874, the **Fire Tower** (Fire Tower Park) assumed great importance for sighting flames and alerting citizens. A watchman would ring a triangle atop the tower and point with a red flag toward the fire (or, at night, wave a lantern); eventually a bell weighing more than a ton replaced the triangle. This wooden tower has been called the "Guardian of the Gulch." The **Bluestone House** (80 South Warren Street) was built of blue granite in 1889 to resemble a castle; it became a whorehouse and an earthquake victim over the years but was saved by renovation in 1976. A red-brick building of 1875, the **U.S. Assay Office** (206 Broadway) drew miners from all over Montana to have their gold assayed and melted into ingots, which could be exchanged for coins at the bank.

The **Lewis and Clark County Courthouse** (228 Broadway) is a Romanesque building built of gray granite in 1885–1887; it functioned as territorial and then state capitol until 1904. Helena's **Original Governor's Mansion** (304 North Ewing Street, 406–444–2694) was built by William Chessman in 1888 and purchased by the state in 1913. This brick Queen Anne mansion with terra-cotta and stone trim, ornate chimneys, turrets, and cupolas served as Montana's executive residence until 1959. Restored to its original appearance and style of furnishings, the house is open for tours. The **Cathedral of Saint Helena** (530 North Ewing Street, 406–442–5825) was begun in 1908 and completed in 1924 in a Viennese Gothic style with two elaborate spires, Bavarian stained glass, and hand-carved ornament.Atop a small hill, the **Montana State Capitol** (Sixth Avenue between Montana Avenue and Roberts Street) is impressive for its massive Classic Revival design, copper-clad dome, and interior paintings by Charles M. Russell (*Lewis and Clark Meeting the Flathead Indians at Ross' Hole*) and Edgar S. Paxson (six canvases on Montana history).

OPPOSITE: *Construction of the Cathedral of Saint Helena, designed by the firm of A. O. Von Herbulis, was funded largely by Thomas Cruse, who had made a fortune mining gold in Marysville. The spires, 218 feet high, are roofed with red tiles. The stained-glass windows were made in Bavaria.*

The architect's drawing for the Montana State Capitol by John H. Kent. Work on the capitol was delayed by accusations that the design competition had been rigged and that the commissioners in charge were taking bribes. Kent's firm was selected in a second competition (detail).

On the west side of Last Chance Gulch are several other noteworthy sites: The west end of the **Colwell Building** of 1888 (Last Chance Mall and Wong Street) is the site where the four Georgians made the original gold discovery in 1864; the long, narrow building matches the dimensions of the mining claim on which it rests. The **Kluge House** (540 West Main Street) is an unusual example of *Fachwerk,* a German style also found in Wisconsin, Missouri, and Texas, which employs logs and half-timbering, with brick infill. The house was built by Emil Kluge in 1873. The **Algeria Temple Shrine/Civic Center** (intersection of Neill, Park, and Benton avenues), designed in 1920 as a Masonic temple, is a Moorish-style building with a minaret, mosaic entry, and grilled windows—an unexpected apparition in the Old West.

Montana Historical Society Museum

About 40,000 objects are in the museum's collections. Prehistoric artifacts include Clovis projectile points from the Anzick Site. Chief Joseph's stirrups are among Plains Indians clothing and artifacts. There is a large collection of costumes and textiles, including a housedress of 1870 and a Salvation Army uniform of 1890, as well as cowboy gear, 600 veterinary tools, gold-and copper-mining artifacts (a rare man-powered three-stamp mill of the 1880s), and smelter tools and protective clothing. Among the transportation collection's seventy-five items are the steering wheel and lantern from a Missouri River steamboat built in 1875 and a Yellowstone park tour bus of 1931. The collection of 700 firearms includes Jim Bridger's Hawken rifle and outlaw Henry Plummer's shotgun. Among 500 pieces of furniture are Father Anthony Ravalli's handmade chair and the back bar from the Mint saloon in Great Falls, once frequented by Charles Russell. There are 200 works by Russell, including 22 major oil paintings; among 1,500 other pieces of mostly Western art are works by Edgar S. Paxson and Maynard Dixon.

LOCATION: 225 North Roberts Street. HOURS: Memorial Day through Labor Day: 8–6 Monday–Friday, 9–5 Saturday–Sunday; Labor Day through Memorial Day: 8–5 Monday–Friday, 9–5 Saturday. FEE: None. TELEPHONE: 406–444–2694.

From 1880 to 1894, **Marysville** (twenty-two miles northwest of Helena off Route 279) produced more gold than any other Montana town. It came from hard-rock mining, especially at the Drumlummon Mine. Still surviving are some false-front buildings, as well as the teetering bleachers of an old athletic field.

TOWNSEND

The Northern Pacific Railroad and the agriculture of the Missouri River valley built Townsend, whose **Broadwater County Museum and Historical Library** (133 North Walnut, 406–266–5252) displays artifacts of local history, including an ore car and gold pans, a furnished homestead cabin and blacksmith shop, and millstones from the area's first mill, earected in 1879.

WHITE SULPHUR SPRINGS

The town got its name from natural hot springs with white sulphur deposits at their edges. Indians knew these waters, and a later resort promoter compared the mineral content to the springs in Baden-Baden, West Germany. The town's dominant feature is the restored **Castle** (310 Second Avenue NE) of 1892, built by Byron Roger Sherman using stone quarried in the Castle Mountains. It is open for tours and serves as the **Meagher County Historical Museum,** displaying period furniture, mineral samples, and clothing.

The blockhouse and other structures are still standing at **Fort Logan** (Route 360, seventeen miles north of White Sulphur Springs). This post defended the freight route from Fort Benton to Helena, the mining operations of Confederate Gulch, and the cattle ranches in the Smith and Upper Musselshell river valleys. Established in 1869 and occupied until 1880, it replaced nearby Camp Baker with a complex of pine-log buildings. The blockhouse, reputedly the last log blockhouse in the West, is notable for its efficient design: Because the upper story rests on the lower story at a forty-five-degree angle, the fort permitted soldiers to shoot in eight directions at once.

The **Castle Historic District** lies thirty-seven miles southeast of White Sulphur Springs (off Route 294). Frame houses and stores still stand in this lead and silver camp, whose peak year was 1891. No mine in Montana produced more lead than the Cumberland, but transporting it was a problem: It was just as costly to ship out the ore as it was to bring in coke for smelters to reduce it. The Jawbone railroad made it halfway up the canyon, then ran out of funding. But the town thrived anyway, with a local sawmill turning out attractive gingerbread for houses and the population reaching 2,000. The editor of *The Whole Truth* newspaper marveled at the "parties, dances, spelling bees and other society affairs in our town"—which was not a typical mining camp, never having recorded a violent death. Saloons were boisterous with the likes of Calamity Jane, who one acquaintance said "was real tall and built like a busted bale of hay." (She came to town with her small daughter and the intention of opening a restaurant but soon grew restless and moved on.) In 1893 the silver panic sent the town reeling, and although the Jawbone laid tracks almost to Castle in 1897, it was too late. Decline set in, and by 1939 the last resident gave up the ghost town.

LIVINGSTON

On the afternoon of July 15, 1806, William Clark and his men rested at a sharp bend in the Yellowstone River—the future site of Livingston. "Clark City" took shape in 1882, when George Carver arrived with a tent and thirty wagon loads of freight, soon attracting 500 people. Then surveyors from the Northern Pacific Railroad laid out another town site called Livingston just four blocks north, and the train's arrival spurred a healthy boom there, especially when the railroad established a major division point and locomotive shops.

Livingston has always been a railroad town, not only for mainte-
nance but also as a passenger hub for tourists traveling to
Yellowstone National Park.

To make a favorable impression, the railroad built a new depot
in 1902, now restored and affiliated with Wyoming's Buffalo Bill
Historical Center as **Depot Center** (200 West Park Street,
406–222–2300). The firm of Reed & Stem, one of the designers of
New York's Grand Central Terminal, employed an Italian villa style
with a curving colonnade. In summer there are exhibits of paintings
by Charles Russell, Frederic Remington, and Thomas Moran; Indian
artifacts and a full-size Crow tepee; antique firearms; and an exhibit
on Yellowstone park, including a turn-of-the-century tour carriage.
Exhibits vary the rest of the year.

Livingston's **Historic Business District** stretches from Depot
Center to Lewis Street, between 2d and Main streets, and contains
hotels and commercial structures, many of them one or two stories

*The Depot Center, built in 1902 by the Northern Pacific Railroad, was designed by the
firm of Reed & Stem who also designed Grand Central Terminal in New York City.*

and made of brick. The **Old Red Light District** (B Street from Clark to Geyser) consists of small turn-of-the-century houses, where at least one brothel was active until the 1970s. A district of Victorian houses is on the west end of town, particularly on South Yellowstone, where merchants and railroad executives built large homes of local stone or wood. The **Park County Museum** (118 West Chinook, 406–222–3506) displays railroad memorabilia, Western rodeo and ranching gear, antique household objects, projectile points, and other items of regional history.

Twenty-five miles south of Livingston, the waters at **Chico Hot Springs** (Route 89, 406–333–4933), long known to the Indians, were used by miners as a laundry and bathtub when gold was discovered up Emigrant Gulch in the late 1800s. The springs are named for a Mexican miner. In 1902 a still-existing wooden **hotel** was built as a hospital for arthritics and other sufferers who came from around the country. Artist Charles Russell was also a regular here. The springs are now part of a resort.

BOZEMAN

The Indians called it by a name meaning "Valley of the Flowers," but it was known as the Gallatin Valley by the time John Bozeman led the first wagon train here in 1864 via his Bozeman Trail from Wyoming. Homesteaders grew food for the mining camps to the southwest, and by 1867 the hamlet of Bozeman had several flour mills and was decreed county seat. Greater prosperity came with larger irrigation projects, an influx of tourists bound for Yellowstone park just ninety miles south, and the 1883 arrival of the Northern Pacific Railroad, which connected the town's farming and commercial life with the East Coast. In 1893 Montana State University was founded; the **Cooperative Extension Building** (1894) is the oldest structure on campus; **Montana Hall** dates to 1896.The **Gallatin County Historical Museum** (317 West Main, 406–585–1311) displays regional historical items in what was once the county jail, a brick building wtih corbeled battlements, designed by architect Fred F. Willson, who worked on many buildings in the city. Stretching south is the **South Willson Historic District,** named for the architect's father, a general; there are forty-eight homes built since 1883. One of 2,800 free libraries funded by Andrew Carnegie, the **Bozeman Carnegie Library** stands at 35 North Bozeman Avenue.

Museum of the Rockies

The museum traces the history of the northern Rocky Mountains from the age of dinosaurs to the era of the Ford automobile. Dinosaur exhibits focus on the pioneering work of curator Jack Horner, whose discovery of the eggs and nests of hadrosaurs (duck-billed dinosaurs) led him to postulate that, contrary to previous ideas, these creatures of 80 million years ago were warm-blooded, intelligent, and lived in herds where they took care of their offspring. On exhibit are the fossilized dinosaur eggs and babies of these plant-eating denizens of the Mesozoic era, as well as the remains of swimming and flying reptiles. It is also possible to observe scientists preparing fossils.

By 1600 the northern Rockies were inhabited by Indians, represented here by a Sioux eagle-feather bonnet, a Crow war shield, a furnished tepee, and other artifacts. The arrival of fur trappers is marked with the collection's guns, trade beads, and beaver hats, as well as artifacts of the settlers who followed: a sheepherder's wagon, a surrey, clothing, a furnished house of the 1930s, and a service station. In addition, a new, world-class planetarium employs computer graphics to simulate three-dimensional travel among the stars.

LOCATION: South Seventh Avenue and Kagy Boulevard, on Montana State University campus. HOURS: Labor Day through Memorial Day: *Museum:* 9–5 Tuesday–Saturday, 1–5 Sunday; *Planetarium:* 11–3 Tuesday–Thursday, 11–9 Friday, 10–8 Saturday, 1–4 Sunday. FEE: Yes. TELEPHONE: 406–994–2251.

The **Gallatin Gateway Inn** (twelve miles south of Bozeman on Route 191, 406–763–4672) was built in 1927 by the Chicago, Milwaukee & St. Paul Railroad as a spot to entertain its passengers bound for Yellowstone National Park. That the dining room accommodated 200 people, although there were just twenty-six bedrooms, seemed logical to the designers of this Spanish Colonial Revival inn, who assumed that most passengers would sleep aboard their Pullman cars after dining and dancing at the hotel. But the automobile age had dawned, and within a decade many travelers came to Yellowstone by car. The hotel ceased to be a paying proposition, despite its handsome design, red-tile roof, and acres of highly promoted gardens. It has since been remodeled and reopened.

THREE FORKS

Missouri Headwaters State Park (seven miles northeast of Three Forks, near Trident) is where three streams join to create the great Missouri River—"an essential point in the geography of this western part of the Continent," declared Lewis and Clark. After making camp and naming the tributary rivers for President Thomas Jefferson, Treasury Secretary Albert Gallatin, and Secretary of State James Madison, the explorers rested here in July 1805. Clark lay ill with a high fever, while Lewis brooded over their lack of food, horses, and contact with Indians who might help. Then the party chose the Jefferson among these "three noble streams" as being most likely to lead them toward the Pacific. By 1810 fur traders Andrew Henry and Pierre Menard of the Missouri Fur Company had arrived, cutting cottonwood trees to build a trading post between the Madison and Jefferson rivers. Their trapping was successful until the Blackfoot—fierce warriors who controlled the region—killed eight of Henry's party, causing him to abandon the post.

In Three Forks is the **Headwaters Heritage Museum** (Main Street), whose treasure is an anvil brought to Montana by the Missouri Fur Company in 1810. Other exhibits include pioneer artifacts, period rooms and shops, Milwaukee Railroad memorabilia, a 700-piece collection of barbed wire, and a mannequin of Sacajawea in authentic Shoshoni garb. Nearby is the **Sacajawea Inn** (Main Street), built in 1882 and expanded in 1910. Named for the Shoshoni woman who accompanied Lewis and Clark, the wooden hotel has a colonnade along the front verandah.

LOGAN

Located seven miles south of Logan in the Madison River valley, the Madison Buffalo Jump (off Route 90) is where hunters from 2000 B.C. until the eighteenth century A.D. stampeded buffalo, or bison, to their deaths over a thirty-foot-high limestone cliff and down the steeply sloping ground below. At the bottom are an old butchering site beside a creek, traces of an Indian village marked by tepee rings, a grave site, an Indian trail, and a lookout point.

OPPOSITE: *Pond that is part of the Madison River system in Gallatin Valley in Missouri Headwaters State Park.*

VIRGINIA CITY

On a May afternoon in 1863, prospectors Bill Fairweather and Henry Edgar decided to see if they could pan enough gold in Alder Gulch to buy some tobacco in town. They made a rich strike, and although their small party tried to keep it quiet when they went to Bannack for supplies, other gold hunters swiftly sniffed out the truth: About 200 men followed them back to the diggings. Within a year there were 10,000 people in Alder Gulch, the biggest placer rush in Montana history, and by 1868 the deposits yielded as much as $40 million in gold.

The hub of a fourteen-mile stretch of frenzied enterprise was Virginia City (originally named Varina for Jefferson Davis's wife, but changed by a judge who took the Union side in the Civil War). Gambling emporiums, cribs (houses of ill repute), and dance halls thrived; in fact, as one historian remarked, some girls learned that they could earn more on the dance floor "than in their usual professional positions." A famous bare-knuckle boxing match, involving a local pugilist who regularly "bruised & mashed to jelly" his opponents' faces, ended in a draw after 158 one-minute rounds. The

Remnants of the mining town of Virginia City, which was for a time the capital of the territory. Murders and thefts by the corrupt county sheriff, Henry Plummer, led to the formation of Montana's feared Vigilantes.

saloonkeeper "Count" Henri Murat was found to be using weighted scales to cheat his customers out of their gold dust at the bar. And yet churches, amateur theatrical companies, and a "Literary Association" also existed in Virginia City—a mixture of the raw and the refined.

Unprepossessing to look at, Virginia City was a bog of muddy streets during wet seasons, a dust cloud in summer. What made it all worthwhile, of course, was gold. The glittering dust was everywhere—Chinese laundrymen regularly panned their wash water after doing the miners' clothes. But gold drew a violent, criminal element, who could operate because of the town's isolation. "Road agents" preyed on ore shipments; to travel on the only road to Bannack was to risk one's life. Most notorious of the outlaws was Henry Plummer, a handsome charmer who got himself installed as county sheriff in Bannack, with authority in Virginia City. One of the West's most remarkable outlaws, he secretly led "the Innocents," a highly organized gang who recognized each other by a password ("I am innocent") and a sign (a neckerchief with a particular knot); they had officers, a secretary, and spies. Because of his position as a lawman, Plummer was able to learn when a rich miner or gold shipment was leaving town, and he so informed his henchmen. Stealing and plundering on the ninety-mile stretch between Alder Gulch and Bannack, Plummer's gang slaughtered at least 102 people in two years.

In response, a group of Masons and others formed the Vigilantes in late 1863, spreading out over the territory. They hanged Plummer's entire gang of twenty-four, plus eight more outlaws. Plummer sobbed and begged for his life, but he and two of his men were left "stiffening in the icy blast" of January. In Virginia City the Vigilantes hanged five of the worst outlaws, including Boone Helm, who once dined on a human leg. Historians Michael Malone and Richard Roeder recount: "Standing with the noose about his neck, Helm looked casually at the still lurching corpse of one of his pals and remarked: 'Kick away, old fellow; I'll be in Hell with you in a minute.'"

The Vigilantes often left their own mysterious symbol attached to the bodies, "3-7-77" (numbers that even today appear on the shoulder patches of Montana highway patrolmen). There is speculation that the numbers were either identifying codes for various Masonic orders or codes relevant to the secret rituals of the Masons. When the Vigilantes made a number of errors, however, such as hanging a "murderer" whose victim later made a full recovery, public protest forced them to disband. Traditional legal institutions moved in, and at the end of 1864, the town's first grand jury returned a decision, then promptly adjourned to the nearest watering hole. That winter, when the price of flour soared astronomically, about 500 armed men ransacked the camp and seized all the flour for distribution to those in need. By 1865 Virginia City had been decreed the second territorial capital, and despite occasional notices in the newspaper warning pedestrians of the dangers of stray bullets, "civilization" was established.

Today Virginia City is a kind of freestanding museum, with five streets of restored and fully furnished buildings. Many are original, dating from the 1860s and 1870s; most are log and frame, others stone and brick. Along wooden sidewalks stand buildings of many styles, from western false-front to Classic Revival and Italianate. **Content Corner** is a stone building, built in 1864, whose second story served as capitol offices for the Montana Territory. Other buildings include a general store filled with merchandise from the 1870s, an assay office, a barbershop, two houses of ill repute, the still-functioning **Madison County Courthouse** of 1876, and the log-and-stone **Vigilante Barn,** where the organization supposedly was founded and which now displays wagons, buggies, and stagecoaches. The **Montana Post Building,** built in 1864, exhibits vintage newspaper equipment in a stone building with Gothic windows. **Gilbert's Brewery** contains tanks, an 1864 steam engine, and other brewing equipment. **Saint Paul's Episcopal Church** of 1902 has two stained-glass windows believed to be of Tiffany glass; the medieval-style stone church serves the oldest Protestant congregation in Montana. The cut-stone **Masonic Temple,** built in 1864 and still used by the lodge, contains many original furnishings.

At the corner of Wallace and Van Buren streets, the Vigilantes hanged Boone Helm and others, who are buried in (yet another) **Boothill Cemetery.** Citizens later established a new cemetery for the "good people" among them gold discoverer Bill Fairweather, who enjoyed riding down Wallace Street, scattering gold dust to the poor. The **Virginia City–Madison County Museum** (Wallace Street) exhibits period furniture and clothing, a chuck wagon, a drugstore, gold-mining material, and other local artifacts. An early Virginia City family established the collections of the **Thompson-Hickman Memorial Museum** (Wallace Street, 406–843–5346), a granite building whose relics include the foot of outlaw "Clubfoot George," displayed under a glass dome, as well as muzzle-loading rifles, Vigilante materials, gold-mining exhibits and ore samples, and other memorabilia from Virginia City.

NEVADA CITY

Located a mile and a half from Virginia City, this was one of a string of towns founded along Alder Gulch during the boom of the early 1860s. In December 1863 George Ives became the first road agent hanged, and general support for this decisive action by the miners' court led to the formation of the Vigilantes. By the 1890s Nevada City had dwindled nearly to a ghost town, with many of its structures hauled away for other uses. For its restoration, buildings were brought from other Montana settlements to supplement the dozen structures that remained, and the front street was re-created to match an 1865 photograph of Nevada City. The fifty buildings are fully furnished, with houses, shops full of merchandise, a music hall containing band organs and player pianos, and other structures.

The **Alder Gulch Work Train Railroad Museum** (Route 287 south of Virginia City, 406–843–5382) displays passenger coaches built in 1906; a train of the 1880s; a roundhouse with two steam engines; a chapel car, equipped with organ, altar, and stained-glass windows; and an observation car used by President Calvin Coolidge. The **Alder Gulch River of Gold** (Route 287, 406–843–5526) is a mining museum with a gold dredge afloat in a pond.

About three miles north of the town of **Laurin** on Route 287 is **Robber's Roost** (406–842–5304), a station on the Bannack–Virginia City stage line. It is said that this is where Sheriff Henry Plummer and his gang of road agents planned many of their murderous capers—although the outlaws were apparently well mannered when drinking and eating here. Known as Pete Daly's place when it was built in 1863, it is a two-story structure of square-hewn logs with a full-length porch and second-floor verandah. A bar and gambling tables occupied the first floor; upstairs was a dance hall. Robber's Roost now contains a small museum.

DILLON

Mrs. Eddy Feris, one of the first residents of this Utah & Northern Railroad town, wrote in 1881: "Of all the dreary looking places I ever saw, Dillon is about the worst." With time, though, trees grew to line the streets, and Dillon became a major hub for wool shipping and cattle ranching, as well as a college town. Successful ranchers and entrepreneurs built houses, civic buildings, and business blocks. Noteworthy are the former **Dillon Tribune Building** (Bannack and

Idaho streets) of 1888, with its pressed-metal facade; **Hotel Metlen** (Railroad Street opposite the depot), a railroad hotel with a mansard roof and dormers; the **Orr Mansion** (Idaho and Orr streets), a Western vernacular version of a Tuscan villa, with a bay window and four decorative chimneys, which was built by a prosperous rancher; and the **B. F. White House** (Orr and Washington streets), a mansion with Queen Anne elements, erected by a bank president and territorial governor.

Main Hall at Montana State Normal School (710 South Atlantic Street) was built of locally fired bricks in 1897. Designed in the Queen Anne style, it has unusual crow-stepped gable ends; the west building was added in 1907. Always a teachers' training facility, it is now part of Western Montana College of the University of Montana. **Beaverhead County Museum** (15 South Montana Street, 406–683–5027) contains local Indian artifacts, mining equipment and ore specimens, and pioneers' household and business articles.

BANNACK

The time was right for a Montana gold rush. Diggings in California and Colorado had all been staked out, so prospectors spread out to find new deposits. Montana's first major strike came in July 1862, when John White tried the gold-laced gravel along Grasshopper Creek. By fall a settlement called Bannack had about 500 freshly minted citizens. The notorious Henry Plummer was Bannack's sheriff until the Vigilantes hanged him here in 1864. Many emigrants had come west to escape the Civil War, and their sympathies were reflected in the naming of local features such as Jeff Davis Gulch and Yankee Flats. With the establishment of Montana Territory in 1864, Bannack became temporary capital. But when the mining excitement moved to Virginia City the next year, the legislature moved there too. In a few years, with ditches to bring water for working the placers, steady but unspectacular mining was revived in the area, and in 1895 an electric dredge began operations, taking out $38,000 in gold in a single week.

Abandoned in 1938 and now preserved as **Bannack State Park** (twenty-five miles southwest of Dillon on Route 278, 406–834–3413), Bannack is a ghost town where log and frame buildings rise from sagebrush and greasewood. The **Courthouse,** built in 1875, served as county seat and later, with remodeling, as the Hotel Meade. In

Bannack, the first territorial capital of Montana, is now a ghost town preserved in Bannack State Park.

1877 citizens took refuge here—the town's only masonry building—when Chief Joseph and his Nez Percé warriors camped near Bannack after the Battle of the Big Hole; however, there was no attack. **Skinner's Saloon,** built in 1863, is one of the few structures surviving from the town's earliest period; here Sheriff Henry Plummer picked up casual information about gold shipments to relay to his cutthroat gang. This outlaw lawman was hanged at the site of **Plummer's Gallows.** Lodge members met on the second story of the **Masonic Temple,** which has a double floor to muffle their secret conversations; a school occupied the first story. When it was built in 1877, **Methodist Church** was the town's first, built by a circuit-riding preacher called "Brother Van"; it is a simple frame building of Carpenter Gothic style. Iron rings mounted in the floor of the **Bannack Jail** were for chaining criminals so they could not escape through the sod roof. A **bootlegger's cabin** produced moonshine as recently as the early 1960s.

THE MONTANA PLAINS

OPPOSITE: *The Chalk Buttes in Custer National Forest in southeastern Montana.*

T he Missouri and Yellowstone rivers flow eastward across the great plains that occupy much of the eastern two- thirds of the state. Little vegetation grows, even at the water's edge. Although a few detached mountain ranges pop up, such as the Bearpaws, where Chief Joseph's band of Nez Percé surrendered in 1877, the landscape is generally a level plain of short grasses. Valleys such as the lovely Judith Basin are tucked here and there. On the eastern side of the state, stretching into North Dakota, is the unearthly landscape of the Badlands.

Dry and windy, ravaged by insects, baked in summer, wracked by blizzards in fall, winter, and spring, the eastern plains of Montana have exacted a toll from those who tried to graze livestock or till the soil there. Surprised by frigid temperatures in the late spring of 1805, William Clark made the first known comment on the state's unpredictable weather—"a verry extraodernary climate, to behold the trees Green & flowers spred on the plain, & Snow an inch deep." In 1927 one rancher commented, as late as May: "Weather man still turning loose a lot of snow. You'd think the son of a bitch would run out of stock some time." Faced with such conditions, few persons or towns have taken root on the plains, compared with the mountainous western province.

The procession of whites into Montana began with Pierre and François de La Vérendrye, French-Canadian brothers who came to find furs and an exploitable northwest river passage to the Pacific. In 1743 they described "shining mountains," probably the Bighorns, toward which they traveled across what seems to have been southeastern Montana. But their broken astrolabe did not take accurate bearings and the trip's journal was vague, so no one, including themselves, knew exactly where they went.

The Missouri River was the state's most important waterway for early explorers and settlers, although one ungrateful traveler compared the water's hue to a "particularly badly-made pea soup." Outsiders came to Montana in a procession typical of the Rockies—explorers, fur trappers, missionaries, miners, cattle ranchers, sheepherders, and sodbusters. And from the first they all sought something of profit, something to take away.

Many of the violent conflicts with the Indians took place in central and eastern Montana, notably Custer's Last Stand at the Battle of Little Bighorn. The population drawn to Montana by the gold boom put tremendous pressure on the Indians and their land.

A pictograph of Custer's Last Stand done by Kicking Bear, an Indian who had fought in the battle. Custer's body is at right in a yellow buckskin outfit. Few events in American history shocked the public as profoundly as the annihilation of Custer's Seventh Cavalry.

Miners violated the Indian reserves during the gold rush, and in response the Sioux and Cheyenne attacked traffic on the Bozeman Trail. Such skirmishes led territorial citizens to cry for protection, so Fort C. F. Smith, the first army post in Montana, was established in 1866 on the upper Bighorn; the next year Fort Shaw was erected where the Mullan Road crossed the Sun River, and Fort Ellis was built near Bozeman.

On the plains the whites brought further pressure to bear by hunting the buffalo, the Native Americans' primary source of meals, clothes, and housing. ("Not by accident," said historian Clark Spence, "did the Indian-head nickel have the bison on the other side.") When the gold seekers arrived, there were perhaps 13 million buffalo on the plains, and in 1877 a rancher reported having to wait in the Yellowstone Valley for three days and nights while the vast northern herd crossed his path. But only twenty-five animals remained when a Smithsonian scientific party surveyed the same region just a decade later. The immense herds had been nearly annihilated by professional hunters, who fanned out over the plains with rifles able to kill a buffalo a thousand yards away. Some hunters butchered the animals to feed railroad laborers, but they left most of the flesh to rot, shipping the hides to leather tanneries back east. (In just two years one Montana steamboat captain transported a

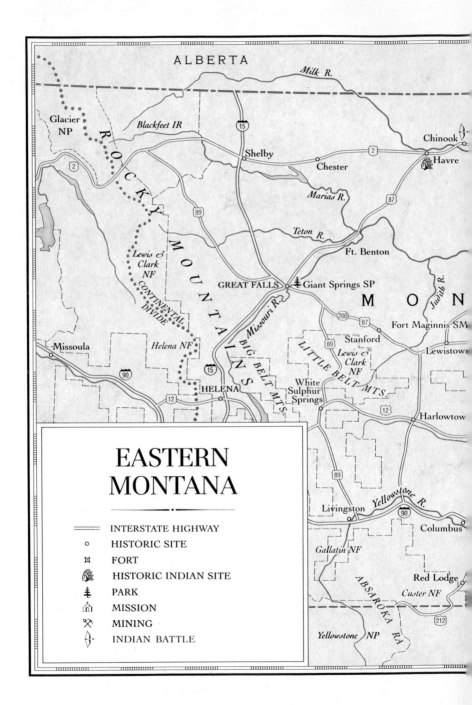

ALBERTA

Milk R.

Glacier
NP

Blackfeet IR

15

Chinook

2

Shelby

Chester

2

Havre

Marias R.

87

89

Teton R.

Ft. Benton

R O C K Y

*Lewis &
Clark
NF*

Missouri R.

CONTINENTAL
DIVIDE

GREAT FALLS

Giant Springs SP

M O N

Judith R.

M O U N T A I N S

200

87

Fort Maginnis SM

Missoula

Helena NF

89

Stanford

*Lewis &
Clark
NF*

LITTLE BELT MTS.

Lewistown

90

BIG BELT MTS.

15

HELENA

White
Sulphur
Springs

12

Harlowtow

12

EASTERN
MONTANA

89

Yellowstone R.

Livingston

90

━━━━ INTERSTATE HIGHWAY

o   HISTORIC SITE

⊞   FORT

      HISTORIC INDIAN SITE

♣   PARK

⌂   MISSION

⚔   MINING

⚲   INDIAN BATTLE

Columbus

Gallatin NF

A B S A R O K A   R A.

Red Lodge

Custer NF

212

Yellowstone NP

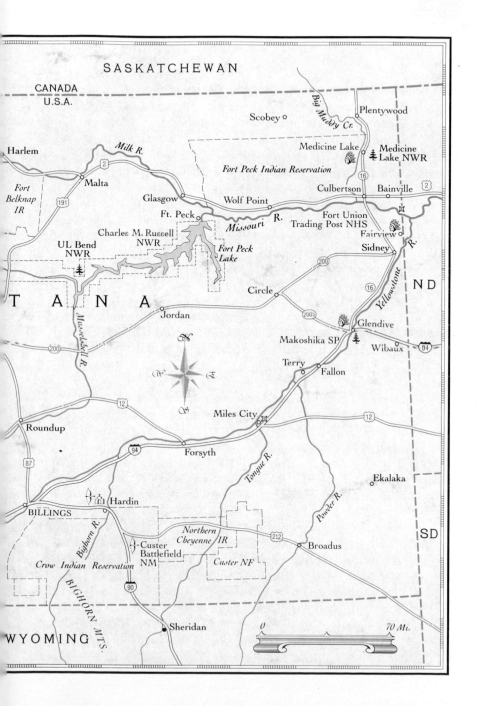

quarter of a million buffalo hides.) The reeking carcasses were soon vulture-picked and weathered, and stacks of bleached skeletons were left scattered across Montana's eastern plains. Needy farmers scavenged the bones to ship east for making fertilizer and bone china.

The slaughter, which began in earnest in about 1870, served to subjugate the Indians by the simple expedient of starving them into dependence on the federal government. The buffalo hunters, said an enthusiastic General Philip Sheridan of the Army of the West, "are destroying the Indians' commissary. . . . For the sake of a lasting peace, let them kill, skin, and sell until the buffalo are exterminated. Then your prairies can be covered with speckled cattle, and the festive cowboy." In 1874 Colonel George Custer's expedition confirmed rumors of gold in the Black Hills of South Dakota, on a reservation given to the Sioux, Cheyenne, and other tribes by the Fort Laramie treaty of 1868. When miners swarmed in despite the army's attempts to prevent them, the federal government tried unsuccessfully to purchase the Black Hills. Angry Indians ranged beyond the reservation to attack settlements and travelers, setting the stage for one of the last acts of Indian resistance to the white invasion—the Battle of the Little Bighorn, or Custer's Last Stand, which left more than 260 soldiers dead.

The Indians' decisive victory, however, led to their ultimate subjugation, because it rallied public opinion and the U.S. Army against them. In 1877 Fort Keogh and Fort Custer were built near the Yellowstone River to garrison more than a thousand soldiers. Meanwhile, Colonel Nelson A. Miles and his "walk-a-heaps" infantrymen fought Crazy Horse, who surrendered in 1877, and also attacked Sitting Bull, who crossed into Canada but later surrendered to the army. The Sioux and Cheyenne troubles were over.

The final campaign against the Indians took place in the north. In 1877 the Nez Percé under Chief Joseph crossed into Montana over the Lolo Trail. Having been displaced from their homeland in the Wallowa Valley of Oregon and ordered onto an Idaho reservation, they were trying to reach sanctuary in Canada. Their arrival in Montana set off a panic among the settlers. Soldiers from Fort Missoula threw up a log barricade in Lolo Canyon, which the Indians easily evaded. The Nez Percé next defeated Colonel John Gibbon in the Big Hole Valley, traversed Yellowstone National Park, and whipped the forces under Colonel Samuel D. Sturgis. Then the refugees crossed the Missouri, but at the Bearpaw Mountains, they were finally cornered by Colonel Nelson A. Miles.

With most of the Indians subjugated, the eastern plains were wide open for new uses. Cattle ranchers had found in Montana a bounty of free grazing land, and they prospered in the 1860s by filling the miners' demand for beef. At the same time, railroads arrived to serve, and be served by, the cattle ranchers. The Utah & Northern (1880), the Northern Pacific (1881), and the Great Northern (1887) connected cow towns with faraway markets and created such instant cities as Great Falls and Havre. But overcrowding of the range, drought, and a bad winter in 1886–1887 ruined many stockmen and wiped out herds. The plains also became pasture for sheep. Billings grew up as the shipping center for a vast wool-producing area, and 50,000 animals were considered just a "fair-sized bunch."

The end of the open range finally was brought about by railroad tracks and homesteaders' barbed wire fences. That chapter in Montana's saga began after the turn of the century, when homesteaders, nicknamed "sodbusters" or "honyockers," started to arrive in droves. High grain prices, land made available under the Enlarged Homestead Act of 1909, boosterism by land companies and the railroads (which had much land to sell), wet years from 1909 to

Members of the Schlenz family threshing wheat southeast of Fallon in 1913. The photograph was taken by Evelyn Cameron, an Englishwoman who settled in Montana in 1890 and recorded the region's transformation from open range to farmland.

1917—all these factors lured hopeful, naive emigrants. One honyock-
er arriving at Dutton inquired where to find the land agent and was
told: "Just go down the street and look like a sucker and [he] will
find you." In the first twenty years of the century, the number of
acres under cultivation in Montana multiplied 2,325 percent, and by
1922 the honyockers owned more than 40 percent of the state. "It's
all grass-side-down now," the artist Charles M. Russell lamented.
"Where once you rode circle . . . a gopher couldn't graze now."

But the homesteaders too would find reasons to lament
—plagues of grasshoppers, droughts, falling wheat prices, and tons
of topsoil blowing away because of improper cultivation. Crops and
farms failed everywhere; three-quarters of the 80,000 people who
arrived during the rush turned around and left, abandoning 11,000
farms before 1925. Montana was the only state in the nation with a
population decline during the twenties. The sodbusters left little
behind but injured land and empty houses whose doors banged in
the wind. Eastern Montana remains one of the least populated
regions of the country. There are no more dreams of beef bonanzas,
but wheat farming has revived, and the people who make their living
here are among the hardiest and proudest on the earth.

This chapter traces a roughly circular path through Eastern
Montana, beginning in Billings and following Route 94 to Wibaux. It
then continues north to Sidney, traces route 16 to Plentywood, moves
west to Scobey, and follows Route 2 to Chester. Next, it proceeds
south to Loma and Fort Benton and concludes in the central portion
of the state.

SOUTHEASTERN MONTANA

BILLINGS

In 1806 William Clark and his party floated down the Yellowstone
River past the site of Billings during their return journey from the
Pacific. The first white settlement, called Coulson, was developed in
1877 by Perry W. "Bud" McAdow, who established irrigated fields, a
sawmill, and a ferry. Businesses and a hotel sprang up, and by 1881
citizens rejoiced that the Northern Pacific was building toward
them, raising hopes that Coulson would be the major station for the

The Louis XVI parlor at the Moss Mansion in Billings. The house was designed for a bank president by an architect who had created some of the most sumptuous hotels in the East.

Yellowstone Valley. But the next year, when McAdow and a real estate promoter named Alderson demanded too high a price for development sites, the Northern Pacific simply established its own town site two miles away, naming it for the man who had secured the railroad's right of way across Montana, company president Frederick Billings. The usual schools, churches, and newspapers cropped up beside the tracks, and in 1883 Billings became county seat. By 1910 three rail lines served the town, which was frequently visited by Buffalo Bill Cody, presidents, and kings.

The **Moss Mansion** (914 Division Street, 406–256–5100·) was designed by Henry J. Hardenburgh, the architect of New York's Plaza Hotel and the original Waldorf-Astoria, as well as the Willard Hotel in Washington, DC. Built of Lake Superior brown sandstone in 1903 in an eclectic style, the house borrows elements from European sources, as seen in the arched Moorish entry (inspired by Granada's Alhambra), the Louis XVI parlor, and the Empire dining room. Original furnishings include Aubusson carpets, rich wood panelling, silk wall coverings, and gilded furniture. Preston B. Moss, a Billings bank president, spent $105,000 to build his mansion. At **Rocky Mountain College** (1511 Poly Drive) stand several noteworthy sandstone buildings, such as the 1915 Prescott Commons.

Boothill Cemetery (Swords Park, Chief Black Otter Trail) was named because many of its occupants died with their boots on, including a sheriff and a number of Indian fighters; the burial ground is the only remnant of old Coulson. The **Old Chamber of Commerce Building** (303 North 27th Street), a brick structure built in 1904 in the Italian Renaissance Revival style, housed the Elks Club and later the chamber of commerce. The **Billings Historic District** (between First and Montana avenues, from 23d to 26th streets) contains numerous old buildings, including the **Rex Hotel** of 1910, built in an ersatz German style and frequented by Buffalo Bill Cody; behind this is the 1912 **Fargo Hotel**. The nearby railroad depot of 1909 served as the main passenger station, with an adjacent beanery.

The **Western Heritage Center** (2822 Montana Avenue, 406–256–6809) occupies the Parmly Billings Library, built in 1901 of sandstone in the Richardsonian Romanesque style with circular towers. It was donated by the son of city namesake Frederick Billings. Exhibits focus on the heritage of the Yellowstone River region: clothing, Native American artifacts, and farming and ranching equipment. The **Austin North House** (Seventh Avenue and North 29th Street, private) was erected in 1903 of sandstone from the local rimrocks and red brick. Its design imitates a castle, with a round turret and battlement, in Victorian Romanesque style. Builder Austin North was an early real estate promoter who tried to establish the Northside district as an elegant residential area.

The **Peter Yegen, Jr., Yellowstone County Museum** (just south of Logan International Airport, 406–256–6811) occupies an 1893 log house where social gatherings often grouped around the large stone fireplace. Downstairs are Indian artifacts, guns, a round-up wagon, saddles, branding irons, a two-headed calf, and dioramas of regional history. Outside rests Old 1031, a Northern Pacific steam engine that traveled 700,000 miles, as well as a bronze statue of silent-movie hero William S. Hart as the "Range Rider of the Yellowstone."

Oscar's Dreamland: Yesteryear Museum (South Frontage Road, exit 446 off Route 90 south of Billings, 406–656–0966) displays antiques and artifacts dating from 1850 to 1930. Among these are a collection of 500 horse-drawn, steam, and gasoline tractors and other farm machinery, and a dozen buildings, including a railroad depot, a jail with a padded cell, and a church boasting the "second-oldest steeple in Billings."

In the eroded sandstone cliffs at **Pictograph Caves State Monument** (seven miles southeast of Billings off Route 90, Lockwood exit, 406–252–4654) are three caves. Each contains pictographs executed in red pigment (made from red ocher, animal grease, and plant resins), black (charcoal and grease), and white (possibly paint obtained through the fur trade). Animals and shield-bearing warriors float eerily across the walls, while later images depict rifles, indicating European contact. Although Middle Cave slopes too sharply for human habitation, Pictograph and Ghost caves reflect four periods of occupation, from paleo-Indian hunter-gatherers to more recent Crow Indians. The vanished residents of this important site left behind stone tools and projectile points, as well as paint applicators from the Shoshoni and Crow.

Indian pictographs are carved in the soft sandstone of **Pompey's Pillar** (28 miles east of Billings off Route 94, 406–875–2166), but the best-known historical graffito is the signature of William Clark inscribed on July 25, 1806—apparently the only physical vestige from the whole Lewis and Clark expedition. While floating down the Yellowstone River, Clark sighted this 150-foot-high block of sandstone and named it after Sacajawea's infant son, Baptiste, whom he had nicknamed "Little Pomp" (Shoshoni for "chief"). Atop the rock, from where Clark saw "emence herds of Buffalows, Elk and wolves," is a view over the distant mountains and the Yellowstone River. While swimming in the river in 1873, George Custer and a large detachment of soldiers were ambushed by Indians, with no injuries.

COLUMBUS

A stagecoach stop on the Yellowstone Trail and later a stone quarry for the state capitol, the settlement had a string of names before choosing Columbus: Eagle's Nest, Sheep Dip (a comment on the local Indian trading post's whiskey), and Stillwater (so dubbed by the Northern Pacific upon its arrival in 1882). Among the town's interesting masonry structures is the **New Atlas Bar Building** (Route 10). The **Beartooth Historical Museum** (Columbus Civic Center) displays a spinning wheel, horseshoes, antique toys, furniture, and clocks from the local area.

RED LODGE

The town of Red Lodge began in 1884 as a mail center for settlers along Red Lodge Creek and developed into a small mining town. Its citizens in 1887 encouraged the Northern Pacific to build a feeder line to obtain nearby coal for the railroad's steam engines. Red Lodge became the hub of Montana's premier coal-producing district, with nearly 5,000 citizens, half of them immigrants from Scotland, Ireland, Finland, Austria, and Italy. The town's commercial center, built from 1893 to 1910 and now known as the **Red Lodge Historic District,** combines vernacular architecture and local materials (stone, brick, wood). Buildings along Broadway include the **Pollard Hotel** of 1893 and the brick **Labor Temple** of 1910. Along Billings Avenue are the **Carbon County Bank** (brick) of 1899 and the **Talmage Building** (masonry) of 1905.

The **Carbon County Museum** (south of Red Lodge on Beartooth Highway) fills a log building with artifacts: rodeo memorabilia, the homestead cabin of Liver Eatin' Johnson (the town's first constable and an Indian fighter for General Nelson Miles), a local hotel register signed by Buffalo Bill Cody, a Finnish rug loom, and the town's first switchboard.

PRYOR

Located on the Crow Indian Reservation, Pryor is the site of the **Chief Plenty Coups State Monument** (one mile west of Pryor off Route 416, 406–252–1289). This Crow war chief promoted good relations with the whites, led scouts for General Crook, and in 1921 traveled to Arlington Cemetery in Virginia, where he made a powerful Armistice Day speech on war and peace. Plenty Coups (*Allek-chear-ahoosh*) adjusted to living on a reservation, occupying a two-story log home with a staircase and wooden floors—very different from the tepee in which it is likely he was born and lived his early life. When he died in 1932, he requested that this house and forty acres be reserved as a park for all people. The memorial complex also includes a log store and the graves of Plenty Coups and two of his wives, as well as the **Chief Plenty Coups Museum,** which displays clothing, medicine bundles, and other Crow artifacts.

OPPOSITE: *Pompey's Pillar, named after the infant son of Sacajawea, the Shoshone woman who took part in the Lewis and Clark expedition. Clark carved his name in the sandstone in 1806.*

HARDIN

Laid out along the Burlington Railroad route by a Nebraska land company, Hardin was opened for settlement in 1906. The 1908 **Becker Hotel** (200 North Center Street), a three-story brick building opposite the Burlington depot, was enlarged in 1917 to accommodate homesteaders coming to the area. A complex at the **Big Horn County Historical Museum and Visitor Center** (east of Hardin, off Route 90, exit 497, 406–665–1671) includes a log cabin, school, farmhouse, mercantile store, filling station, church, and depot with railroad cars. The main building houses a visitor center and exhibits on local history.

Custer Battlefield National Monument

After the Sioux and Northern Cheyenne refused to heed a government ultimatum to return to their reservation in early 1876, the U.S. Army was sent to persuade them. Three expeditions entered southeastern Montana under the commands of General George

Stone tablets mark the spots where George Armstrong Custer and his men fell in battle on June 25, 1876. The placements are conjectural. In 1877 Custer's remains were removed and sent to West Point.

Crook, General John Gibbon, and General Alfred Terry (whose column included General George Custer with the Seventh Cavalry). They had orders to crush the Indians in a three-pronged attack. But the Plains Indians were savage fighters, splendid horsemen who could match the skills of any cavalry, and Sitting Bull, Chief Gall, and Crazy Horse were formidable leaders. In the Battle of the Rosebud, Crazy Horse defeated Crook and put his troops out of the campaign.

Figuring that the Indians would move to the Little Bighorn Valley, Terry and Gibbon approached from the north, up the Yellowstone and Bighorn rivers. Meanwhile, Custer traveled up Rosebud Creek and followed a major Indian trail toward the Little Bighorn to find and attack the village before the Indians could flee. On June 25 Custer, believing that the 600 soldiers of his Seventh Cavalry could conquer the 800 braves he expected, divided his regiment into three battalions. Captain Frederick Benteen was sent to nearby bluffs to scout, while Major Marcus Reno moved across the river to attack the village—but both leaders ended up on the bluffs in retreat. Meanwhile, Custer also advanced on the encampment, soon learning that he had miscalculated: The village housed perhaps 8,000 Sioux and Cheyenne, including 1,500 to 2,000 warriors. They killed Custer and all 210 men under his immediate command within an hour.

The rest of this hot Sunday afternoon in June, Reno and Benteen's companies sustained a bloody siege behind defense lines on the bluffs. As one soldier recalled: "When the firing commenced . . . I said to Jones, 'Let's get off our coats.' He didn't move. I reached down and turned him over. He was dead, shot through the heart." Another private watched an Indian sharpshooter pick off the three soldiers to his right one by one before he and other army men fired "a deadly volley . . . I think we put an end to that Indian." After two days the siege ended, and the Indians slipped away, so suddenly that the troops were wary of a trick. The reason became clear the next morning, when Terry and Gibbon's forces came marching up the river.

Because the Indians' triumph only provoked the government to force them onto reservations more harshly, it has been said that Custer's Last Stand was also the last stand of the Sioux and Cheyenne. The national monument includes the Reno-Benteen

OVERLEAF: *A section of the Little Bighorn River where Major Marcus Reno's detachment fought.*

Battlefield and the "Last Stand" site on Custer Hill. There are guided tours of the battlefield as well as a visitor center containing museum exhibits on the battle. Ranger talks cover subjects from Plains Indian life to archaeological work at the site.

> LOCATION: 18 miles south of Hardin, off Route 90 on the Crow Indian Reservation. HOURS: October through May: 8–4:30 Daily; June through August: 8–8 Daily; September: 8–6 Daily. FEE: Yes. TELEPHONE: 406–638–2621.

About twenty-three miles south of Hardin on Route 313 stands **Saint Xavier Mission Chapel,** on the Crow Indian Reservation. Jesuit missionaries arrived here in 1887 and used a single tent for holding services, cooking meals, and sleeping until they could erect this wooden chapel and adjacent school, which are still in use.

FORSYTH

Located on the Yellowstone River, the town is named for General James Forsyth, who alighted from a steamboat on the site in 1875 before a town existed. By 1882 Forsyth had become enough of a settlement to receive its own post office. The **Rosebud County Pioneer Museum** (1300 Main Street) displays pioneer memorabilia and photographs. The **Rosebud County Courthouse** (1200 block of Main Street) is a Classic Revival building of 1911, with a copper dome, murals, and stained glass.

MILES CITY

Miles City came about, according to historian Clark Spence, "primarily to sell pop-skull whiskey to the soldiers at Fort Keogh." Businessmen started a settlement in 1876–1877 to serve the recently established fort; when the fort moved in 1878, the town also moved to its present location where the Tongue River flows into the Yellowstone. This was a good place to ford the Yellowstone and a logical trading hub on a major route across the northern plains. Soon it became the area's most important settlement. In 1879 one observer came to the town of 350 residents and twenty saloons, noting "as many thieves as any town of its size in the world." Buffalo hunters operated just north of Miles City in the lower Yellowstone Valley. "The bottoms are literally sprinkled with carcasses," reported explorer and scientist Granville Stuart with disgust, ". . . all murdered for their hides which are piled like cordwood all along the way." The Northern Pacific's arrival in 1881 boosted this bloody enterprise even more, and in 1882 the railroad shipped 200,000 hides. (So complete was the carnage that only one carload was shipped in 1884.) At the same time, Miles City developed into eastern Montana's leading cow town. It had already been a stopping place for cattle drovers on the trail from Texas, and now it became a railhead for shipping herds east from all over the region. The town was also a major exporter of sheep—one entrepreneur was waiting for the Northern Pacific's first train with a herd of 6,000 woolies. By 1918 Miles City was the largest horse market in the world due to the demand brought about by the First World War, with sales lasting for days and thousands of horses sold. Sales dropped drastically, however, once the war ended.

The city was neatly divided in the early era, with the south side of Main Street an unbroken stretch of gambling halls, saloons, and dance halls; on the north side lived the "decent folk." After a series of fires, the town rebuilt itself largely in locally made brick. Among historic structures in Miles City are the **Post Office** (106 North 7th), built in 1916 in a Renaissance Revival style; the **Miles City Laundry** (8th and Bridge), completed in 1912 and operated continuously ever since; the Queen Anne house at **1005 Palmer,** built in 1887 and occupied by pioneer ranchers; the **George Miles House** (28 South Lake), erected in 1898 by General Nelson A. Miles's nephew, who had brought the first sheep to the area in 1876; and the **Water Works Building** (Pumping Plant Road) of 1911, whose tanks are now occupied by the Custer County Art Center galleries.

Fort Keogh (two miles southwest of Miles City off Routes 10 and 12) was established in 1876 as a military base to bring the Sioux and Northern Cheyenne to their knees after the Battle of the Little Bighorn; it was named for one of Custer's fallen officers. To patrol eastern Montana, Colonel (later General) Nelson A. Miles commanded the Fifth Infantry and other soldiers, whom he drilled for prolonged winter marches. In the fall of 1876, Miles and his 500 foot soldiers defeated Sitting Bull at Cedar Creek, scattering the Indian camps and driving the chief north. As winter came on, Miles had his men sew long underwear out of woolen blankets and then marched in pursuit, again defeating Sitting Bull, who retreated to Canada. (Miles later kept close watch on the border, blocked Sitting Bull's people from hunting buffalo in the United States, and forced

the starving remnants to surrender in 1881.) Miles and his "walk-a-heaps" troops battled Crazy Horse to a draw in early 1877, killed Lame Deer in May, and helped complete the conquest of the Sioux and Northern Cheyenne. From Fort Keogh he set out after Chief Joseph and his Nez Percé in September 1877, defeating them at Bear's Paw. Soldiers stayed at the fort until 1908, when it was converted to the range and livestock experiment station of the U.S. Department of Agriculture. The only traces of the fort are two officers' quarters, a warehouse, and the parade ground.

One of the frame officers' quarters buildings was moved to the **Range Rider's Museum** (Routes 10 and 12, 406–232–6146). The museum stands on the site of the original cantonment of Fort Keogh, which served as a temporary camp until the fort could be erected nearby. Early range life in eastern Montana is portrayed through a log cabin, a reproduction of Miles City of the 1880s, photographs and pioneer artifacts, military and cowboy memorabilia, and a collection of 400 guns, from elephant rifles to dueling pistols.

BROADUS

This cow town lies on the Powder River, which has been described as "a mile wide and an inch deep, too wet to plow and too thick to drink." When a post office was established here in 1900, Washington bureaucrats mistakenly dropped one *d* in the name of the Broaddus family of settlers. The family's donations of a buggy, piano, and icebox formed the nucleus of the **Powder River Historical Museum** (East Wilson Street), which also displays two 1931 Fords, the old county jail, and a chuck wagon. **Mac's Museum** (Powder River High School, 500 North Trautman, 406–436–2658) contains seashells, minerals, and Indian artifacts collected by pioneer Mac McCurdy.

TERRY

Founded on the Yellowstone River in 1882, Terry is the home of the **Prairie County Museum** (Logan Avenue), whose regional exhibits include tools, machines, a school, a library, pictures depicting local scenery, a hospital with reconstructed rooms, and a Victorian stone outhouse in the back. The museum occupies the old State Bank of Terry, which has marble floors and fine panelling.

OPPOSITE: *A bedroom at the Range Rider's Museum displays a variety of late nineteenth- and early twentieth-century household artifacts.*

BAKER

The history of Fallon County comes to life at the **O'Fallon Historical Museum** (1st Street West and 10th, 406–778–3256) with a collection of settlers' memorabilia—a stuffed 4,000-pound steer, household goods, clothing, and military artifacts—all housed in the old jail.

GLENDIVE

Glendive is an alteration of the name Glendale, which was given to a nearby creek by the famous Irish sportsman Sir George Gore. In the mid-1850s this wealthy hunter passed through Montana on a Wild West safari with forty servants, a string of wagons filled with luxurious amenities, and Jim Bridger as guide; the aptly named Gore killed so many animals with his little arsenal for sport that the Indians were appalled. In 1881 the Northern Pacific's arrival created a construction boom, and within a few years the town was a rail center for shipping cattle and buffalo hides. Regional history lives on at the **Frontier Gateway Museum** (one mile east of Glendive off Route 94, on Belle Prairie Route, 406–365–8168); a complex of eight buildings, it has a main street restored to its 1881 appearance, farm machinery, a school, and a blacksmith shop. The **Charles Krug House** (103 North Douglas Street, private) is a brick Classic Revival home built in 1907 that belonged to the area's first millionaire, a cattle baron.

An earthlodge village at the **Hagen Site** (five miles south of Glendive off Sidney Highway) was occupied by Crow Indians before they became buffalo-hunting nomads. A 1938 excavation uncovered a ten-acre midden area with a house site, storage pits, a burial mound, and hoes made of bison shoulder bones, all indicating a farming culture.

WIBAUX

Located in the badlands of eastern Montana, Wibaux was named for pioneer rancher Pierre Wibaux, a Frenchman from a wealthy background who settled here in 1883. After the severe winter of 1886–1887, he organized an investment company in France and bought out the surviving herds, building his herd to 100,000 head.

OPPOSITE: *Saint Peter's Catholic Church in Wibaux, erected in 1885.*

The town became a center where stockmen (including Theodore Roosevelt) drove their cattle for shipping, and in one year it exported 1.5 million sheep.

The **Wibaux Home/Office Building** (Orgain Avenue and Wibaux Street) of 1892 served Pierre Wibaux as an office and home; the grounds around the frame clapboard building once were landscaped with arbors, ponds, and a grotto. The building is now headquarters of the **Wibaux County Museum** (406–795–8112). **Saint Peter's Catholic Church** (East Orgain Avenue) was dedicated in 1885 and enlarged later using native lava rock. At the **Centennial Car Museum** (East Orgain Avenue, 406–795–2289), a railroad car from the 1964 Montana Territorial Centennial Train now contains Indian and settlers' artifacts—among them a human bone with an arrow through it, an old slot machine, and one of Pierre Wibaux's rifles. The **Gateway Gallery** (310 Beaver Street, 406–795–8207), located in the Reverend and Mrs. Harry Heidt's home, displays a private collection of 1,200 arrowheads found by the Heidt family, along with scrapers, knives, petrified wood, and eastern Montana fossils.

EKALAKA

Once nicknamed Puptown (perhaps for the dogs who congregated in town during winter), this settlement got a post office in 1885 and took the Sioux name of Sitting Bull's niece Ijkalaka, who married a settler. The town grew from a single barroom: Although Claude Carter had intended to build elsewhere, he supposedly bogged his wagon in the mud here and declared, "Hell, any place in Montana is a good place to build a saloon." The **Carter County Museum** (100 Main Street, 406–775–6886) occupies a stone garage built in 1926 and displays locally discovered dinosaur fossils, including one complete skeleton of the duck-billed anatosaur and skulls of the three-horned triceratops and dome-headed pachycephalosaur. The archaeology section displays artifacts dating back to the earliest paleo-Indians who occupied this area over 11,000 years ago. The collection also includes an 1880s post office, furniture, and cowpunchers' saddles and spurs.

One of Montana's earliest cattle companies had a circle brand, which inspired the name of this old-time cowpunchers' town of **Circle** around the turn of the century. Grazing cattle changed the terrain nearby, and by the 1910s homesteaders with their plows had again refashioned the land. At the **McCone County Museum** (Route 200 South, 406–485–2414) exhibits trace regional history through ranching gear and farm machinery.

The farm and oil center of **Sidney** houses the **MonDak Heritage Center** (120 Third Avenue SE, 406–482–3500). Fossils and dinosaur bones, a Winchester rifle collection, a homesteader's shack, a turn-of-the-century town, and a service station with a Model A Ford are on exhibit.

MISSOURI   RIVER   REGION

FORT UNION TRADING POST
NATIONAL HISTORIC SITE

In 1829 John Jacob Astor's American Fur Company built a fortified trading post on the Missouri River near the mouth of the Yellowstone. Twenty feet from the river stood a high palisade enclosing barracks, storehouses, workshops, and a trading room for the Indians, all constructed of cottonwood logs. Historian Kent Ruth noted, "It was a formidable structure physically, a popular ren-

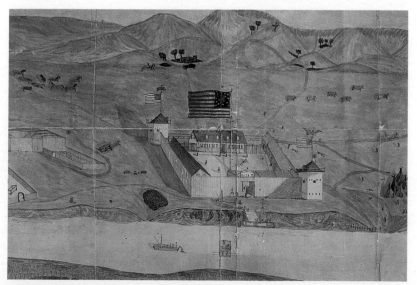

A drawing of Fort Union in the 1850s (detail).

dezvous for travelers socially, and one of the most important fur trading houses in the United States commercially." Here Indians swapped pelts of beaver, mink, and marten for rifles and ammunition, trinkets, and whiskey. And, although an 1832 law forbade the liquor trade because of its devastating effect on the tribes, the fort's lordly factor, Kenneth McKenzie, decided to stay competitive by building a corn whiskey distillery. (His rivals' complaints later forced him to return to simple smuggling to obtain supplies.) The first steamboat arrived at the fort in 1832, but the coming of the *Saint Peters* five years later had more impact, for it brought the smallpox that decimated 15,000 Indians up and down the river. The sojourning Maximilian, prince of Wied, wrote: "The destroying angel has visited the unfortunate sons of the wilderness with terrors never known . . . and has converted the extensive hunting grounds [and] peaceful settlements . . . into desolate and boundless cemeteries." Others who visited the fort included artists George Catlin and Karl Bodmer, who painted it in the 1830s, and Father De Smet, John James Audubon, and Jim Bridger in the next decade. By the 1860s the fur trade had long declined; the now dilapidated fort served briefly as a supply camp for General Alfred Sully's expedition against the Sioux in 1864. Three years later Fort Union was abandoned—its kitchen torn down to fuel the steamboat *Miner,* half the remaining buildings dismantled to build nearby Fort Buford, and the rest scavenged by wood hawks selling firewood.

Today the fort is partially reconstructed to its appearance in 1851: four palisades, two stone bastions, the trade house, and the home of the factor, which serves as visitor center and museum. Original artifacts include trade baubles, Indian weapons and clothing, furs, firearms, and tableware.

LOCATION: 11 miles north of Fairview on the Montana–North Dakota border, via Routes 200, 58, and 1804. HOURS: 9–5:30 Daily, 8–8 in summer. FEE: None. TELEPHONE: 701–572–9083.

Bainville, laid out after the turn of the century, is the home of the **Bainville Historical Association Museum** (Clinton Avenue, 406–769–2127), which displays the household objects and shop tools of early settlers in the area, as well as a restored 1920s fire truck.

Located in the **Medicine Lake National Wildlife Refuge** is the **Tepee Hills Site** (seven miles east of Medicine Lake off Route 16, 406–789–2305). In the hills around the lake are tepee rings that may be 4,000 years old. These circles of rocks mark sites where lodges once stood and indicate long habitation by people who came for the hunting, water, and fuel available.

Plentywood is said to have been named when a cattle outfit found firewood, rare on the plains, alongside a creek where the town now lies. The **Sheridan County Museum** (east of town on Route 16, summer only) has collected antique threshing machines and tractors, as well as homestead items.

Located in a grain-growing and ranching region, **Scobey** took shape around the Great Northern station after the turn of the century. On the twenty acres of the **Daniels County Museum and Pioneer Town** (Second Avenue West and Seven County Road, seven blocks west of Main Street, 406–487–5965) are forty buildings dating to the early 1900s, among them a bank, saloon, ladies' shop, fire station, funeral home, watch-repair shop, and two churches; also displayed are vintage automobiles and tractors. A early trading post and cow town, **Wolf Point** supposedly got its name from the hundreds of frozen wolf carcasses carried in one winter by hunters and piled alongside the river awaiting the steamboat. The **Wolf Point Area Historical Society Museum** (220 Second Avenue South, 406–653–1912) has Indian, ranching, and homesteading displays.

It is hard to imagine greater isolation than the town of **Jordan**, which was dubbed "the lonesomest town in the world" in 1930. Roads were mere ruts (often bogged with mud), a proposed railroad connection never materialized, there was no telephone service until 1935, and the local newspaper editor used to get his news of the world on a shortwave radio. Three decades after the town was settled in 1901, there were 1,000 farms in the county, but just eight had running water. The **Garfield County Museum** (Route 200 and Brusett Road, 406–557–2517) displays local homestead articles, an old-time fire engine, fossils, and a fiberglass replica of a triceratops unearthed north of town in 1965.

FORT PECK

Fort Peck began in 1867 as an Indian agency and trading post under proprietors E. H. Durfee and Campbell K. Peck. "Among the supplies they issued were 100-pound sacks of flour emblazoned on each side with great red circles composed of the words 'Durfee and Peck,'" according to government historians. "The Indians adopted the sacks for war dress, merely cutting holes for the arms and neck. The Hunkpapa, a Sioux tribe, especially valued the bright red circles as 'good medicine.'" After controlling commerce with the Sioux and Assiniboine for twelve years, the post was abandoned. Today's settlement of Fort Peck began in 1933 as a government-planned town for workers at the **Fort Peck Dam** (406–526–3431), which was built to aid navigation on the Missouri River, reduce flooding, and generate power. Since its completion in 1940, it has been the world's largest hydraulic earth-fill dam, its main dike containing 126 million cubic yards of material and the resulting lake stretching 134 miles, with a shoreline of 1,600 miles—longer than California's coast. The dam and reservoir have been called "the largest man-made alteration on the Montana landscape." There is a visitor center at the dam, and tours are offered. The **Fort Peck Museum** (Power Plant Number 1, adjacent to visitor center, 406–526–3411) displays more than 400 fossils found in the vicinity by early dam workers in their off-hours: bones of flesh-and plant-eating dinosaurs, fossilized plants (including a palm leaf and petrified figs from an earlier subtropical era), and the remains of armored fishes and other denizens of ancient seas. Recreation for 1930s workers on the dam was provided by movies at the **Fort Peck Theatre** (Main Street, 406–526–9943), an Arts and Crafts–style wooden chalet that now houses a summer theatrical company.

GLASGOW

First named, prosaically, "Siding 45" by the Great Northern Railway, Glasgow was retitled for the Scottish city in 1888, a year after its founding. By then it had eight saloons, a store, and three restaurants. Although it became a railroad hub for shipping stock and farm products, its real boom came after 1932 with the building of the Fort Peck Dam, which inflated the town's population and restored a Wild West atmosphere so colorful that *Life* magazine ran a cover story on the subject in its first issue in 1936. The **Pioneer Museum** (Route 2 West, 406–228–8692) has collected Indian materials (elk-hide tepee), pioneer items (farm machinery, furniture), a Great Northern caboose, a cherrywood saloon bar, a general store, musical instruments, and old Victrolas.

OPPOSITE: *The Fort Peck Theatre, built to entertain workers at the Fort Peck Dam in the 1930s.*

MALTA

When the time came to give this town a more distinguished name than Siding 44, a Great Northern Railway worker spun a globe and came up with the name of the Mediterranean island. Malta was the heart of a vast cattle domain from 1870 to 1900. The town's old Carnegie Library now houses the **Phillips County Historical Museum** (133 South 1st Street West, 406–654–1037), with cowboy gear, Indian artifacts, and homesteaders' items.

LANDUSKY

On the flank of the Little Rocky Mountains stands a ghost town now protected as the **Landusky Historic District** (south of Harlem off Route 66). The town began with a gold strike in 1893 by Powell "Pike" Landusky, as rough a customer as the Wild West ever produced. Legend has it that once, when taken prisoner by the Sioux, he picked up a frying pan and battered a warrior so mightily that the band backed off, leaving Pike with two of their horses to appease his evil spirit. Later a Blackfoot shot him in the jaw: "Staggering with pain and loss of blood, Pike . . . broke off the shattered section of jaw with four teeth in it, still raging as he threw it in the corner," reported Lambert Florin, a historian of the era. One day in 1894 he went to a Landusky saloon and got into a brawl with Harvey "Kid" Curry, a local rancher and rustler. Pike drew his gun, which misfired; Curry drilled him with a .45 revolver. Kid Curry fled town, later joining the "Wild Bunch" alongside Butch Cassidy and the Sundance Kid.

Eight miles east of Landusky stands the **Zortman Historic District** (off Route 191), named for the prospector Pete Zortman, discoverer of the Alabama mine in the early 1890s. Two miles north, the Ruby Gulch mine produced high-grade ore that was processed by a huge cyanide mill and turned into gold bricks. A 1936 fire swept across the mountains to Zortman, erasing much of the town, but it has been revived as a tourist attraction.

Chinook—the Indian name means "warm winter wind"—has been a cattle ranchers' shipping center and a sodbusters' commercial hub. Area history is the focus at the **Blaine County Museum** (501 Indiana, 406–357–2590), whose collections emphasize the homesteading period around 1910. The exhibits include a furnished settler's shack, farming tools, doctor's office, one-room school, and Indian beadwork.

CHIEF JOSEPH BATTLEGROUND
OF THE BEAR'S PAW STATE MONUMENT

The last engagement of the Nez Percé War took place here in the fall of 1877. The battle is commemorated by a roadside marker sixteen miles south of Chinook on Route 240. When the government ordered the Nez Percé from Oregon's Wallowa Valley, those who refused to go to the reservation in Idaho fled the U.S. Army into Montana, fighting a number of battles along the way. Finally, believing that they had eluded the last of General Oliver O. Howard's pursuing soldiers, the Indians camped near the Bearpaw Mountains, only forty-two miles south of the Canadian border. They felt safe: Howard was trailing them distantly as usual, which is why the Indians called him "General Day after Tomorrow." But they could not have guessed that he had telegraphed Fort Keogh, asking

Chief Looking Glass, killed in the battle at Bear's Paw, was one of the last casualties in the Nez Percé war.

Colonel Nelson A. Miles to bring infantry and cavalry soldiers on a diagonal route to cut the Indians off. On September 30, 1877, Miles's forces attacked the camp and stole most of the Nez Percé horses, although Indian sharpshooters dispatched sixty of the soldiers. Miles then launched a siege with his artillery. During peace negotiations, he violated the white flag by capturing Chief Joseph but was thwarted when the Indians seized one of Miles's own officers and forced an exchange. After several days of battle, Howard's forces arrived, and the Nez Percé chiefs debated surrender. Looking Glass had been killed, White Bird decided to flee with his band to Canada, and on October 5 Joseph chose to give up with 417 of his people. According to legend, Chief Joseph uttered a powerful and beautiful speech of surrender: "The old men are all dead. . . . It is cold and we have no blankets. The little children are freezing to death. . . . I want to have time to look for my children and see how many of them I can find; maybe I shall find them all among the dead. Hear me, my chiefs, I am tired. My heart is sick and sad. From where the sun now stands, I will fight no more, forever." Although scholars believe that Chief Joseph probably did not utter these words, and although he was only one of several Nez Percé chiefs, he became celebrated as the "Red Napoleon" who had led a 1,700-mile retreat with his women, children, and elders over impossibly rugged terrain, beat back the U.S. Army, and brilliantly outfoxed its generals.

In a report to the U.S. Senate, General William Tecumseh Sherman later summarized the Nez Percé campaign as "one of the most extraordinary Indian wars of which there is any record. The Indians throughout displayed a courage and skill that elicited universal praise. They abstained from scalping; let captive women go free . . . and fought with almost scientific skill, using advance and rear guards, skirmish lines and field fortifications." But he recommended that the Nez Percé never be allowed to return to Oregon or Idaho. Although Joseph's surrender had been based on assurances from Miles and Howard that his band could go to Idaho's Lapwai Reservation, instead the Nez Percé ended up being shunted to Kansas and Oklahoma, returning to the Northwest only in 1885.

HAVRE

In 1887 James J. Hill surveyed the Milk River valley and picked this site, which had abundant water, as a station on the Manitoba (Great Northern) line and a branch point to Great Falls. During what Hill called "a long and hard summer's work," his crews laid three-and-a-quarter miles of track daily, or 550 miles in all, from Minot, North Dakota, to Great Falls via Havre. Originally called Bull Hook Bottoms, at Hill's command the settlement was renamed for a French settler's hometown. A Great Northern caboose and other railroading items are displayed at the **H. Earl Clack Museum** (Hill County Fairgrounds, on Route 2, 406–265–9641); also featured are fossils, farm machinery, and dioramas of the early West. The museum has also gathered several historical buildings such as a windmill, homestead house, post office, and a U.S. Signal Corps weather station. The museum conducts tours of the **Wahkpa Chu'gn Buffalo Jump and Archaeological Site** where, from 50 B.C. to A.D. 1850, Indians stampeded herds of bison off a cliff and butchered them. An enclosure for small herds offered another way to trap and kill the animals. Also known as the "Too-Close-For-Comfort-Site," the locale has yielded bison bones, projectile points, and evidence of a campsite. The collections at **Northern Montana College** (300 11th Street West, 406–265–3700) include fossils and Plains Indians artifacts.

Several of original fort buildings still stand at **Fort Assiniboine** (six miles southwest of Havre on Route 87, 406–265–4383), built between 1879 and 1883 as a base for patrols of the Canadian border

Original brick buildings at Fort Assiniboine.

(so Sitting Bull's Sioux could not cross back into Montana) and the Milk River valley; it later became a regimental training center and in the 1930s served as a camp for transients. It is in use today as the site of an agricultural research station, established in 1913.

Until a railroad built tracks into the region, ranchers had to drive their stock to the railhead in North Dakota, often stopping over on Cottonwood Creek at **Chester.** The Great Northern duly arrived; in 1907 it decided to straighten a bend in the line, so the whole town had to pick up and move from the north side of the tracks to the south side. The **Liberty County Museum** (2d Street and Madison Avenue, 406–759–5256) displays old machinery, a one-room schoolhouse, a country store, military and medical items, costumes, and Indian artifacts.

LOMA

Lewis and Clark spent a June night in 1805 near the spot where the Marias and Missouri rivers meet. They were surprised to find this confluence of rivers, the northern branch turbulent and muddy from the spring runoff, the southern branch sparkling clear. Lewis wrote of this episode: "An interesting question was now to be determined; which of these rivers was the Missouri. To mistake the stream at this period of the season, two months of the traveling season having now elapsed, and to ascend such stream to the Rocky mountain or perhaps much further before we could inform ourselves whether it did approach the Columbia or not, and then be obliged to return and take the other stream would not only loose us the whole of this season but would probably so dishearten the party that it might defeat the expedition altogether." Lewis and Clark split up to explore the two rivers separately. They met again on this spot on June 8 and made their momentous decision—correctly. They identified the southern branch as the Missouri and named the northern branch Marias after Lewis's cousin, Maria Wood—in whom Lewis had more than a passing interest, commenting that the river's muddy waters "but illy comport with the pure celestial virtues and amiable qualifications of that lovely fair one." Twenty-six years later the American Fur Company built a trading post here called Fort Piegan, but the fur merchants were driven out by hostile Indians, who promptly burned it. The town of Loma, a stop on the Great Northern line, took its name from a telegraphers' contraction of Lower Marias. The **Earth Science Museum** (106 Main Street,

406–739–4357) has exhibits on railroad history, including twisted rails and other scraps from a Great Northern train that was pulling a carload of dynamite in 1897 and blew up. Also displayed are items from the Fort Benton–Fort Assiniboine trail (such as a ball and chain hammered off by an unknown person), Indian artifacts, minerals, and western petrified woods. The **House of a Thousand Dolls** (106 1st Street, 406–739–4338) overflows with dolls, dated 1860–1980 and made of bisque, cloth, and plastic.

FORT BENTON

On a wide, grassy bank on the Missouri River stood a fort that served the twilight of the fur trade and then saw the golden dawn of steamboat days. The American Fur Company established the post in 1846 as Fort Lewis, moved it across the river in 1848 as Fort Clay, and renamed it in 1850 for Senator Thomas Hart Benton, the firm's champion in Congress. Although the fur era was fading, the adobe fort grew into a vital trading hub because of its location at the head

A railroad bridge crosses the Missouri River at Fort Benton.

of navigation on the Missouri. In 1860 the first steamboats arrived, the *Chippewa* and *Key West,* carrying soldiers who set off on the new Mullan Road that ran west toward Walla Walla, Washington. When gold was discovered in Montana in 1862, a transportation network was already in place. In the peak year of 1867, Fort Benton's docks bustled with 39 steamboats, 8,061 tons of freight, and 10,000 passengers—remarkable numbers, considering that Fort Benton was the most isolated port in the nation. To obtain whiskey, Indians flocked to the "Alcohol Springs," as one traveler called Fort Benton. Along the waterfront a raucous settlement grew up. "Walk in the middle of the street and mind your own business,"· newcomers were advised. "This is a tough town." A historian, declared that "Fort Benton's sidewalks were at times so thickly carpeted with discarded playing cards that it was difficult to see the wood planking."

The American Fur Company quit doing business here in 1869. Within a few years, the wild town grew quiet again, a casualty of the mining decline and especially the building of the transcontinental railroad, which siphoned off freight traffic from the river. The fort became a military post with few real duties. In 1875, however, the the town revived as such merchants as I. G. Baker and T. C. Power transferred river freight northward on the Whoop-Up Trail to remote posts in Canada. The flow of illegal whiskey to the Indians from Fort Benton was so profuse that the Northwest (now Royal Canadian) Mounted Police was called in to plug it.

The **Fort Benton Landmark District** encompasses the historic section of town. Old Fort Park contains a **blockhouse and ruins** of the fort's adobe walls, as well as the adjacent **Fort Benton Museum of the Upper Missouri** (1801 Front Street), whose exhibits include Indian tools and clothing, a model of Fort Benton made of adobe from the original fort, frontier relics (such as a trapper's cabin, gold scale, and an oxen yoke), steamboat displays, a saloon bar, cowboy gear, and Northwest Mounted Police equipment. Across the street from the museum is the **Lewis and Clark memorial,** a bronze statue of the explorers and their Indian interpreter, Sacajawea. Among the district's nineteenth-century buildings is the **Chouteau House** (1614 Front Street, 406–622–3842), the town's original luxury inn, established in 1868 as the Thwing Hotel and reconstructed of brick in

OPPOSITE: *Among the frontier relics preserved at the Fort Benton Museum of the Upper Missouri are this buffalo robe and powder horn.*

1903; the bar still operates. Next door stands the **I. G. Baker House** (1608 Front Street), a restored 1867 adobe built by an early Fort Benton merchant whose enterprises included steamboats, bull teams, and trading posts as distant as the Arctic Circle; the house later became officers' quarters during the fort's military era. Clapboard siding was added in 1876. Along the old **levee** (Front Street) interpretive signs discuss the days when bales and barrels of freight were stacked on the riverfront.

A brick Italianate pile built in 1882, the **Grand Union Hotel** (14th and Front streets) was one of the most luxurious hostelries in Montana; at three stories, it is still Fort Benton's tallest building. Topped with a clocktower, the **Chouteau County Courthouse** (Franklin between 13th and 14th streets) was built of local brick in 1884; the courtroom preserves its original furnishings. At 14th and Choteau streets stands **Saint Paul's Episcopal Church,** which in 1880 replaced a saloon and the courthouse as a center for worship. One of the state's oldest masonry buildings, the Romanesque Gothic church has restored its original altar, benches, and stained-glass windows. In 1880 the two-story, brick **C. E. Conrad Home** (16th and Washington streets, private) was built by one of the partners in the I. G. Baker Company. The **Montana Agricultural Center and Museum of the Northern Great Plains** (21st and Washington streets) depicts three farm generations—the homestead period, the "dirty '30s," and the present—and the advancement of farming technology.

C E N T R A L   M O N T A N A

Settlement started in **Stanford** in 1880, when two brothers bought a 100,000-acre spread to run sheep. Stanford became a stage stop and cowboy social center, frequented by painter Charles Russell when he worked on local ranches. Early relics of the area—a hand-powered washing machine, an old fire engine, buttons, clothing, and 2,030 sets of salt-and-pepper shakers—are on display at the **Judith Basin Museum** (203 First Avenue South, 406–566–2281).

Platted after the Great Northern came through in 1907, **Windham** rose (and later sagged) as a hub for ranchers and homesteaders. The **Sod Buster Museum** (five miles southeast of Windham on Route 87, 406–423–5358) displays a sodbuster's plow and collections of Indian artifacts, ranching gear, and barbed wire; outside are a log cabin homestead and a blacksmith shop.

The Sod Buster Museum near Windham features displays of farming gear such as this nineteenth-century wagon.

In the 1880s Charles M. Russell came to **Utica** to ride in the Judith Basin roundups. A better painter than builder, Russell erected a mismade cabin in a gulch above town, supposedly his first Western home and first studio; it has since disappeared. Homestead-era artifacts are on display at the **Utica Museum** (Main Street, 406–423–5208), including furniture, dishes, tools, saddles, farm machinery, and an 1880s wagon.

LEWISTOWN

Mixed-blood French and Indians, known as metis, settled Lewistown in about 1879. The town took its name from Fort Lewis, which had been established earlier two miles away. A ranching center, Lewistown had its wild times. In a main-street shootout, townsmen turned their Winchesters on two rustlers, Edward "Longhair" Owen and Charles "Rattlesnake Jake" Fallon, who "continued firing until they could no longer pull a trigger." During the homestead era after the turn of the century, Lewistown boomed because it lay in a district of nearly 6.5 million acres of public land thrown open to land seekers. Entrepreneurs who profited from the trading boom of 1905–1919 built homes in the **Silk Stocking Historic District,** which

includes large houses in the 200 block of West Boulevard and the 300 block of Third Avenue North. The **Central Montana Museum** (403 Northeast Main Street, 406–538–5436) features exhibits of Indian clothing and beadwork and pioneer relics, including blacksmith tools, cowboy gear, and guns.

Once a gathering spot for cattle herds grazing in the Musselshell River valley, the town of **Roundup** received a post office in 1883. When the Milwaukee Railroad arrived in 1908, it decided to develop coal mines nearby, which brought more people and prosperity. A replica of a coal tunnel is part of the **Musselshell Valley Historical Museum** (524 First StreetWest, 406–323–1403), along with fossils, pioneer artifacts, a post office and school, and the operating room of an old hospital. On the premises is the 1884 log home of an English cattle baron, moved to the site.

HARLOWTON

Located on bluffs along the Musselshell River, this town was the starting point for the Milwaukee Road's electric line heading west over the mountains to Idaho. (On the way downhill, an electric engine could recharge up to 60 percent of the power it had consumed going up.) A **Milwaukee Road Electric Locomotive,** made by General Electric in 1915, is at the intersection of Central Avenue and Route 12. Already in place to serve rail travelers, the **Graves Hotel** (Central Avenue, 406–632–4301) was built in 1908 of local sandstone, with a wooden cornice and a cast-iron turret and dome. The hotel overlooks the former **Milwaukee Road Complex,** including the unrestored 1909 wooden depot and roundhouse. The **Upper Musselshell Historical Society Museum** (11 South Central Avenue, 406–632–5519) displays Indian arrowheads, stone hammers, and garments, a restored country store, and a rural schoolroom.

In the shadow of the Crazy Mountains, the intriguingly named hamlet of **Twodot** (thirteen miles west of Harlowton off Route 12) was founded by stockman George "Two Dot" Wilson. He branded his cattle with two dots—on the shoulder and thigh—a marking difficult for rustlers to modify. An old railroad station and other weathered buildings still stand.

OPPOSITE: *The county courthouse in Lewistown, once a wild cattle town and now a quiet agricultural center.*

NOTES ON ARCHITECTURE

GOTHIC REVIVAL

After about 1830 darker colors, asymmetry, broken skylines, verticality, and the pointed arch began to appear. New machinery produced carved and pierced trim along the eaves. Roofs became steep and gabled; porches became more spacious. Oriel and bay windows were common and there was greater use of stained glass.

ITALIANATE

CRESTED BUTTE CITY HALL, CO

The Italianate style began to appear in the 1840s, both in a formal, balanced "palazzo" style and in a picturesque "villa" style. Both had round-headed windows and arcaded porches. Commercial structures were often made of cast iron, with a ground floor of large arcaded windows and smaller windows on each successive rising story.

QUEEN ANNE

GREENOUGH MANSION, MT

The Queen Anne style emphasized contrasts of form, texture, and color. Large encircling verandahs, tall chimneys, turrets, towers, and a multitude of textures are typical of the style. The ground floor might be of stone or brick, the upper floors of stucco, shingle, or clapboard. Specially shaped bricks and plaques were used for decoration. Panels of stained glass outlined or filled the windows. The steep roofs were gabled or hipped, and other elements, such as pediments, Venetian windows, and front and corner bay windows, were typical.

SHINGLE STYLE

CONRAD MANSION, MT

The Shingle Style bore the stamp of a new generation of professional architects led by Henry Hobson Richardson (1838–1886). Sheathed in wooden shingles, its forms were smoothed and unified. Verandahs, turrets, and complex roofs were sometimes used, but they were thoroughly integrated into a whole that emphasized uniformity of surface rather than a jumble of forms. The style was a domestic and informal expression of what became known as Richardsonian Romanesque.

RICHARDSON ROMANESQUE

HUERFANO COUNTY COURTHOUSE, CO

Richardson Romanesque made use of the massive forms and ornamental details of the Romanesque: rounded arches, towers, stone and brick facing. The solidity and gravity of masses were accentuated by deep recesses for windows and entrances, by rough stone masonry, stubby columns, strong horizontals, rounded towers with conical caps, and botanical, repetitive ornament.

RENAISSANCE REVIVAL OR BEAUX ARTS

In the 1880s and 1890s, American architects who had studied at the Ecole des Beaux Arts in Paris brought a new Renaissance Revival to the United States. Sometimes used in urban mansions, but generally reserved for public and academic buildings, it borrowed from three centuries of Renaissance detail—much of it French—and put together picturesque combinations from widely differing periods. The Beaux Arts style gave rise to the "City Beautiful" movement, whose most complete expression was found in the late nineteenth- and early twentieth-century world's fairs in Chicago and San Francisco.

ECLECTIC PERIOD REVIVALS

MIRAMONT CASTLE, CO

During the first decades of the twentieth century, revivals of diverse architectural styles became popular in the United States, particularly for residential buildings. Architects designed Swiss chalets, half-timbered Tudor houses, and Norman chateaux with equal enthusiasm. In Europe such architecture is found in the countryside; in America the styles were transplanted to the suburbs.

I N D E X

Numbers in *italics* indicate illustrations; numbers in **boldface** indicate maps.

Adams, J.C., Stone Barn, 367
Alamosa, CO, 92
Alder Gulch River of Gold, 409
Alder Gulch Work Train Railroad Museum, 409
Alexander House, 300
Algeria Temple Shrine/Civic Center, 398
Almo, ID, 285, *285, 286-87,*288
Alta Ranger Station, 382
Anaconda, MT, 388-89, *390,* 391
Anaconda-Deer Lodge County Courthouse, 389, *390*
Anasazi, 25, 75, 101
Anasazi Heritage Center, 106
Animas Museum, 109
Antonito, CO, 92
Appaloosa Museum, 342
Arapaho, 25, 33, 34, 79, 118
Arapaho Museum, 236
Arlington, WY, 187
Arts Chateau, 394
Ashcroft, CO, 147
Aspen, CO, 142, 144, *144,* 145, *146,* 147, *147*
Astor House Hotel, 55
Atlas Theater, 173
Avery House, 120

B'Nai Israel Synagogue, Butte, MT, 394
Baca House, 89
Bagley, John, House, 276
Bainville, MT, 438
Bainville Historical Association Museum, 438
Baker, I. G., House, 450
Baker, Jim, Cabin, 187
Baker, MT, 434
Bank Museum, 242
Bannack, MT, 410-411, *411*
Bannack Jail, 411
Bannack State Park, 410, *411*
Bannock County Historical Museum, 278
Bates, Katherine Lee, 131
Bean, Luther, Museum, 92
Bear Canon Cemetery, 66
Bear River Battleground, 284
Beartooth Historical Museum, 423
Beaverhead County Museum, 410
Becker Hotel, 426
Bent's Old Fork National Historic Site, 79, *80,* 81
Bielenberg Home, 387

Big Hole National Battlefield, 382-83, *384, 385*
Big Horn, WY, 252-53
Big Horn County Historical Museum and Visitor Center, 426
Bighorn Canyon National Recreation Area, *30*
Billings, MT, 420-23, *421*
Bingham County Historical Museum, 281
Black Canyon of the Gunnison National Monument Park, *96,* 97
Blackfoot, ID, 281-82, *281*
Blaine County Historical Museum, 311
Blaine County Museum, 442
Bloom House, 89
Blue Jay Inn, 66
Bluestone House, 397
Boise, ID, *270,* 296-298, *296-97, 299,* 300-302, *303,* 304
Boise Basin Museum, 310
Bonanza, ID, 325
Bonner County Historical Museum, 347
Boothill Cemetery, Virginia City, MT, 408
Boulder, CO, 53-54
Boulder Historical Society Museum, 54
Bozeman, MT, 402-03
Bozeman Carnegie Library, 402
Breckenridge, CO, 136-37
Breckenridge Mining Camp Museum, 137
Briarhurst, 132
Bridger, Jim, 24, 29, 71, 159, *159,* 167, 188, 192, 194, 198, 202, 215, 226, 248, 438
Bridger Road Dry Creek Crossing, 248
Broadmoor Hotel, *124,* 125
Broadus, MT, 433
Broadwater County Museum and Historical Library, 399
Brown, Henry C., 39, 40
Brown, Molly, 44-45; House Museum, 44, *44, 45*
Brown Palace Hotel, *38,* 39
Browning, MT, 368, *369*
Buffalo, WY, 250-52, *251*
Buffalo Bill Dam, 247
Buffalo Bill Historical Center, 242-45, *243, 244*
Buffalo Bill Memorial Museum and Grave, CO, 56, *56*
Buffalo Bill Museum, 244
Buffalo Creek, CO, 66
Burgdorf Hot Springs, 327
Bush Mansion, 300

Butte, MT, 391-94, *393*
Butte, Anaconda & Pacific Railway Depot, 391
Butte-Silver Bow City-County Courthouse, 393, *393*
Byers-Evans House, 43

Calamity Jane, 211, 254
Camp Rock, 285
Campbell County Rockpile Museum, 256
Canon City, CO, 84-85, *86-87,* 88
Canon City Municipal Museum, 85, 88
Canyon County Historical Museum, 304
Carbon County Bank, 425
Carbon County Museum, Rawlins, CO, 187
Carbon County Museum, Red Lodge, MT, 425
Carson, Kit, 24, 40, 71, 75, 78, 81, 91, 136, 202, 265; Museum, 79
Carter County Museum, 436
Cascade County Courthouse, 366
Cascade County Historical Museum and Archives, 366
Casey, Edmond Thomas, 122
Casper, WY, 209-11
Cassidy, Butch, 99, 165, 179, 276
Castle Garden, *238,* 239, *239*
Castle Historic District, 400
Castle Rock, CO, 67
Cataldo, ID, 343-44, *345*
Cathedral of Saint Helena, Helena, MT, *396,* 397
Cavendish, ID, *340-41*
Centennial, WY, 179-80
Centennial Car Museum, 436
Centennial Village Museum, 119
Central City, CO, 57
Central City Opera, 57
Central Montana Museum, 453
Central Presbyterian Church, Denver, CO, 40
Challis, ID, *318,* 323, *324,* 325-26
Chautauqua Park, 54
Chester, MT, 446
Cheyenne, WY, 169-74, *171, 173, 174,* 175-76
Cheyenne Frontier Days Old West Museum, 175
Cheyenne Indians, 25, 33, 79, 118
Chico Hot Springs, 402
Chimney Rock, CO, *108,* 109
Chinook, MT, 442
Chouteau County Courthouse, 450

298: David R. Frazier Photolibrary, Boise, ID
299, 303, 306: John Marshall
307: Idaho State Historical Society, Negative No. 83-37.22, Photo Courtesy Arthur A. Hart
308-309, 312: John Marshall
315: Idaho State Historical Society, Negative No. 1289, Photo Courtesy Arthur A. Hart
318: David Muench
321, 323, 324, 328-329: John Marshall
330: Idaho State Historical Society, Negative No. 1260
332-333: Smithsonian Institution
334: National Park Service, Harper's Ferry Center, Harper's Ferry, WV
335: Idaho State Historical Society, Negative No. 63-221.24, Photo by Jane Gay
338, 340-341: John Marshall
342: Arthur A. Hart, Boise, ID
345: John Marshall
348: Mark E. Gibson
351: Missouri Historical Society, St. Louis, MO
356: C. M. Russell Museum, Great Falls, MT
358-359: Library of Congress

360-361: John Reddy
364: Milwaukee Public Museum of Milwaukee County, WI
365: C. M. Russell Museum
367: Jeff Gnass/West Stock
369: Museum of the Plains Indians, Browning, MT, Photographs Courtesy of The Science Museum, St. Paul, MN
370: Russell Lamb
371, 373, 374, 377, 378, 379, 380, 384, 386, 387, 389, 390, 393, 396: John Reddy
398: Montana Historical Society, Helena, MT
401: John Reddy
404: Jeff Gnass
406: Ralph Hunt Williams/West Stock
411: Larry Ulrich
412: John Reddy
415: Southwest Museum, Los Angeles, CA
419: Donna M. Lucey
421: John Reddy, courtesy of the Moss Mansion
424: David Muench
426: Russell Lamb
428-429: Jeff Gnass/West Stock
432, 435: Michael Crummett, Billings, MT
437: Jesuit Missouri Province Archives, St. Louis, MO

441: Michael Crummett
443: Smithsonian Institution
445: Michael Crummett
447, 449, 451: John Reddy
452: Michael Crummett
453 (left): Michael Sales/Image Bank
453 (right, top and bottom): John Reddy
454 (left), 454 (right): Kevin Beebe
Back Cover: Mark E. Gibson

The editors gratefully acknowledge the assistance of Ann J. Campbell, Virginia Dooley, Moira Duggan, Fonda Duvanel, Julia Ehrhardt, Rick Ewing, Ann ffolliott, Lydia Howarth, Brigid A. Mast, Carol A. McKeown, Martha Schulman, Stephen Summers, Linda Venator, and David N. Wetzel.

The author dedicates this book to his parents, Jerry and Mugs Dunn.

Composed in New Caledonia and ITC New Baskerville by Graphic Arts Composition, Inc., Philadelphia, Pennsylvania. Printed and bound by Toppan Printing Company, Ltd., Tokyo, Japan.